FULLMETAL ALCHEMIST
VOL. 2

Story and Art by Hiromu Arakawa

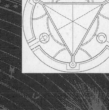

Translation/Akira Watanabe
Touch-up Art & Lettering/Wayne Truman
Design/Amy Martin
Editor/Jason Thompson
Series Consultant/Egan Loo

Editor in Chief, Books/Alvin Lu
Editor in Chief, Magazines/Marc Weidenbaum
VP of Publishing Licensing/Rika Inouye
VP of Sales/Gonzalo Ferreyra
Sr. VP of Marketing/Liza Coppola
Publisher/Hyoe Narita

Printed in the U.S.A.

Published by VIZ Media, LLC
P.O. Box 77010
San Francisco, CA 94107

10 9 8
First printing, June 2005
Eighth printing, May 2008

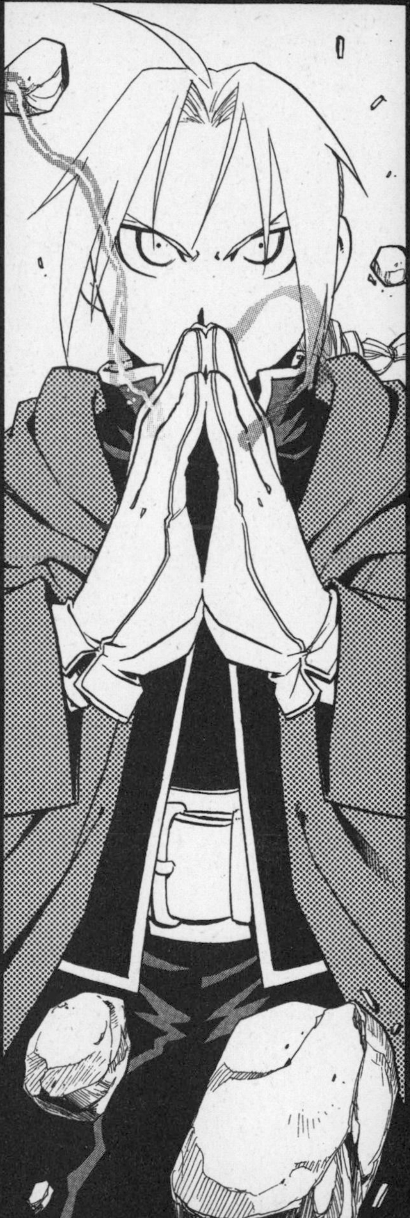

鋼の錬金術師

FULLMETAL ALCHEMIST

2

荒川弘
HIROMU ARAKAWA

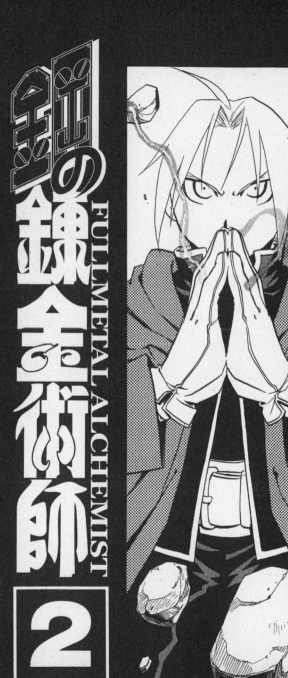

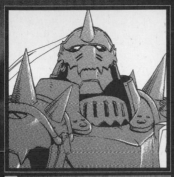

□ アルフォンス・エルリック

Alphonse Elric

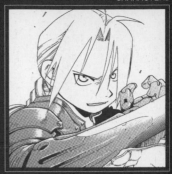

□ エドワード・エルリック

Edward Elric

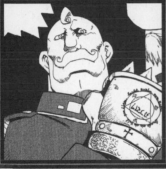

□ アレックス・ルイ・アームストロング

Alex Louis Armstrong

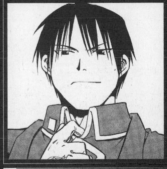

□ ロイ・マスタング

Roy Mustang

Using a forbidden alchemical ritual, the Elric
brothers attempted to bring their dead mother back
to life. But the ritual went wrong, consuming
Edward Elric's leg and Alphonse Elric's entire body.
At the cost of his arm, Edward was able to graft
his brother's soul into a suit of armor. Equipped
with mechanical "auto-mail" to replace his missing
limbs, Edward becomes a state alchemist, serving
the military on deadly missions. Now, the two
brothers roam the world in search of a way
to regain what they have lost...

鋼の錬金術師
FULLMETAL ALCHEMIST

CHARACTERS
FULLMETAL ALCHEMIST

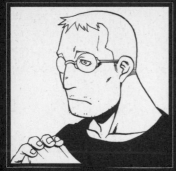

□ ショウ・タッカー

Shou Tucker

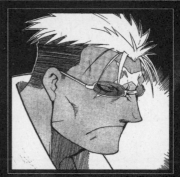

□ 傷の男（スカー）

Scar

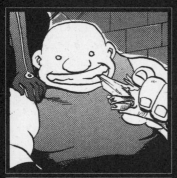

□ グラトニー

Gluttony

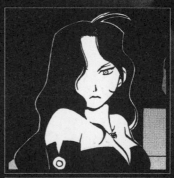

□ ラスト

Lust

OUTLINE
FULLMETAL ALCHEMIST

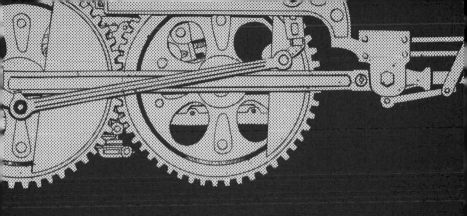

CONTENTS

Chapter 5: The Alchemist's Suffering 7

Chapter 6: The Right Hand of Destruction 53

Chapter 7: After the Rain 99

Chapter 8: The Road of Hope 139

Extra 183

Preview 188

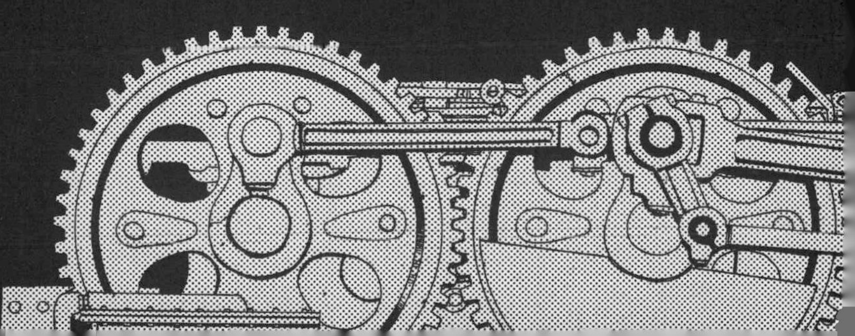

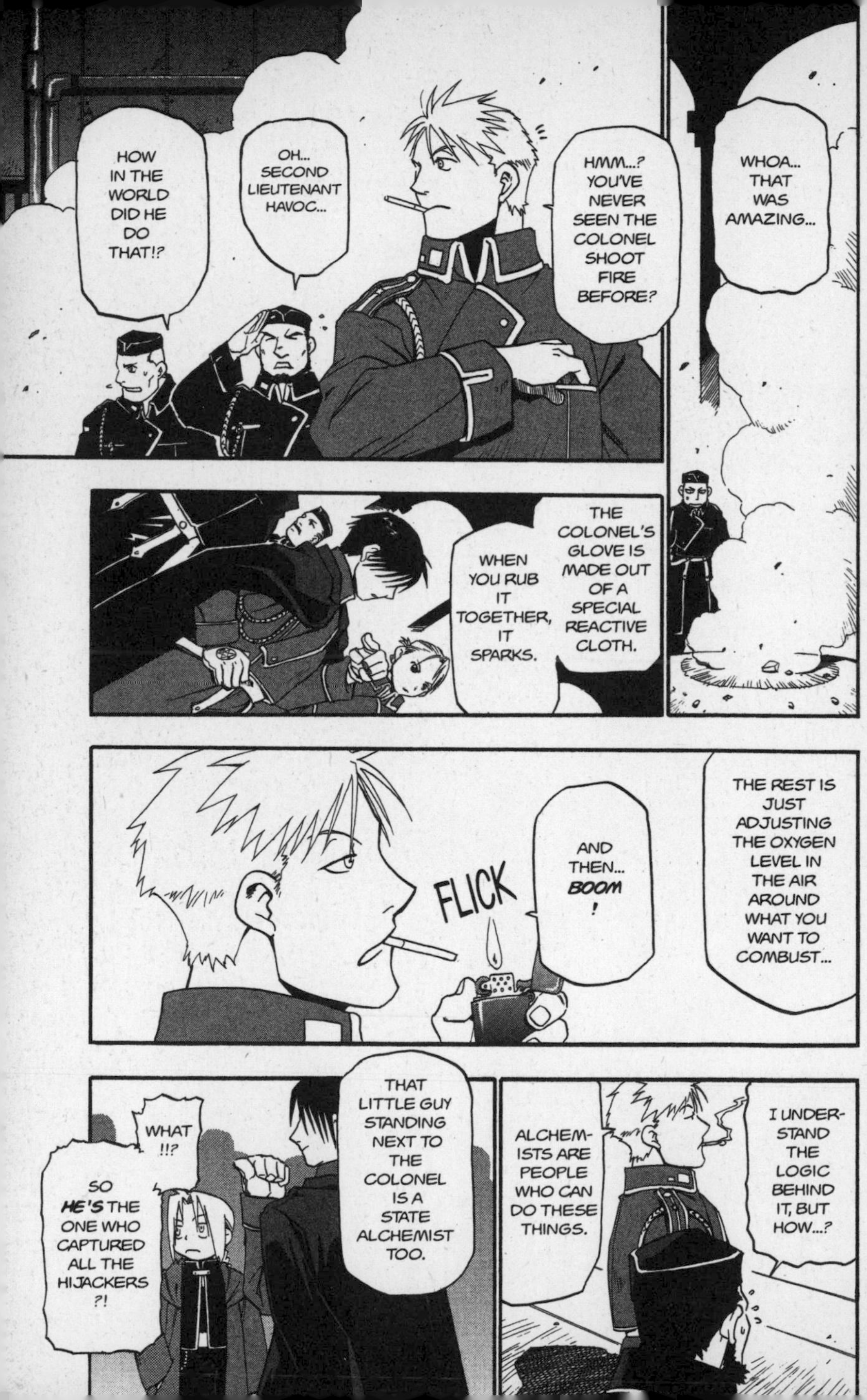
WHOA... THAT WAS AMAZING...
HMM...? YOU'VE NEVER SEEN THE COLONEL SHOOT FIRE BEFORE?
OH... SECOND LIEUTENANT HAVOC...
HOW IN THE WORLD DID HE DO THAT!?
THE COLONEL'S GLOVE IS MADE OUT OF A SPECIAL REACTIVE CLOTH.
WHEN YOU RUB IT TOGETHER, IT SPARKS.
THE REST IS JUST ADJUSTING THE OXYGEN LEVEL IN THE AIR AROUND WHAT YOU WANT TO COMBUST...
AND THEN... ***BOOM*** !
FLICK
I UNDER-STAND THE LOGIC BEHIND IT, BUT HOW...?
ALCHEM-ISTS ARE PEOPLE WHO CAN DO THESE THINGS.
THAT LITTLE GUY STANDING NEXT TO THE COLONEL IS A STATE ALCHEMIST TOO.
WHAT !!?
SO ***HE'S*** THE ONE WHO CAPTURED ALL THE HIJACKERS ?!

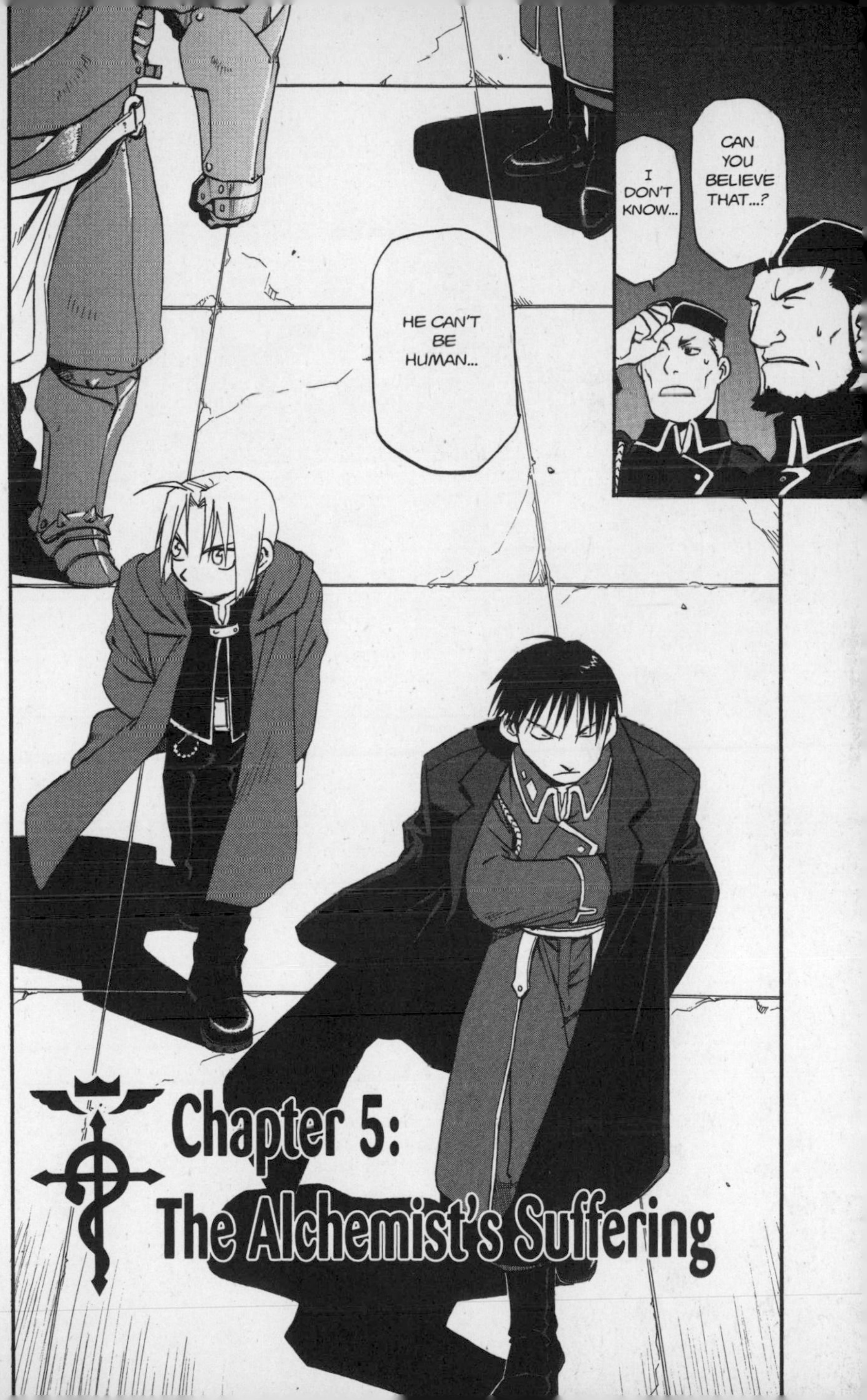
CAN YOU BELIEVE THAT...?
I DON'T KNOW...
HE CAN'T BE HUMAN...
Chapter 5:
The Alchemist's Suffering

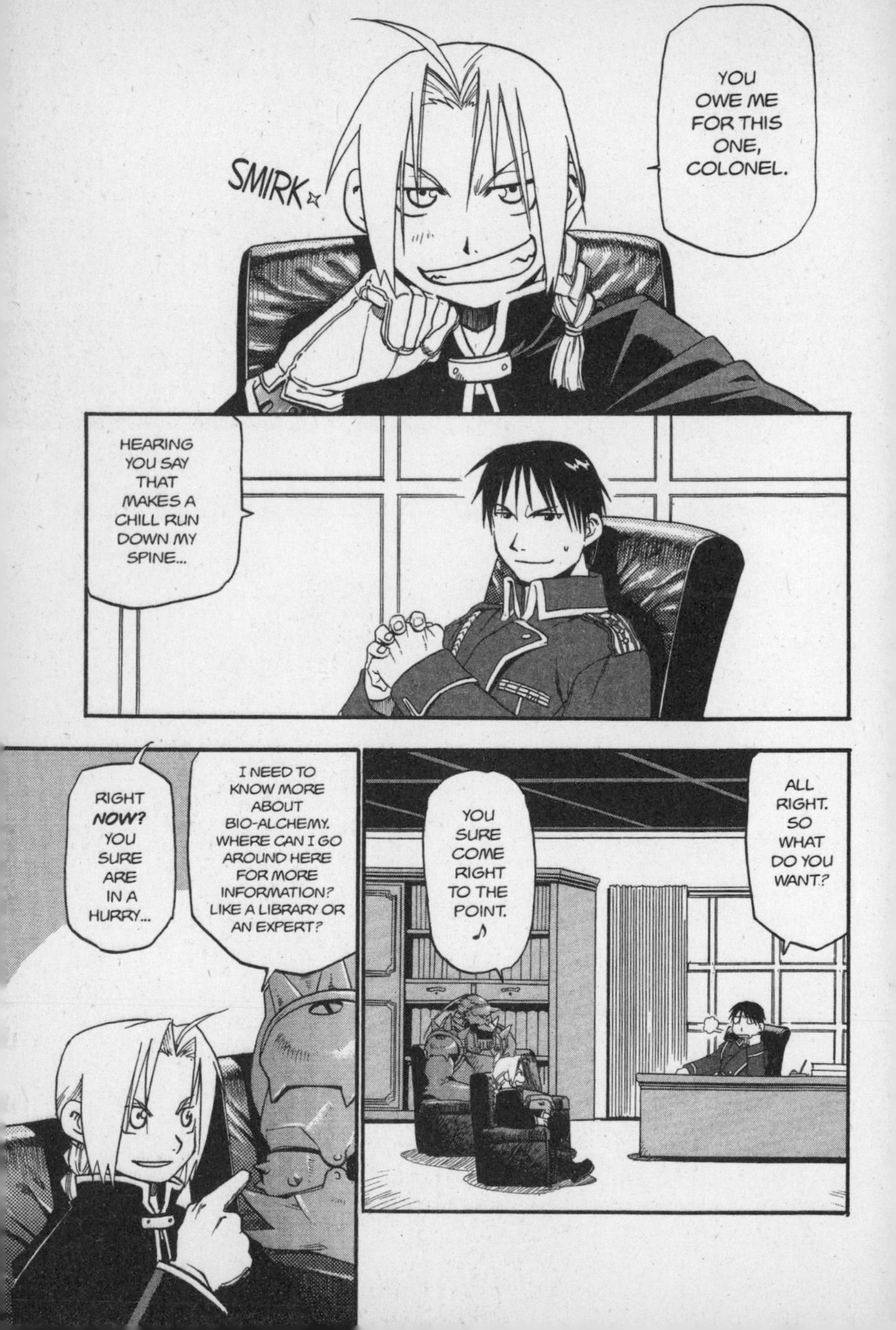
YOU OWE ME FOR THIS ONE, COLONEL.
SMIRK
HEARING YOU SAY THAT MAKES A CHILL RUN DOWN MY SPINE...
ALL RIGHT. SO WHAT DO YOU WANT?
YOU SURE COME RIGHT TO THE POINT. ♪
I NEED TO KNOW MORE ABOUT BIO-ALCHEMY. WHERE CAN I GO AROUND HERE FOR MORE INFORMATION? LIKE A LIBRARY OR AN EXPERT?
RIGHT *NOW?* YOU SURE ARE IN A HURRY...

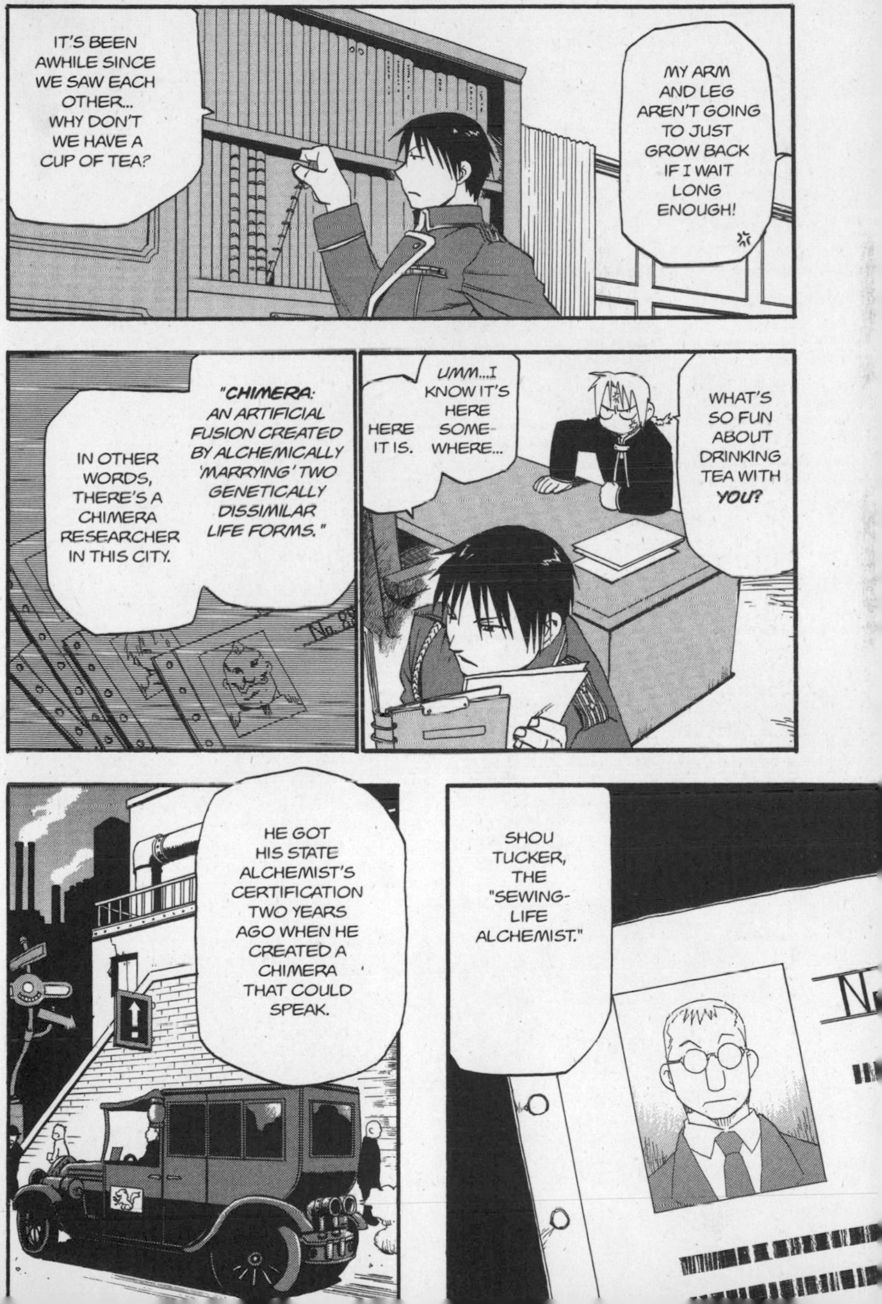
MY ARM AND LEG AREN'T GOING TO JUST GROW BACK IF I WAIT LONG ENOUGH!
IT'S BEEN AWHILE SINCE WE SAW EACH OTHER... WHY DON'T WE HAVE A CUP OF TEA?
WHAT'S SO FUN ABOUT DRINKING TEA WITH *YOU?*
UMM...I KNOW IT'S HERE SOME-WHERE...
HERE IT IS.
*"**CHIMERA**: AN ARTIFICIAL FUSION CREATED BY ALCHEMICALLY 'MARRYING' TWO GENETICALLY DISSIMILAR LIFE FORMS."*
IN OTHER WORDS, THERE'S A CHIMERA RESEARCHER IN THIS CITY.
SHOU TUCKER, THE "SEWING-LIFE ALCHEMIST."
HE GOT HIS STATE ALCHEMIST'S CERTIFICATION TWO YEARS AGO WHEN HE CREATED A CHIMERA THAT COULD SPEAK.

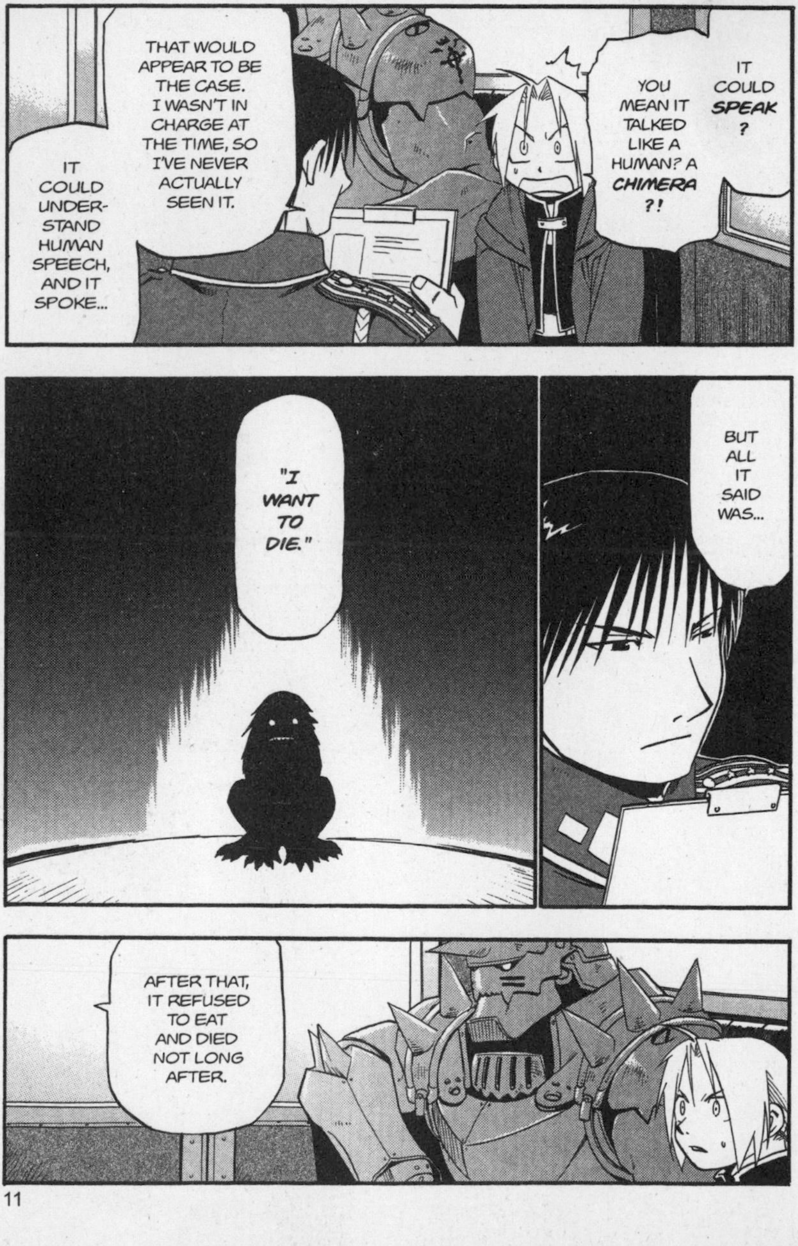
IT COULD SPEAK?
YOU MEAN IT TALKED LIKE A HUMAN? A CHIMERA?!
THAT WOULD APPEAR TO BE THE CASE. I WASN'T IN CHARGE AT THE TIME, SO I'VE NEVER ACTUALLY SEEN IT.
IT COULD UNDER-STAND HUMAN SPEECH, AND IT SPOKE...
BUT ALL IT SAID WAS...
"I WANT TO DIE."
AFTER THAT, IT REFUSED TO EAT AND DIED NOT LONG AFTER.

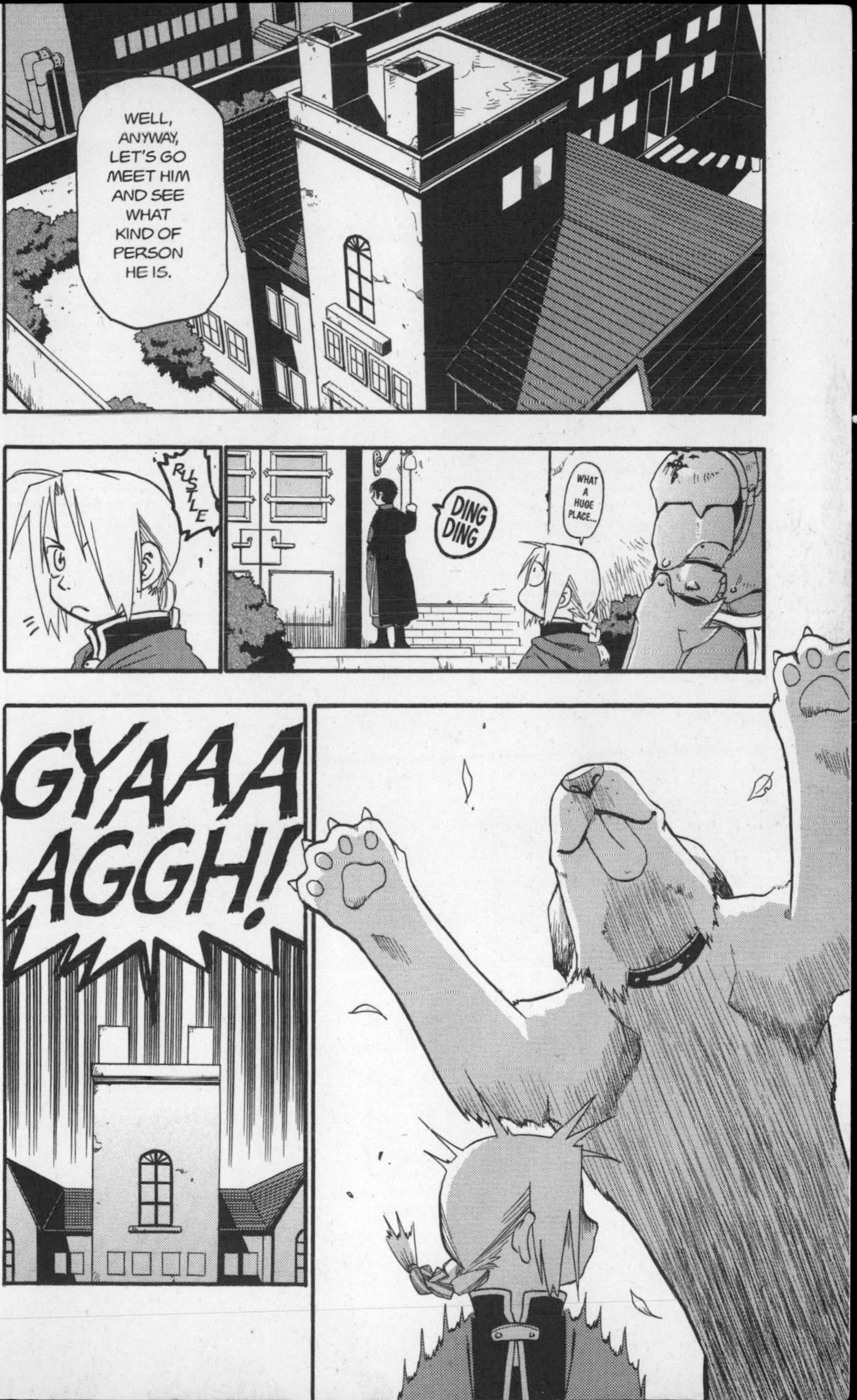
WELL, ANYWAY, LET'S GO MEET HIM AND SEE WHAT KIND OF PERSON HE IS.
WHAT A HUGE PLACE...
DING DING
RUSTLE
GYAAA AGGH!

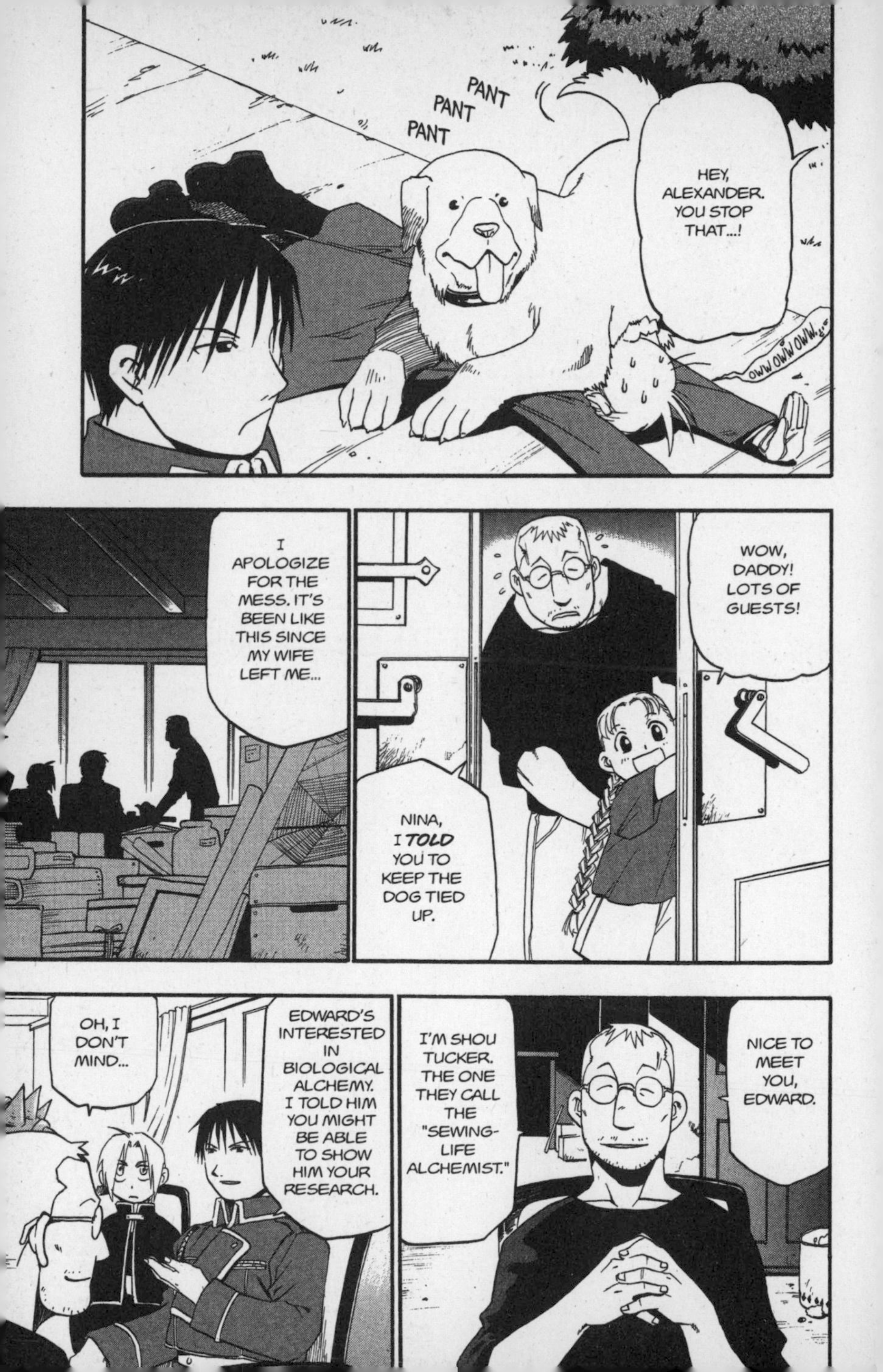

PANT
PANT
PANT
HEY, ALEXANDER. YOU STOP THAT...!
OWW OWW OWW...
WOW, DADDY! LOTS OF GUESTS!
NINA, I ***TOLD*** YOU TO KEEP THE DOG TIED UP.
I APOLOGIZE FOR THE MESS. IT'S BEEN LIKE THIS SINCE MY WIFE LEFT ME...
NICE TO MEET YOU, EDWARD.
I'M SHOU TUCKER. THE ONE THEY CALL THE "SEWING-LIFE ALCHEMIST."
EDWARD'S INTERESTED IN BIOLOGICAL ALCHEMY. I TOLD HIM YOU MIGHT BE ABLE TO SHOW HIM YOUR RESEARCH.
OH, I DON'T MIND...

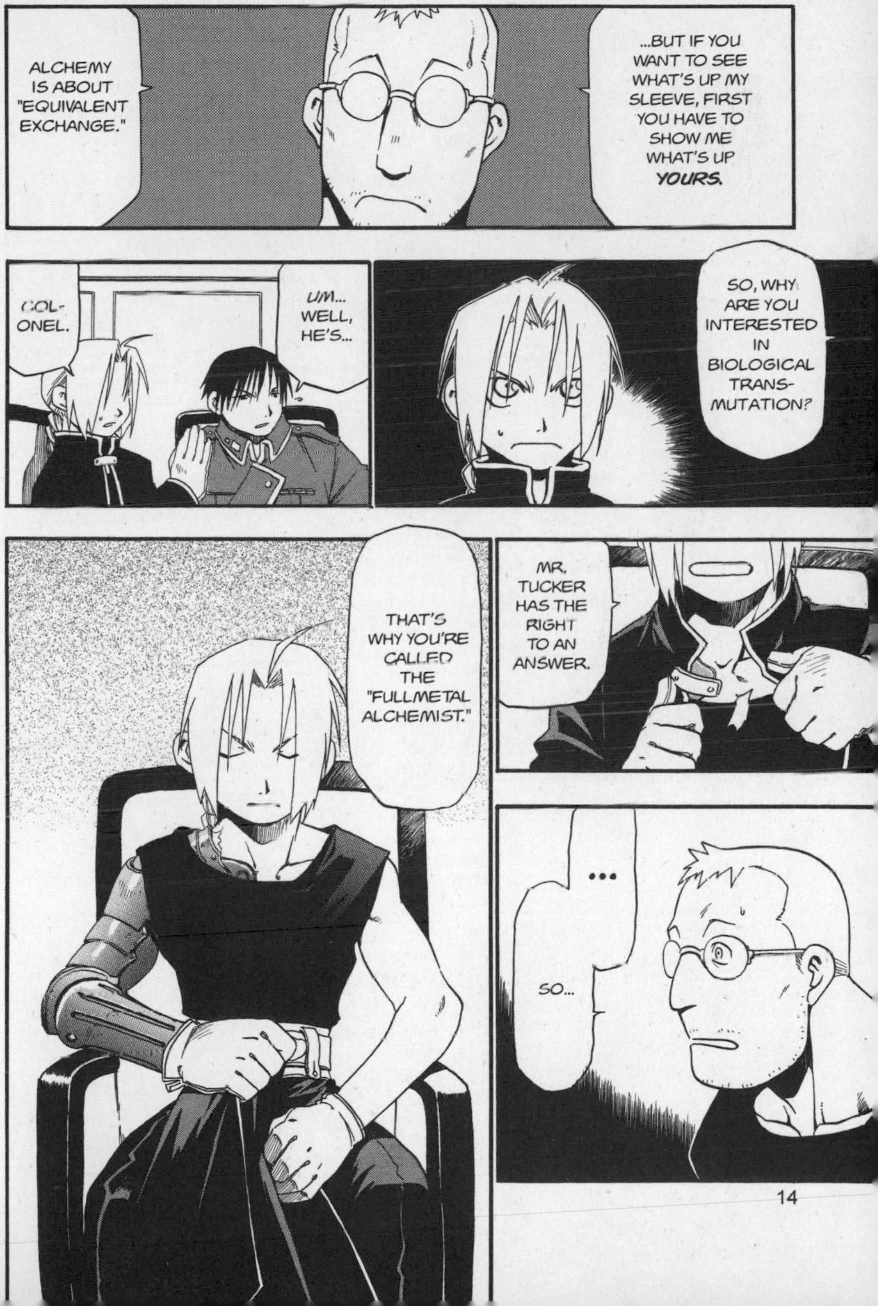
ALCHEMY IS ABOUT "EQUIVALENT EXCHANGE."
...BUT IF YOU WANT TO SEE WHAT'S UP MY SLEEVE, FIRST YOU HAVE TO SHOW ME WHAT'S UP *YOURS.*
SO, WHY ARE YOU INTERESTED IN BIOLOGICAL TRANS-MUTATION?
UM... WELL, HE'S...
COL-ONEL.
MR. TUCKER HAS THE RIGHT TO AN ANSWER.
...
SO...
THAT'S WHY YOU'RE CALLED THE "FULLMETAL ALCHEMIST."

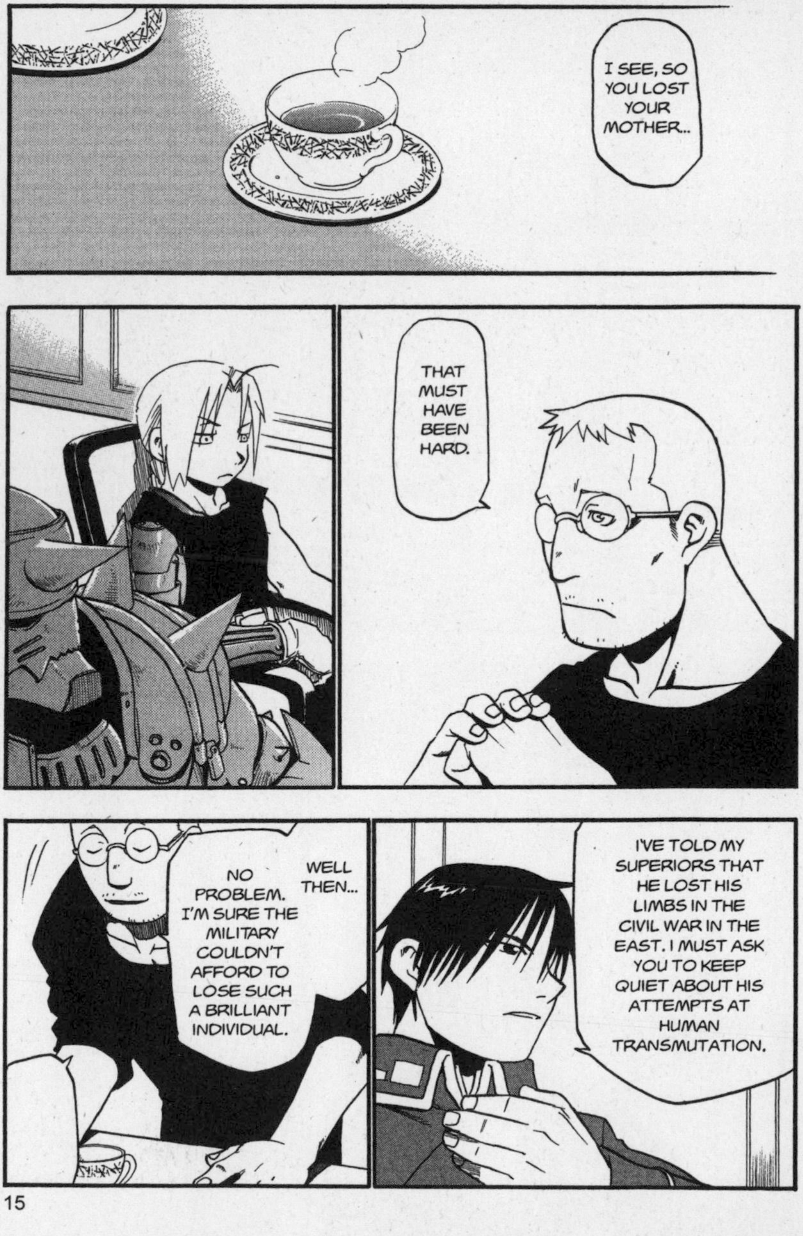
I SEE, SO YOU LOST YOUR MOTHER...
THAT MUST HAVE BEEN HARD.
I'VE TOLD MY SUPERIORS THAT HE LOST HIS LIMBS IN THE CIVIL WAR IN THE EAST. I MUST ASK YOU TO KEEP QUIET ABOUT HIS ATTEMPTS AT HUMAN TRANSMUTATION.
WELL THEN...
NO PROBLEM. I'M SURE THE MILITARY COULDN'T AFFORD TO LOSE SUCH A BRILLIANT INDIVIDUAL.

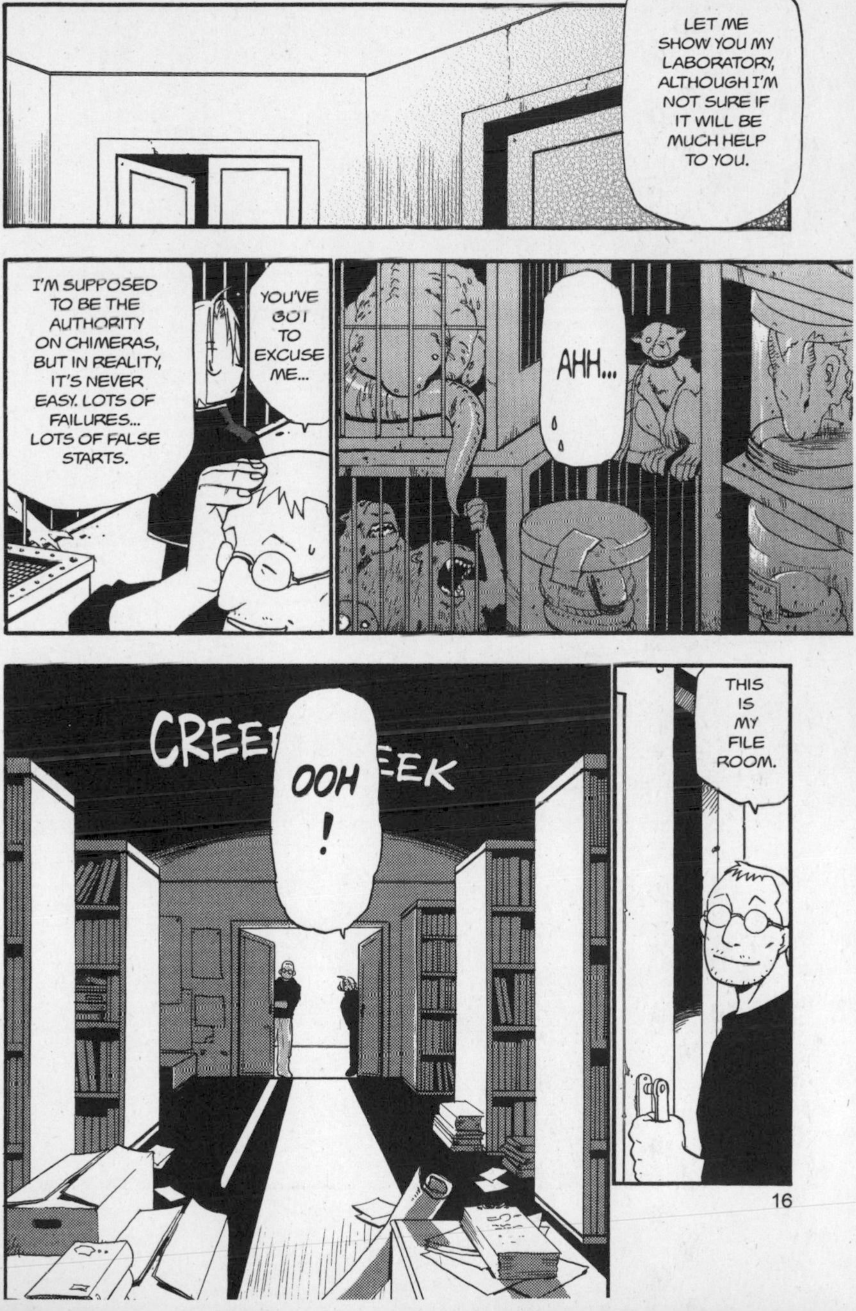
LET ME SHOW YOU MY LABORATORY, ALTHOUGH I'M NOT SURE IF IT WILL BE MUCH HELP TO YOU.
AHH...
YOU'VE GOT TO EXCUSE ME...
I'M SUPPOSED TO BE THE AUTHORITY ON CHIMERAS, BUT IN REALITY, IT'S NEVER EASY. LOTS OF FAILURES... LOTS OF FALSE STARTS.
THIS IS MY FILE ROOM.
CREE
EEK
OOH!

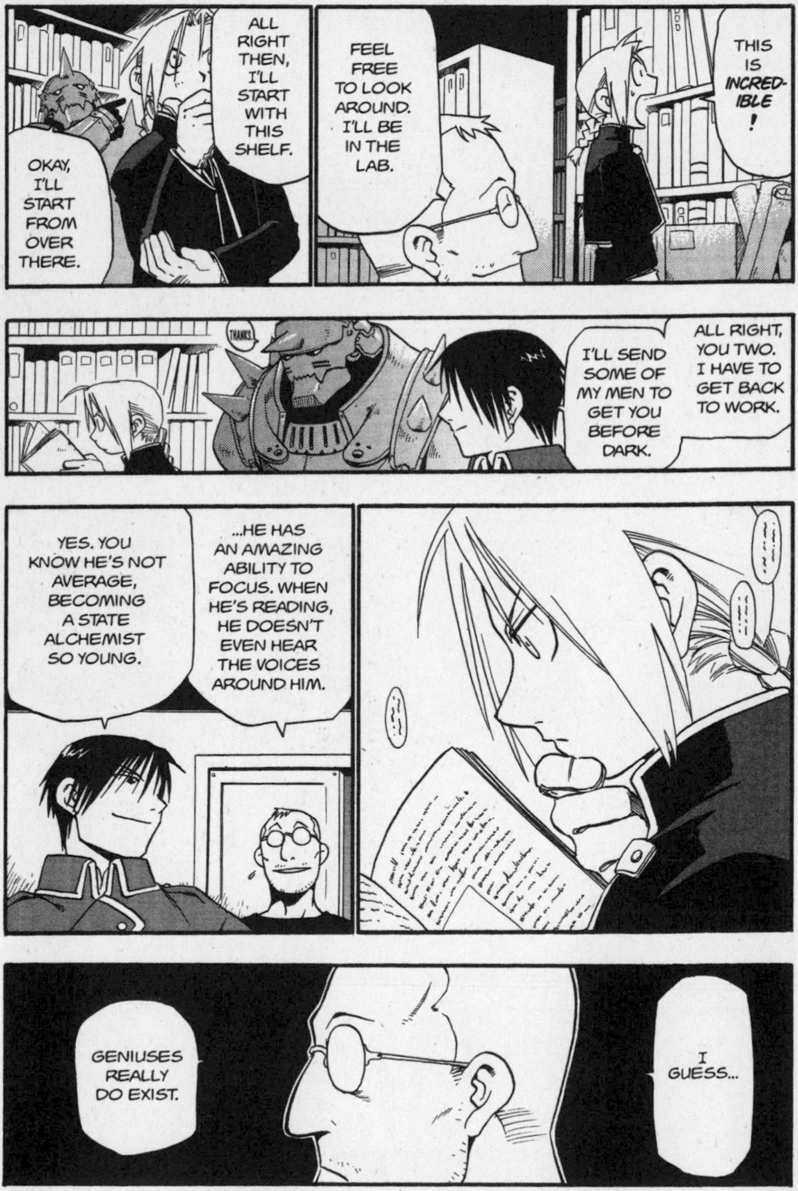
THIS IS INCREDIBLE!
FEEL FREE TO LOOK AROUND. I'LL BE IN THE LAB.
ALL RIGHT THEN, I'LL START WITH THIS SHELF.
OKAY, I'LL START FROM OVER THERE.
ALL RIGHT, YOU TWO. I HAVE TO GET BACK TO WORK.
I'LL SEND SOME OF MY MEN TO GET YOU BEFORE DARK.
THANKS.
...HE HAS AN AMAZING ABILITY TO FOCUS. WHEN HE'S READING, HE DOESN'T EVEN HEAR THE VOICES AROUND HIM.
YES. YOU KNOW HE'S NOT AVERAGE, BECOMING A STATE ALCHEMIST SO YOUNG.
I GUESS...
GENIUSES REALLY DO EXIST.

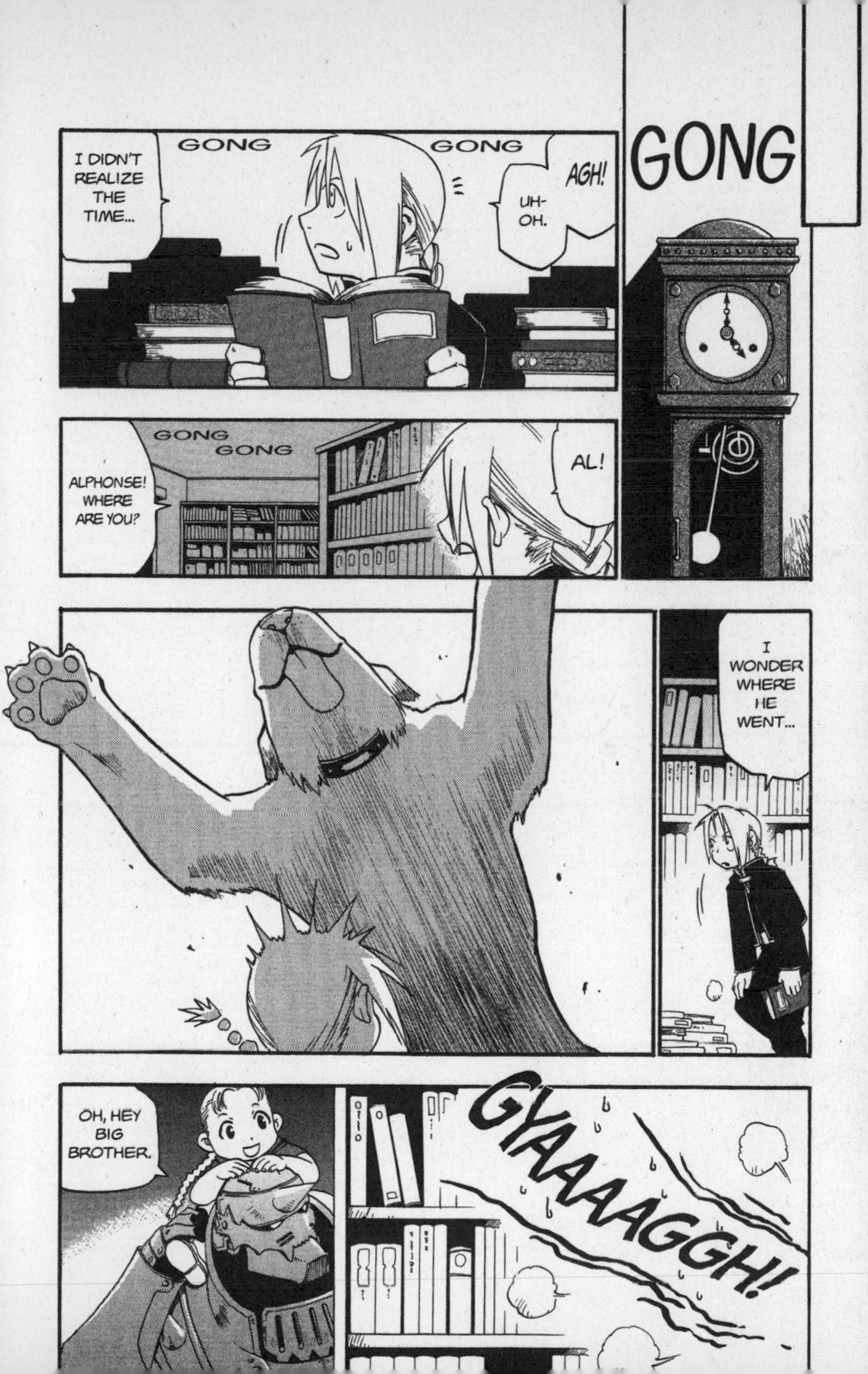
GONG
GONG
GONG
AGH!
UH-OH.
I DIDN'T REALIZE THE TIME...
AL!
GONG
GONG
ALPHONSE! WHERE ARE YOU?
I WONDER WHERE HE WENT...
GYAAAAGGH!
OH, HEY BIG BROTHER.

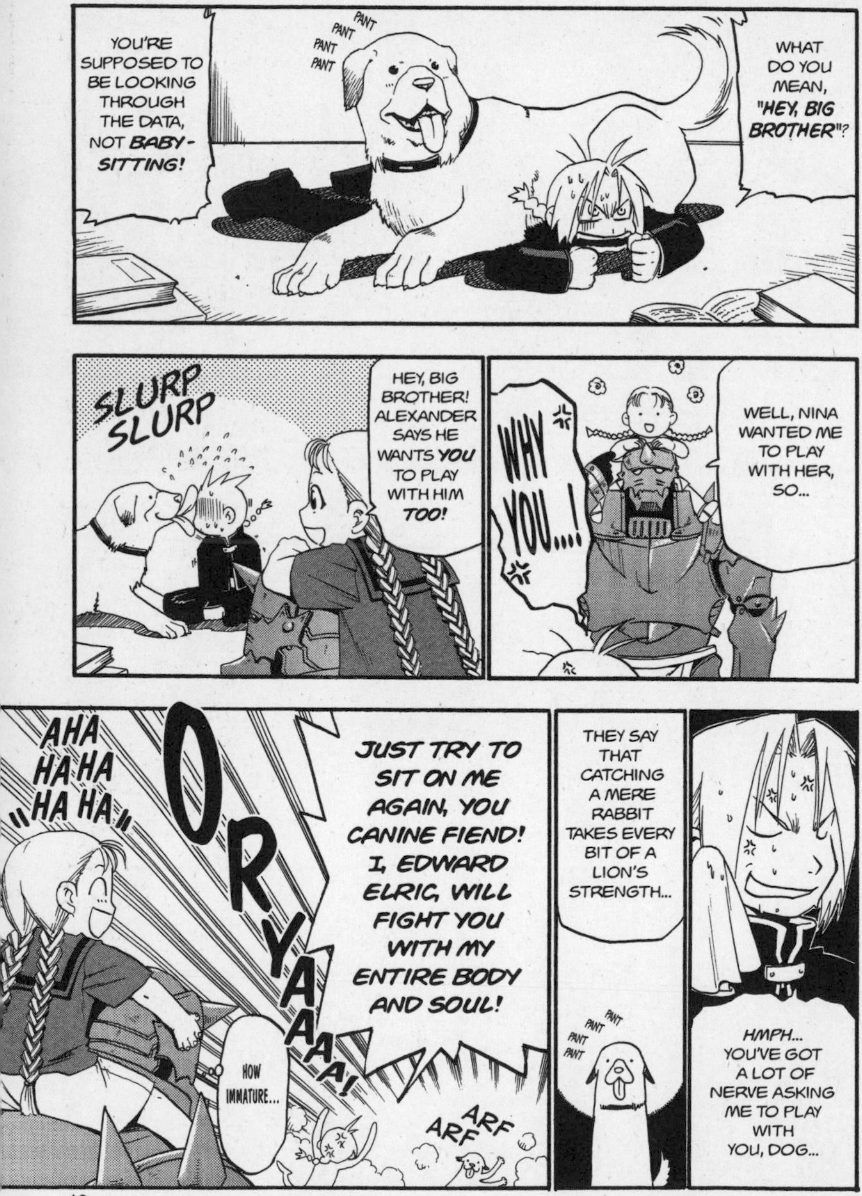
WHAT DO YOU MEAN, "HEY, BIG BROTHER"?
PANT PANT PANT PANT
YOU'RE SUPPOSED TO BE LOOKING THROUGH THE DATA, NOT BABY-SITTING!
WELL, NINA WANTED ME TO PLAY WITH HER, SO...
WHY YOU...!
HEY, BIG BROTHER! ALEXANDER SAYS HE WANTS YOU TO PLAY WITH HIM TOO!
SLURP SLURP
HMPH... YOU'VE GOT A LOT OF NERVE ASKING ME TO PLAY WITH YOU, DOG...
THEY SAY THAT CATCHING A MERE RABBIT TAKES EVERY BIT OF A LION'S STRENGTH...
PANT PANT PANT
JUST TRY TO SIT ON ME AGAIN, YOU CANINE FIEND! I, EDWARD ELRIC, WILL FIGHT YOU WITH MY ENTIRE BODY AND SOUL!
ORYAAAA!
AHA HA HA HA HA
HOW IMMATURE...
ARF ARF

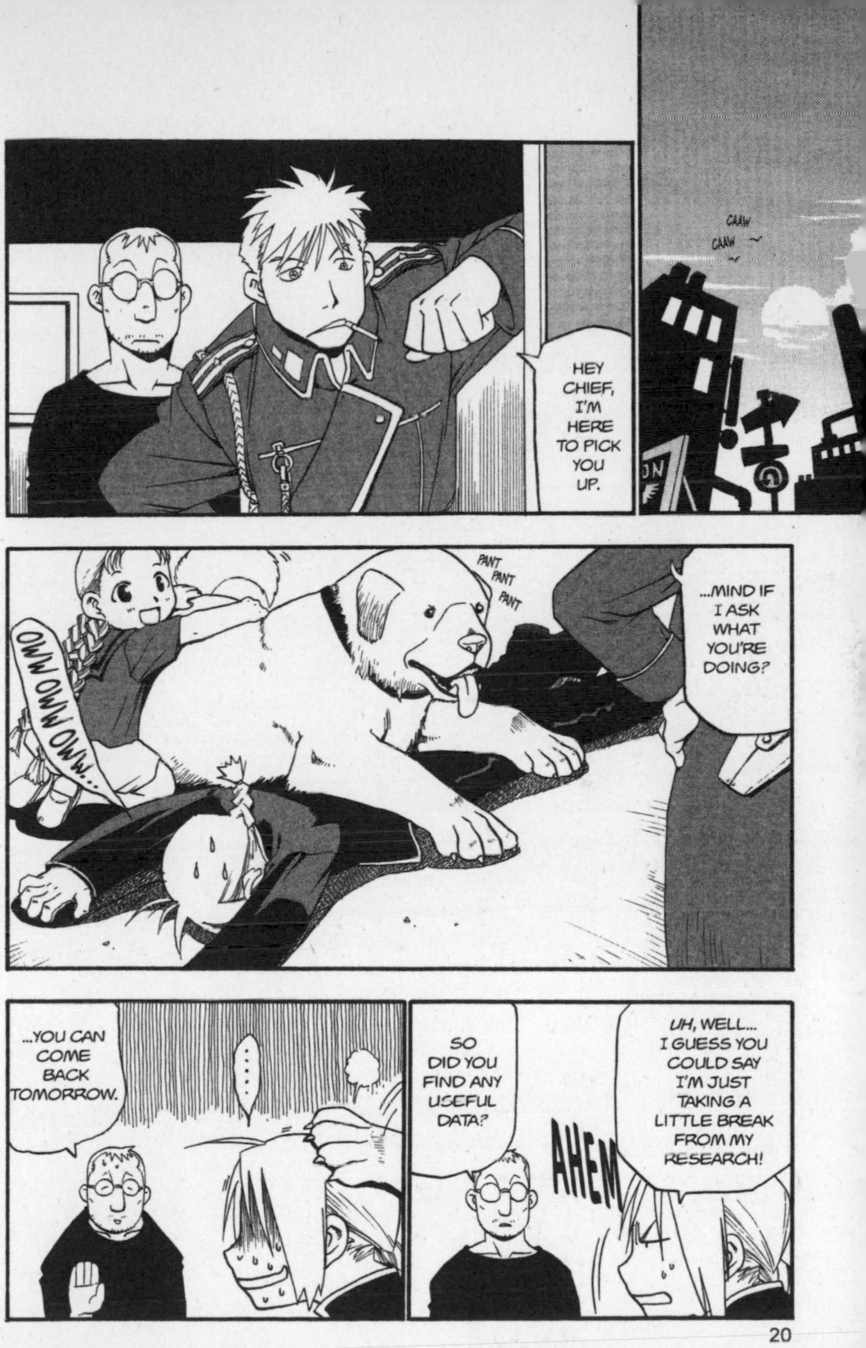
CAAW
CAAW
HEY CHIEF, I'M HERE TO PICK YOU UP.
...MIND IF I ASK WHAT YOU'RE DOING?
PANT PANT PANT
OWW OWW OWW...
UH, WELL... I GUESS YOU COULD SAY I'M JUST TAKING A LITTLE BREAK FROM MY RESEARCH!
AHEM
SO DID YOU FIND ANY USEFUL DATA?
......
...YOU CAN COME BACK TOMORROW.

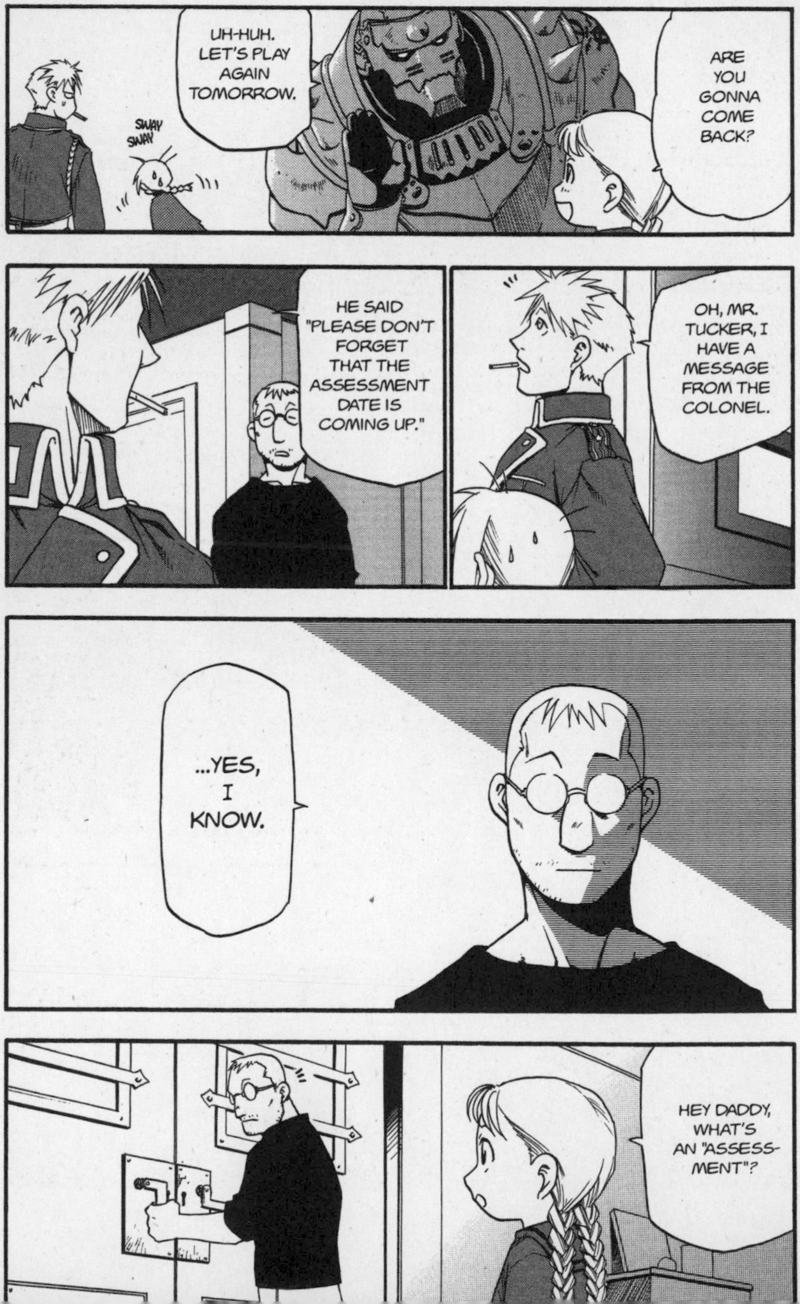
ARE YOU GONNA COME BACK?
UH-HUH. LET'S PLAY AGAIN TOMORROW.
SWAY SWAY
OH, MR. TUCKER, I HAVE A MESSAGE FROM THE COLONEL.
HE SAID "PLEASE DON'T FORGET THAT THE ASSESSMENT DATE IS COMING UP."
...YES, I KNOW.
HEY DADDY, WHAT'S AN "ASSESSMENT"?

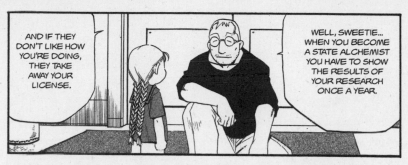

WELL, SWEETIE... WHEN YOU BECOME A STATE ALCHEMIST YOU HAVE TO SHOW THE RESULTS OF YOUR RESEARCH ONCE A YEAR.
AND IF THEY DON'T LIKE HOW YOU'RE DOING, THEY TAKE AWAY YOUR LICENSE.
DADDY'S EVALUATION WASN'T VERY GOOD LAST YEAR...
SO UNLESS I DO SOMETHING GREAT THIS YEAR, I WON'T BE A STATE ALCHEMIST ANYMORE.
WHAAAT? YOU'LL DO GREAT, DADDY! YOU'RE ALWAYS STUDYING A LOT!
I KNOW, SWEETIE. BUT IF THEY DON'T LIKE ME, THERE'S NOTHING ELSE LEFT THAT I CAN DO...
THAT'S RIGHT...
THERE'S NOTHING ELSE I CAN DO...

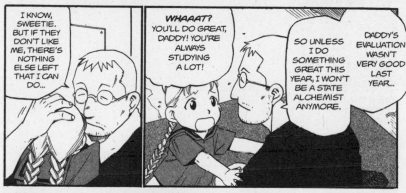

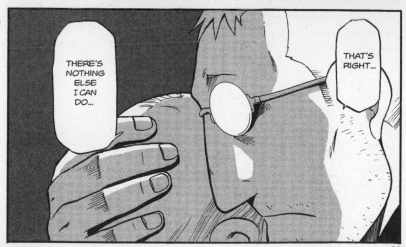

HMM... SO YOUR MOM LEFT TWO YEARS AGO...
UH-HUH. DADDY SAID SHE WENT BACK TO HER PARENTS' HOUSE.
REALLY? IT MUST BE LONELY LIVING IN A BIG HOUSE LIKE THIS WITH JUST THE TWO OF YOU.
NO, IT'S NOT!
DADDY'S NICE TO ME, AND I HAVE ALEXANDER TOO!
BUT...
LATELY DADDY'S ALWAYS IN HIS LABORATORY WITH THE DOOR LOCKED... SO IT'S A *LITTLE* LONELY.

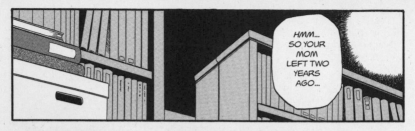

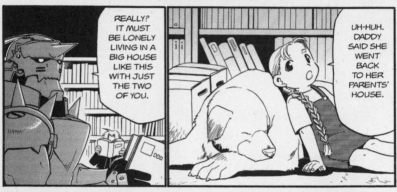

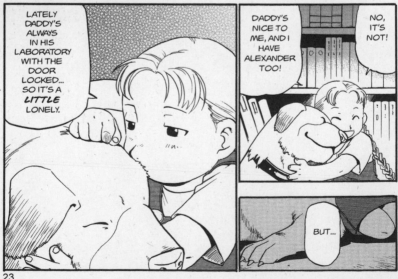

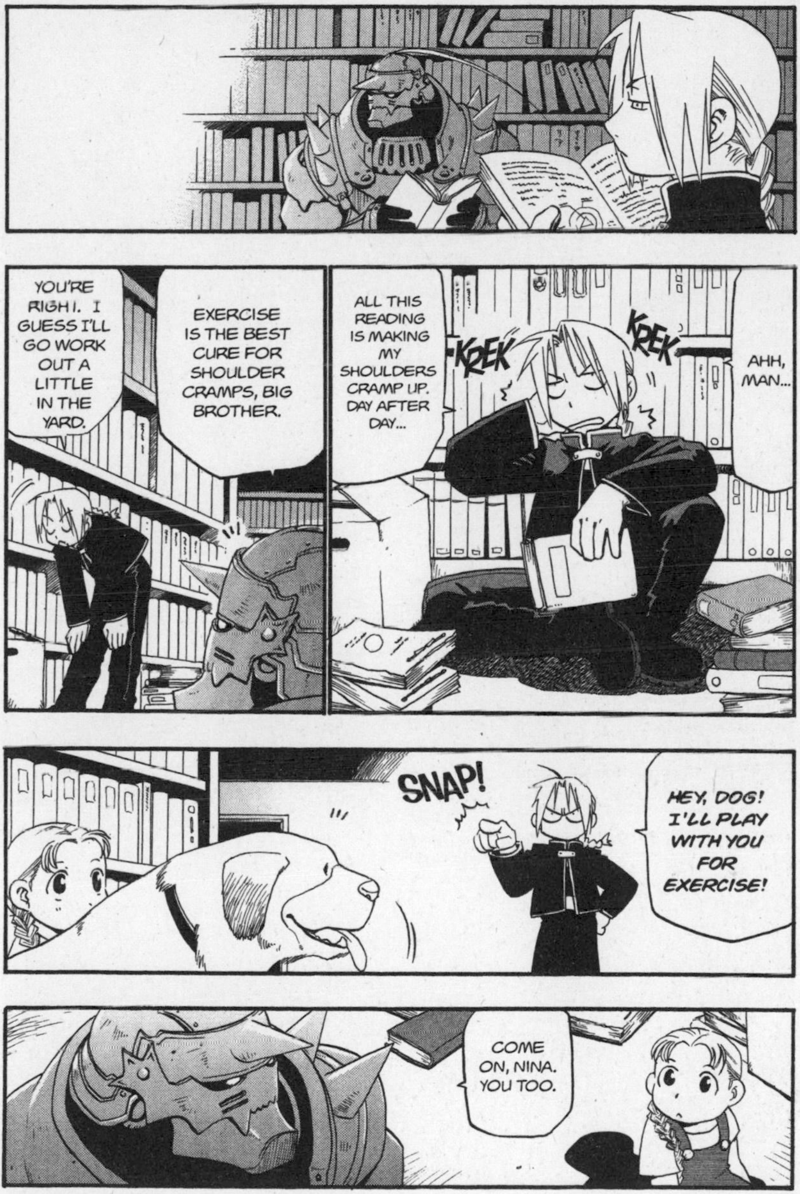
AHH, MAN...
KREK
KREK
ALL THIS READING IS MAKING MY SHOULDERS CRAMP UP. DAY AFTER DAY...
EXERCISE IS THE BEST CURE FOR SHOULDER CRAMPS, BIG BROTHER.
YOU'RE RIGHT. I GUESS I'LL GO WORK OUT A LITTLE IN THE YARD.
HEY, DOG! I'LL PLAY WITH YOU FOR EXERCISE!
SNAP!
COME ON, NINA. YOU TOO.

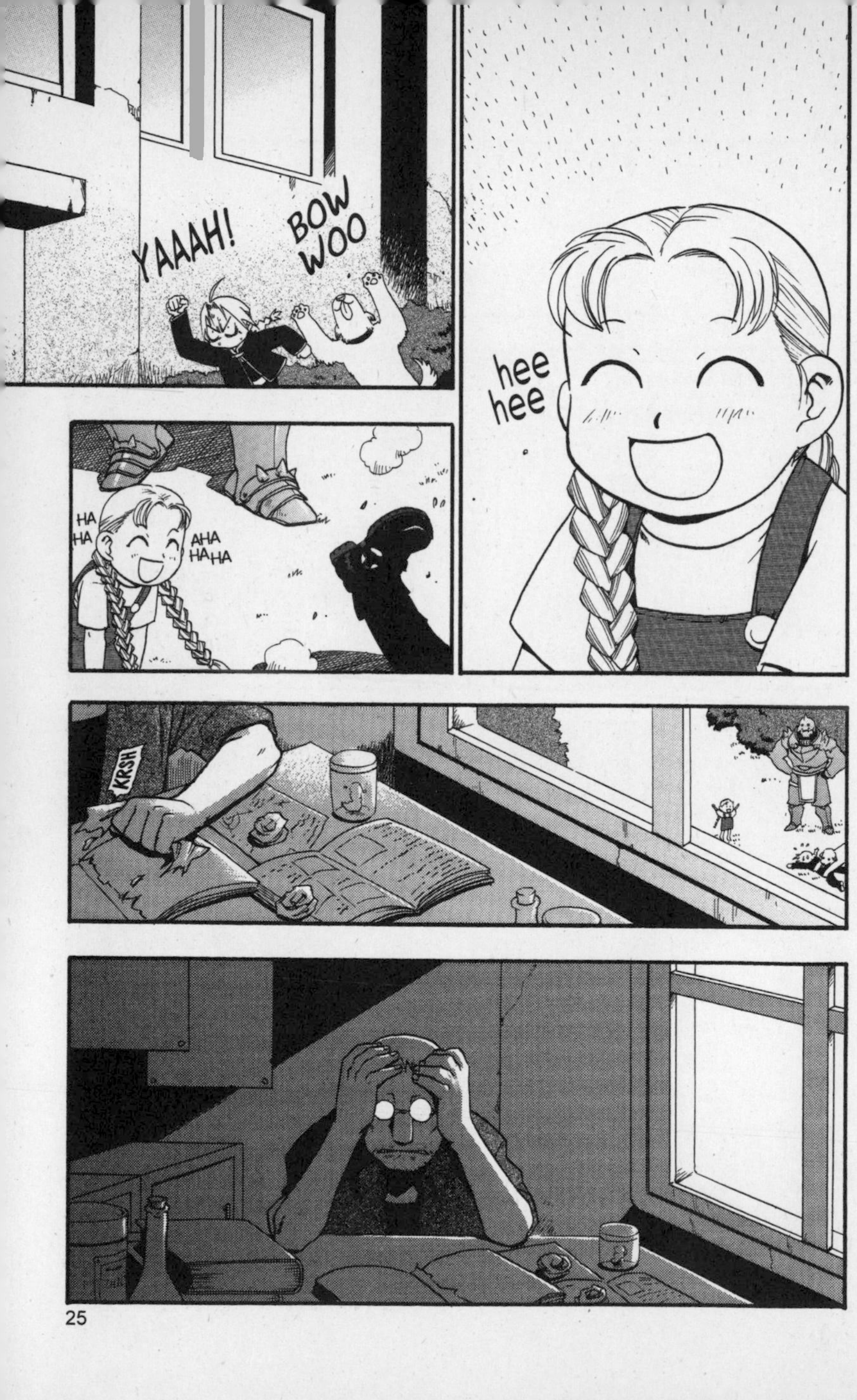

hee hee
YAAAH!
BOW WOO
HA HA
AHA HAHA
KRSH

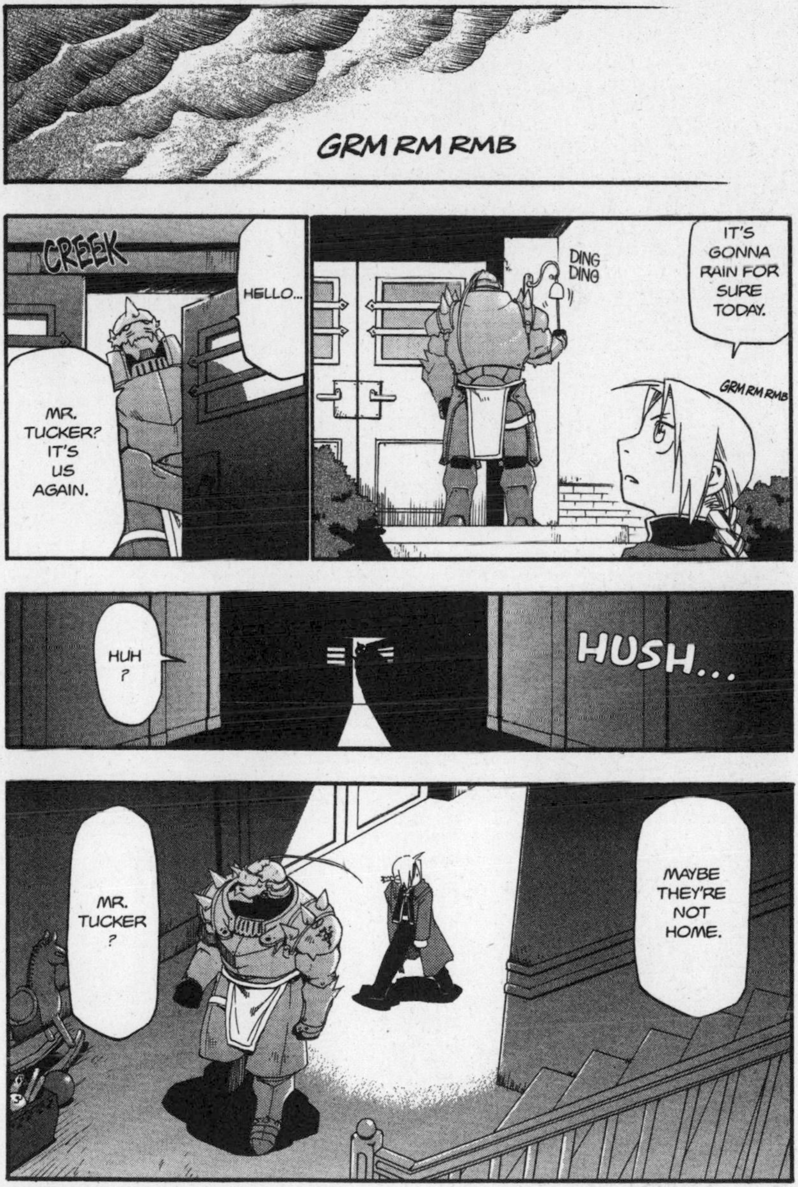
GRM RM RMB
IT'S GONNA RAIN FOR SURE TODAY.
DING DING
GRM RM RMB
HELLO...
CREEK
MR. TUCKER? IT'S US AGAIN.
HUSH...
HUH?
MAYBE THEY'RE NOT HOME.
MR. TUCKER?

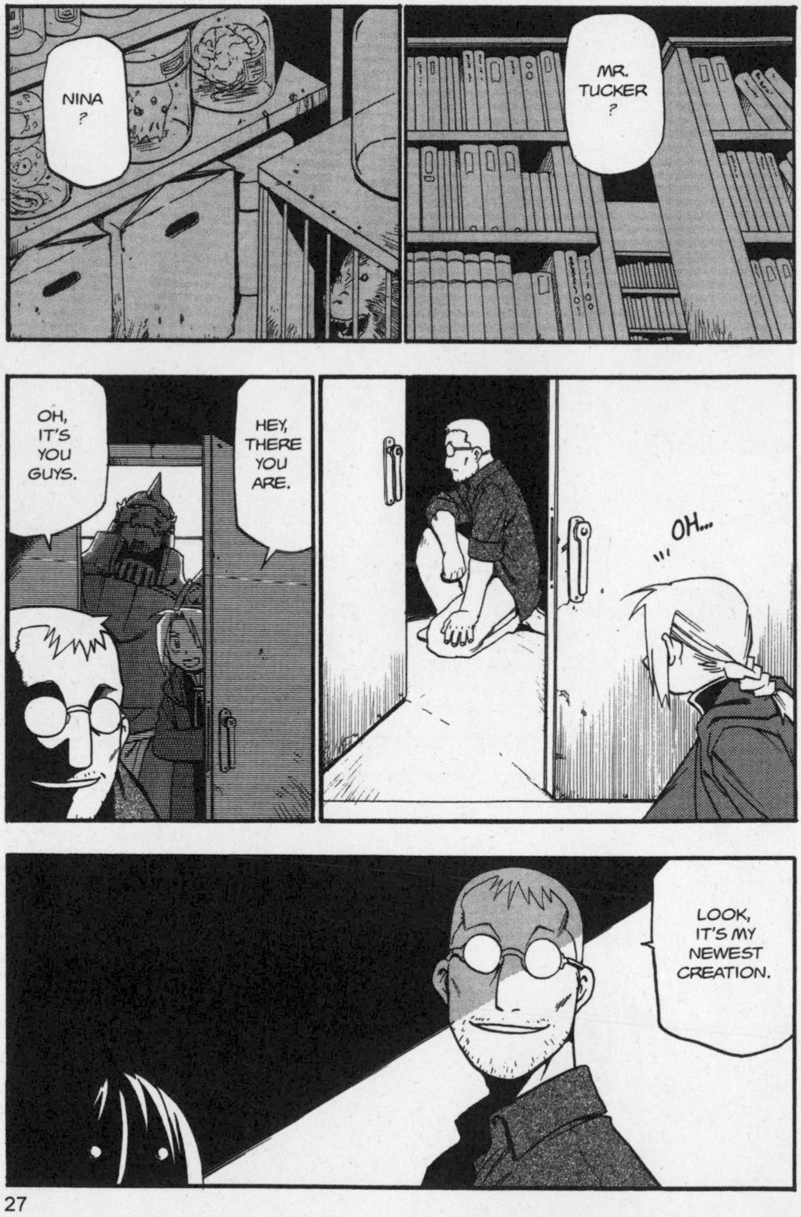
MR. TUCKER ?
NINA ?
OH...
HEY, THERE YOU ARE.
OH, IT'S YOU GUYS.
LOOK, IT'S MY NEWEST CREATION.

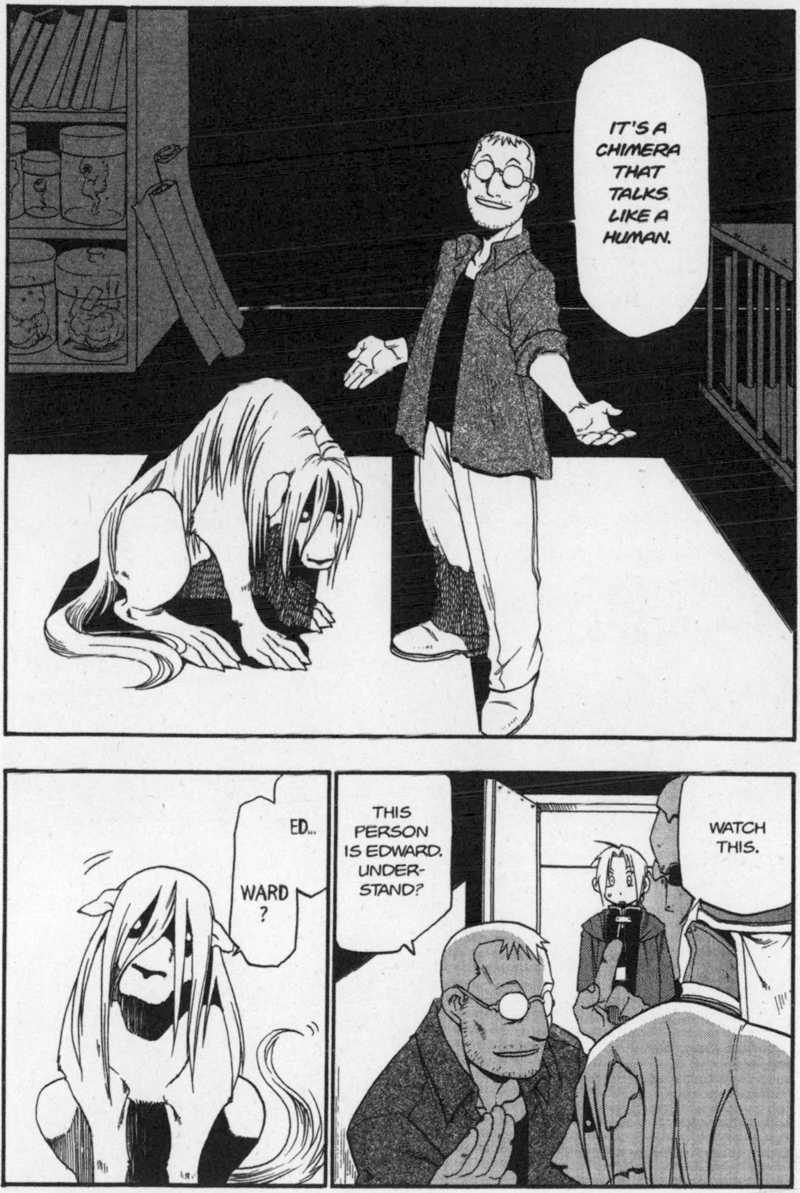
IT'S A CHIMERA THAT TALKS LIKE A HUMAN.
WATCH THIS.
THIS PERSON IS EDWARD. UNDER-STAND?
ED...
WARD?

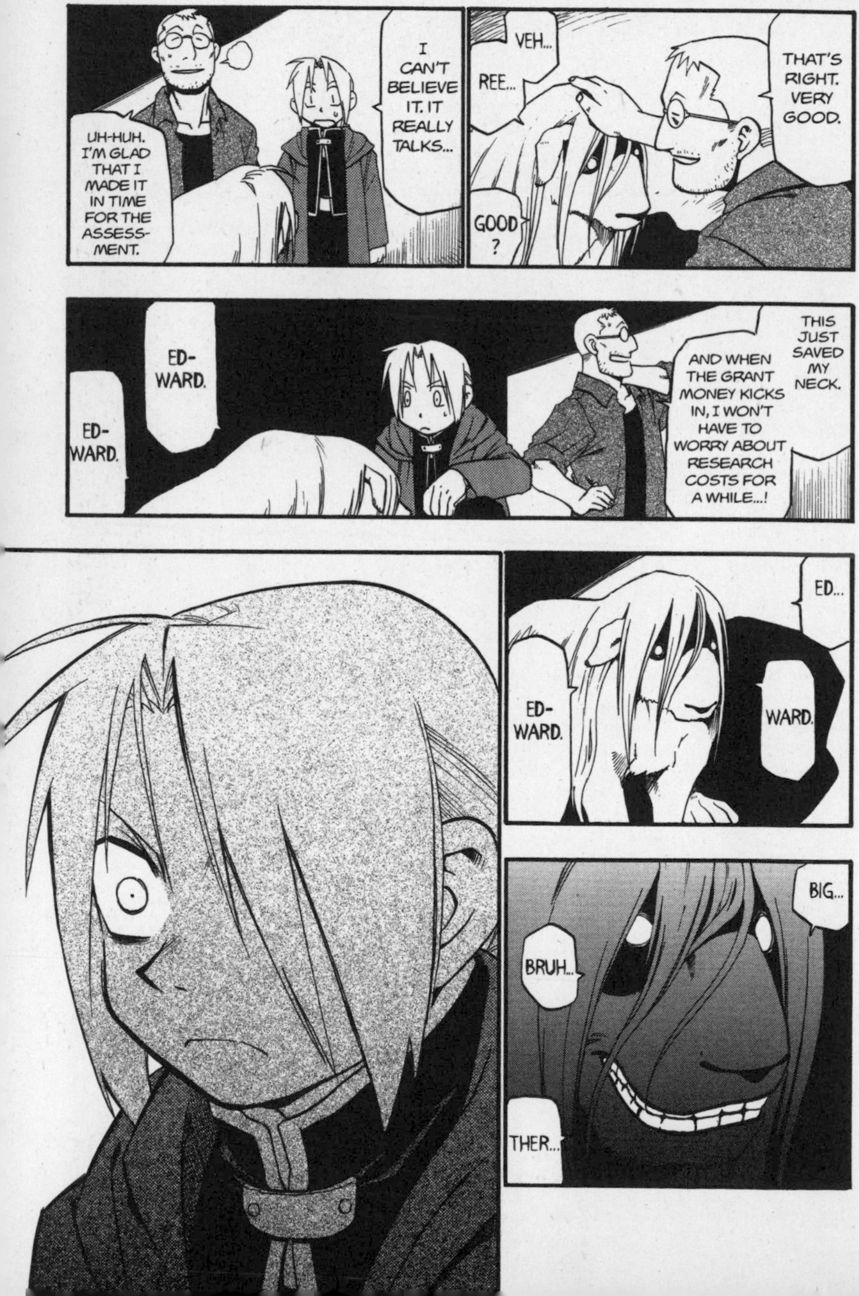
VEH...
REE...
GOOD?
THAT'S RIGHT. VERY GOOD.
I CAN'T BELIEVE IT. IT REALLY TALKS...
UH-HUH. I'M GLAD THAT I MADE IT IN TIME FOR THE ASSESS-MENT.
THIS JUST SAVED MY NECK.
AND WHEN THE GRANT MONEY KICKS IN, I WON'T HAVE TO WORRY ABOUT RESEARCH COSTS FOR A WHILE...!
ED-WARD.
ED-WARD.
ED...
WARD.
ED-WARD.
BIG...
BRUH...
THER...

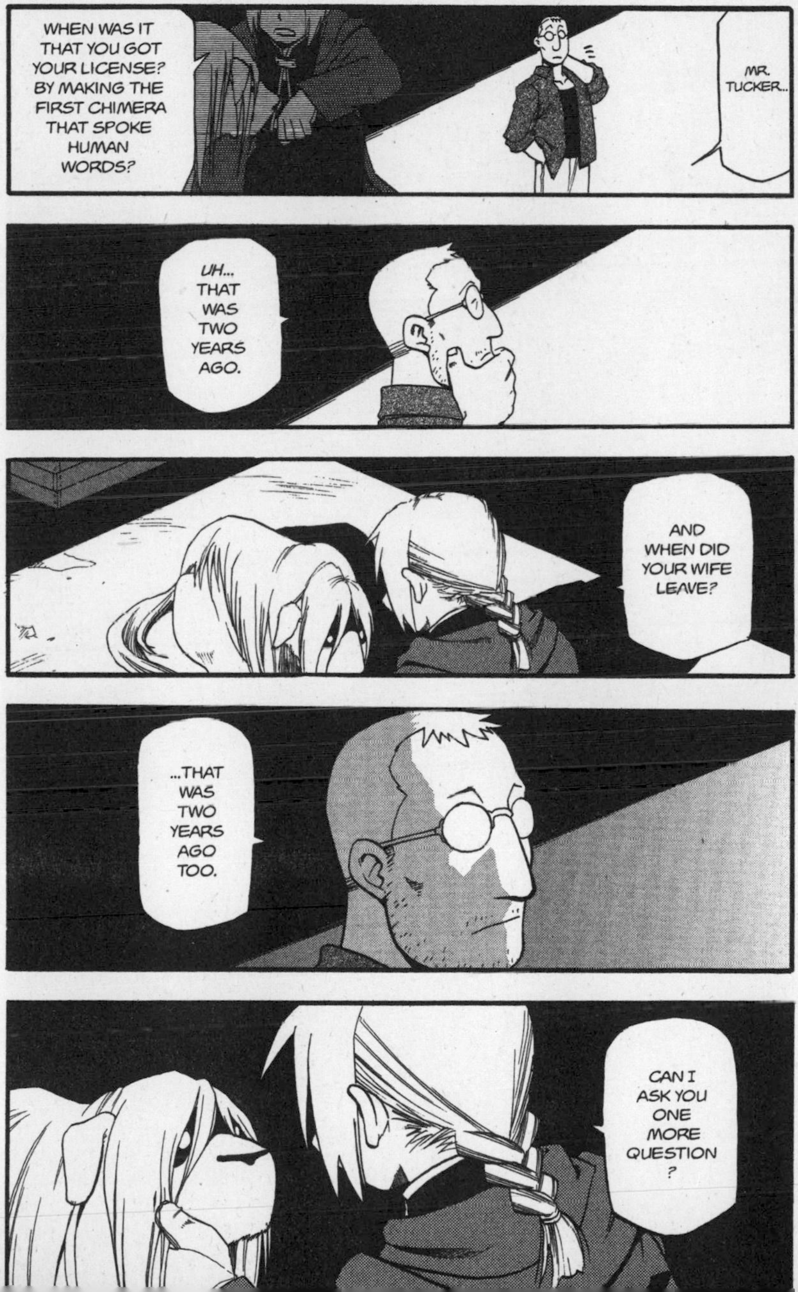
MR. TUCKER...
WHEN WAS IT THAT YOU GOT YOUR LICENSE? BY MAKING THE FIRST CHIMERA THAT SPOKE HUMAN WORDS?
UH... THAT WAS TWO YEARS AGO.
AND WHEN DID YOUR WIFE LEAVE?
...THAT WAS TWO YEARS AGO TOO.
CAN I ASK YOU ONE MORE QUESTION ?

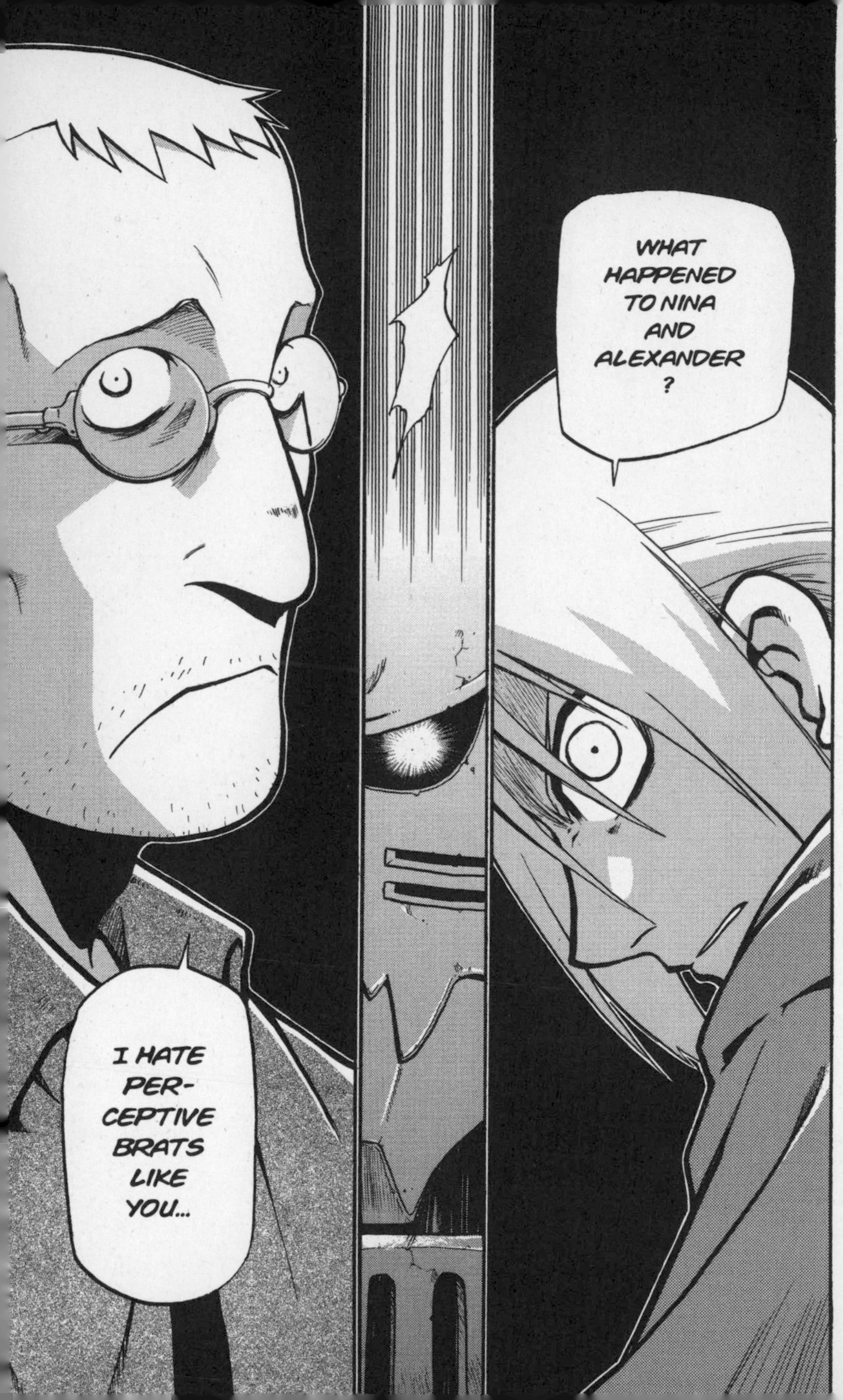
WHAT HAPPENED TO NINA AND ALEXANDER?
I HATE PER-CEPTIVE BRATS LIKE YOU...

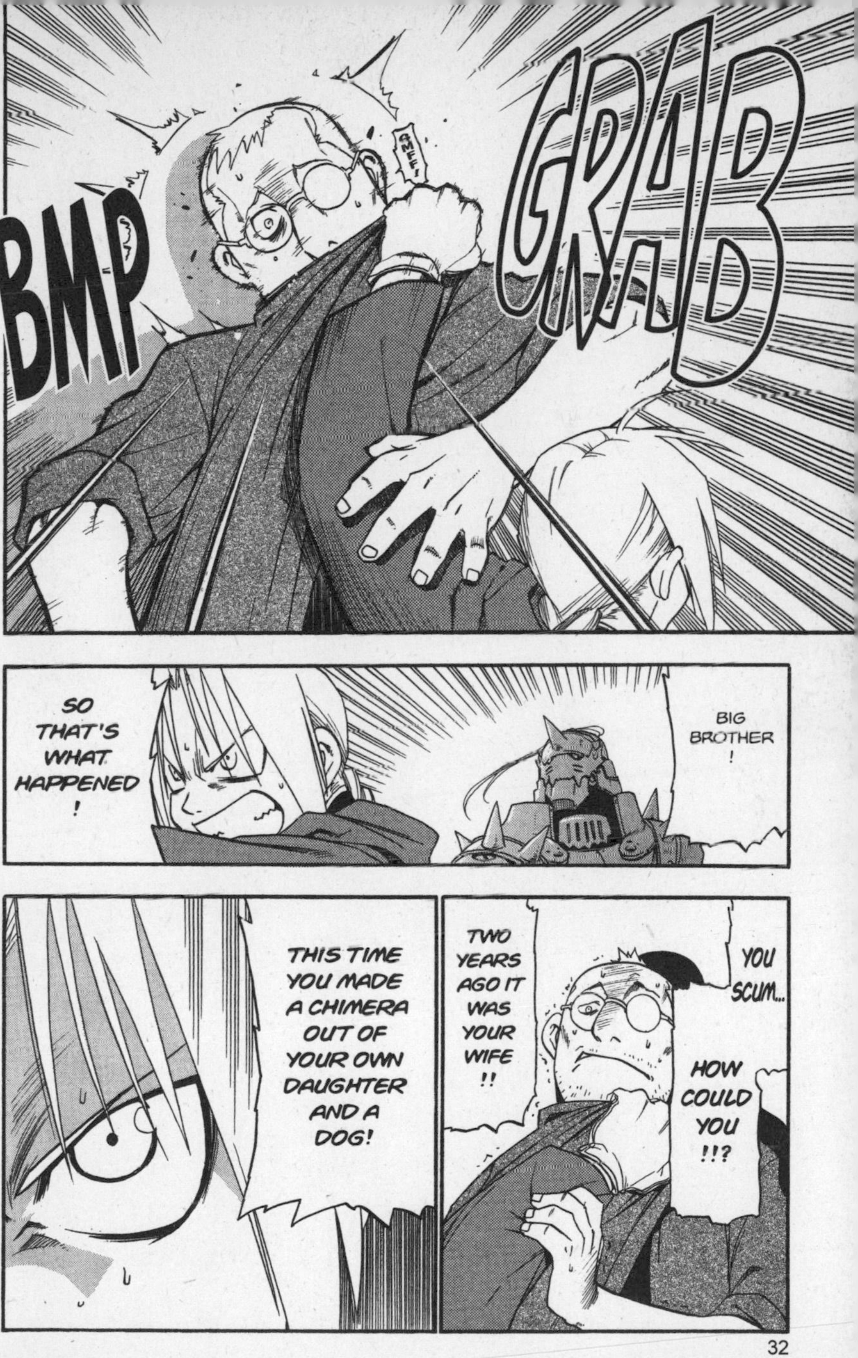
GRAB
GMFF!
BMP
BIG BROTHER !
SO THAT'S WHAT HAPPENED !
YOU SCUM...
TWO YEARS AGO IT WAS YOUR WIFE !!
HOW COULD YOU !!?
THIS TIME YOU MADE A CHIMERA OUT OF YOUR OWN DAUGHTER AND A DOG!

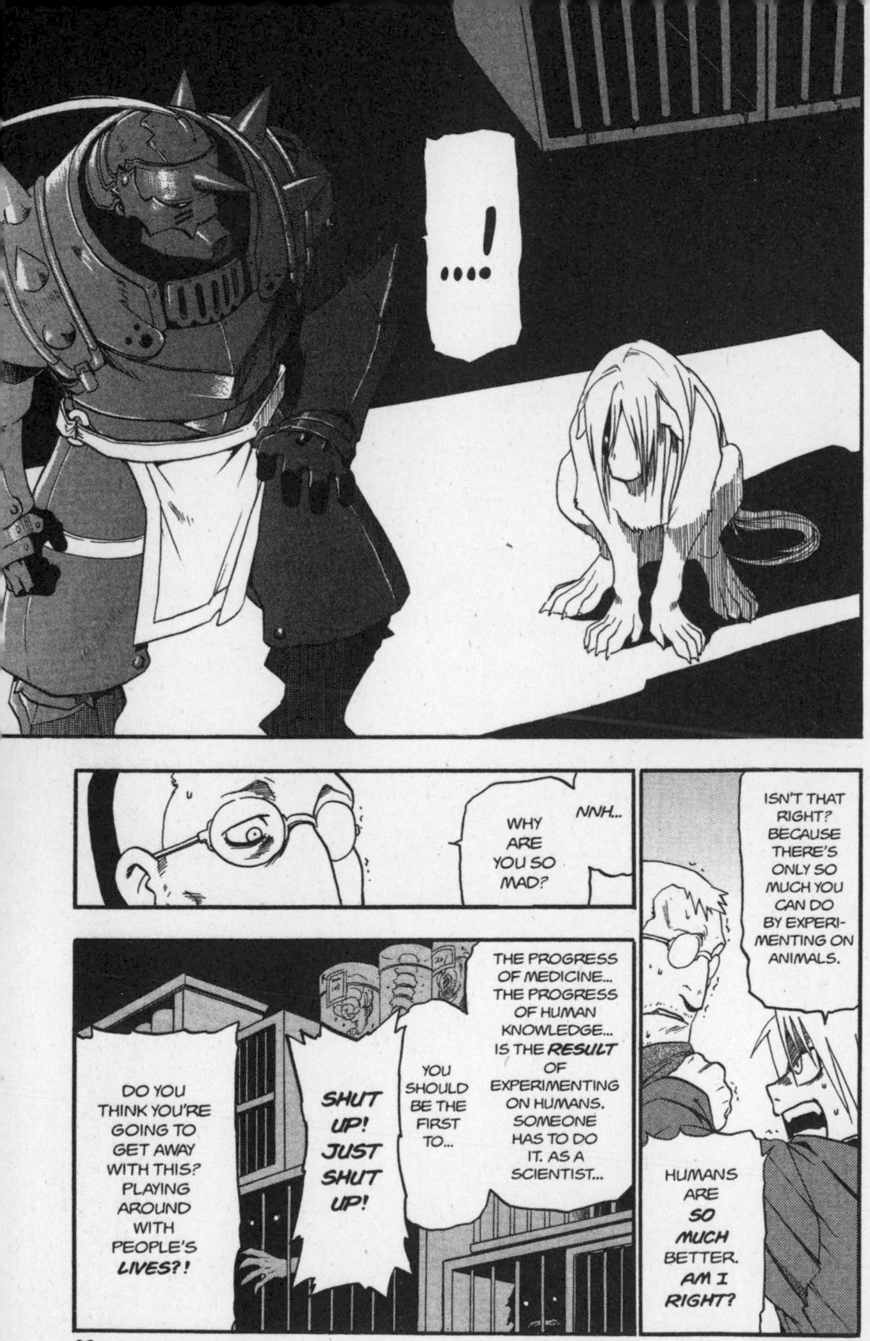
....!
ISN'T THAT RIGHT? BECAUSE THERE'S ONLY SO MUCH YOU CAN DO BY EXPERIMENTING ON ANIMALS.
HUMANS ARE SO MUCH BETTER. AM I RIGHT?
NNH...
WHY ARE YOU SO MAD?
THE PROGRESS OF MEDICINE... THE PROGRESS OF HUMAN KNOWLEDGE... IS THE RESULT OF EXPERIMENTING ON HUMANS. SOMEONE HAS TO DO IT. AS A SCIENTIST...
YOU SHOULD BE THE FIRST TO...
SHUT UP! JUST SHUT UP!
DO YOU THINK YOU'RE GOING TO GET AWAY WITH THIS? PLAYING AROUND WITH PEOPLE'S LIVES?!

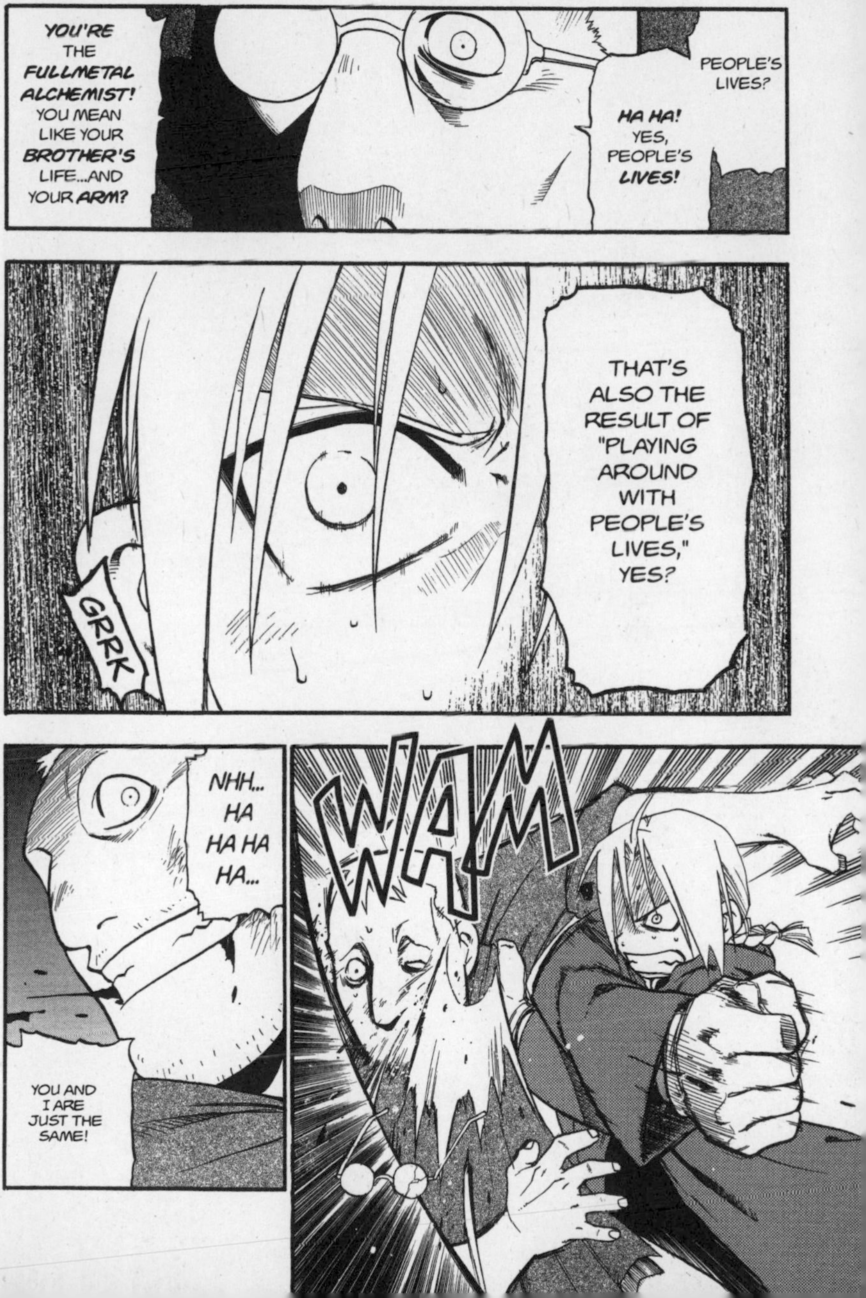
PEOPLE'S LIVES?
HA HA! YES, PEOPLE'S LIVES!
YOU'RE THE FULLMETAL ALCHEMIST! YOU MEAN LIKE YOUR BROTHER'S LIFE...AND YOUR ARM?
THAT'S ALSO THE RESULT OF "PLAYING AROUND WITH PEOPLE'S LIVES," YES?
GRRK
WAM
NHH... HA HA HA HA...
YOU AND I ARE JUST THE SAME!

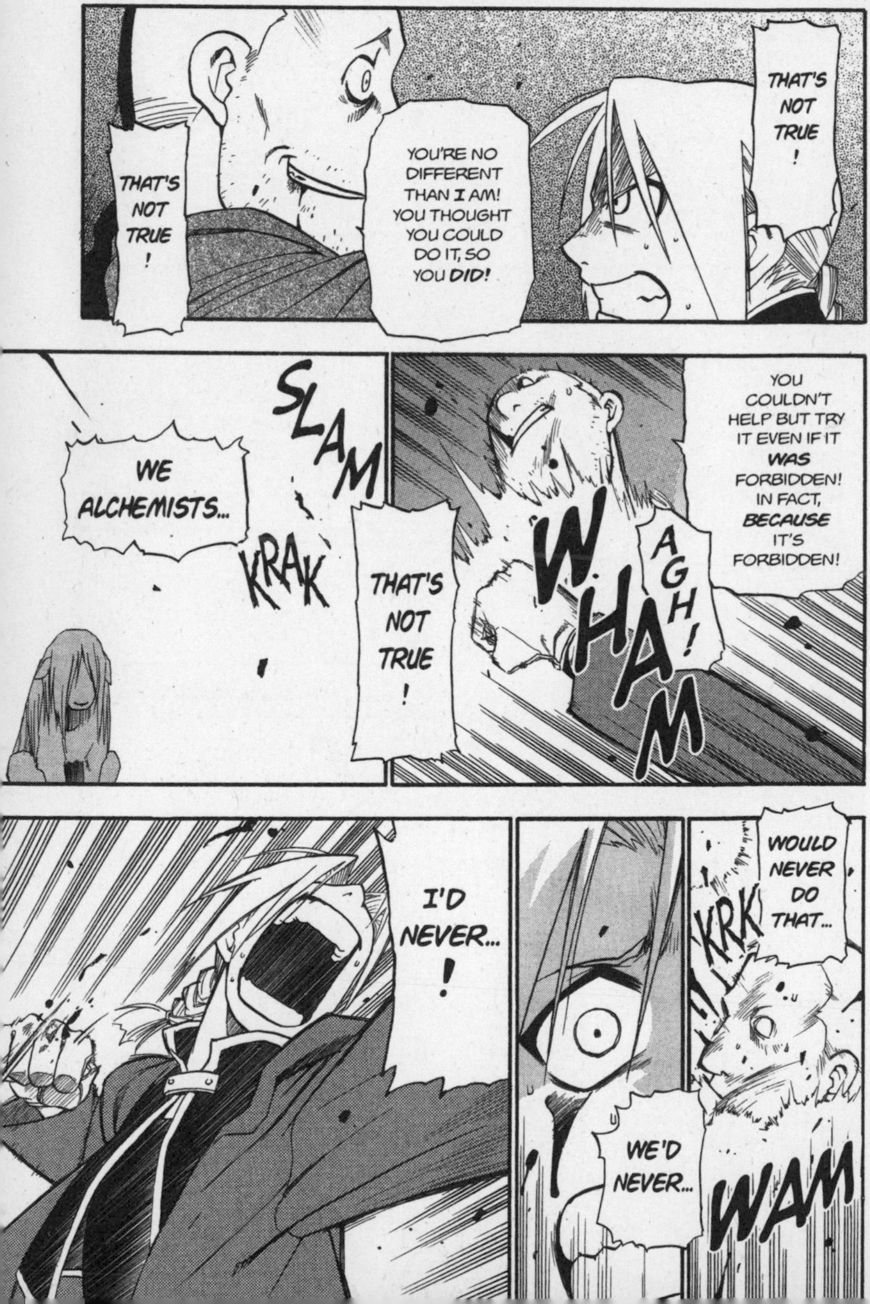
THAT'S NOT TRUE!
YOU'RE NO DIFFERENT THAN I AM! YOU THOUGHT YOU COULD DO IT, SO YOU DID!
THAT'S NOT TRUE!
YOU COULDN'T HELP BUT TRY IT EVEN IF IT WAS FORBIDDEN! IN FACT, BECAUSE IT'S FORBIDDEN!
AGH!
WHAM
THAT'S NOT TRUE!
SLAM
WE ALCHEMISTS...
KRAK
WOULD NEVER DO THAT...
KRK
WAM
WE'D NEVER...
I'D NEVER...!

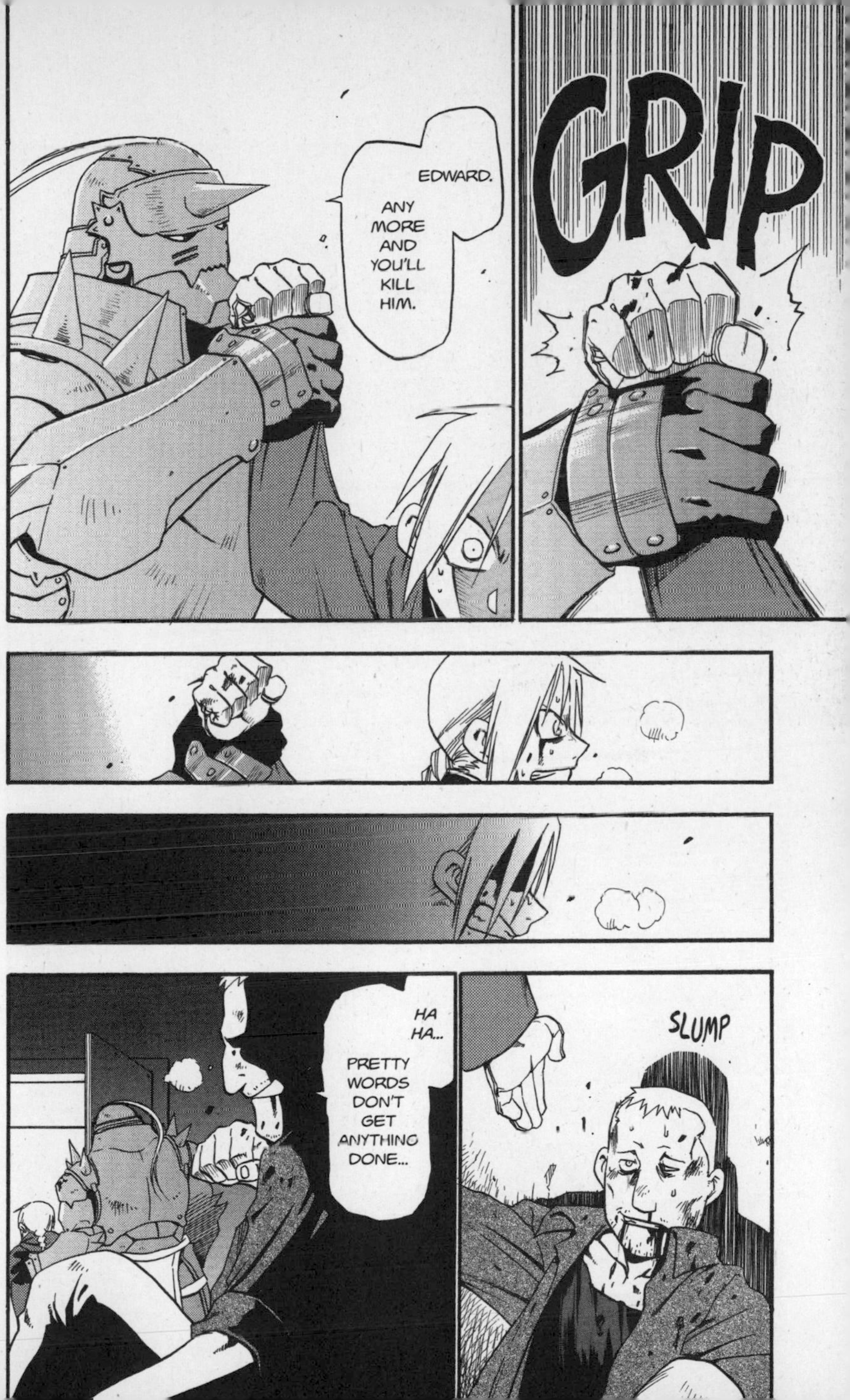
GRIP
EDWARD.
ANY MORE AND YOU'LL KILL HIM.
SLUMP
HA HA...
PRETTY WORDS DON'T GET ANYTHING DONE...

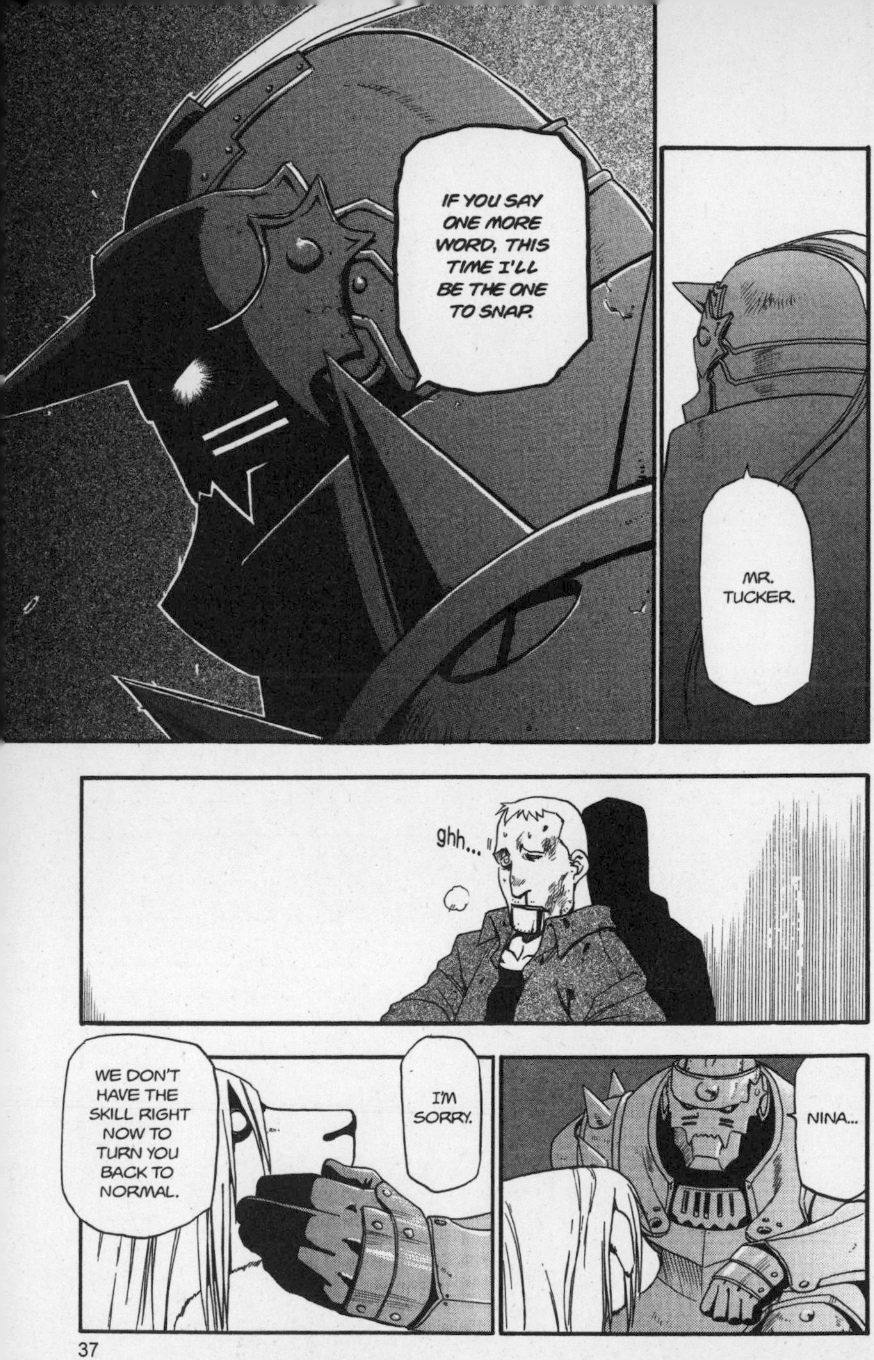
MR. TUCKER.
IF YOU SAY ONE MORE WORD, THIS TIME I'LL BE THE ONE TO SNAP.
ghh...
NINA...
I'M SORRY.
WE DON'T HAVE THE SKILL RIGHT NOW TO TURN YOU BACK TO NORMAL.

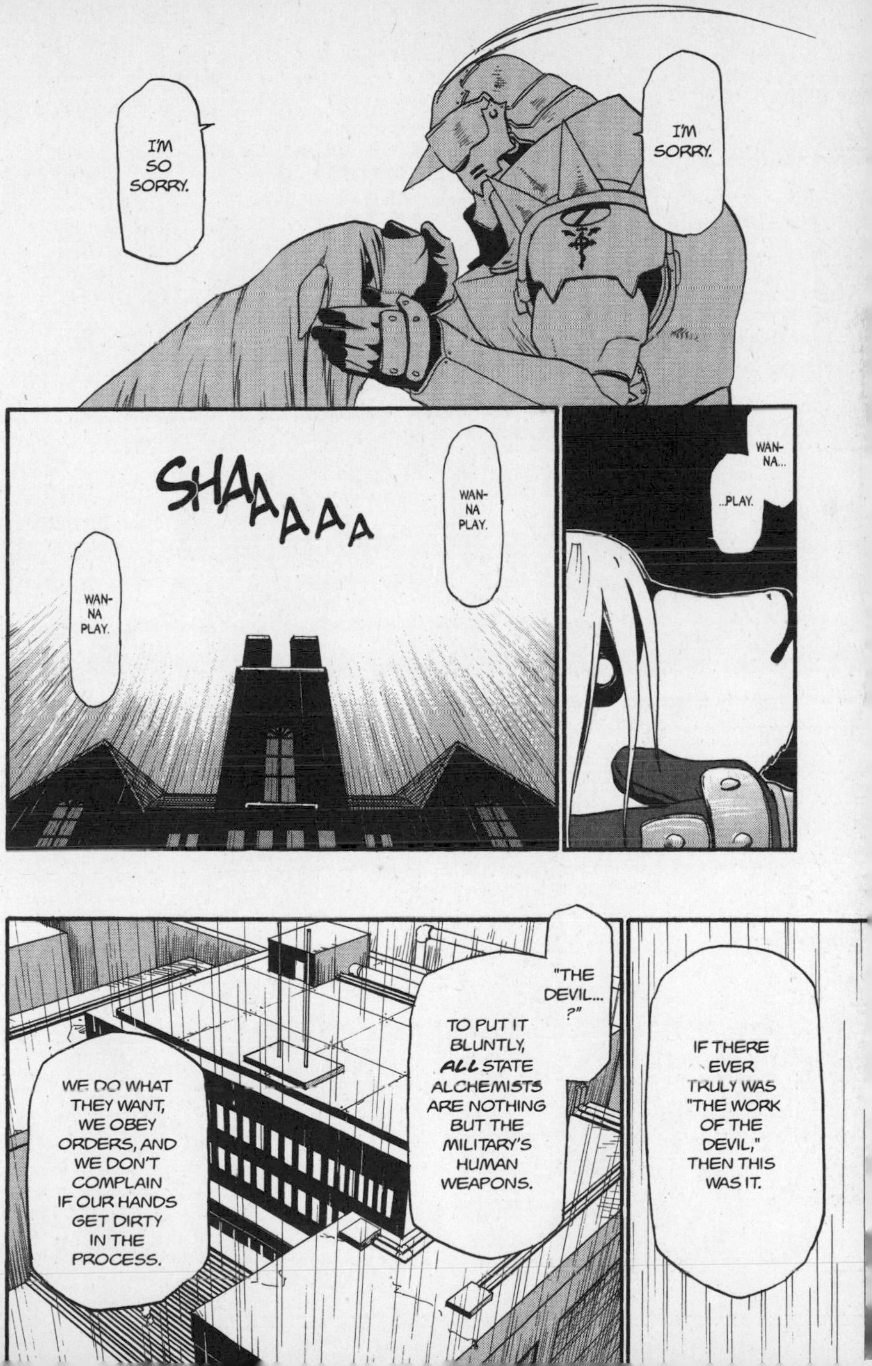
I'M SORRY.
I'M SO SORRY.
WAN-NA...
...PLAY.
WAN-NA PLAY.
SHAAAAAA
WAN-NA PLAY.
IF THERE EVER TRULY WAS "THE WORK OF THE DEVIL," THEN THIS WAS IT.
"THE DEVIL... ?"
TO PUT IT BLUNTLY, ALL STATE ALCHEMISTS ARE NOTHING BUT THE MILITARY'S HUMAN WEAPONS.
WE DO WHAT THEY WANT, WE OBEY ORDERS, AND WE DON'T COMPLAIN IF OUR HANDS GET DIRTY IN THE PROCESS.

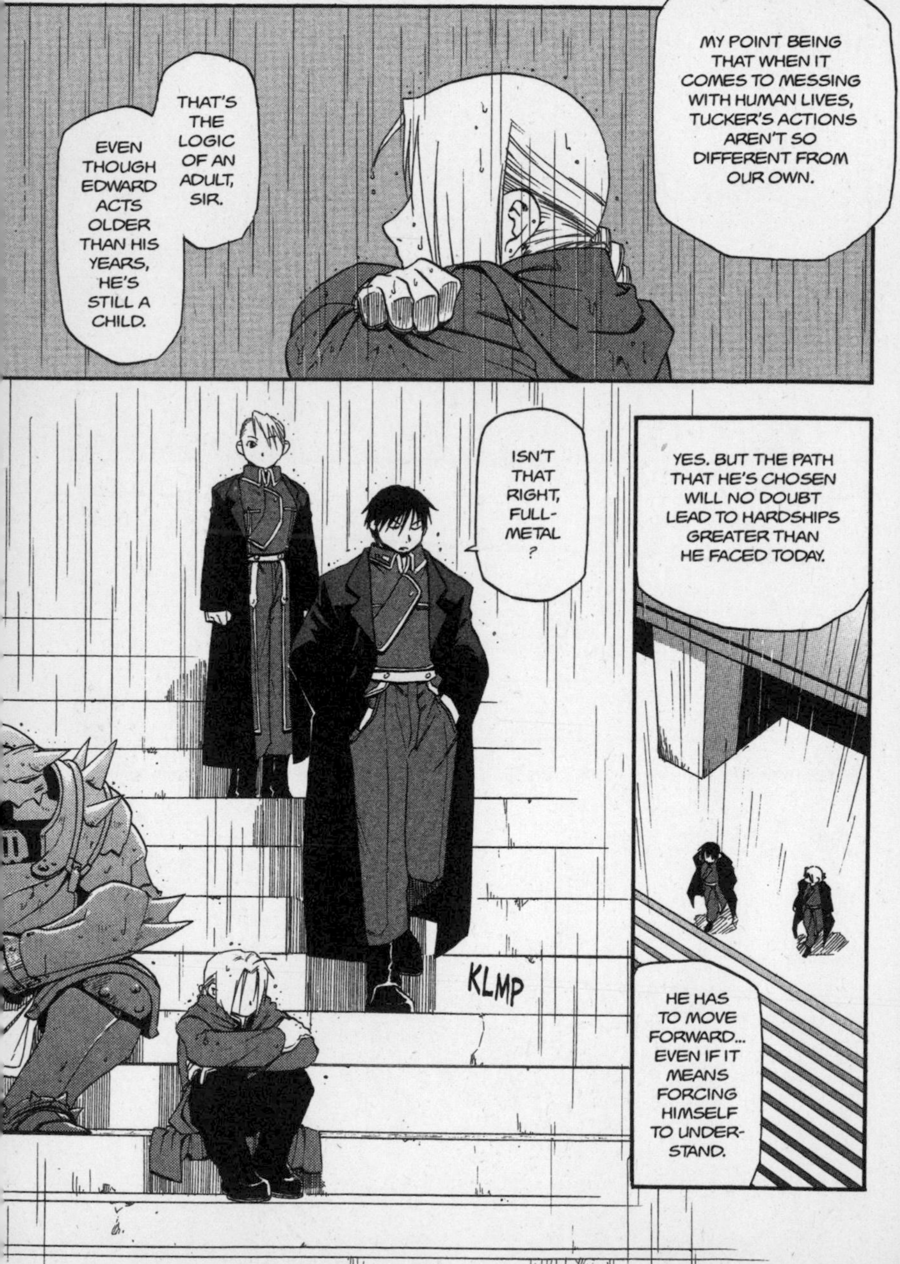
MY POINT BEING THAT WHEN IT COMES TO MESSING WITH HUMAN LIVES, TUCKER'S ACTIONS AREN'T SO DIFFERENT FROM OUR OWN.
THAT'S THE LOGIC OF AN ADULT, SIR.
EVEN THOUGH EDWARD ACTS OLDER THAN HIS YEARS, HE'S STILL A CHILD.
YES. BUT THE PATH THAT HE'S CHOSEN WILL NO DOUBT LEAD TO HARDSHIPS GREATER THAN HE FACED TODAY.
HE HAS TO MOVE FORWARD... EVEN IF IT MEANS FORCING HIMSELF TO UNDERSTAND.
ISN'T THAT RIGHT, FULL-METAL?
KLMP

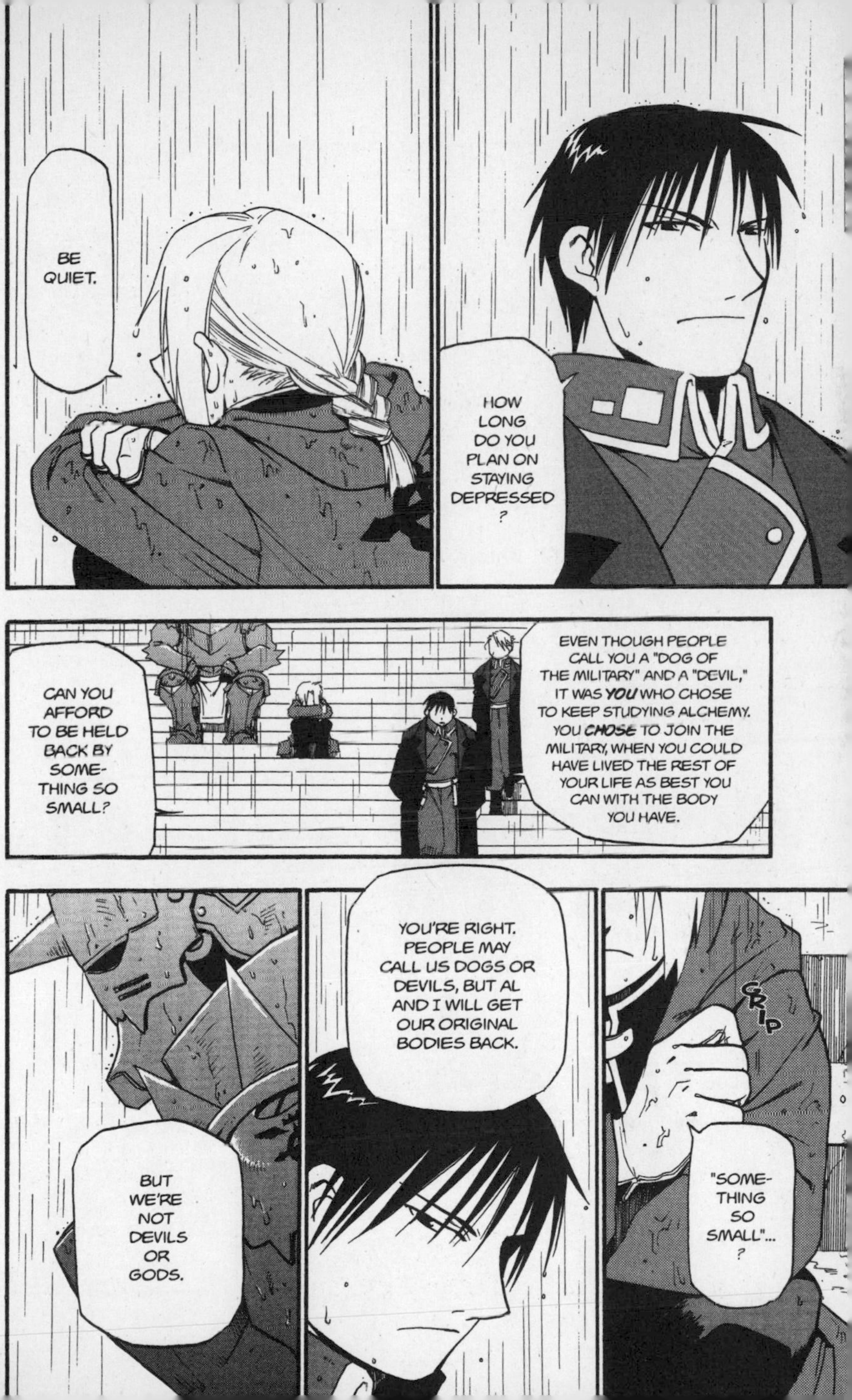
HOW LONG DO YOU PLAN ON STAYING DEPRESSED?
BE QUIET.
EVEN THOUGH PEOPLE CALL YOU A "DOG OF THE MILITARY" AND A "DEVIL," IT WAS *YOU* WHO CHOSE TO KEEP STUDYING ALCHEMY. YOU *CHOSE* TO JOIN THE MILITARY, WHEN YOU COULD HAVE LIVED THE REST OF YOUR LIFE AS BEST YOU CAN WITH THE BODY YOU HAVE.
CAN YOU AFFORD TO BE HELD BACK BY SOME-THING SO SMALL?
GRIP
"SOME-THING SO SMALL"...?
YOU'RE RIGHT. PEOPLE MAY CALL US DOGS OR DEVILS, BUT AL AND I WILL GET OUR ORIGINAL BODIES BACK.
BUT WE'RE NOT DEVILS OR GODS.

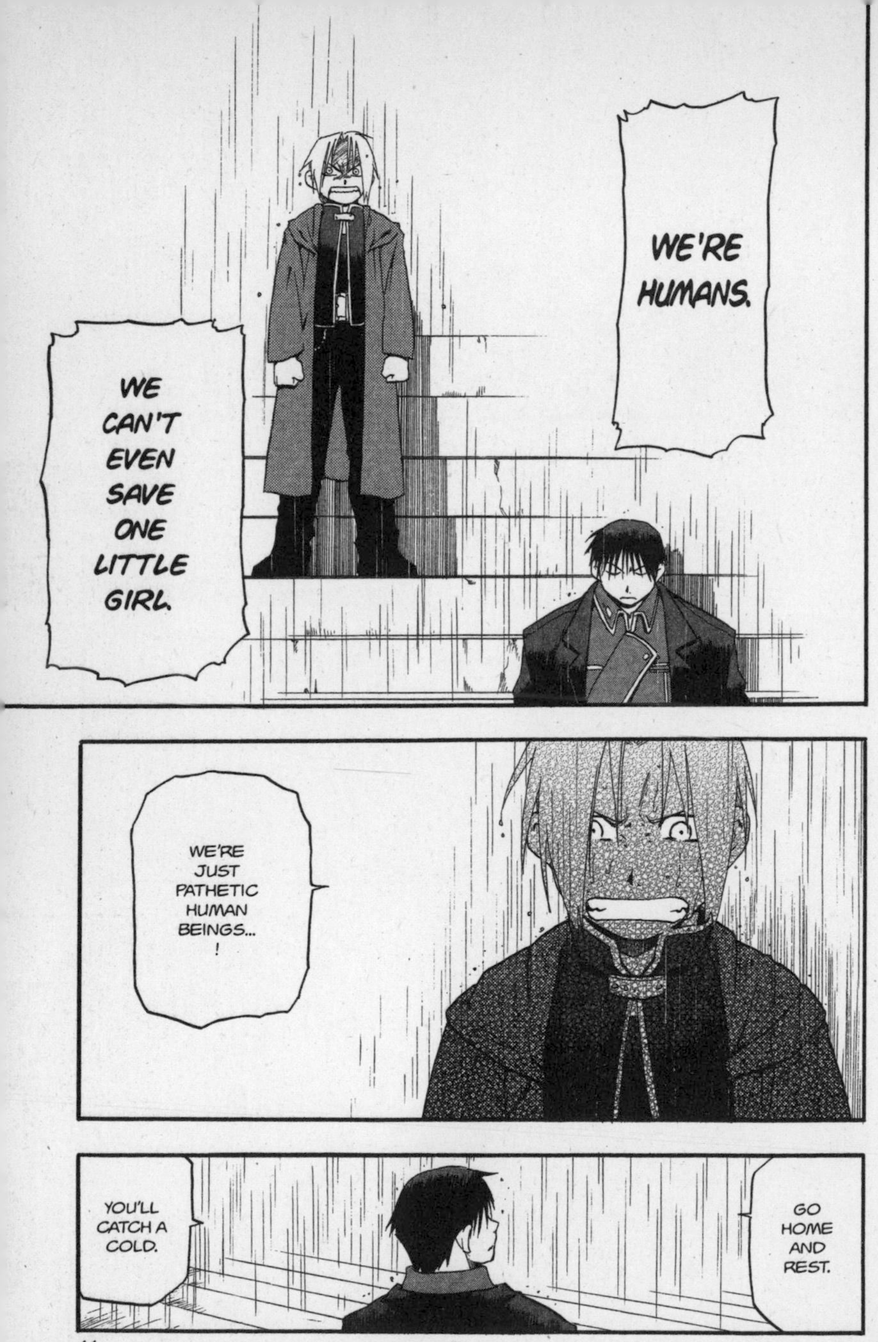
WE'RE HUMANS.
WE CAN'T EVEN SAVE ONE LITTLE GIRL.
WE'RE JUST PATHETIC HUMAN BEINGS...!
GO HOME AND REST.
YOU'LL CATCH A COLD.

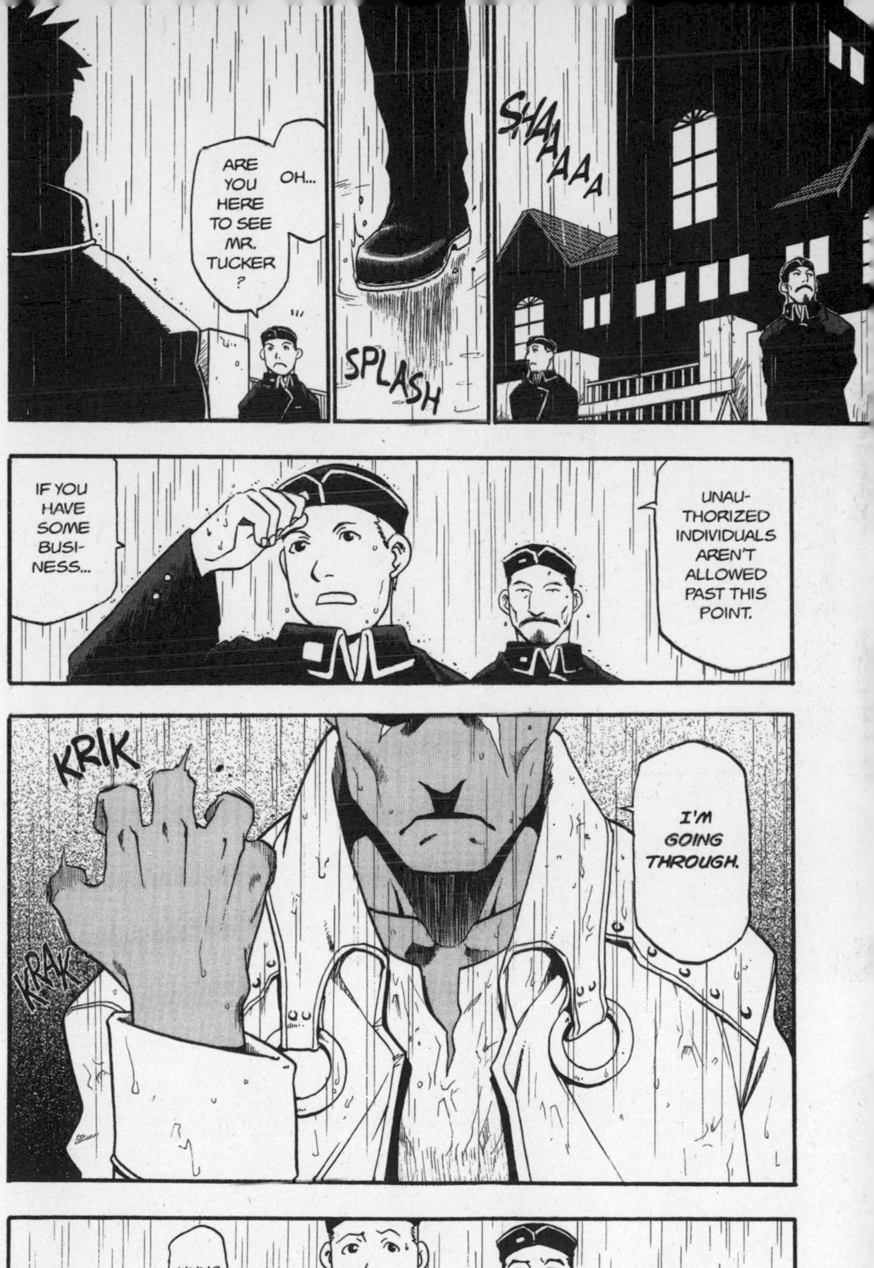
SHAAAAA
SPLASH
OH...
ARE YOU HERE TO SEE MR. TUCKER?
UNAUTHORIZED INDIVIDUALS AREN'T ALLOWED PAST THIS POINT.
IF YOU HAVE SOME BUSINESS...
I'M GOING THROUGH.
KRIK
KRAK
HUH?

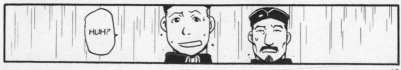

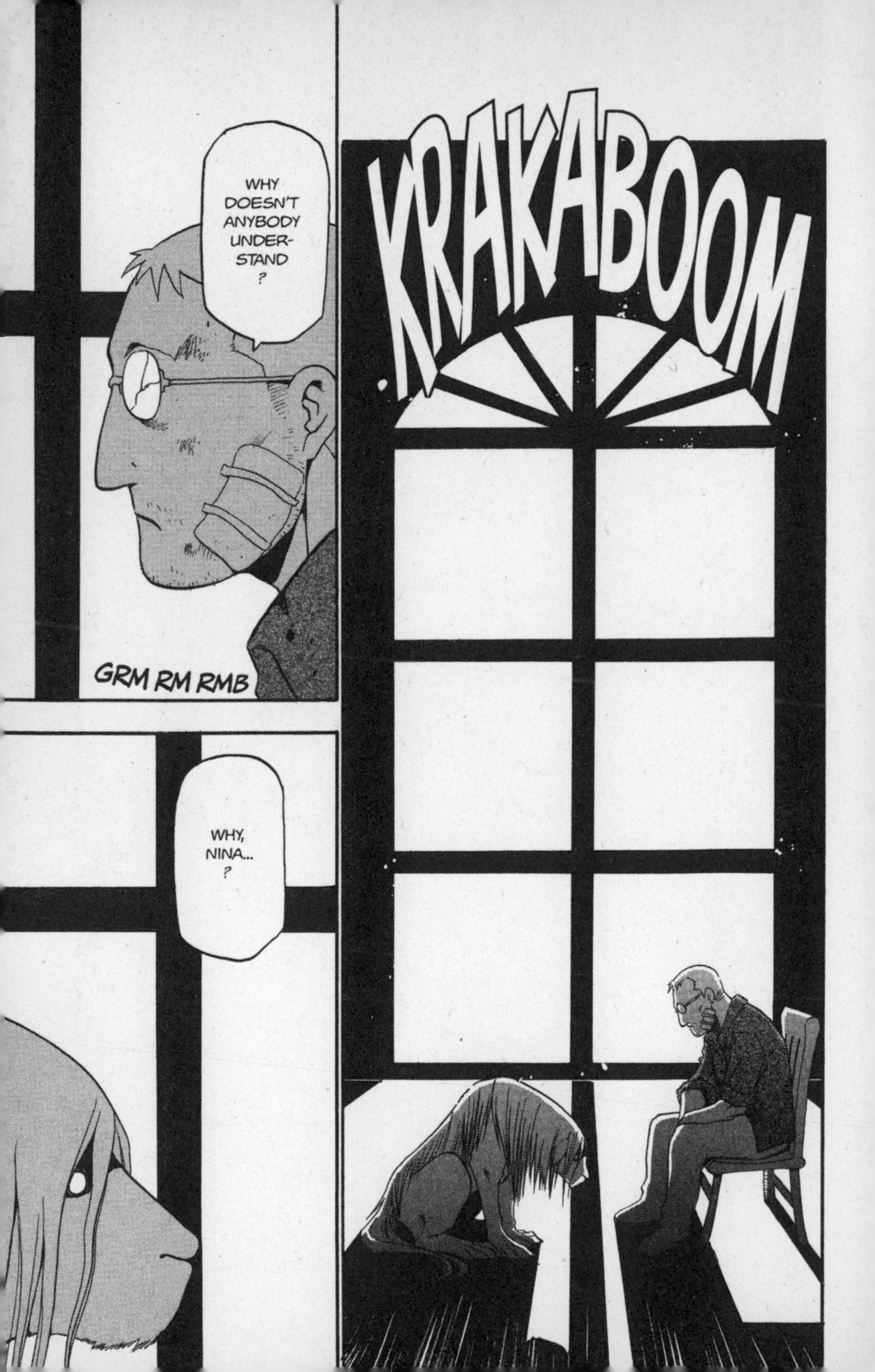
KRAKABOOM
WHY DOESN'T ANYBODY UNDER-STAND?
GRM RM RMB
WHY, NINA...?

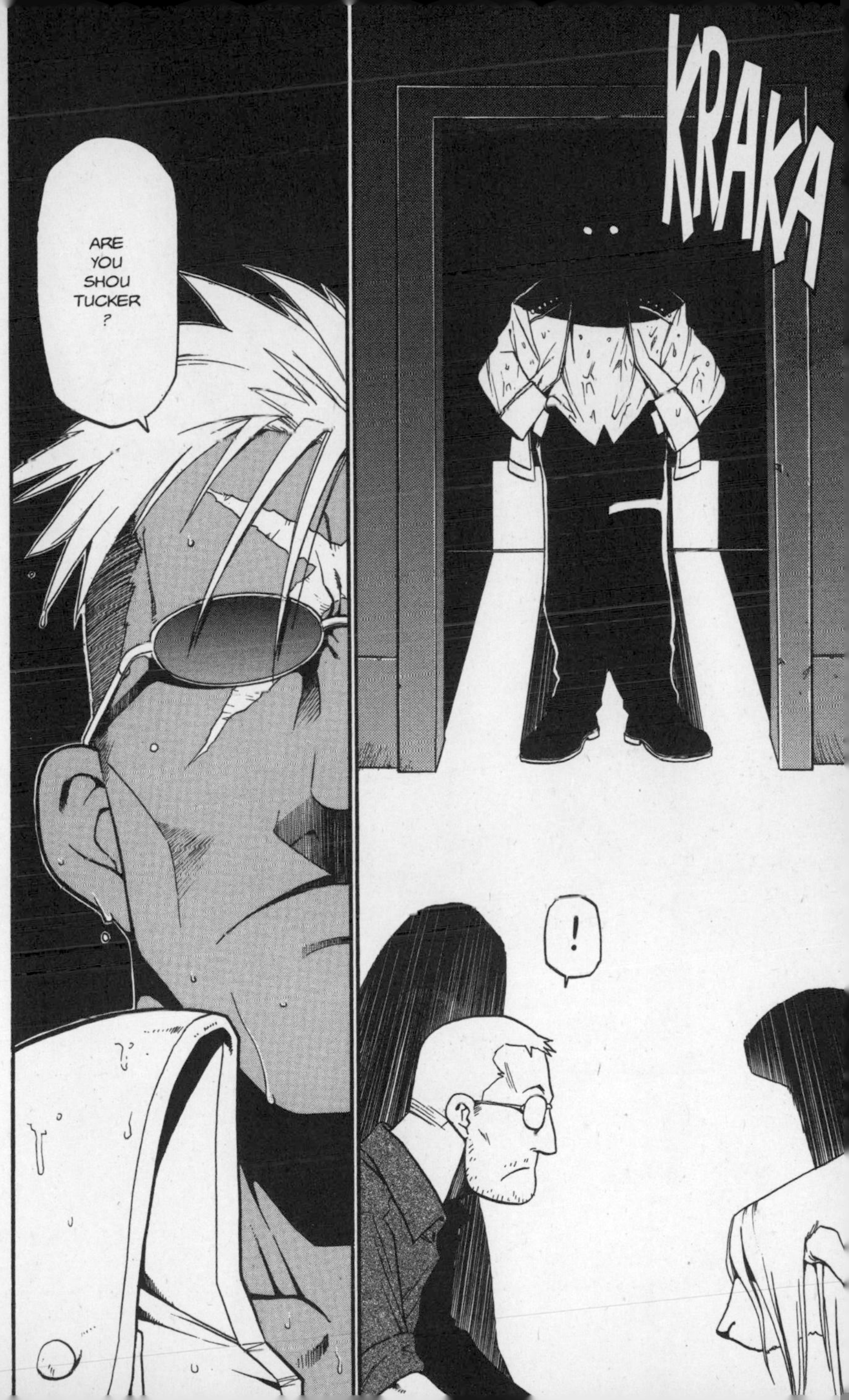
KRAKA
!
ARE YOU SHOU TUCKER ?

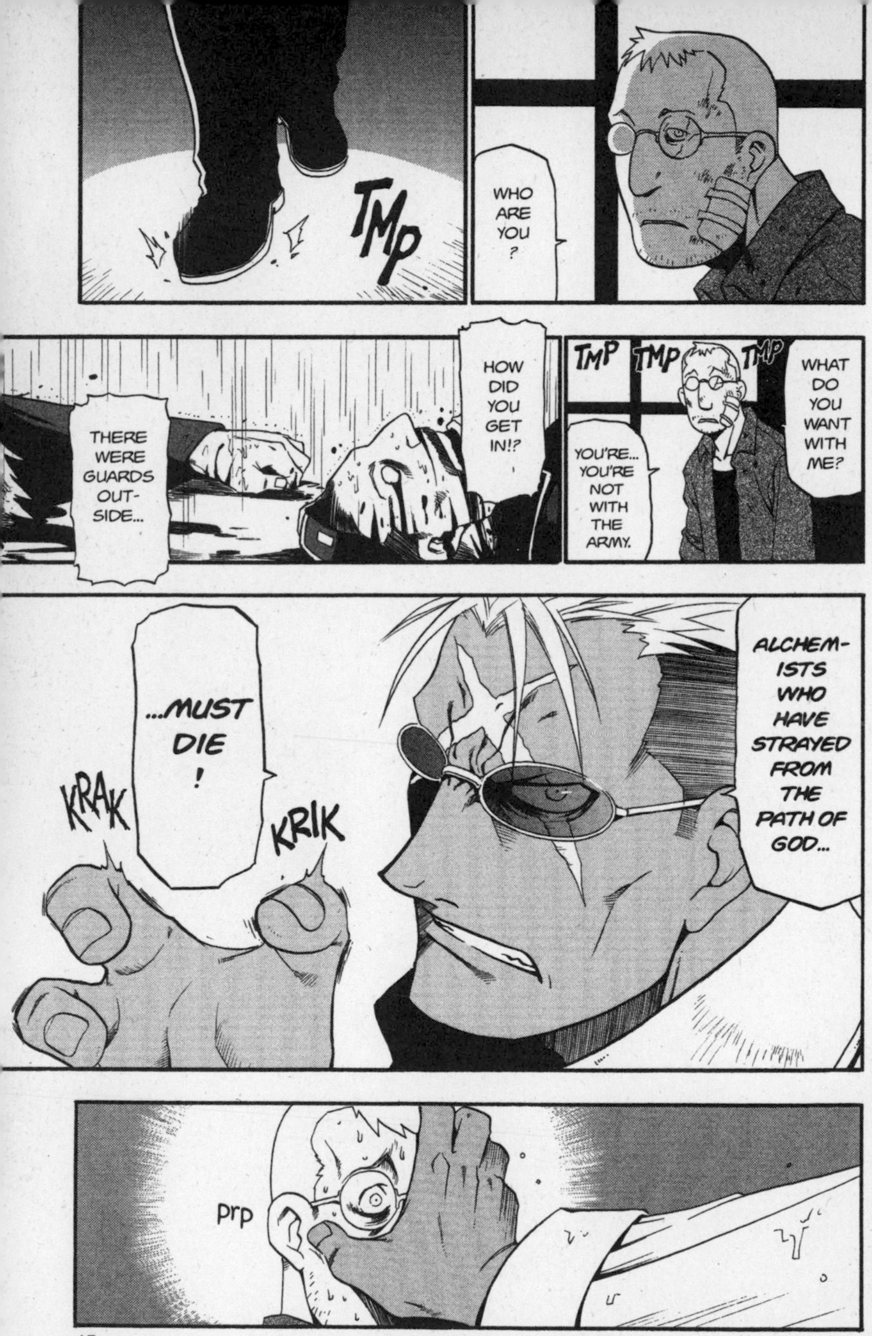
WHO ARE YOU ?
TMP
TMP TMP TMP
WHAT DO YOU WANT WITH ME?
YOU'RE... YOU'RE NOT WITH THE ARMY.
HOW DID YOU GET IN!?
THERE WERE GUARDS OUT-SIDE...
ALCHEM-ISTS WHO HAVE STRAYED FROM THE PATH OF GOD...
KRIK
...MUST DIE !
KRAK
prp

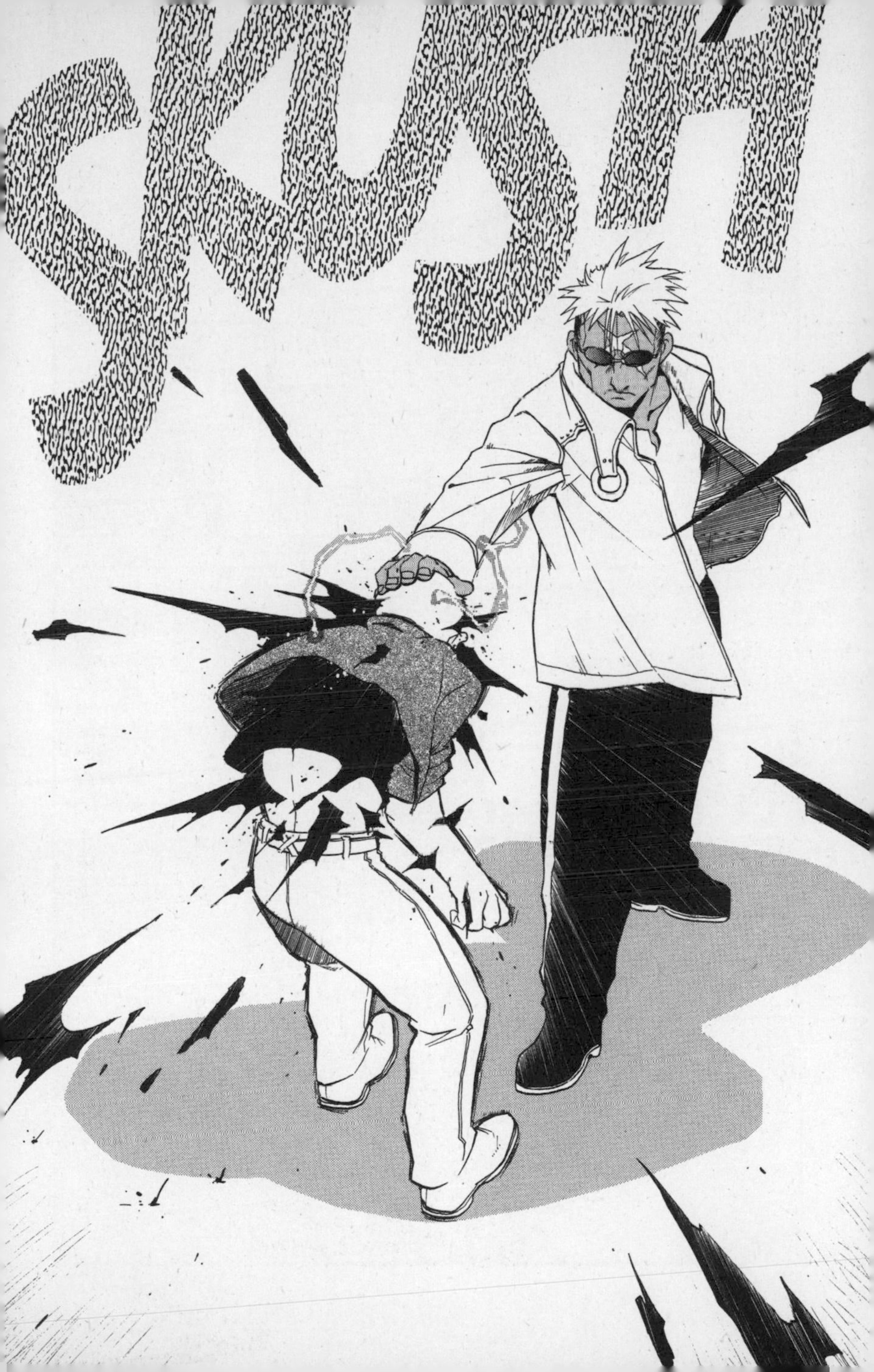
SKUSH!

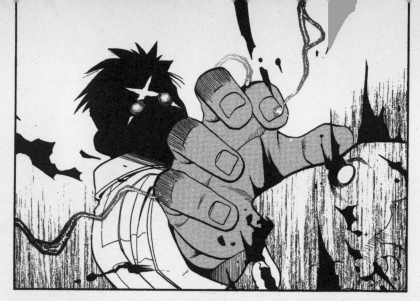

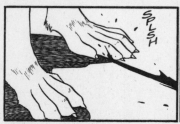

SPLSH

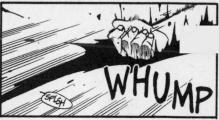

SPLSH

WHUMP

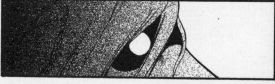

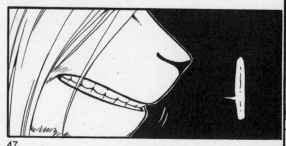

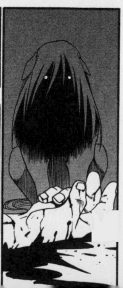

DA-DA...
DAD-DY.
DAD-DY.
DAD-DY.
DAD-DY.
...HOW AW-FUL.
NOW THAT HE'S DONE THIS TO YOU, THERE'S NO WAY TO CHANGE YOU BACK TO NORMAL.

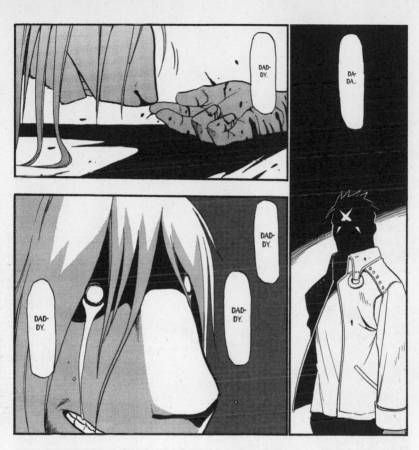

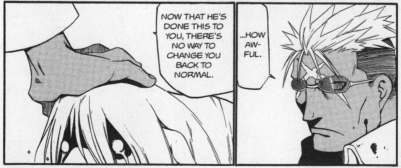

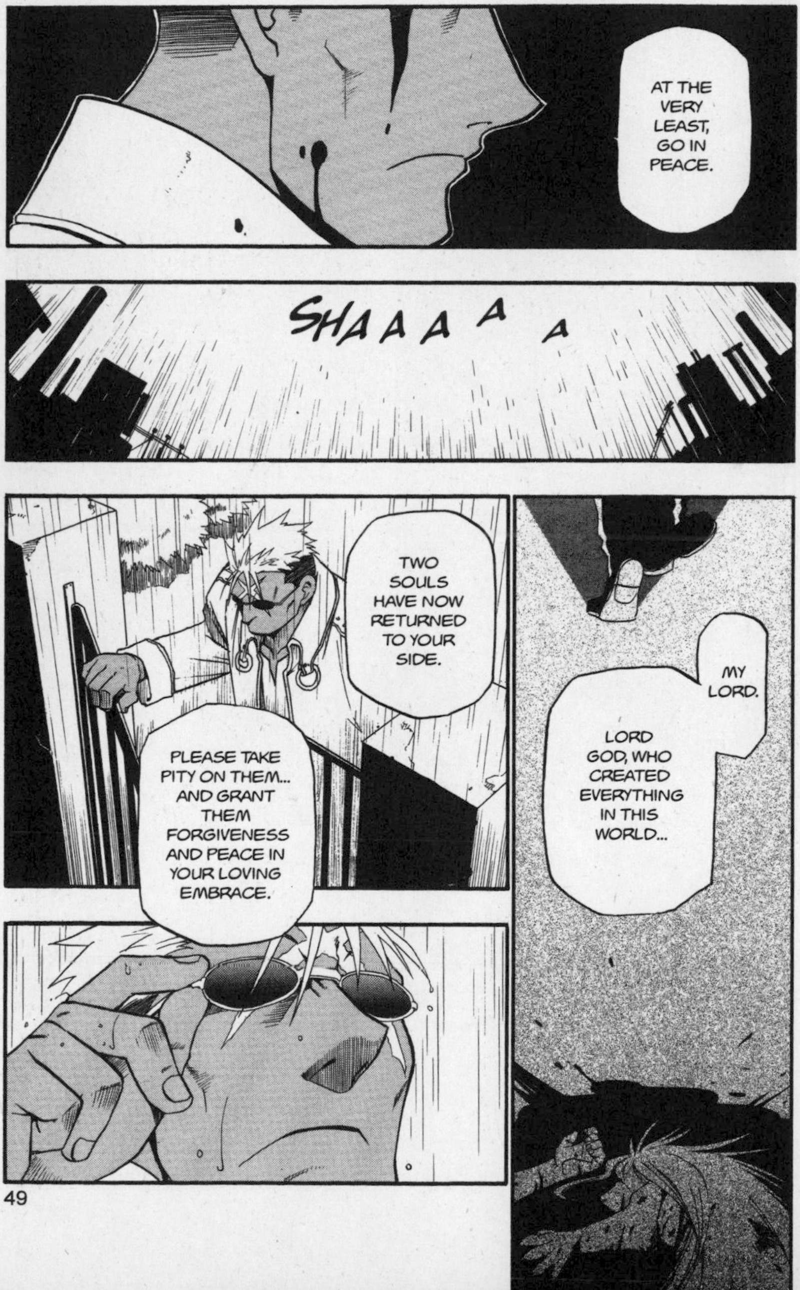
AT THE VERY LEAST, GO IN PEACE.
SHAAAAA
MY LORD.
LORD GOD, WHO CREATED EVERYTHING IN THIS WORLD...
TWO SOULS HAVE NOW RETURNED TO YOUR SIDE.
PLEASE TAKE PITY ON THEM... AND GRANT THEM FORGIVENESS AND PEACE IN YOUR LOVING EMBRACE.

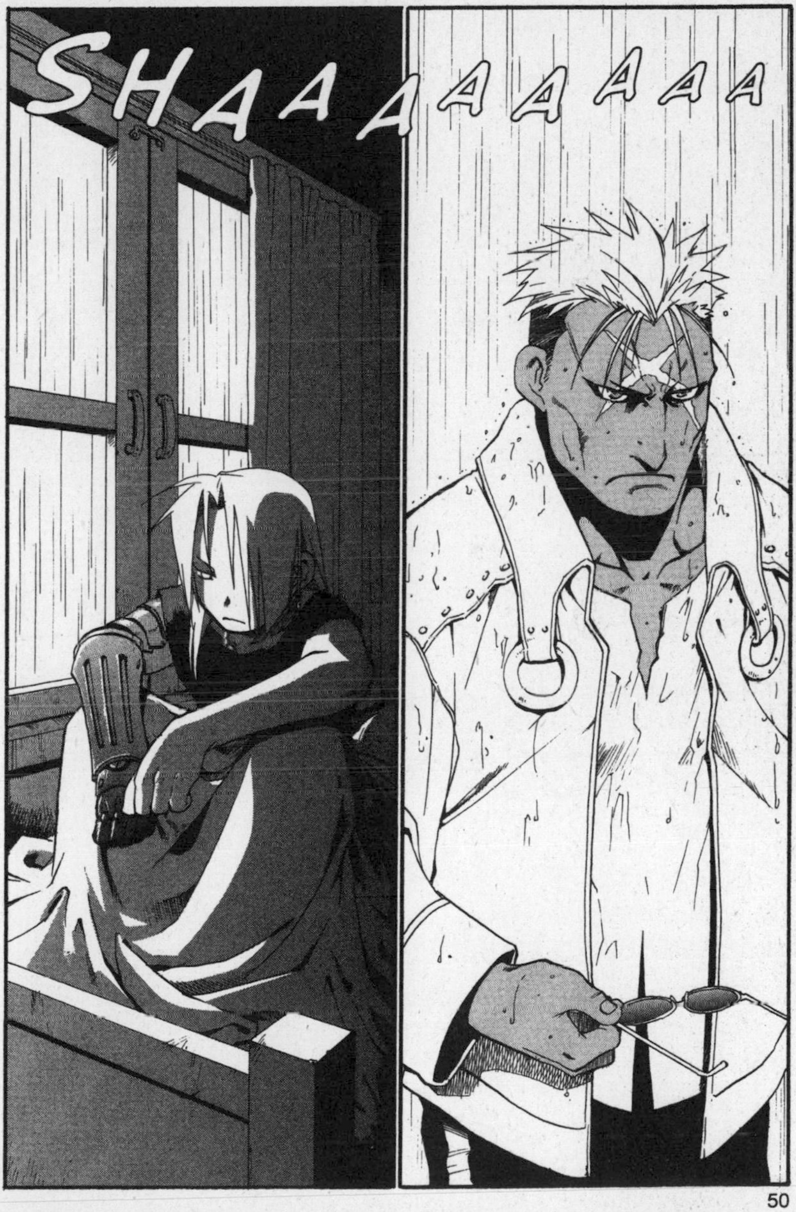
SHAAAAAAAAA

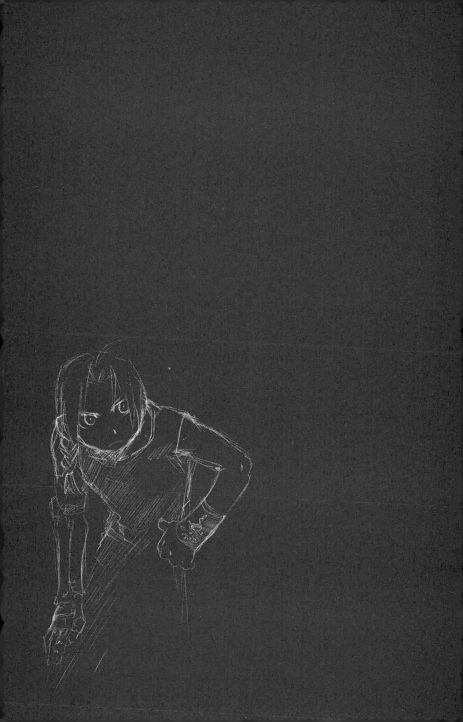

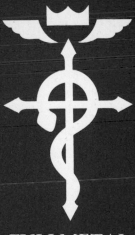

FULLMETAL
ALCHEMIST

Chapter 6: The Right Hand of Destruction

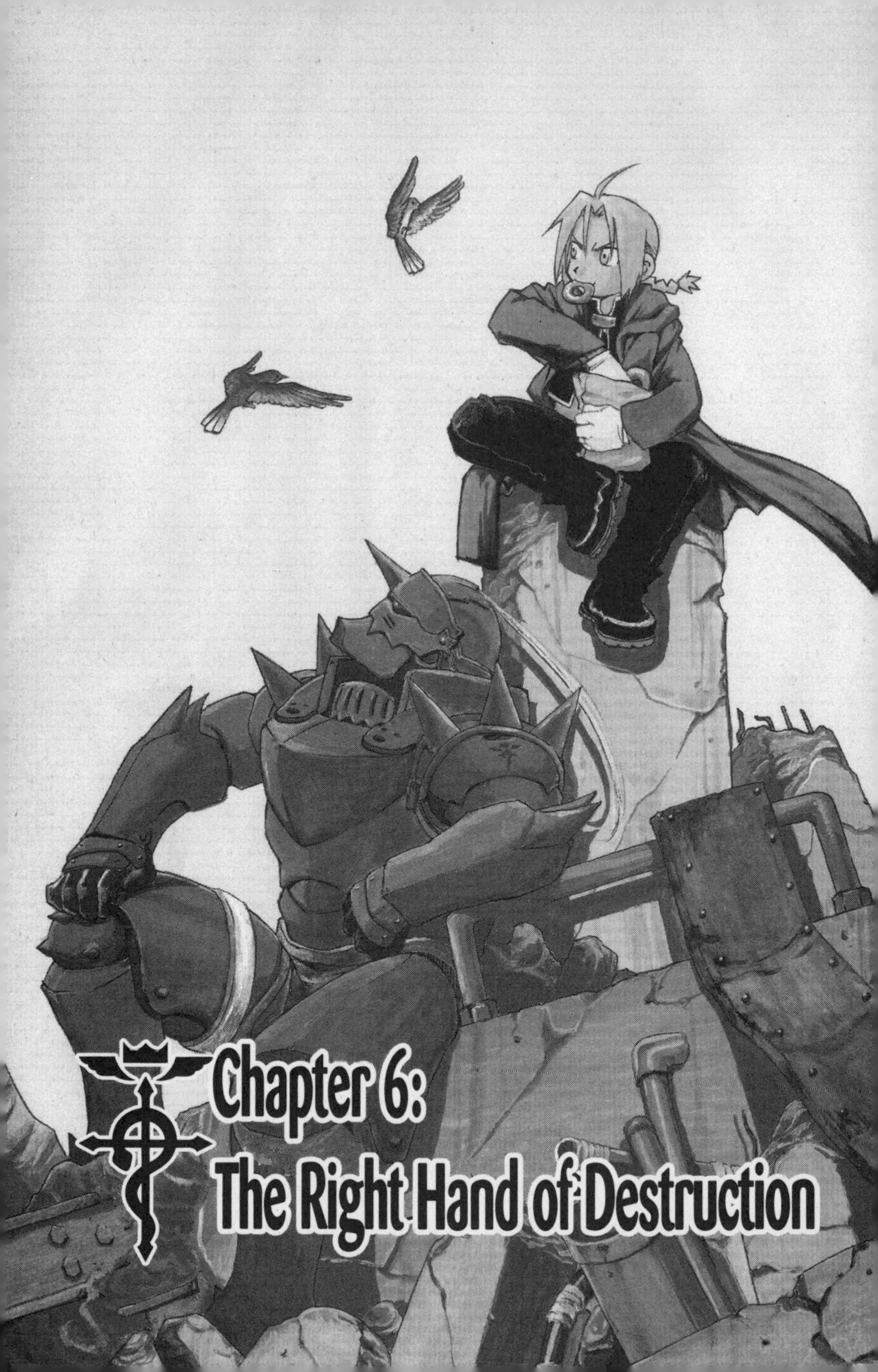

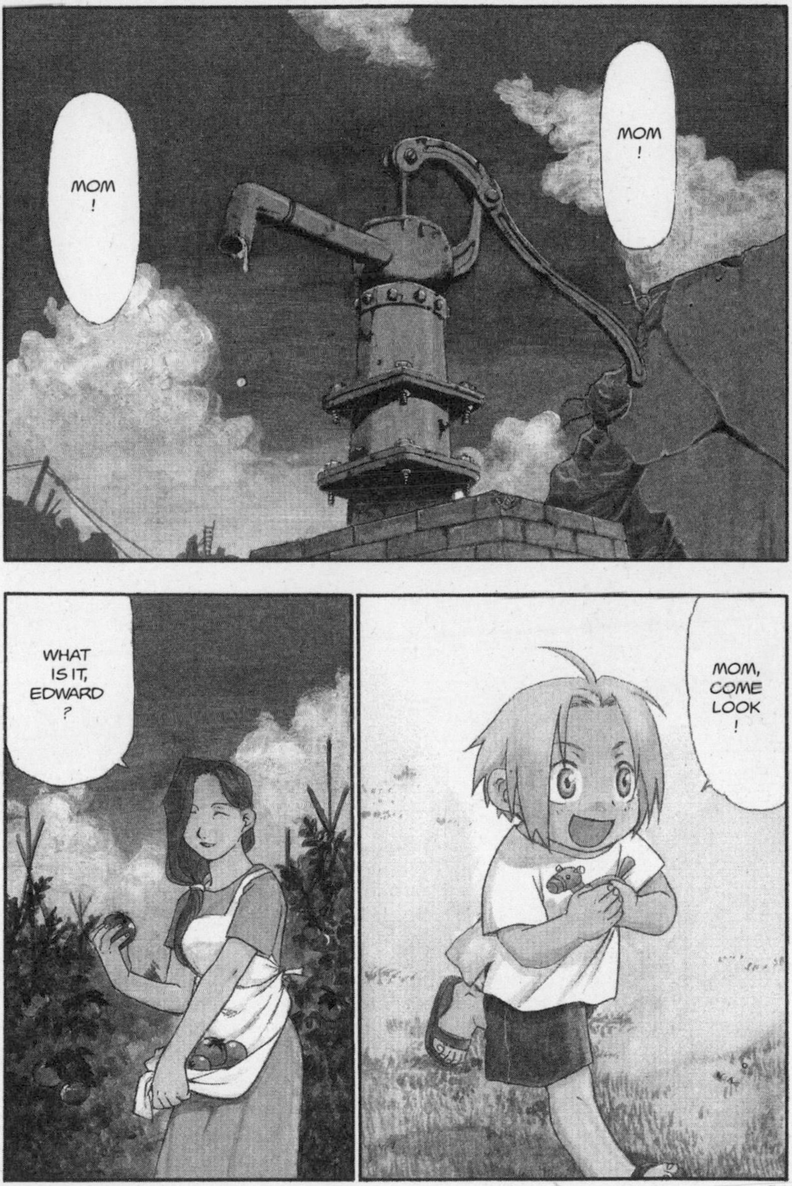
MOM!
MOM!
MOM, COME LOOK!
WHAT IS IT, EDWARD?

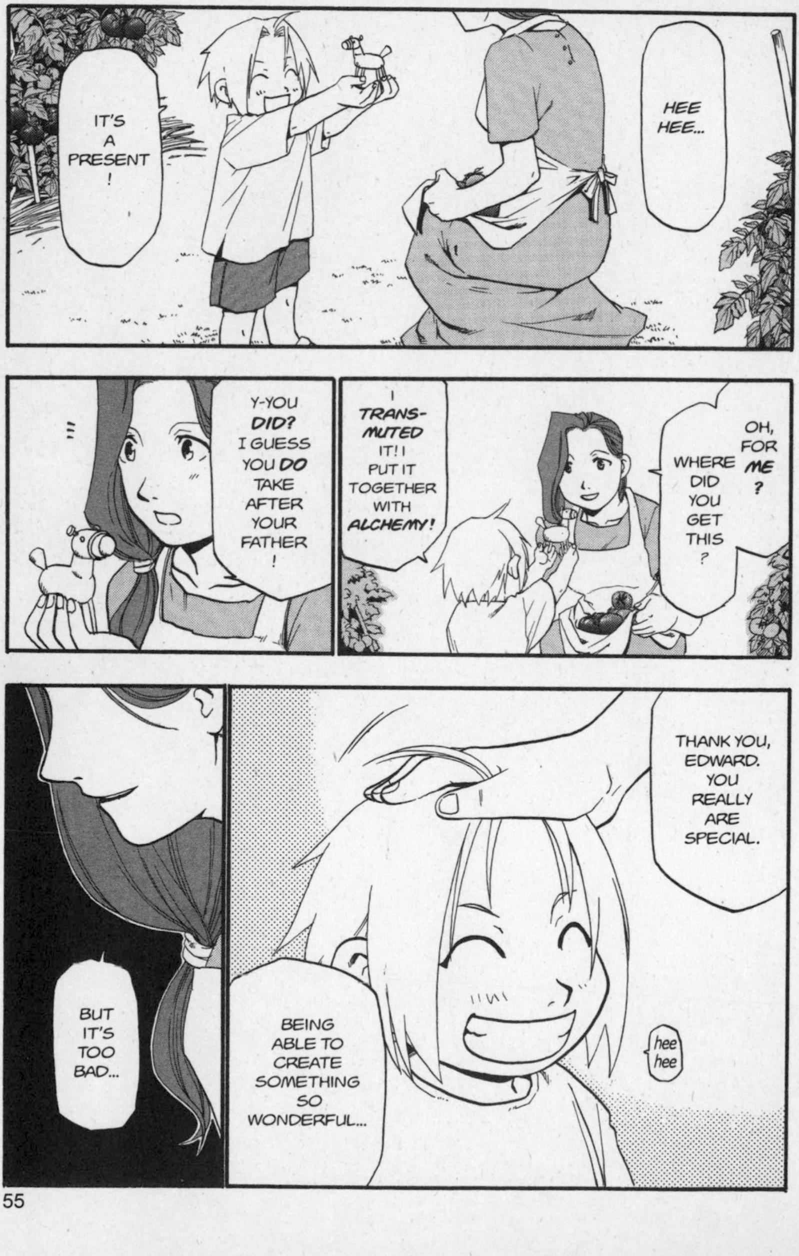
HEE HEE...
IT'S A PRESENT!
OH, FOR ME?
WHERE DID YOU GET THIS?
I TRANSMUTED IT! I PUT IT TOGETHER WITH ALCHEMY!
Y-YOU DID? I GUESS YOU DO TAKE AFTER YOUR FATHER!
THANK YOU, EDWARD. YOU REALLY ARE SPECIAL.
hee hee
BEING ABLE TO CREATE SOMETHING SO WONDERFUL...
BUT IT'S TOO BAD...

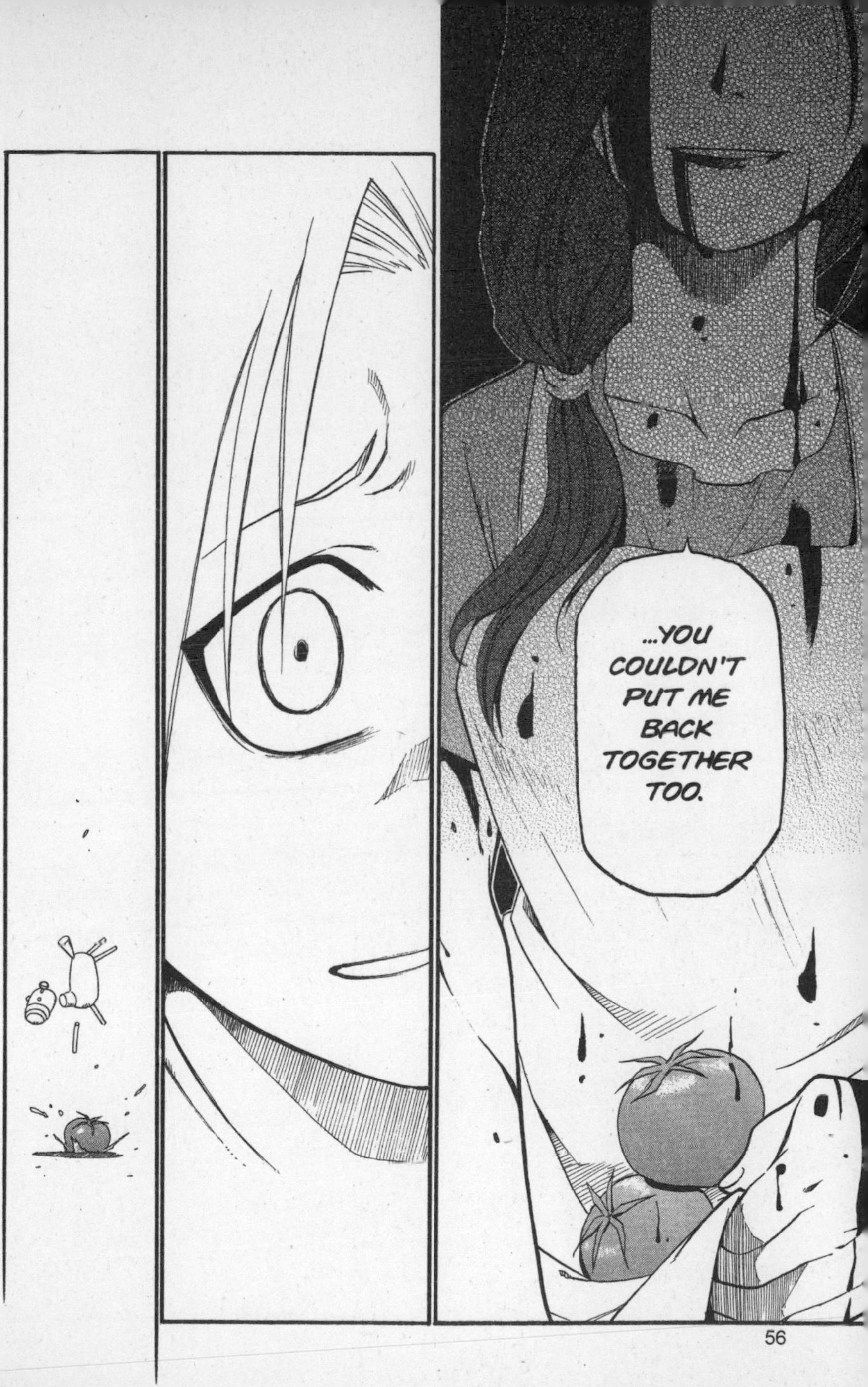
...YOU COULDN'T PUT ME BACK TOGETHER TOO.

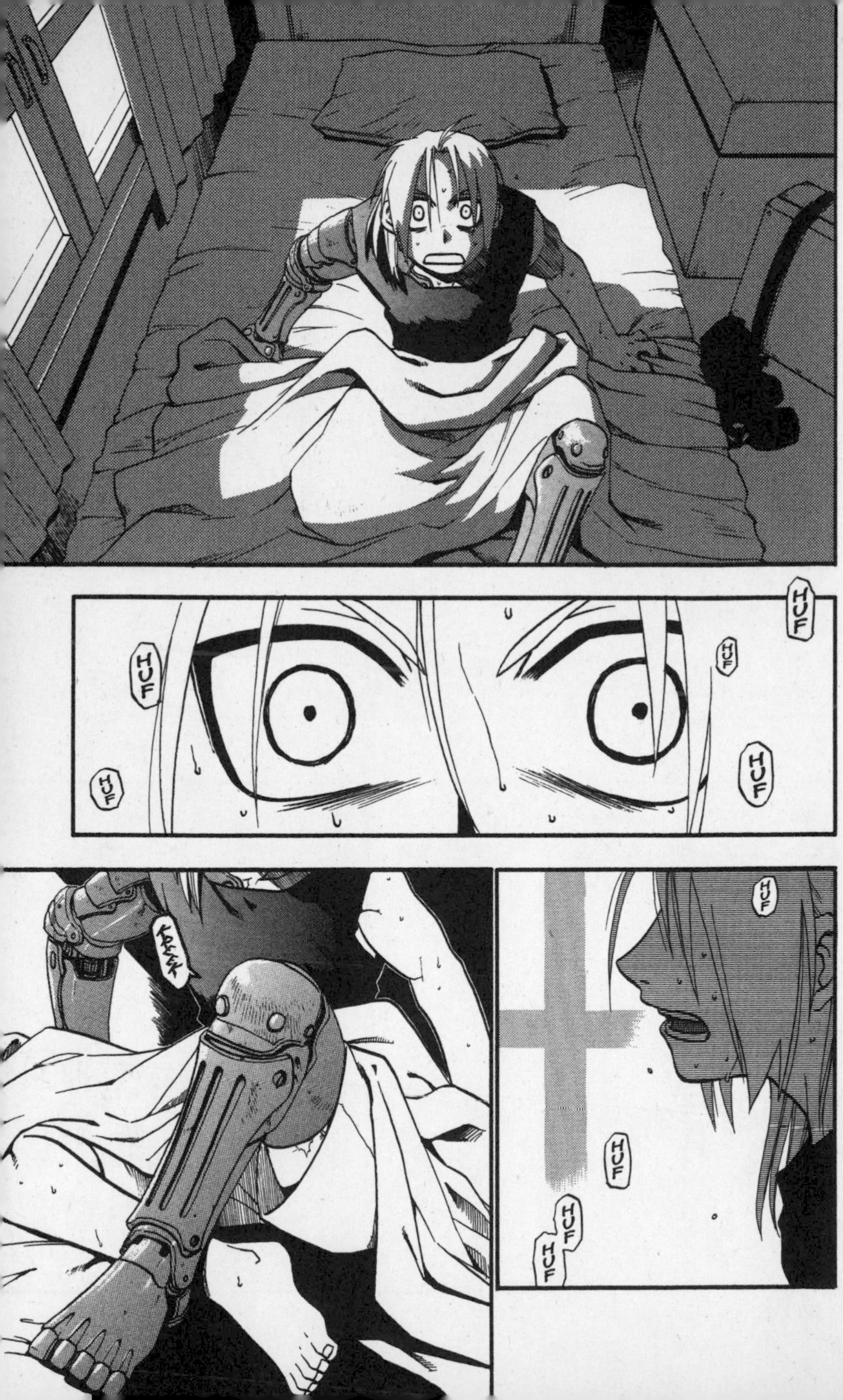
HUF
HUF
HUF
HUF
HUF
HUF
HUF
HUF
HUF
KREEK

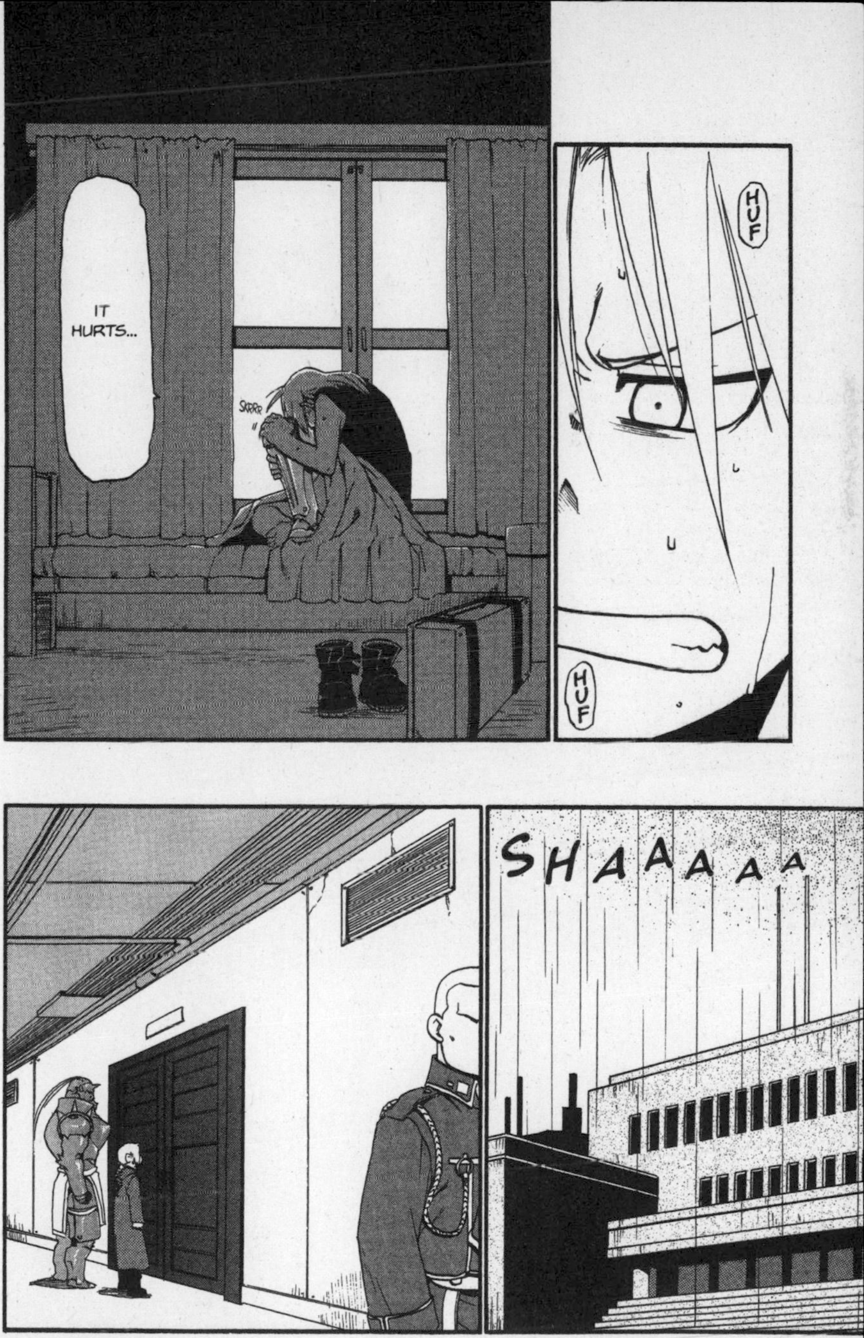
HUF
HUF
IT HURTS...
SKRRR
SHAAAAA

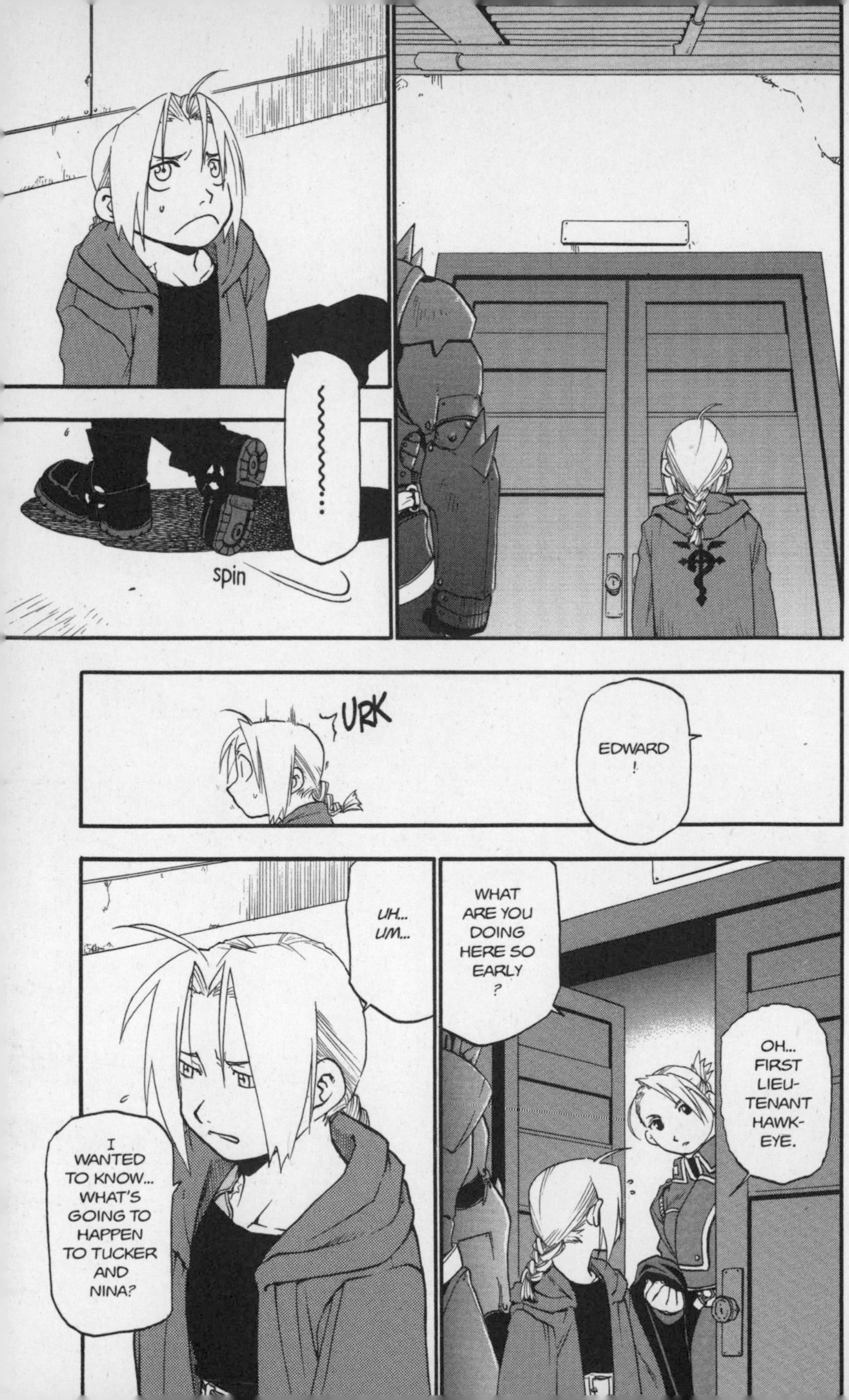
......
spin
EDWARD!
URK
OH... FIRST LIEUTENANT HAWKEYE.
WHAT ARE YOU DOING HERE SO EARLY?
UH... UM...
I WANTED TO KNOW... WHAT'S GOING TO HAPPEN TO TUCKER AND NINA?

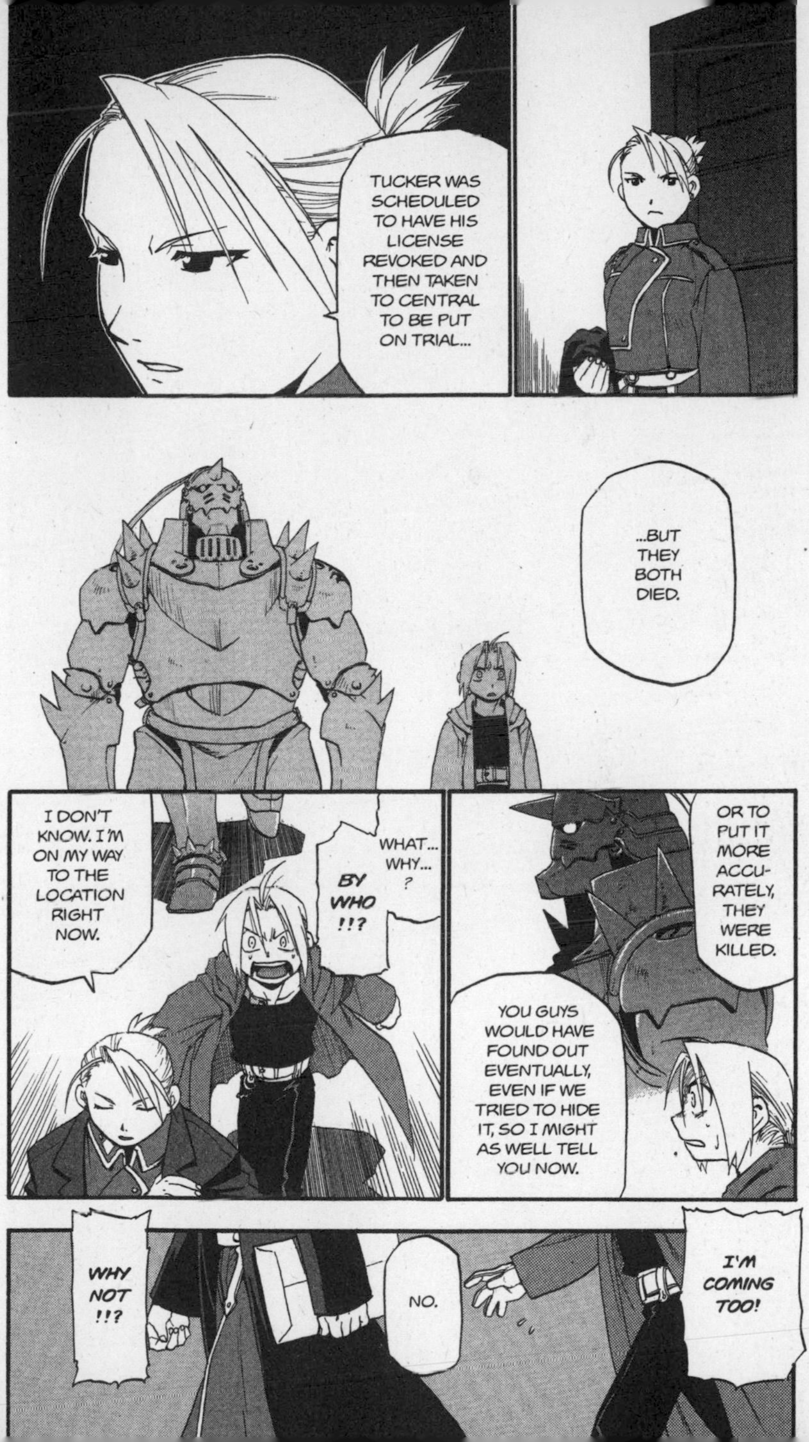
TUCKER WAS SCHEDULED TO HAVE HIS LICENSE REVOKED AND THEN TAKEN TO CENTRAL TO BE PUT ON TRIAL...
...BUT THEY BOTH DIED.
OR TO PUT IT MORE ACCU-RATELY, THEY WERE KILLED.
YOU GUYS WOULD HAVE FOUND OUT EVENTUALLY, EVEN IF WE TRIED TO HIDE IT, SO I MIGHT AS WELL TELL YOU NOW.
WHAT... WHY...?
BY WHO!!?
I DON'T KNOW. I'M ON MY WAY TO THE LOCATION RIGHT NOW.
I'M COMING TOO!
NO.
WHY NOT!!?

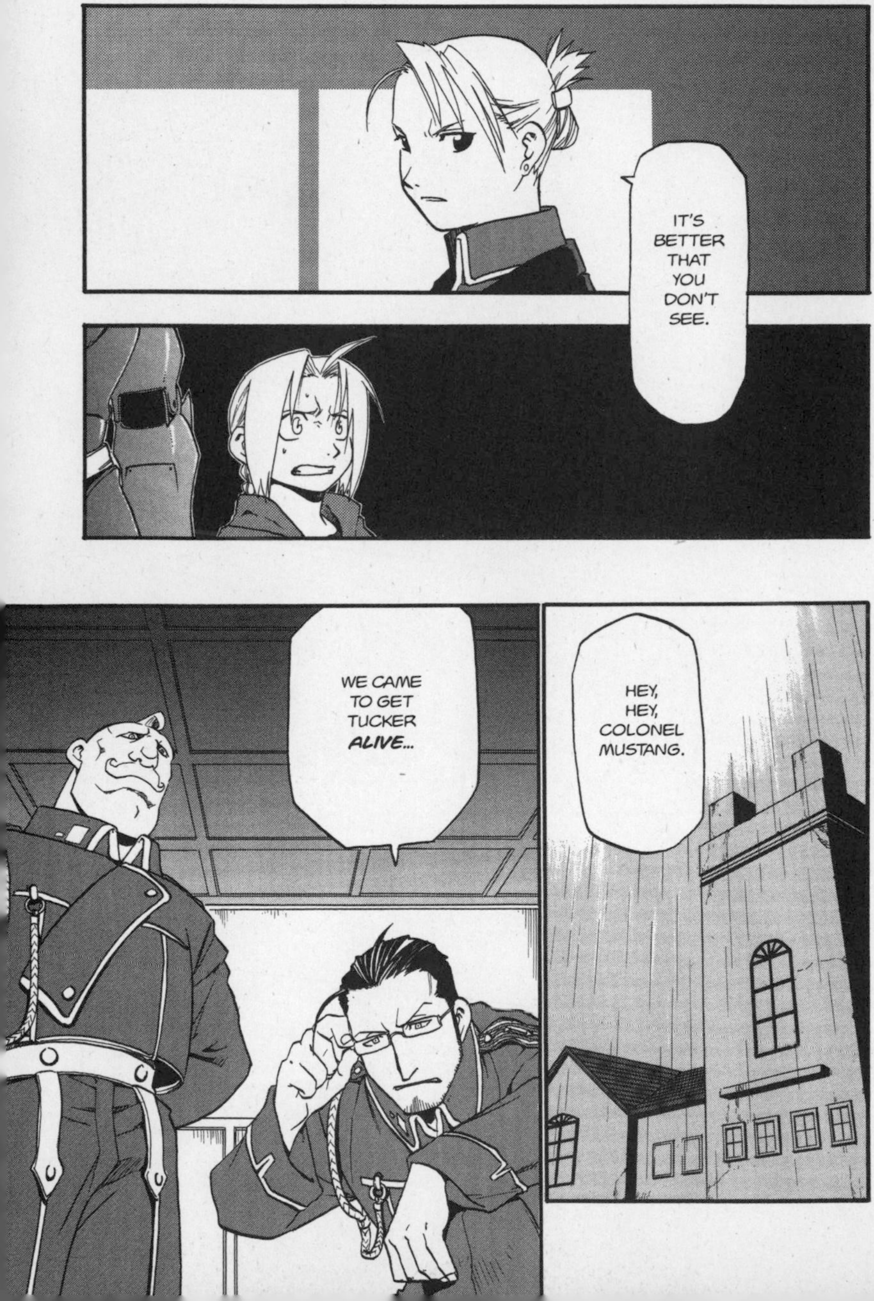
IT'S BETTER THAT YOU DON'T SEE.
HEY, HEY, COLONEL MUSTANG.
WE CAME TO GET TUCKER *ALIVE...*

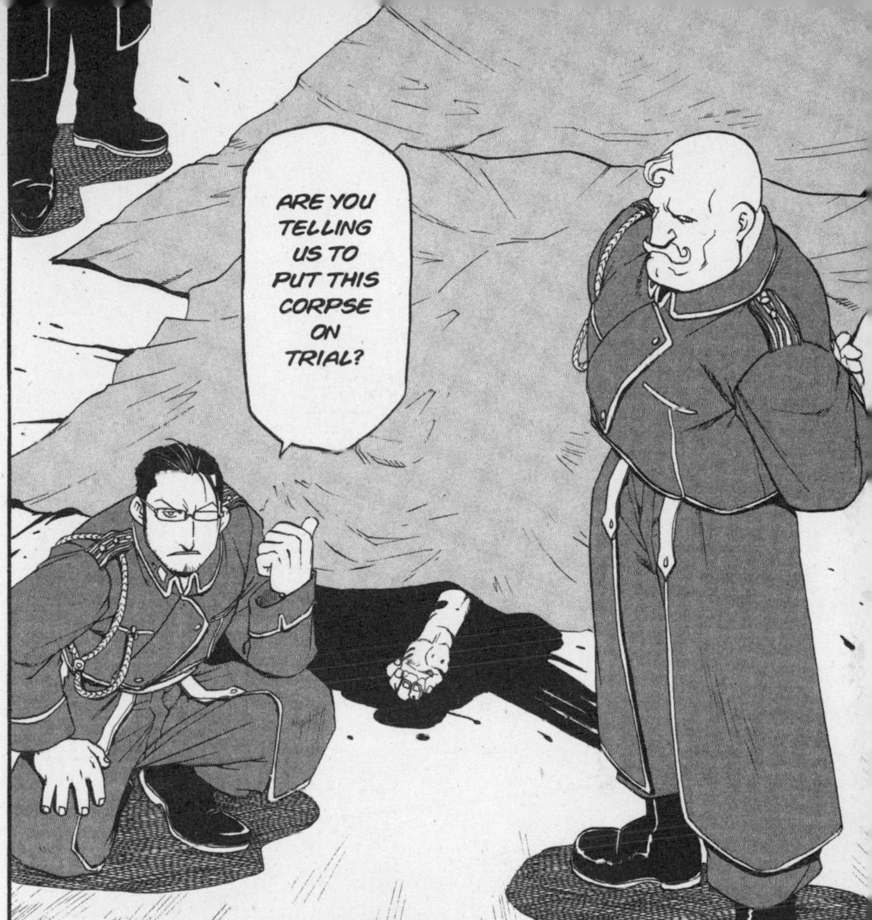
ARE YOU TELLING US TO PUT THIS CORPSE ON TRIAL?

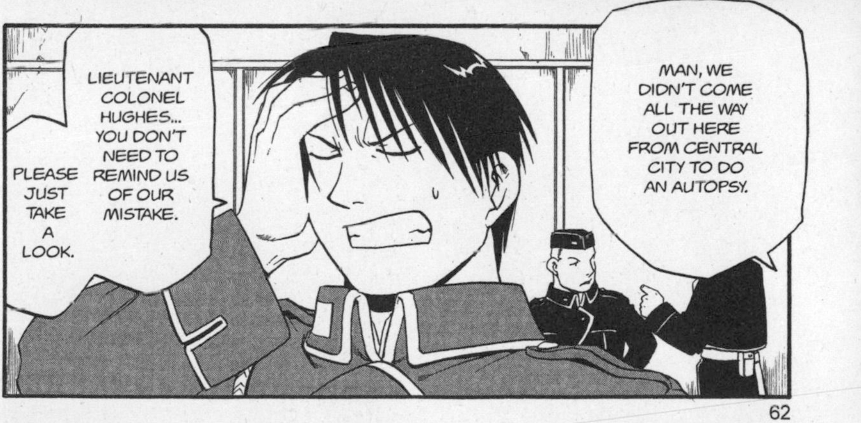
MAN, WE DIDN'T COME ALL THE WAY OUT HERE FROM CENTRAL CITY TO DO AN AUTOPSY.
LIEUTENANT COLONEL HUGHES... YOU DON'T NEED TO REMIND US OF OUR MISTAKE.
PLEASE JUST TAKE A LOOK.

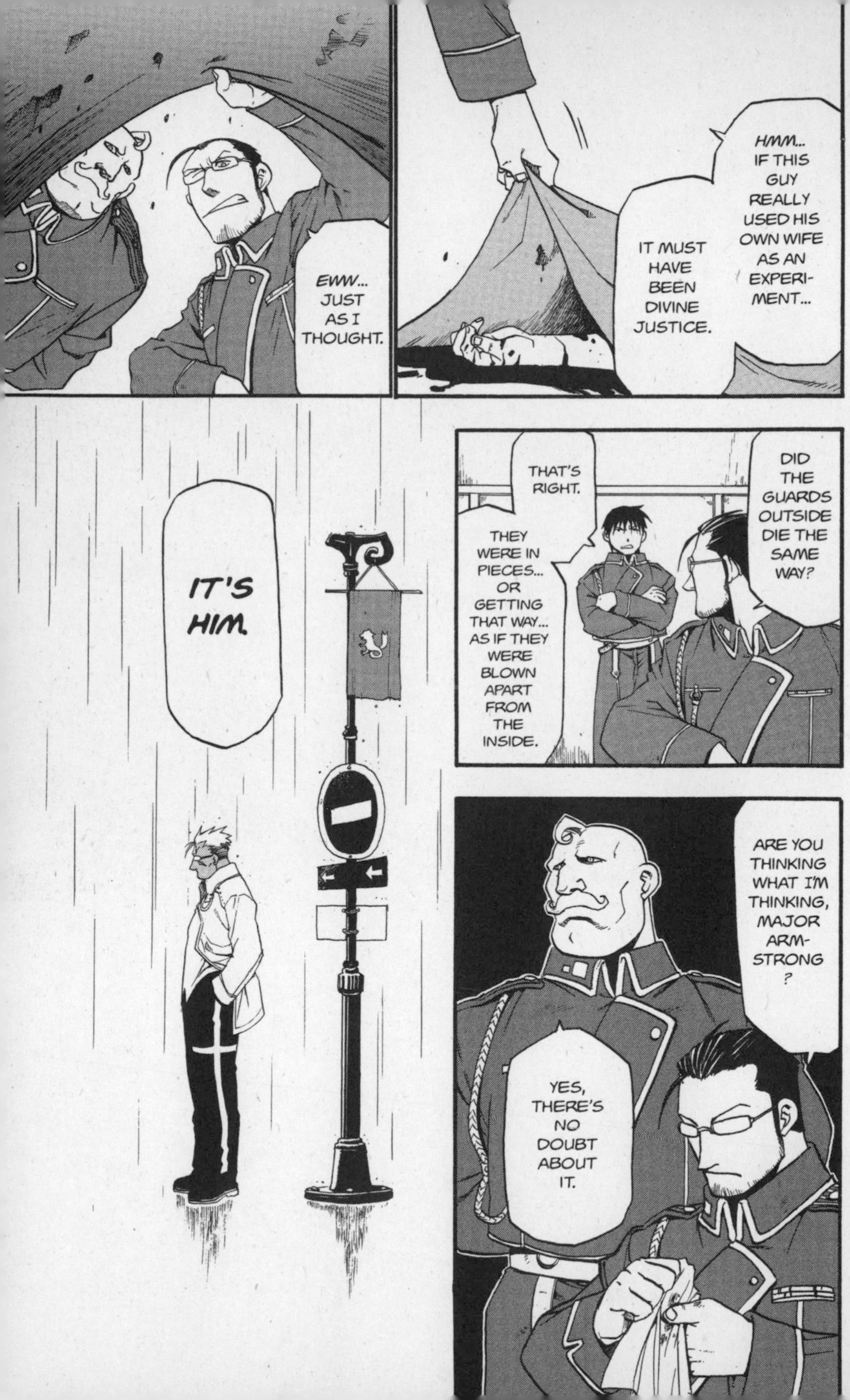
HMM... IF THIS GUY REALLY USED HIS OWN WIFE AS AN EXPERIMENT...
IT MUST HAVE BEEN DIVINE JUSTICE.
EWW... JUST AS I THOUGHT.
DID THE GUARDS OUTSIDE DIE THE SAME WAY?
THAT'S RIGHT.
THEY WERE IN PIECES... OR GETTING THAT WAY... AS IF THEY WERE BLOWN APART FROM THE INSIDE.
ARE YOU THINKING WHAT I'M THINKING, MAJOR ARMSTRONG?
YES, THERE'S NO DOUBT ABOUT IT.
IT'S HIM.

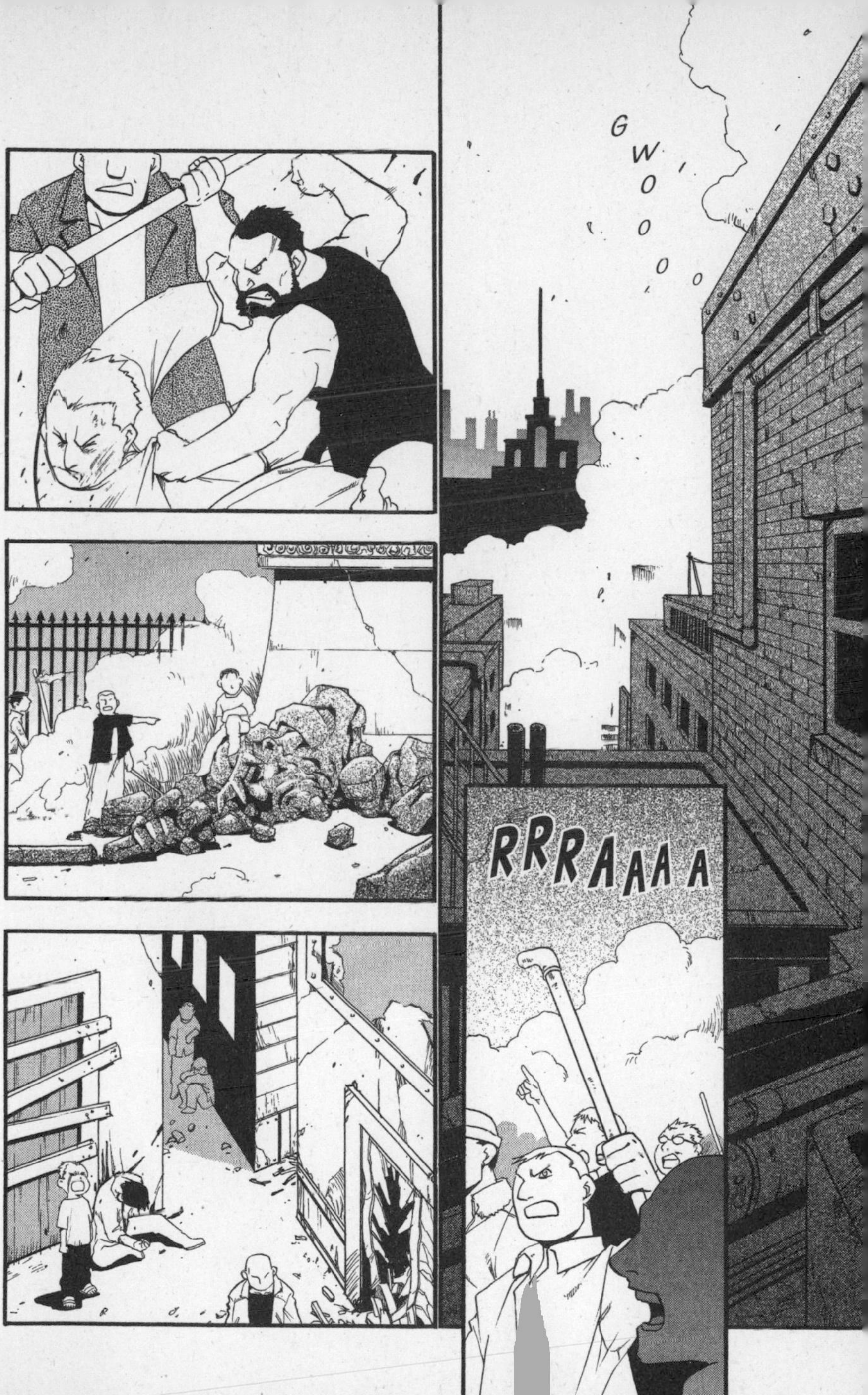
GWOOOOO
RRRAAAA

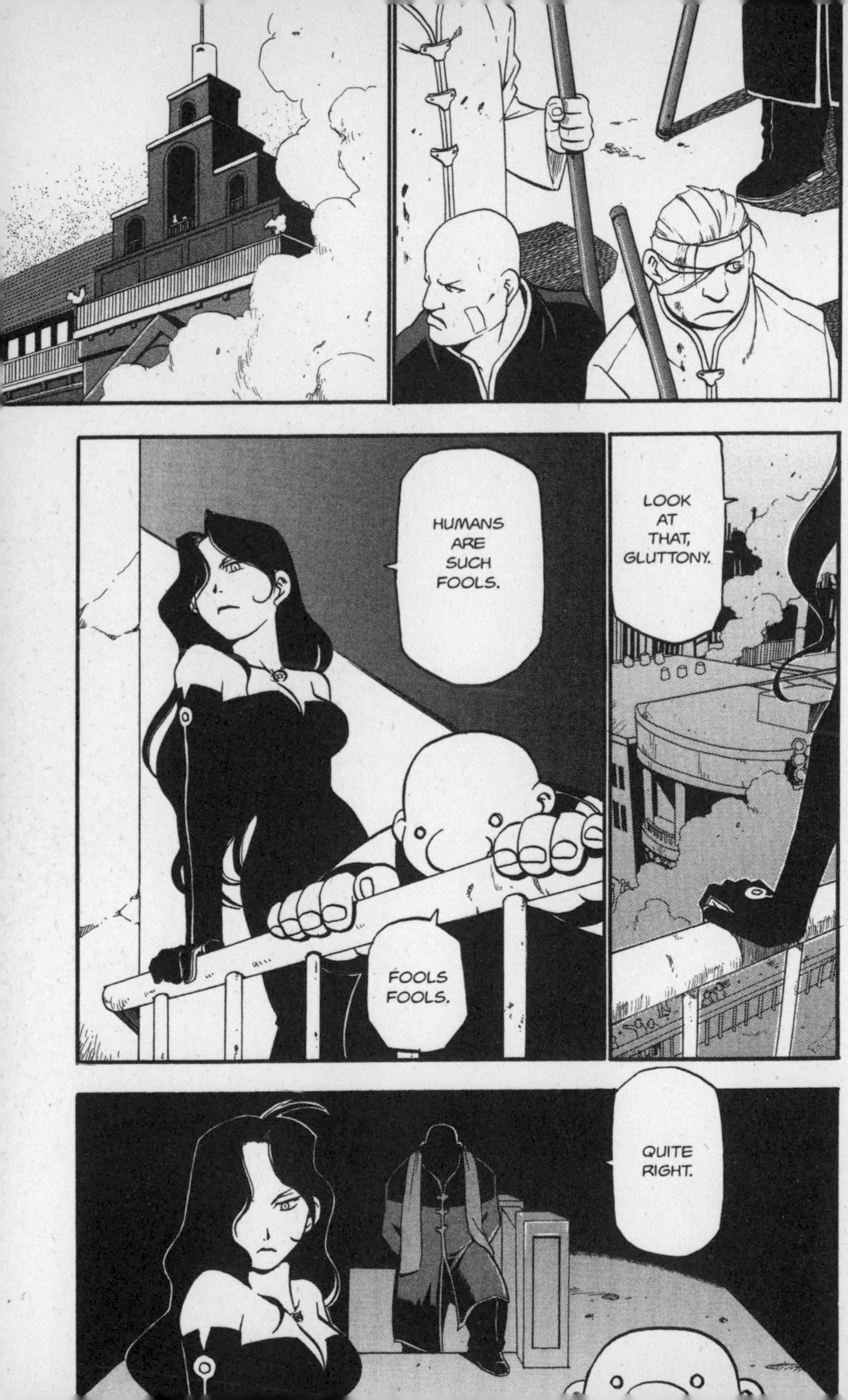
LOOK AT THAT, GLUTTONY.
HUMANS ARE SUCH FOOLS.
FOOLS FOOLS.
QUITE RIGHT.

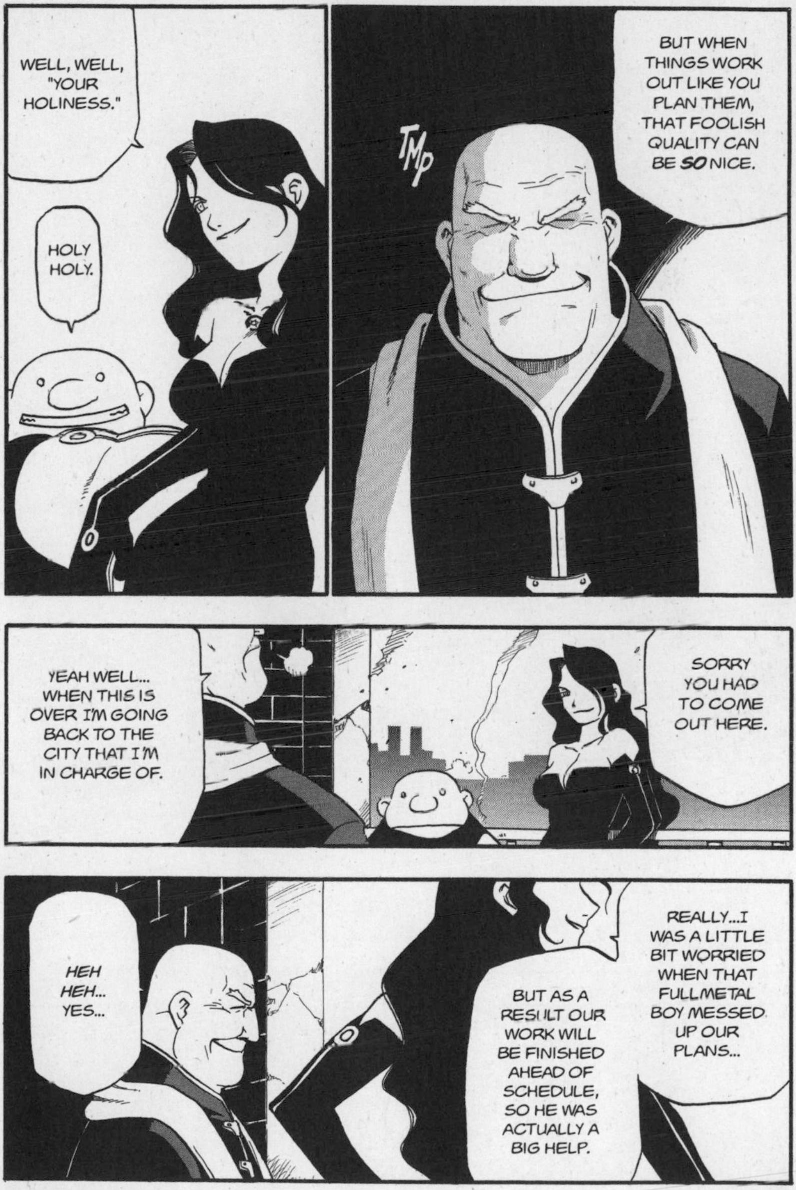
BUT WHEN THINGS WORK OUT LIKE YOU PLAN THEM, THAT FOOLISH QUALITY CAN BE SO NICE.
TMP
WELL, WELL, "YOUR HOLINESS."
HOLY HOLY.
SORRY YOU HAD TO COME OUT HERE.
YEAH WELL... WHEN THIS IS OVER I'M GOING BACK TO THE CITY THAT I'M IN CHARGE OF.
REALLY...I WAS A LITTLE BIT WORRIED WHEN THAT FULLMETAL BOY MESSED UP OUR PLANS...
BUT AS A RESULT OUR WORK WILL BE FINISHED AHEAD OF SCHEDULE, SO HE WAS ACTUALLY A BIG HELP.
HEH HEH... YES...

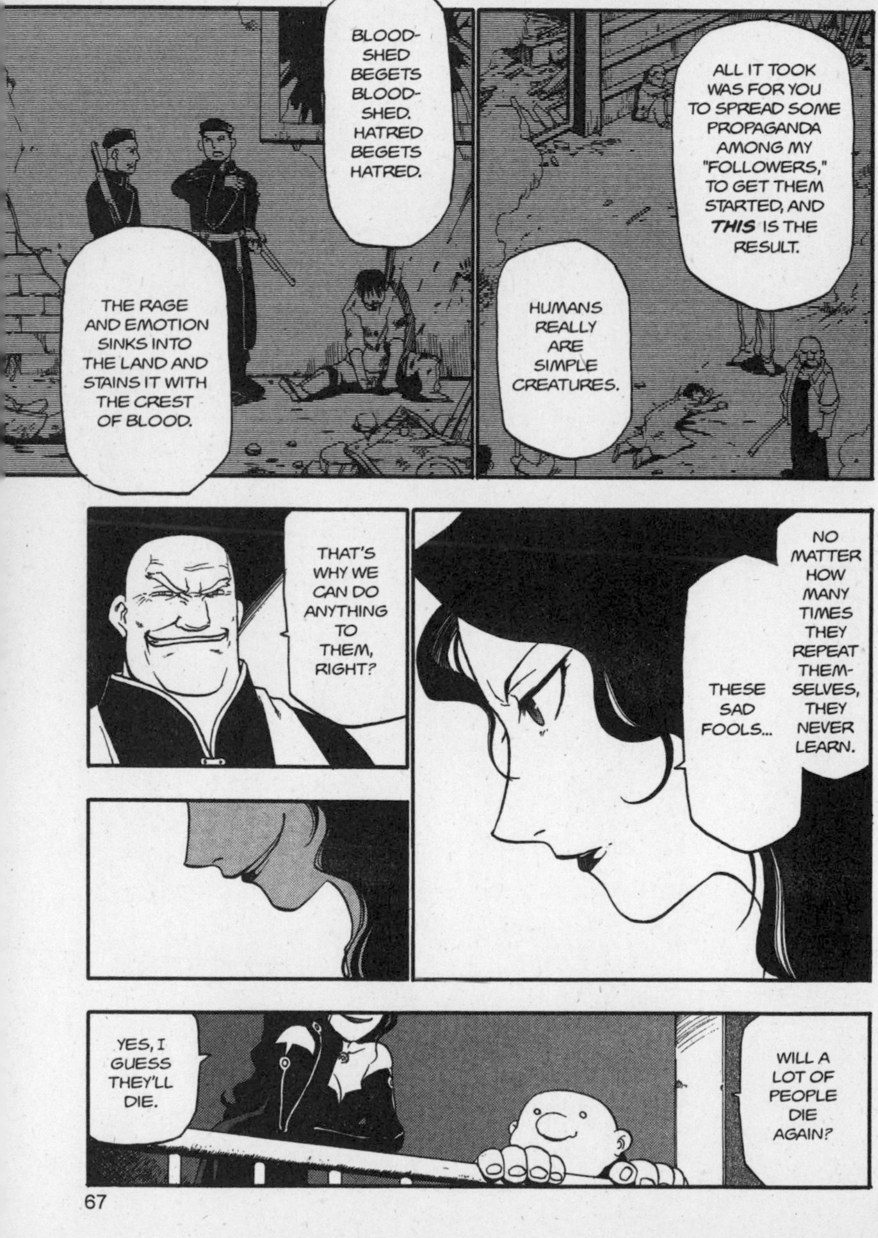
ALL IT TOOK WAS FOR YOU TO SPREAD SOME PROPAGANDA AMONG MY "FOLLOWERS," TO GET THEM STARTED, AND **THIS** IS THE RESULT.
HUMANS REALLY ARE SIMPLE CREATURES.
BLOODSHED BEGETS BLOODSHED. HATRED BEGETS HATRED.
THE RAGE AND EMOTION SINKS INTO THE LAND AND STAINS IT WITH THE CREST OF BLOOD.
NO MATTER HOW MANY TIMES THEY REPEAT THEMSELVES, THEY NEVER LEARN.
THESE SAD FOOLS...
THAT'S WHY WE CAN DO ANYTHING TO THEM, RIGHT?
WILL A LOT OF PEOPLE DIE AGAIN?
YES, I GUESS THEY'LL DIE.

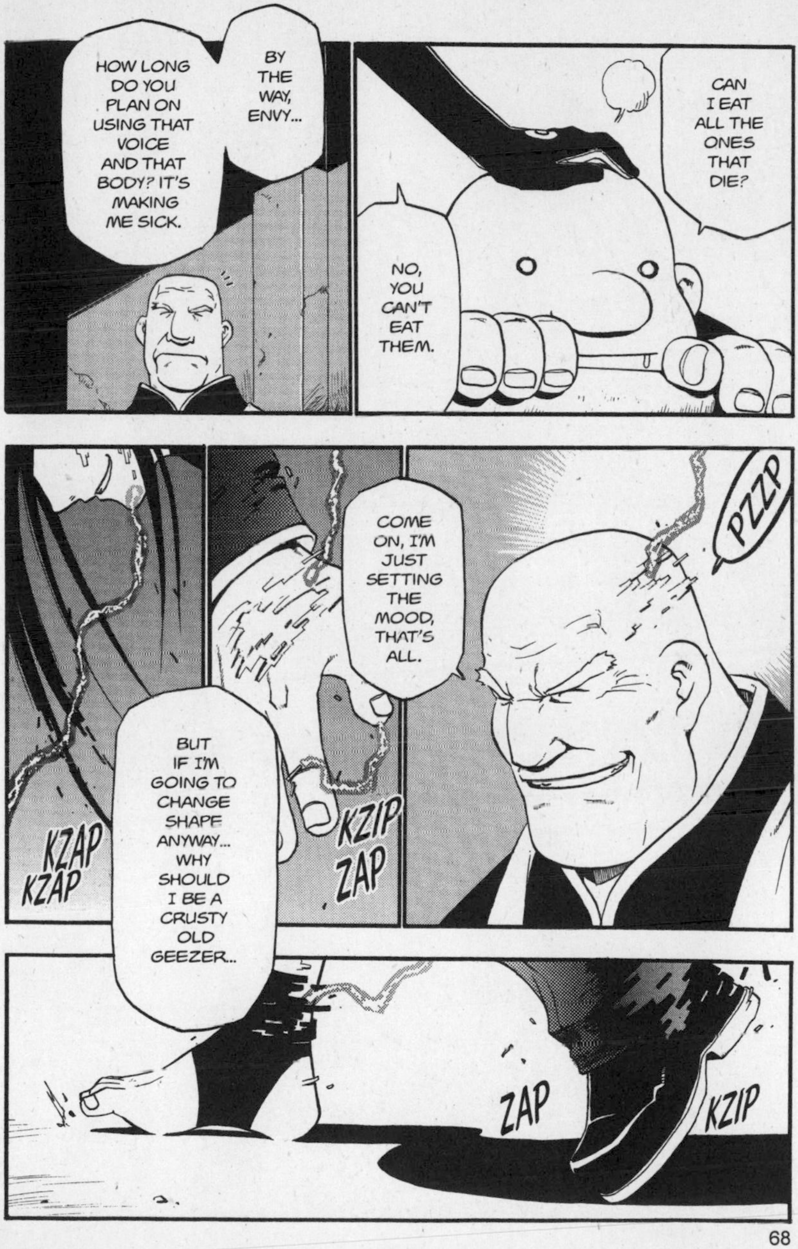
CAN I EAT ALL THE ONES THAT DIE?
NO, YOU CAN'T EAT THEM.
BY THE WAY, ENVY...
HOW LONG DO YOU PLAN ON USING THAT VOICE AND THAT BODY? IT'S MAKING ME SICK.
PZZP
COME ON, I'M JUST SETTING THE MOOD, THAT'S ALL.
KZIP ZAP
KZAP KZAP
BUT IF I'M GOING TO CHANGE SHAPE ANYWAY... WHY SHOULD I BE A CRUSTY OLD GEEZER...
KZIP
ZAP

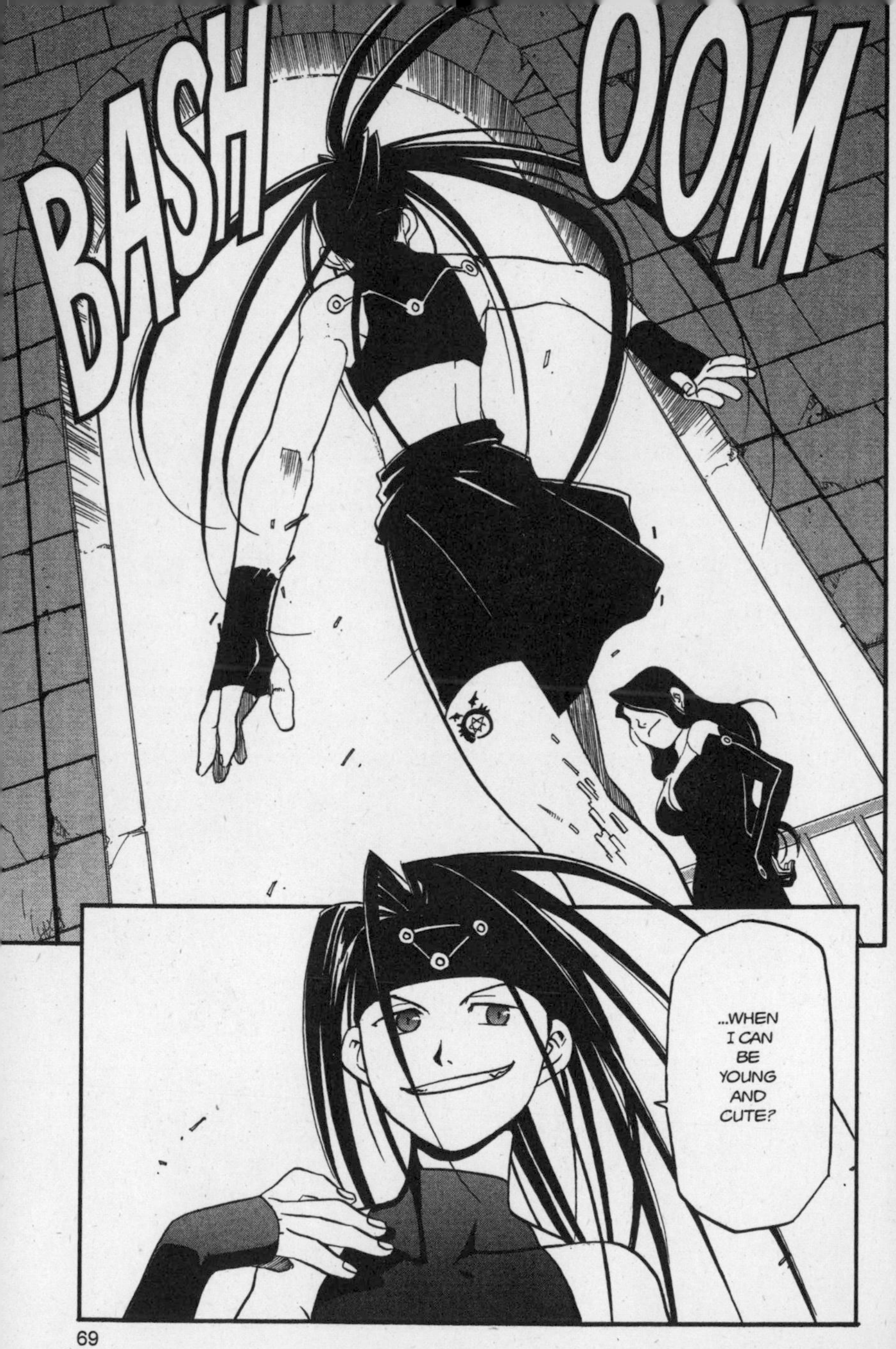
BASH OOM
...WHEN I CAN BE YOUNG AND CUTE?

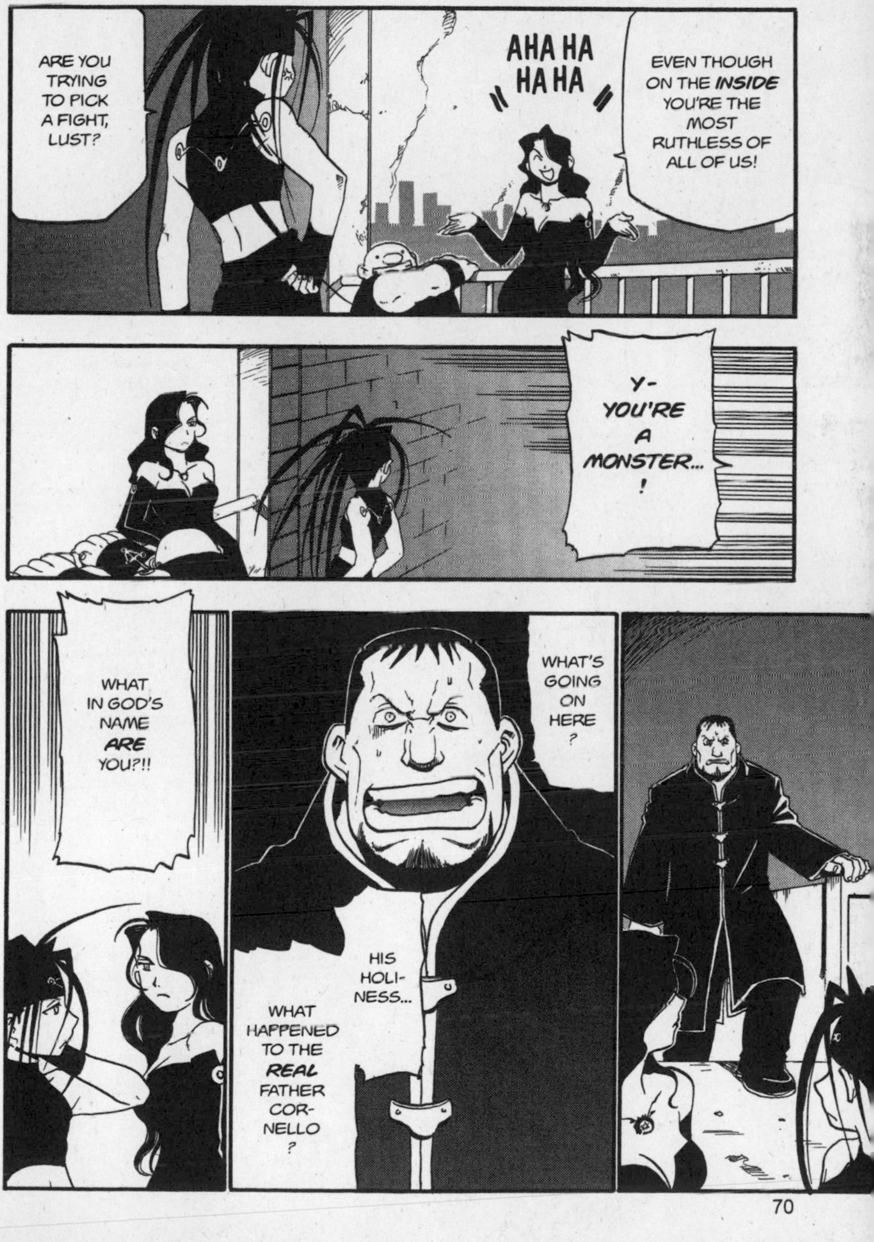
EVEN THOUGH ON THE *INSIDE* YOU'RE THE MOST RUTHLESS OF ALL OF US!
AHA HA HA HA
ARE YOU TRYING TO PICK A FIGHT, LUST?
Y- *YOU'RE* A *MONSTER*... !
WHAT'S GOING ON HERE?
HIS HOLINESS...
WHAT HAPPENED TO THE *REAL* FATHER CORNELLO?
WHAT IN GOD'S NAME *ARE* YOU?!!

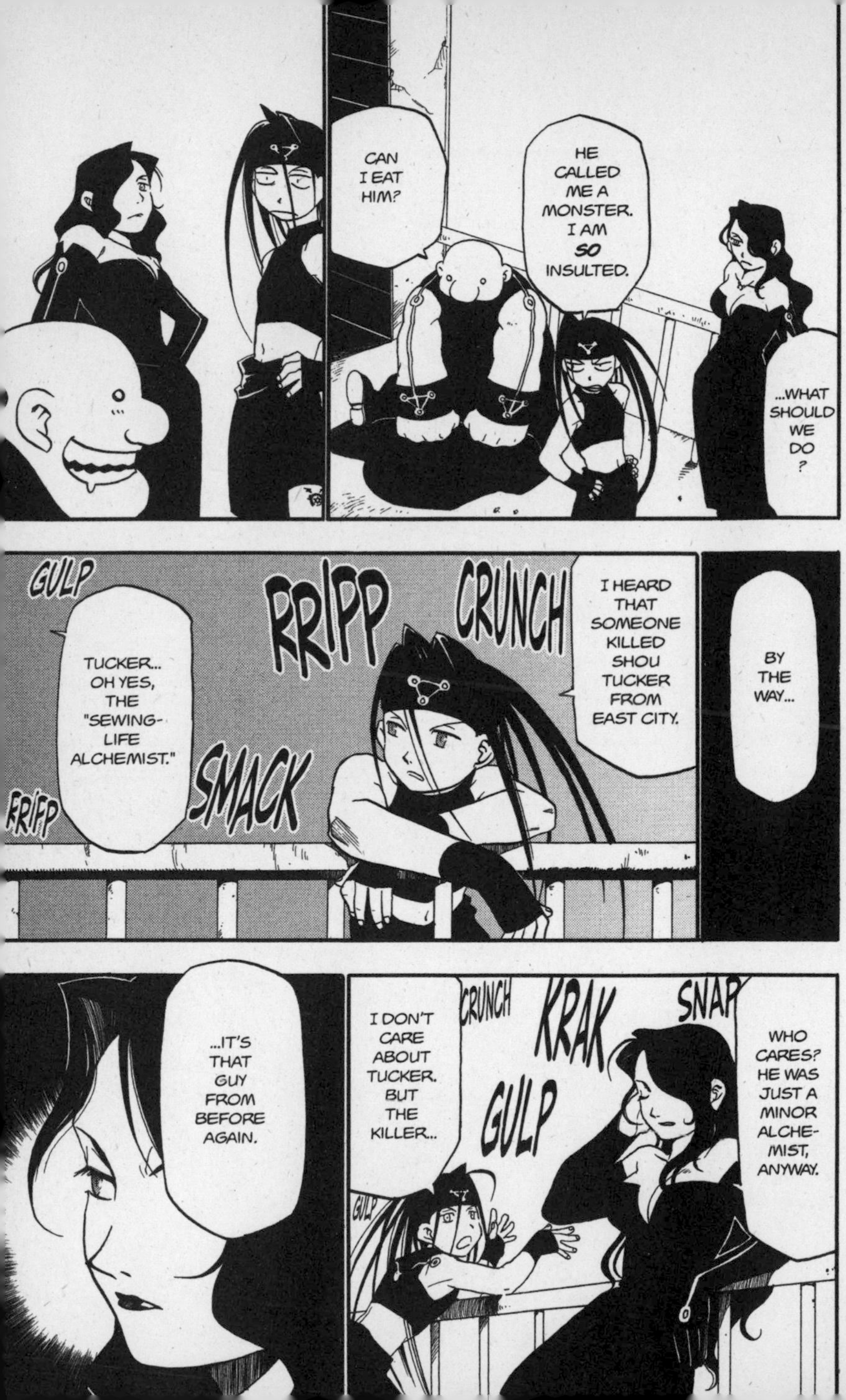
HE CALLED ME A MONSTER. I AM SO INSULTED.
...WHAT SHOULD WE DO?
CAN I EAT HIM?
BY THE WAY...
I HEARD THAT SOMEONE KILLED SHOU TUCKER FROM EAST CITY.
CRUNCH
RRIPP
SMACK
GULP
TUCKER... OH YES, THE "SEWING-LIFE ALCHEMIST."
KRIPP
SNAP
WHO CARES? HE WAS JUST A MINOR ALCHEMIST, ANYWAY.
KRAK
CRUNCH
GULP
I DON'T CARE ABOUT TUCKER. BUT THE KILLER...
GULP
...IT'S THAT GUY FROM BEFORE AGAIN.

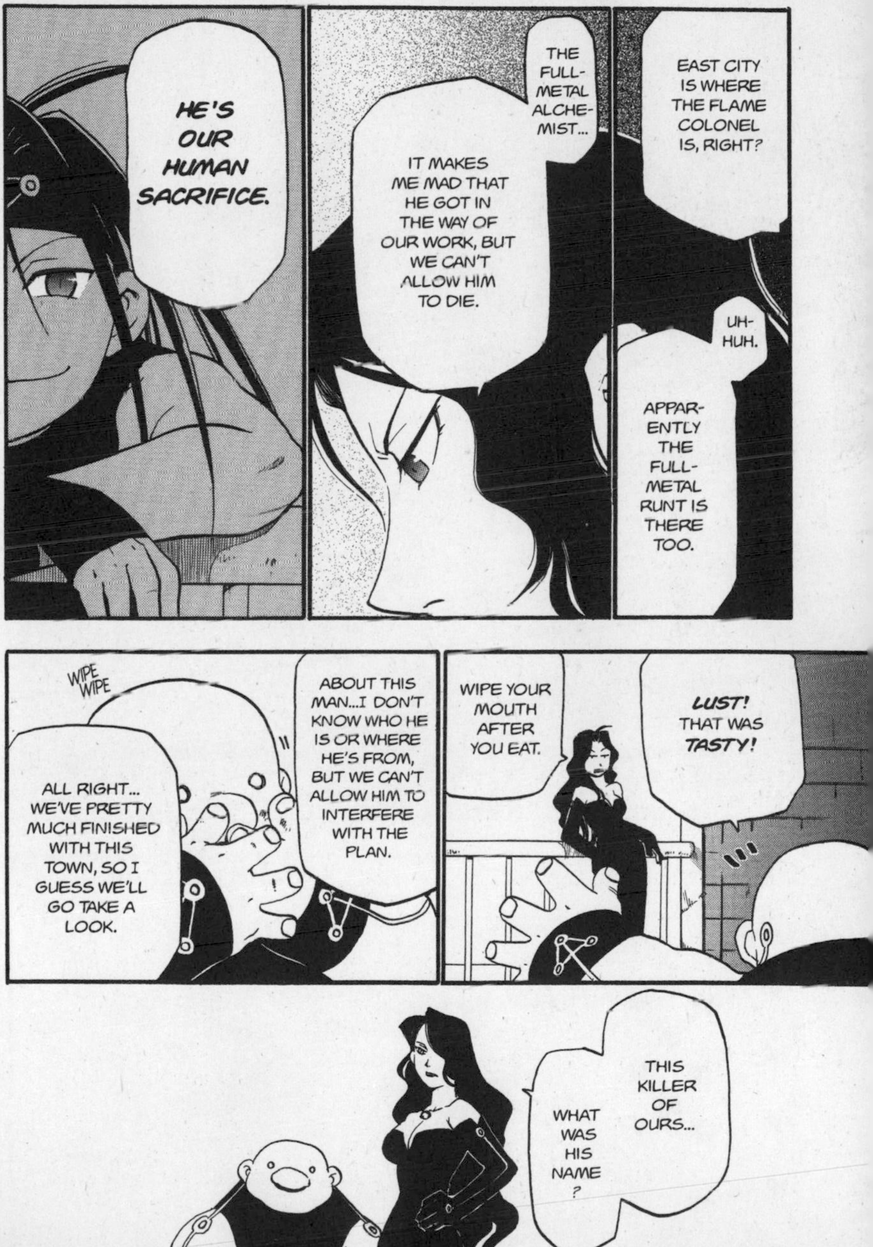
EAST CITY IS WHERE THE FLAME COLONEL IS, RIGHT?
UH-HUH.
APPARENTLY THE FULLMETAL RUNT IS THERE TOO.
THE FULLMETAL ALCHEMIST...
IT MAKES ME MAD THAT HE GOT IN THE WAY OF OUR WORK, BUT WE CAN'T ALLOW HIM TO DIE.
HE'S OUR HUMAN SACRIFICE.
LUST! THAT WAS TASTY!
WIPE YOUR MOUTH AFTER YOU EAT.
ABOUT THIS MAN...I DON'T KNOW WHO HE IS OR WHERE HE'S FROM, BUT WE CAN'T ALLOW HIM TO INTERFERE WITH THE PLAN.
WIPE WIPE
ALL RIGHT... WE'VE PRETTY MUCH FINISHED WITH THIS TOWN, SO I GUESS WE'LL GO TAKE A LOOK.
THIS KILLER OF OURS...
WHAT WAS HIS NAME?

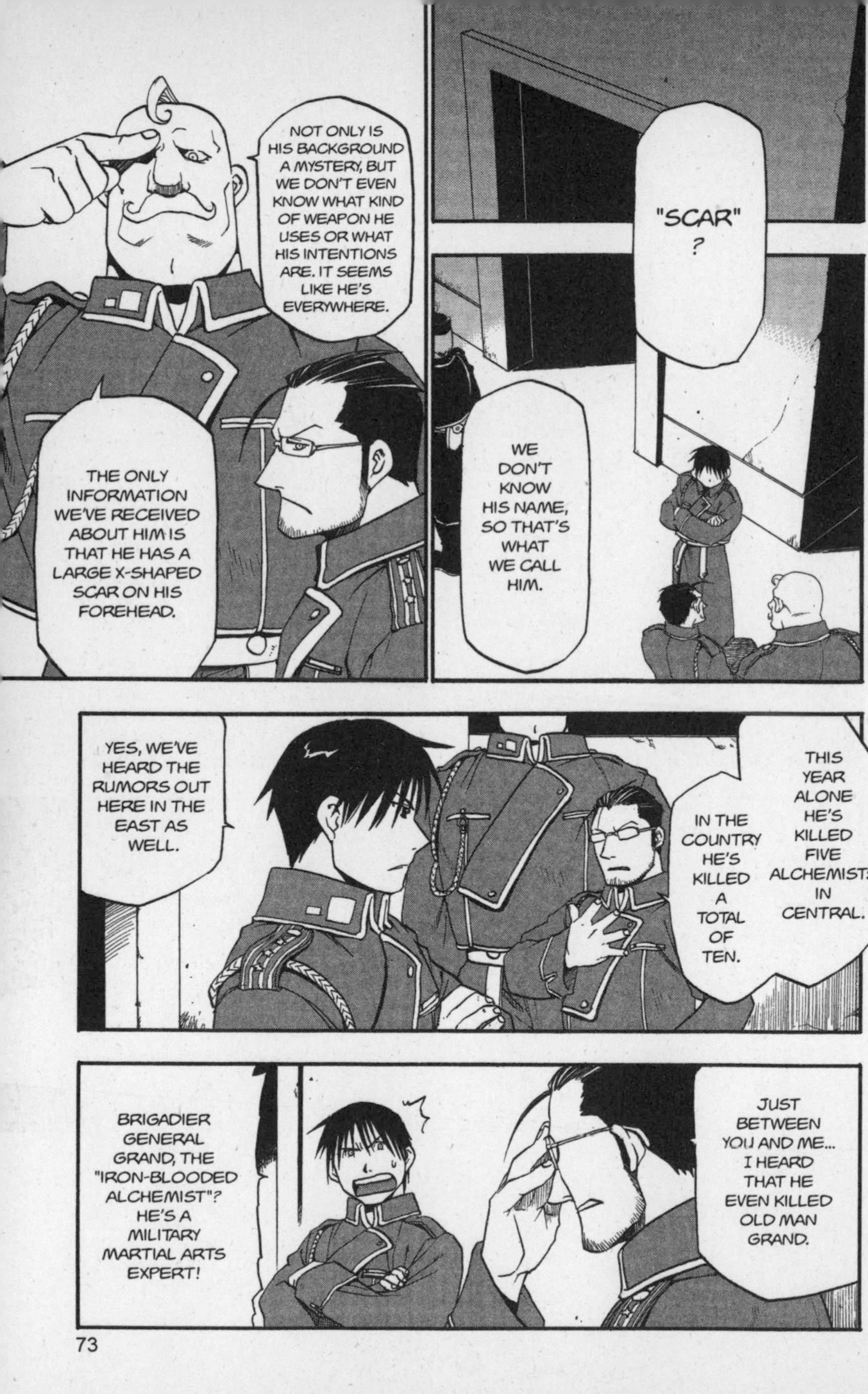
"SCAR"?
WE DON'T KNOW HIS NAME, SO THAT'S WHAT WE CALL HIM.
NOT ONLY IS HIS BACKGROUND A MYSTERY, BUT WE DON'T EVEN KNOW WHAT KIND OF WEAPON HE USES OR WHAT HIS INTENTIONS ARE. IT SEEMS LIKE HE'S EVERYWHERE.
THE ONLY INFORMATION WE'VE RECEIVED ABOUT HIM IS THAT HE HAS A LARGE X-SHAPED SCAR ON HIS FOREHEAD.
THIS YEAR ALONE HE'S KILLED FIVE ALCHEMISTS IN CENTRAL.
IN THE COUNTRY HE'S KILLED A TOTAL OF TEN.
YES, WE'VE HEARD THE RUMORS OUT HERE IN THE EAST AS WELL.
JUST BETWEEN YOU AND ME... I HEARD THAT HE EVEN KILLED OLD MAN GRAND.
BRIGADIER GENERAL GRAND, THE "IRON-BLOODED ALCHEMIST"? HE'S A MILITARY MARTIAL ARTS EXPERT!

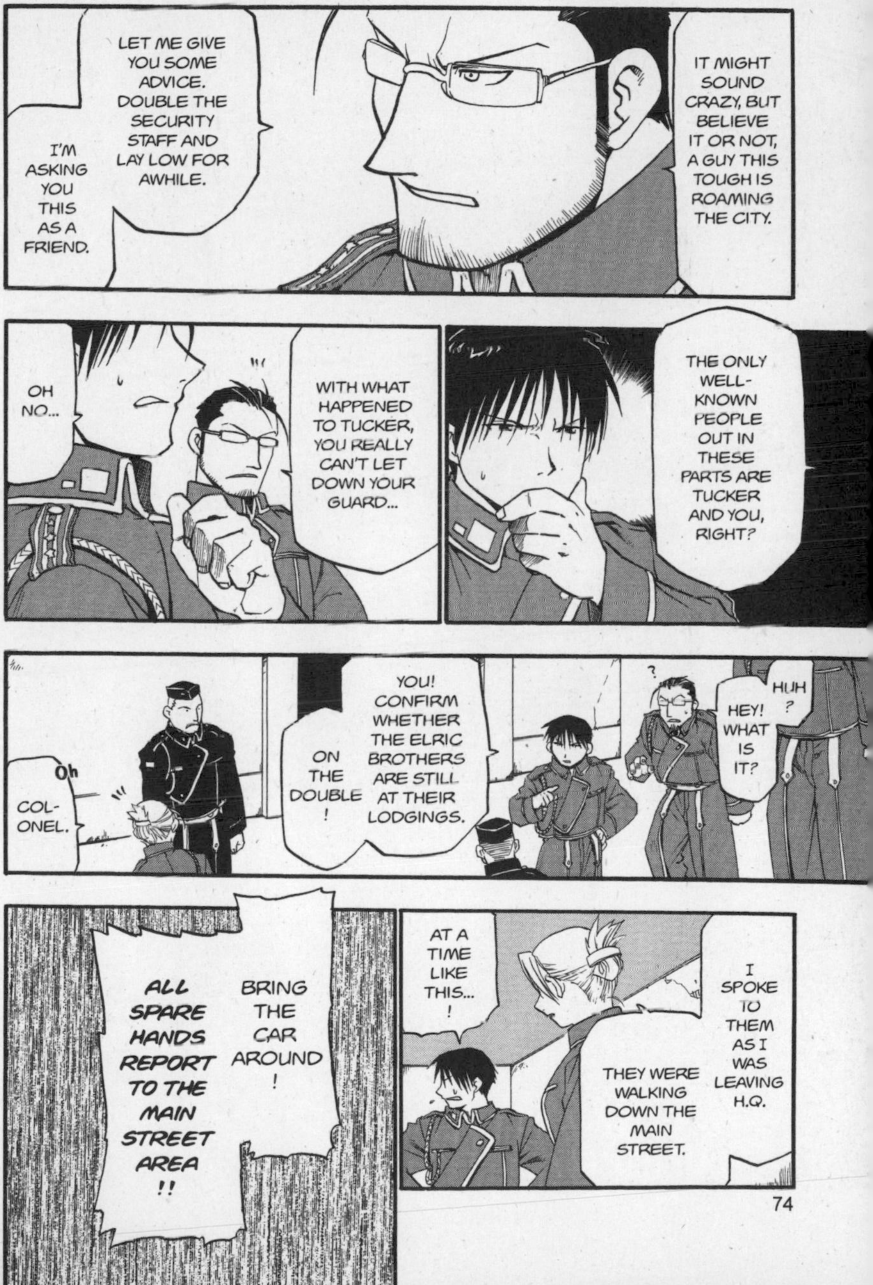
IT MIGHT SOUND CRAZY, BUT BELIEVE IT OR NOT, A GUY THIS TOUGH IS ROAMING THE CITY.
LET ME GIVE YOU SOME ADVICE. DOUBLE THE SECURITY STAFF AND LAY LOW FOR AWHILE.
I'M ASKING YOU THIS AS A FRIEND.
THE ONLY WELL-KNOWN PEOPLE OUT IN THESE PARTS ARE TUCKER AND YOU, RIGHT?
WITH WHAT HAPPENED TO TUCKER, YOU REALLY CAN'T LET DOWN YOUR GUARD...
OH NO...
HUH?
HEY! WHAT IS IT?
YOU! CONFIRM WHETHER THE ELRIC BROTHERS ARE STILL AT THEIR LODGINGS.
ON THE DOUBLE!
Oh
COL-ONEL.
I SPOKE TO THEM AS I WAS LEAVING H.Q.
THEY WERE WALKING DOWN THE MAIN STREET.
AT A TIME LIKE THIS...!
BRING THE CAR AROUND!
ALL SPARE HANDS REPORT TO THE MAIN STREET AREA!!

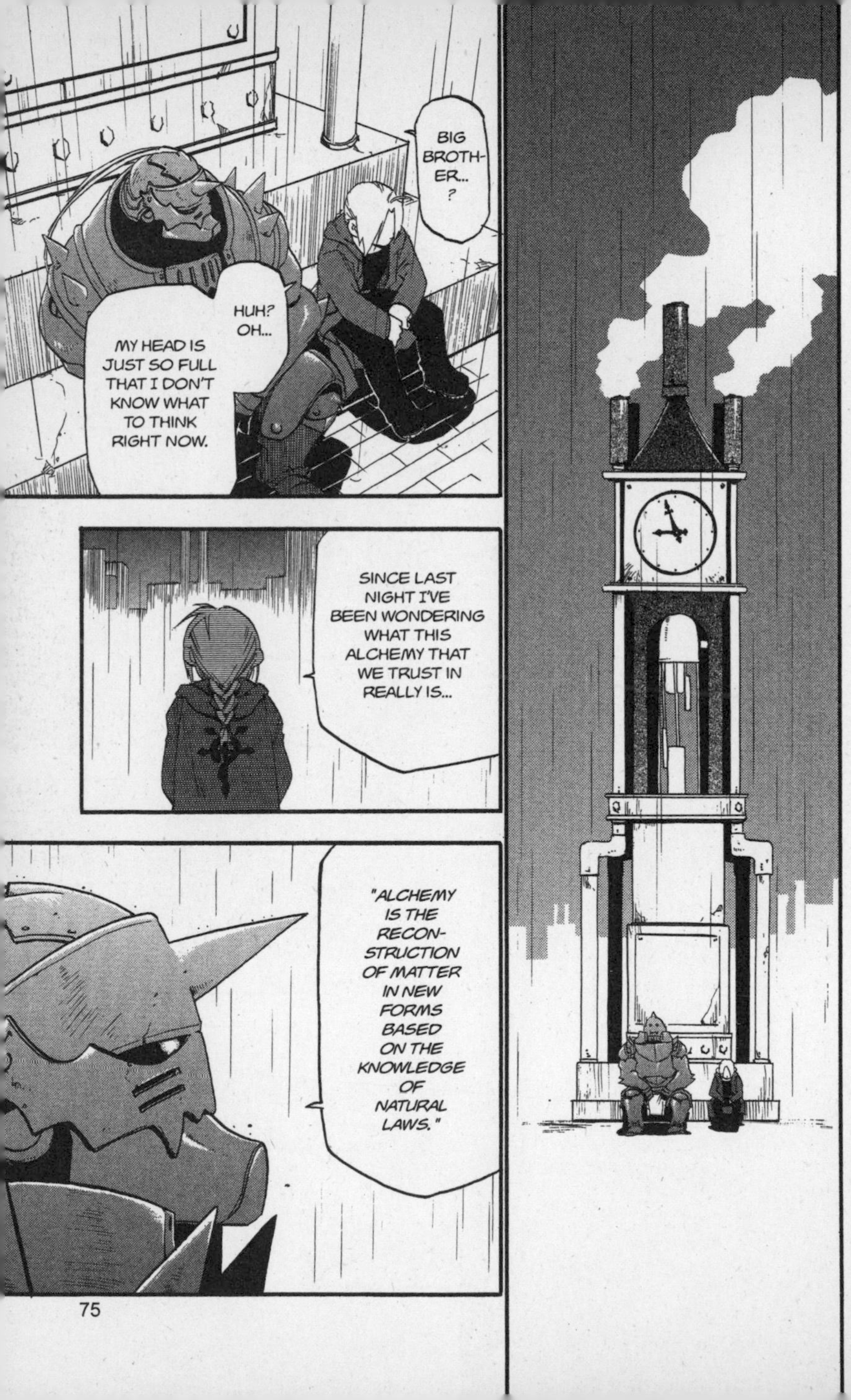
BIG BROTH-ER... ?
HUH? OH...
MY HEAD IS JUST SO FULL THAT I DON'T KNOW WHAT TO THINK RIGHT NOW.
SINCE LAST NIGHT I'VE BEEN WONDERING WHAT THIS ALCHEMY THAT WE TRUST IN REALLY IS...
"ALCHEMY IS THE RECON-STRUCTION OF MATTER IN NEW FORMS BASED ON THE KNOWLEDGE OF NATURAL LAWS."

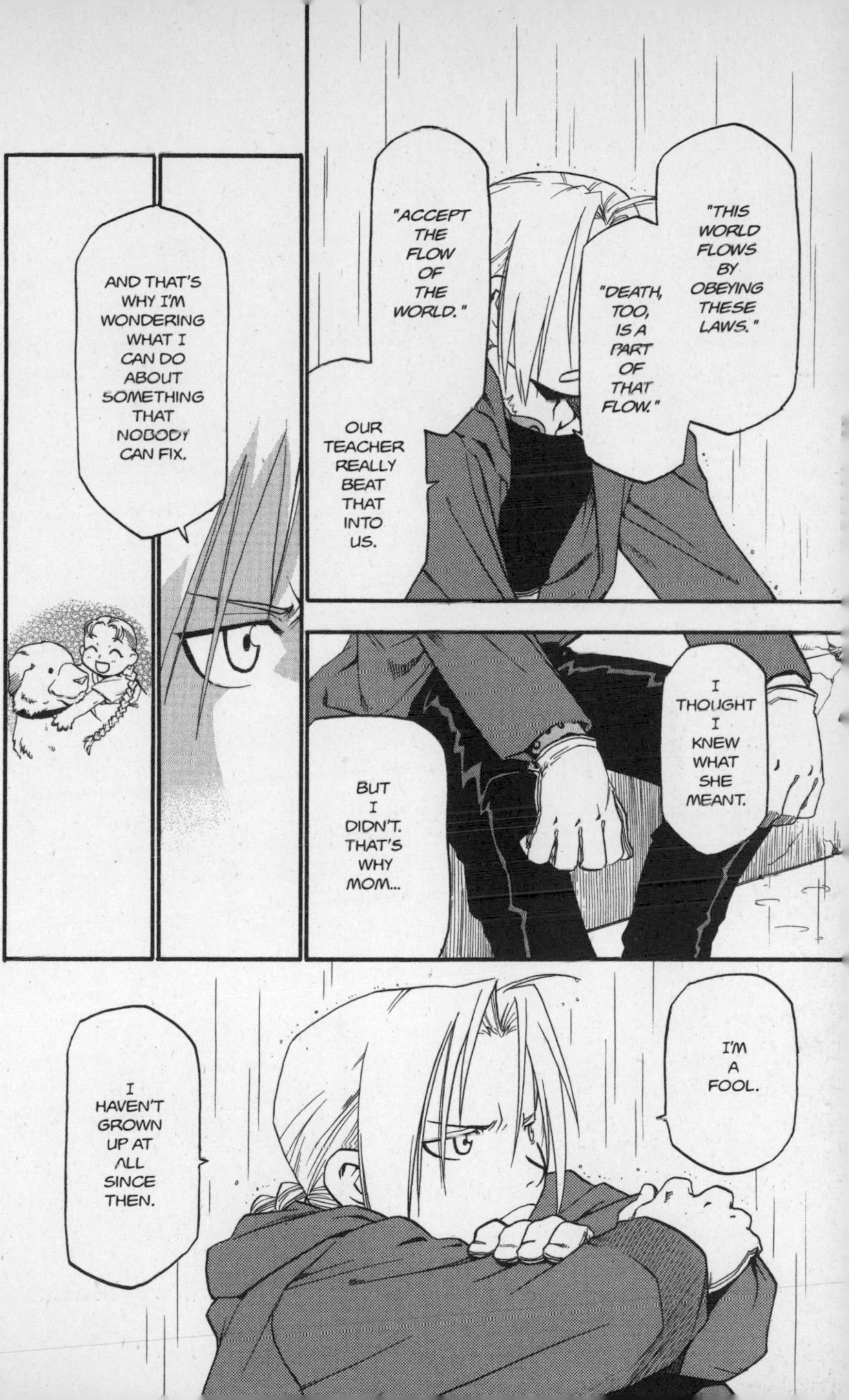
"THIS WORLD FLOWS BY OBEYING THESE LAWS."
"DEATH, TOO, IS A PART OF THAT FLOW."
"ACCEPT THE FLOW OF THE WORLD."
OUR TEACHER REALLY BEAT THAT INTO US.
I THOUGHT I KNEW WHAT SHE MEANT.
BUT I DIDN'T. THAT'S WHY MOM...
AND THAT'S WHY I'M WONDERING WHAT I CAN DO ABOUT SOMETHING THAT NOBODY CAN FIX.
I'M A FOOL.
I HAVEN'T GROWN UP AT ALL SINCE THEN.

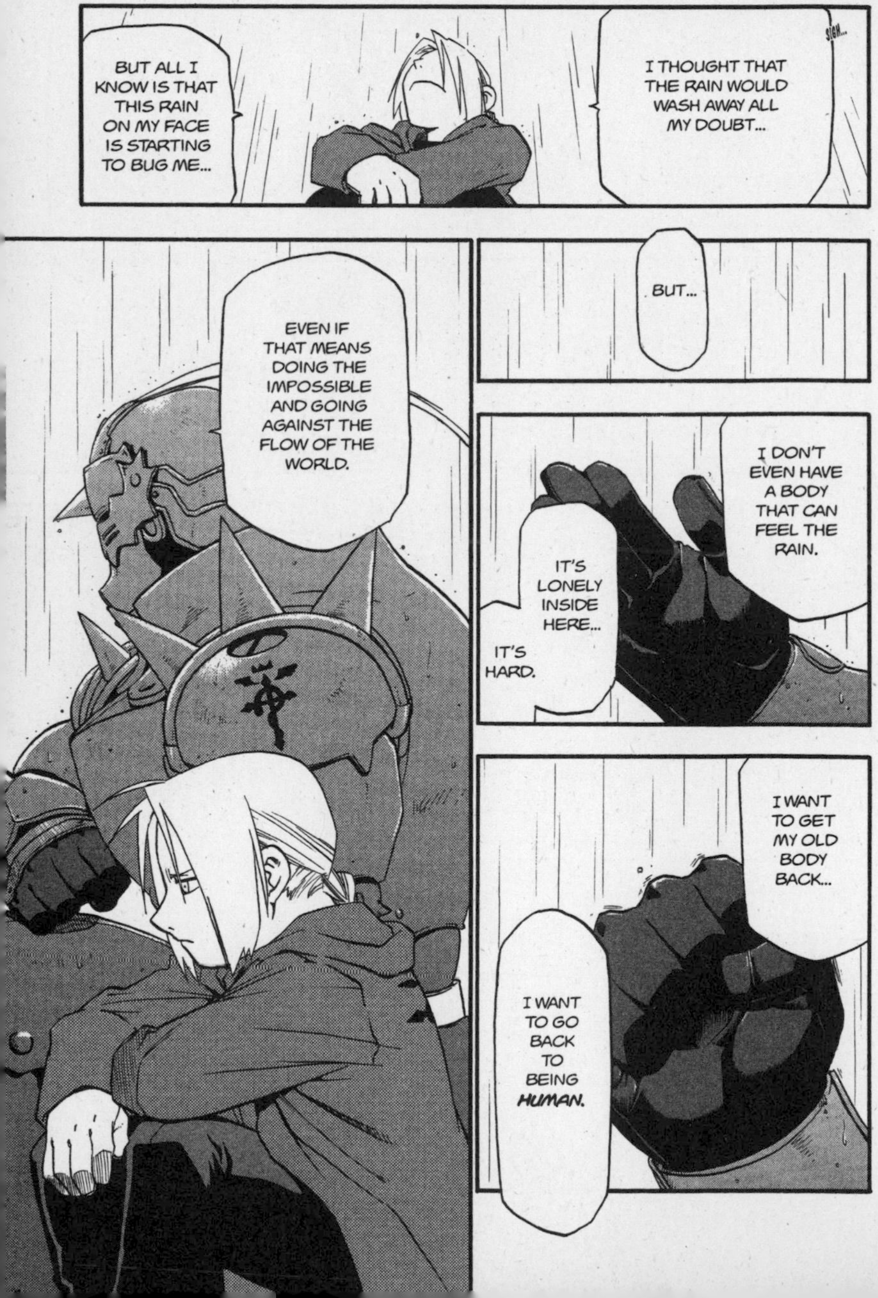
SIGH...
I THOUGHT THAT THE RAIN WOULD WASH AWAY ALL MY DOUBT...
BUT ALL I KNOW IS THAT THIS RAIN ON MY FACE IS STARTING TO BUG ME...
BUT...
I DON'T EVEN HAVE A BODY THAT CAN FEEL THE RAIN.
IT'S LONELY INSIDE HERE...
IT'S HARD.
I WANT TO GET MY OLD BODY BACK...
I WANT TO GO BACK TO BEING ***HUMAN***.
EVEN IF THAT MEANS DOING THE IMPOSSIBLE AND GOING AGAINST THE FLOW OF THE WORLD.

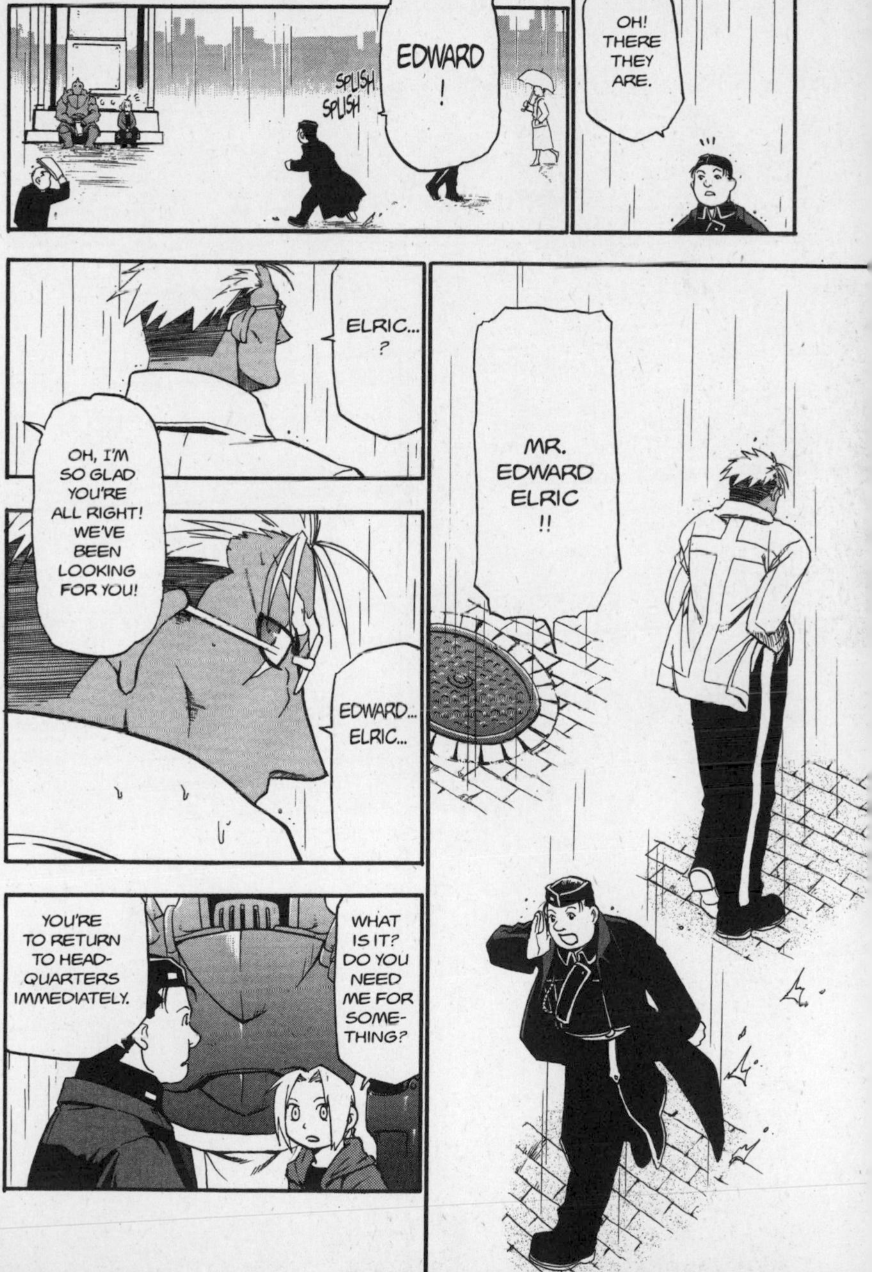
OH! THERE THEY ARE.
EDWARD !
SPLISH
SPLISH
MR. EDWARD ELRIC !!
ELRIC... ?
OH, I'M SO GLAD YOU'RE ALL RIGHT! WE'VE BEEN LOOKING FOR YOU!
EDWARD... ELRIC...
WHAT IS IT? DO YOU NEED ME FOR SOME-THING?
YOU'RE TO RETURN TO HEAD-QUARTERS IMMEDIATELY.

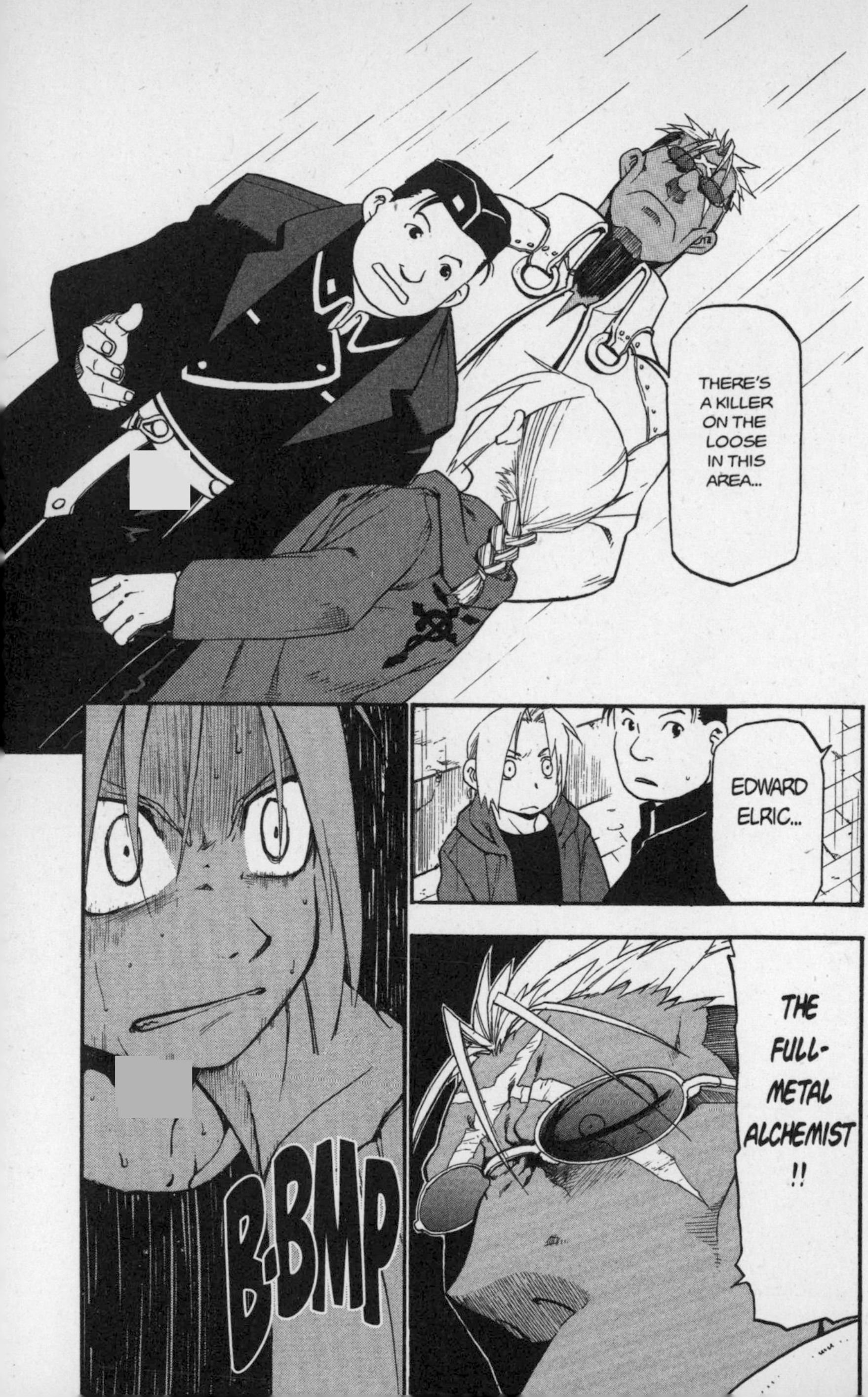
THERE'S A KILLER ON THE LOOSE IN THIS AREA...
EDWARD ELRIC...
THE FULL-METAL ALCHEMIST !!
B-BMP

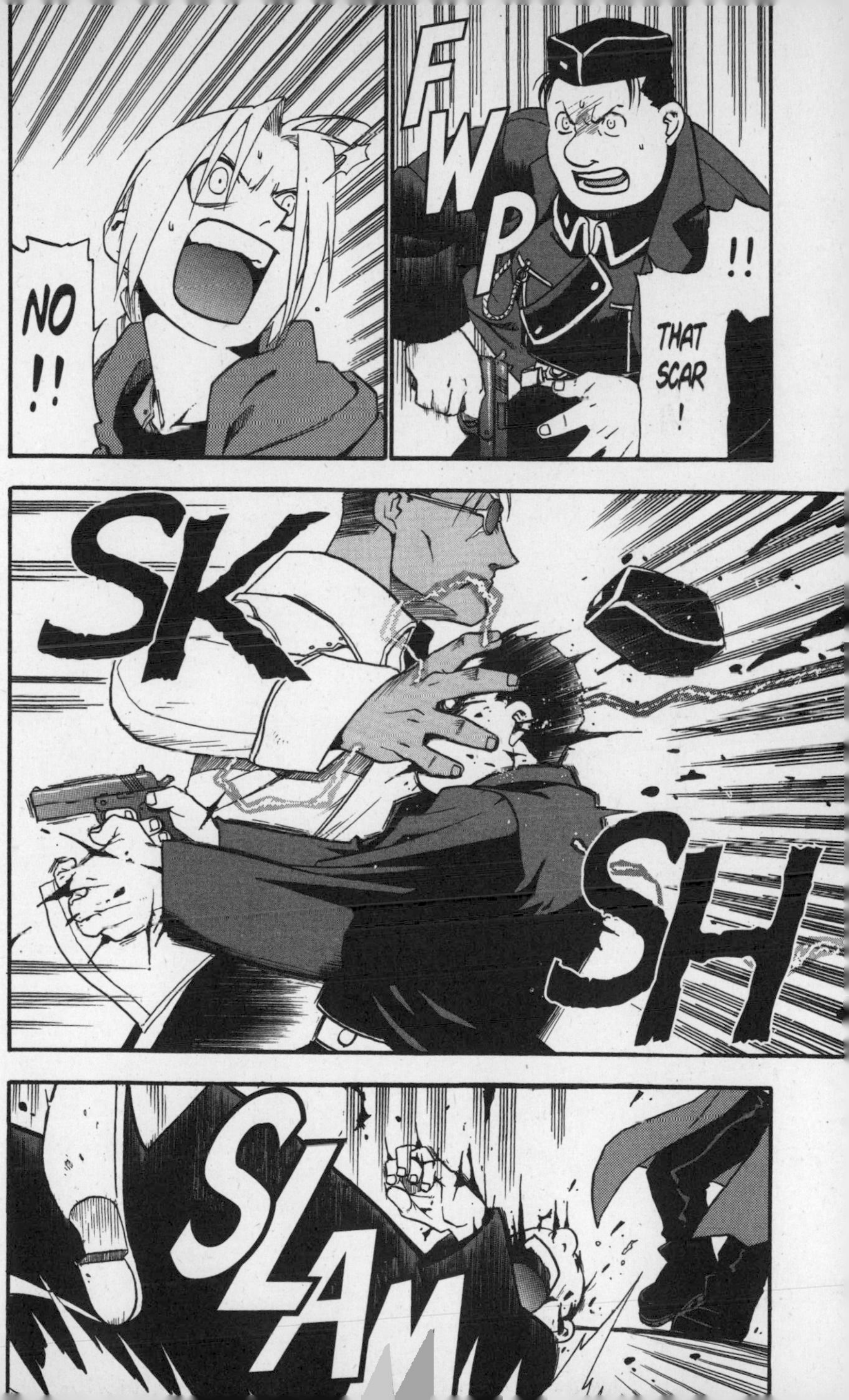
FWP
!!
THAT SCAR !
NO !!
SK
SH
SLAM

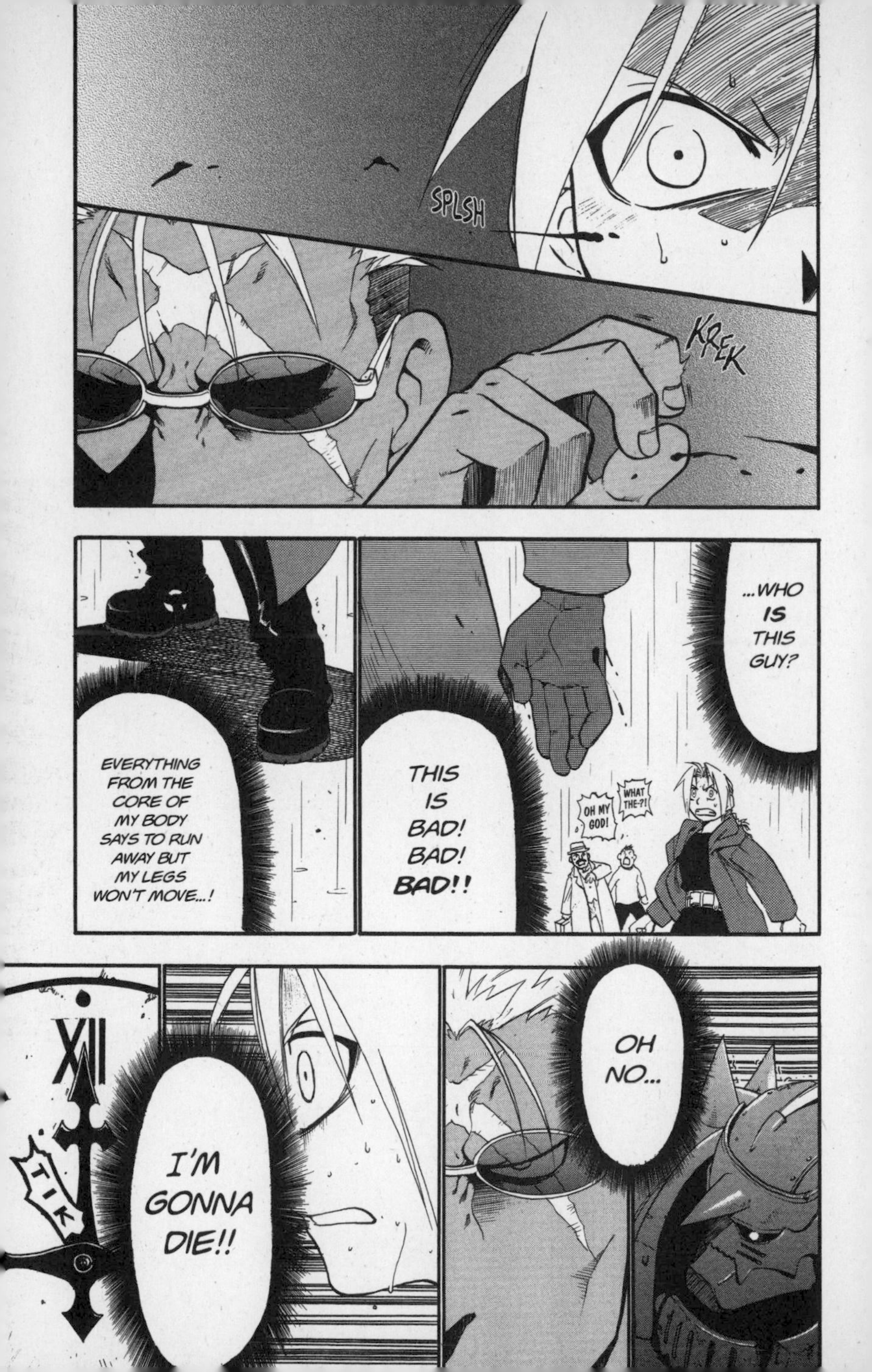
SPLSH
KREK
...WHO IS THIS GUY?
WHAT THE-?!
OH MY GOD!
THIS IS BAD! BAD! BAD!!
EVERYTHING FROM THE CORE OF MY BODY SAYS TO RUN AWAY BUT MY LEGS WON'T MOVE...!
OH NO...
I'M GONNA DIE!!
XII
TIK

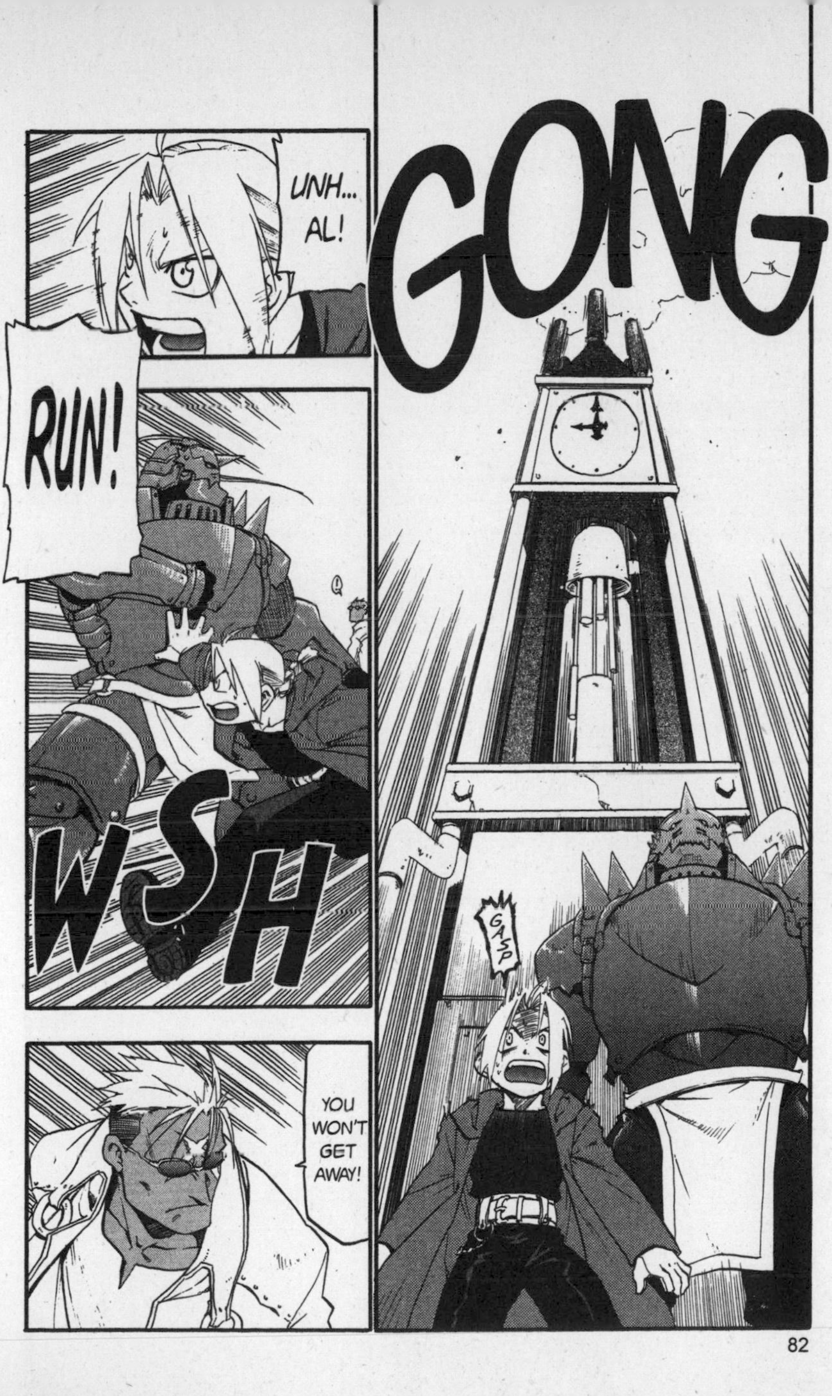
GONG
GASP
UNH... AL!
RUN!
WSH
YOU WON'T GET AWAY!

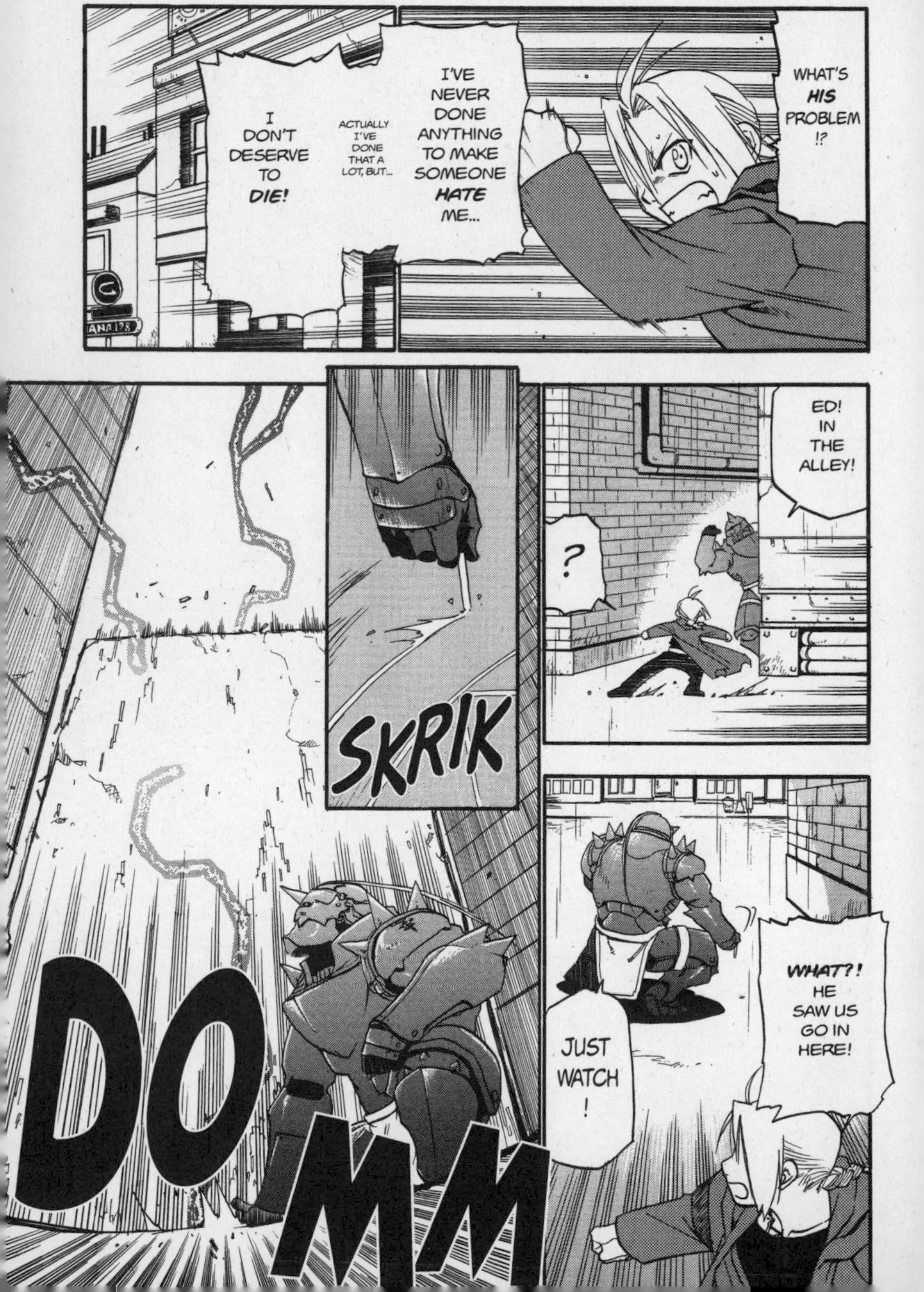
WHAT'S HIS PROBLEM !?
I'VE NEVER DONE ANYTHING TO MAKE SOMEONE HATE ME...
ACTUALLY I'VE DONE THAT A LOT, BUT...
I DON'T DESERVE TO DIE!
ED! IN THE ALLEY!
?
WHAT?! HE SAW US GO IN HERE!
JUST WATCH!
SKRIK
DOMM

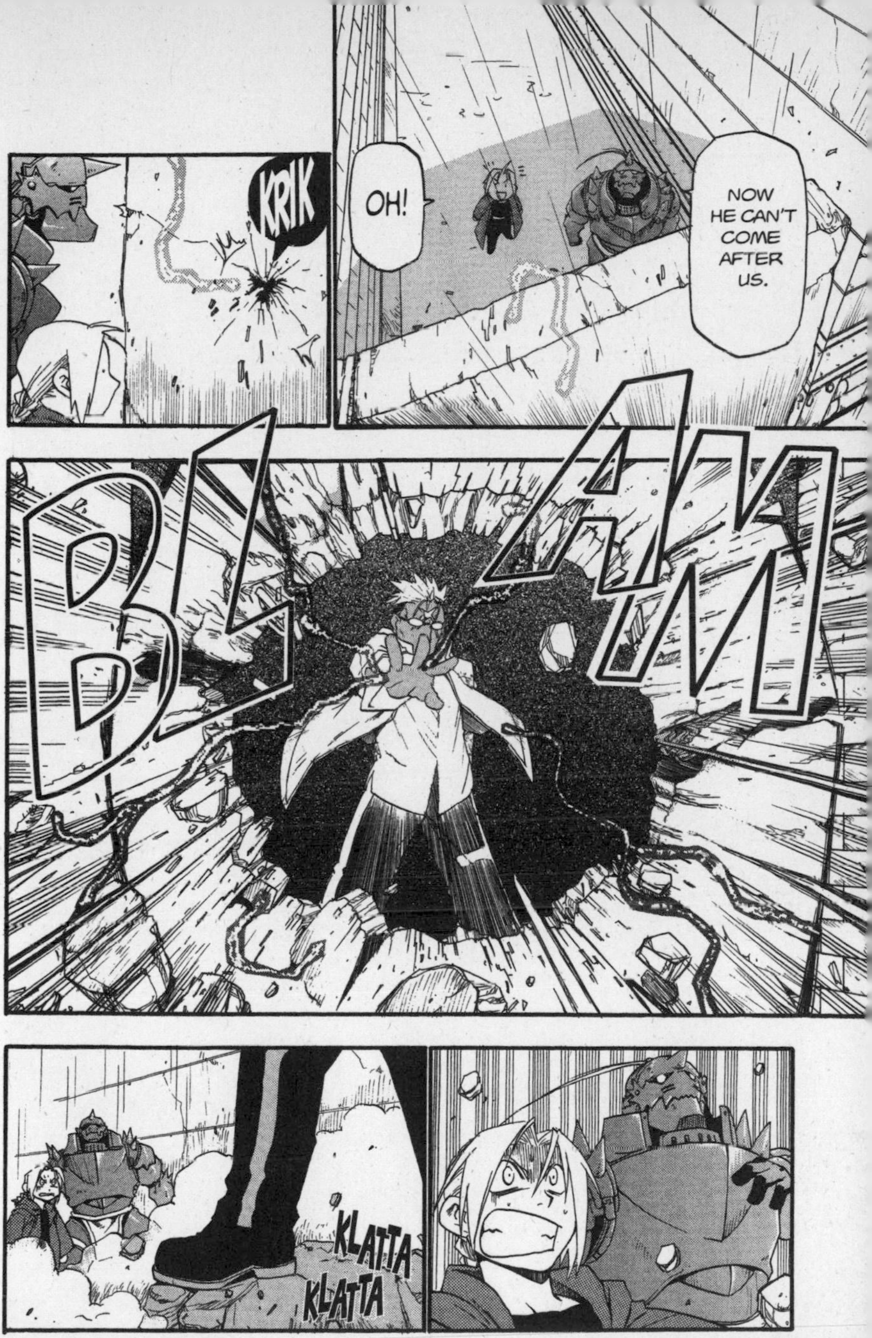
NOW HE CAN'T COME AFTER US.
OH!
KRIK
BLAM
KLATTA KLATTA

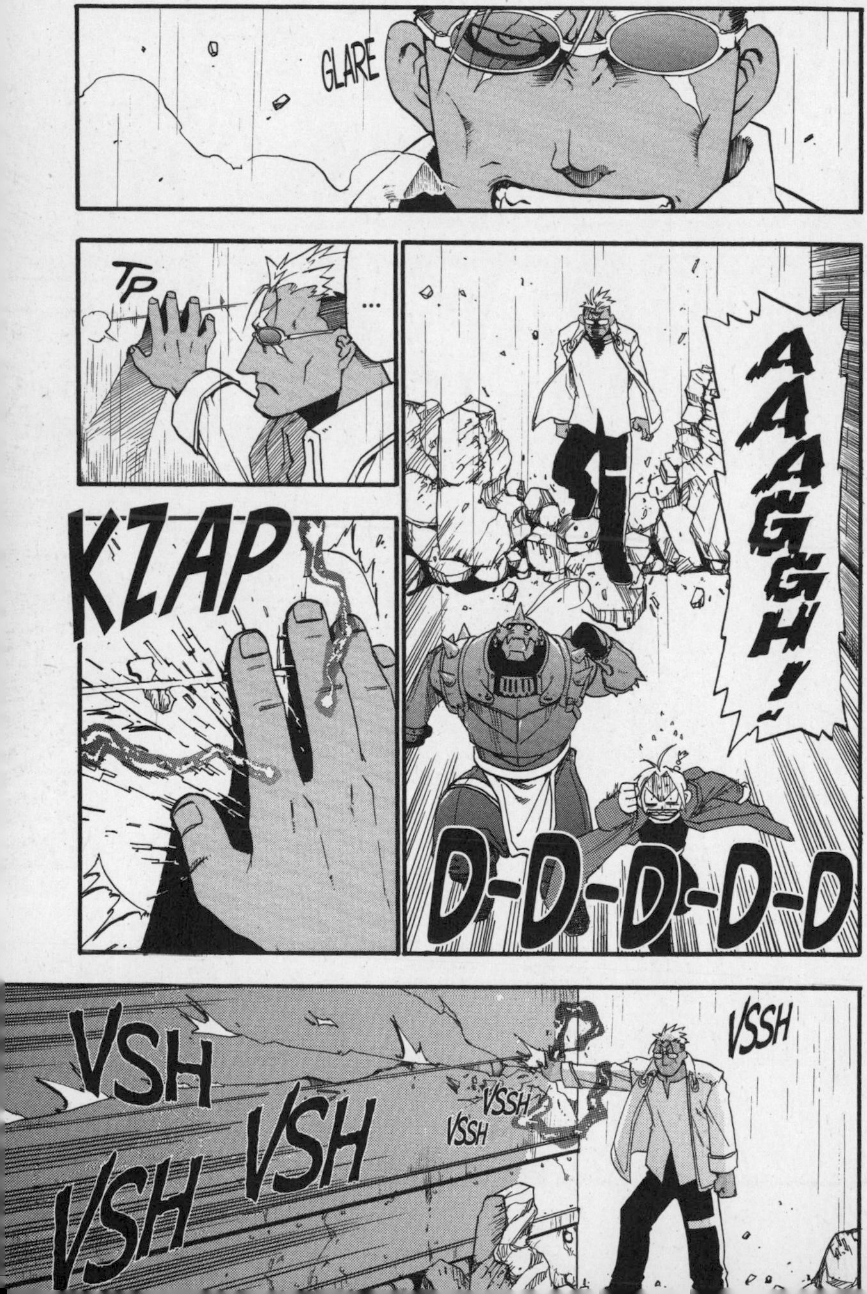
GLARE
AAAAGH!!
D-D-D-D-D
TP
...
KZAP
VSSH
VSSH
VSSH
VSH
VSH
VSH

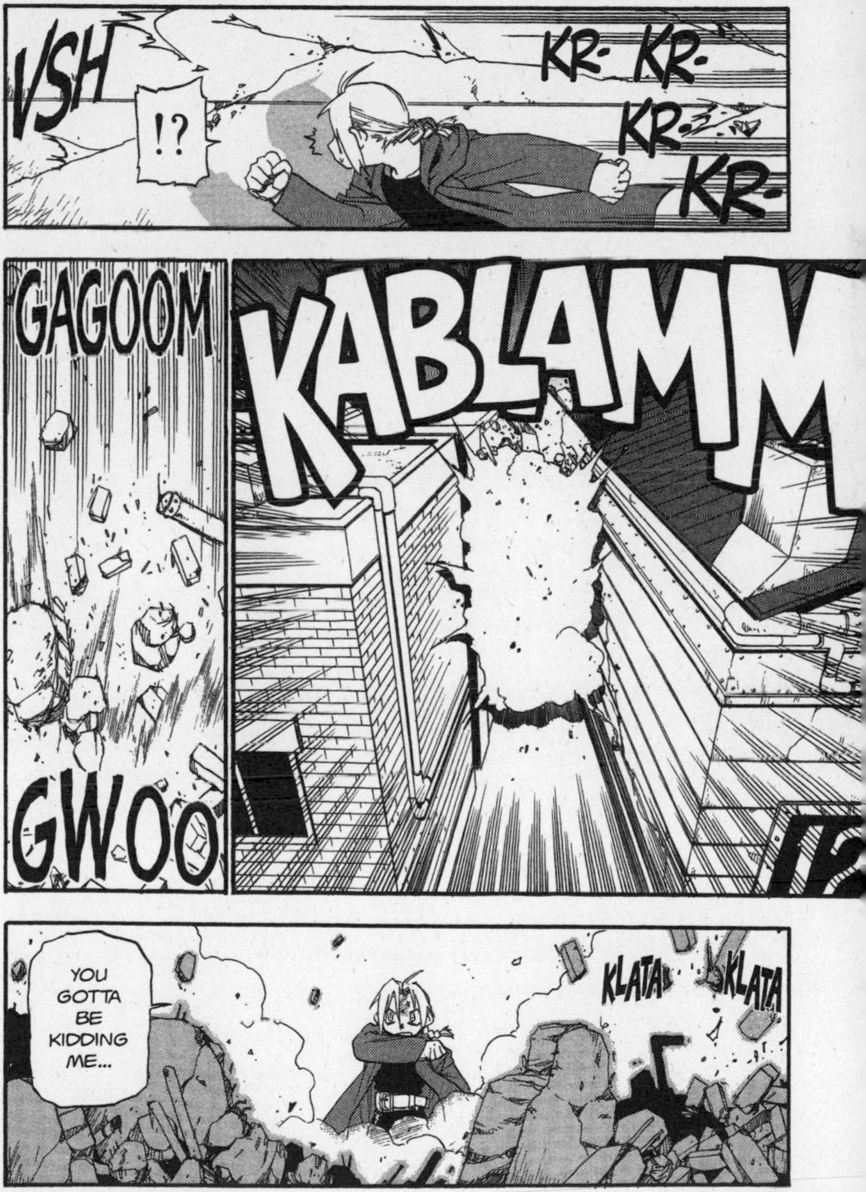
KR- KR- KR- KR-
!?
VSH
KABLAMM
GAGOOM
GWOO
KLATA KLATA
YOU GOTTA BE KIDDING ME...

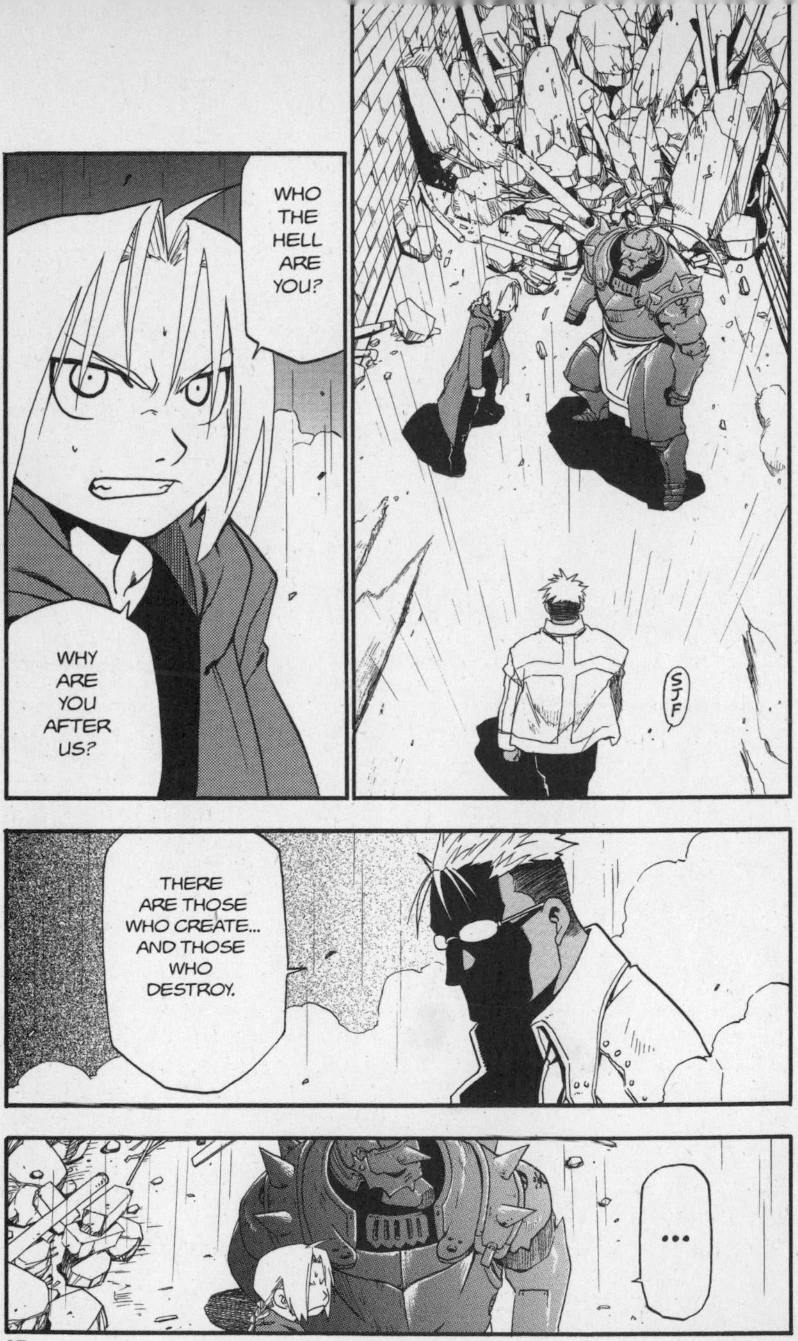
SJF
WHO THE HELL ARE YOU?
WHY ARE YOU AFTER US?
THERE ARE THOSE WHO CREATE... AND THOSE WHO DESTROY.
...

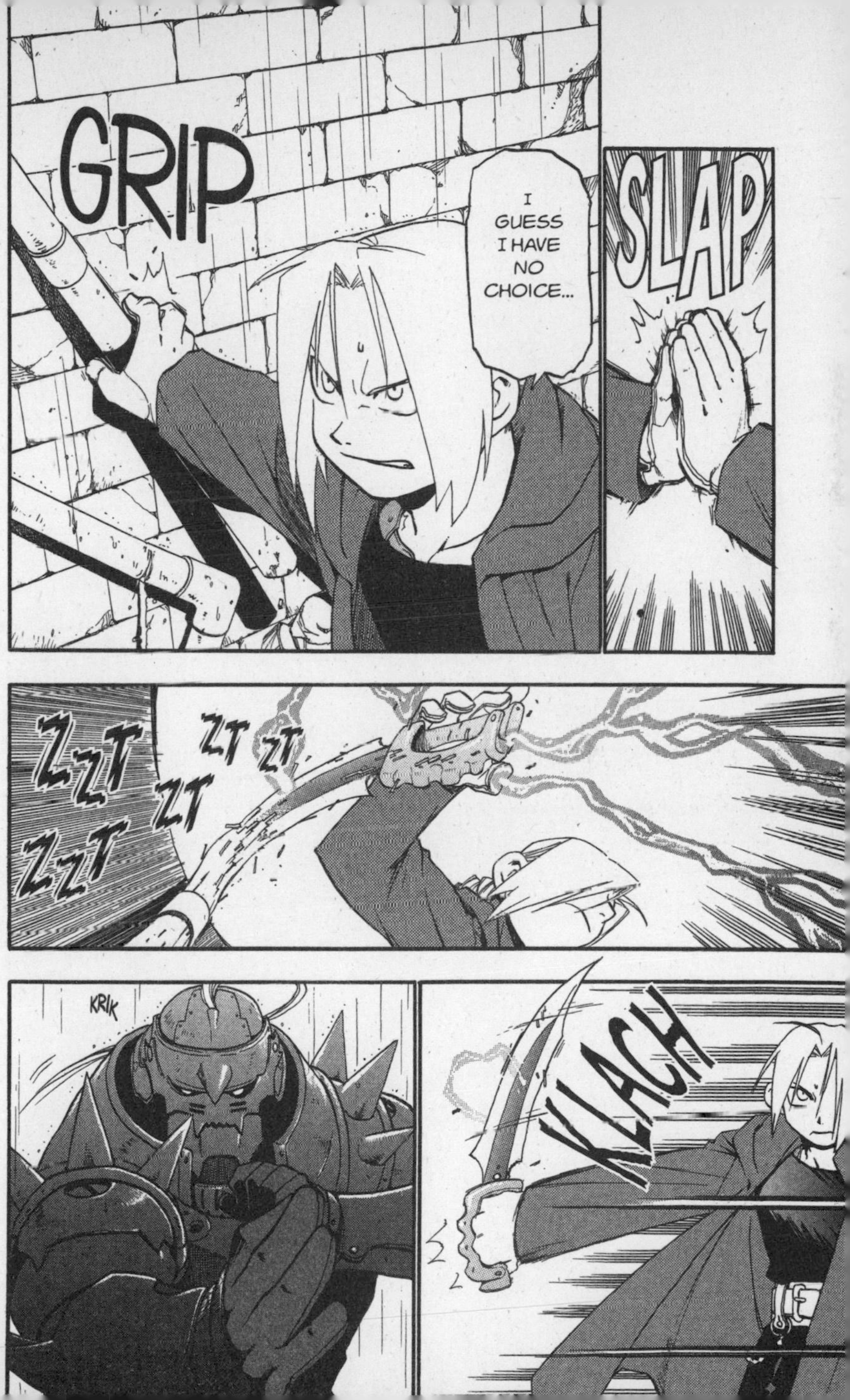
SLAP
GRIP
I GUESS I HAVE NO CHOICE...
ZZT ZZT ZZT ZZT ZZT ZZT
KLACH
KRIK

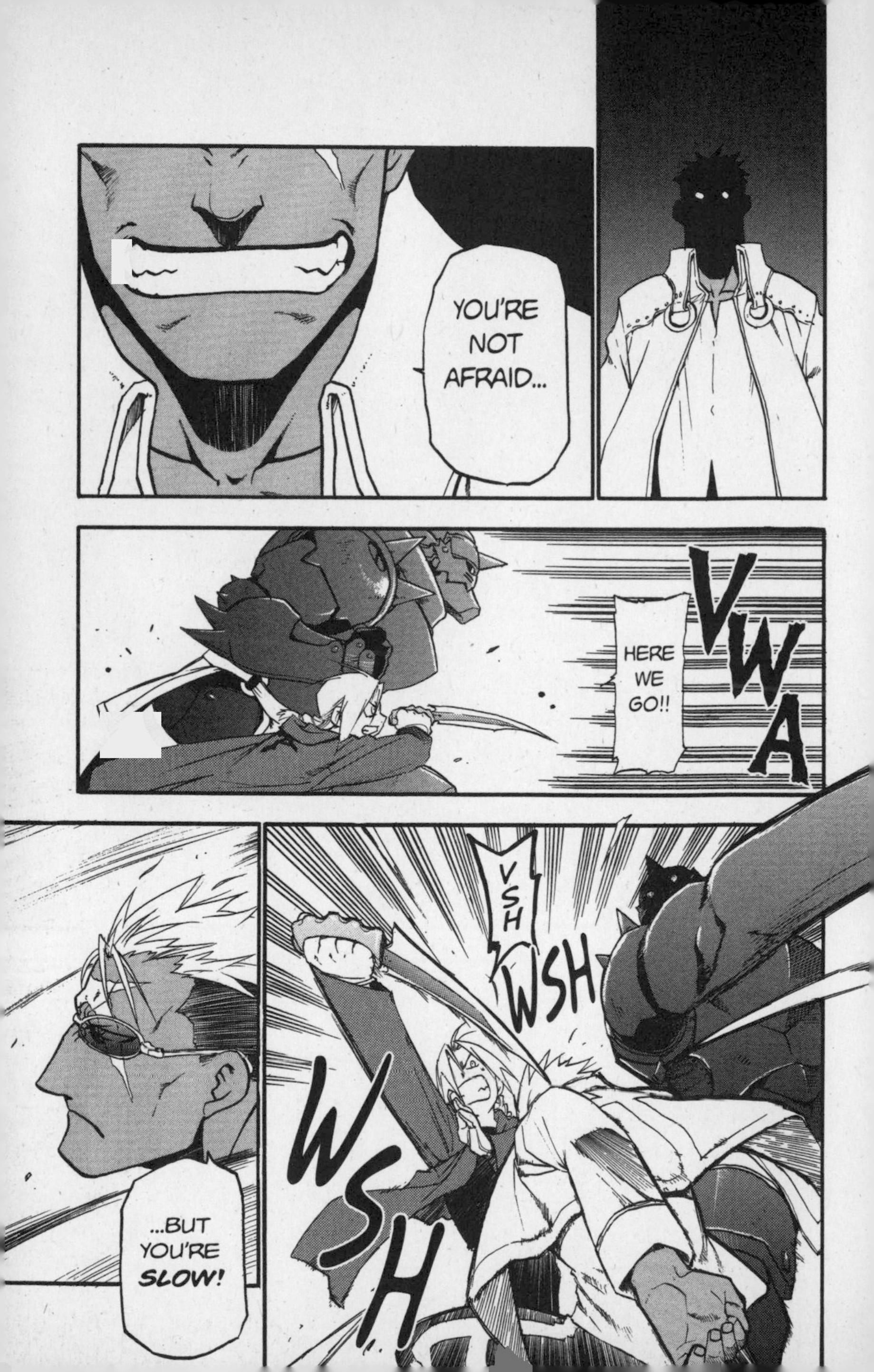
YOU'RE NOT AFRAID...
VWA
HERE WE GO!!
VSH
WSH
WSH
...BUT YOU'RE SLOW!

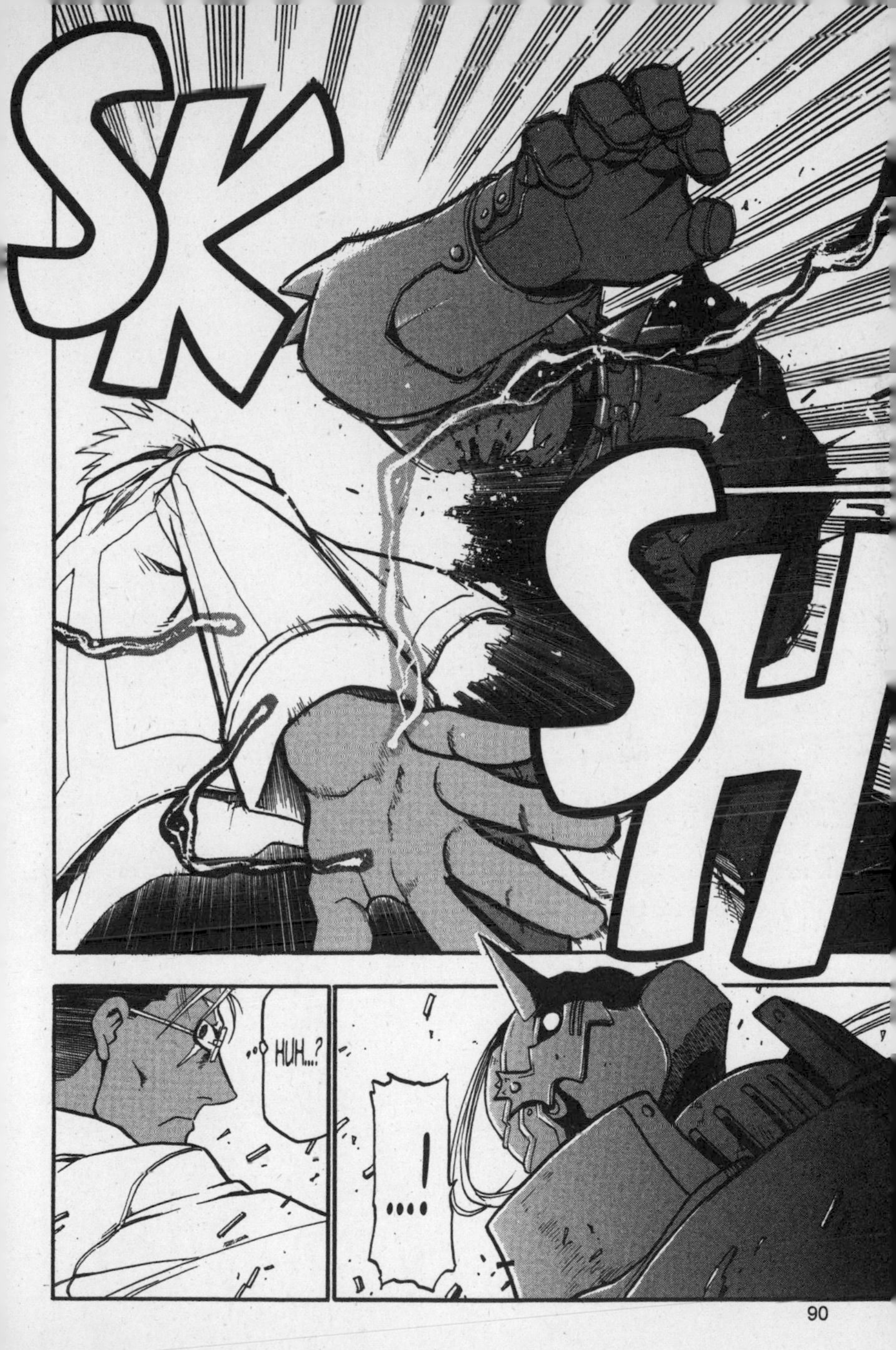
SK
SH
!
....
HUH...?

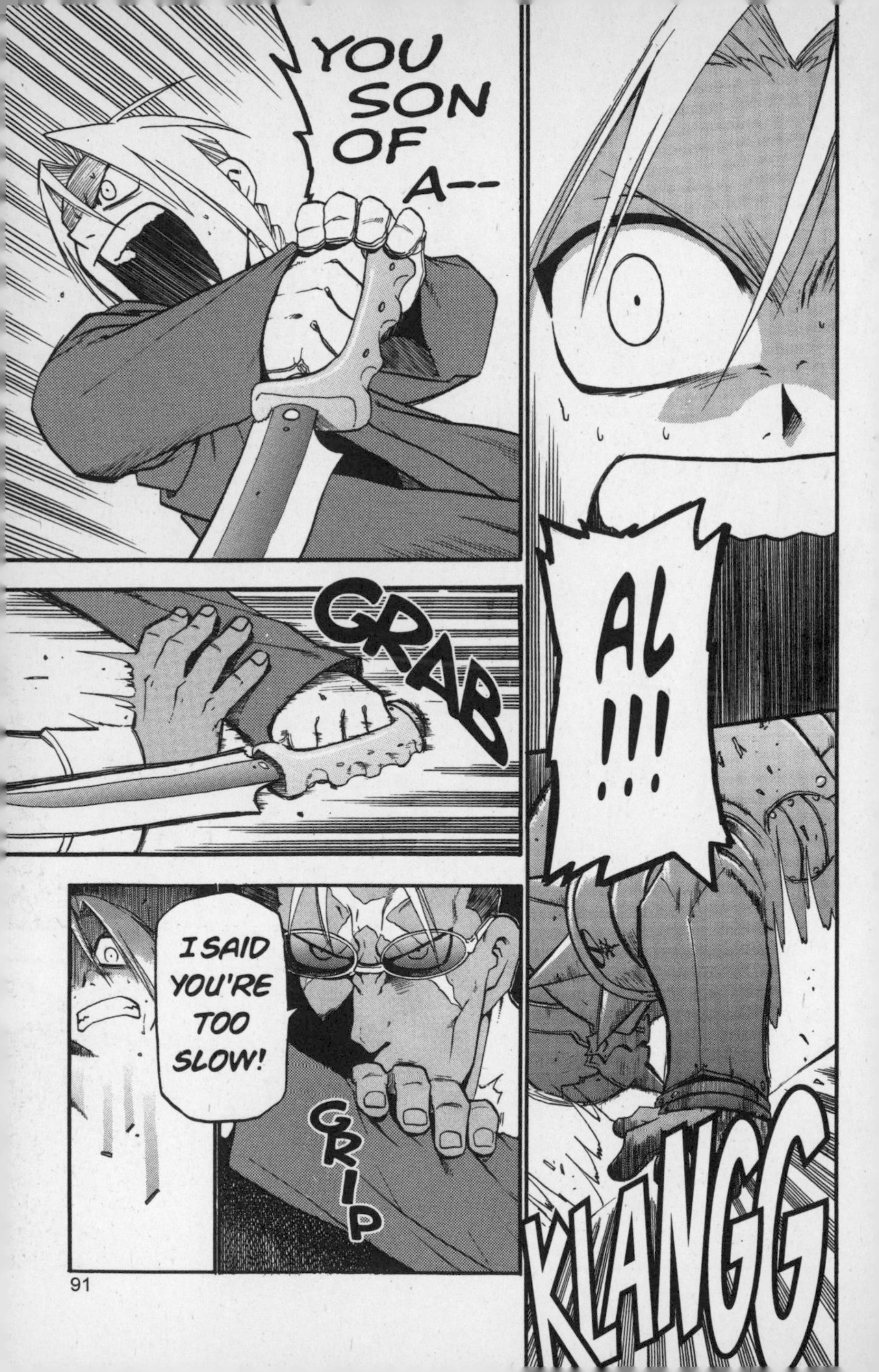
AL!!!
KLANGG
YOU SON OF A--
GRAB
I SAID YOU'RE TOO SLOW!
GRIP

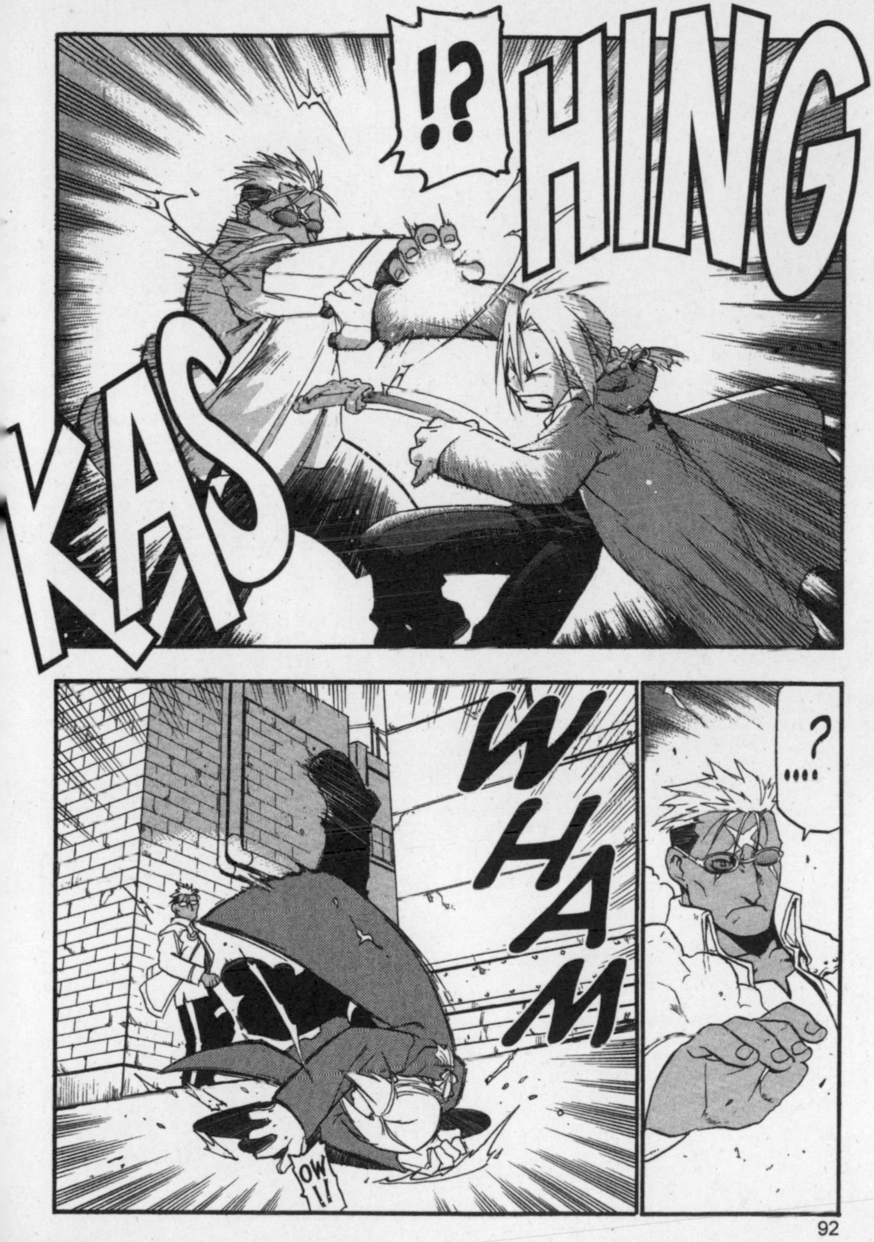
!?
KAS HING
....?
WHAM
OW!!

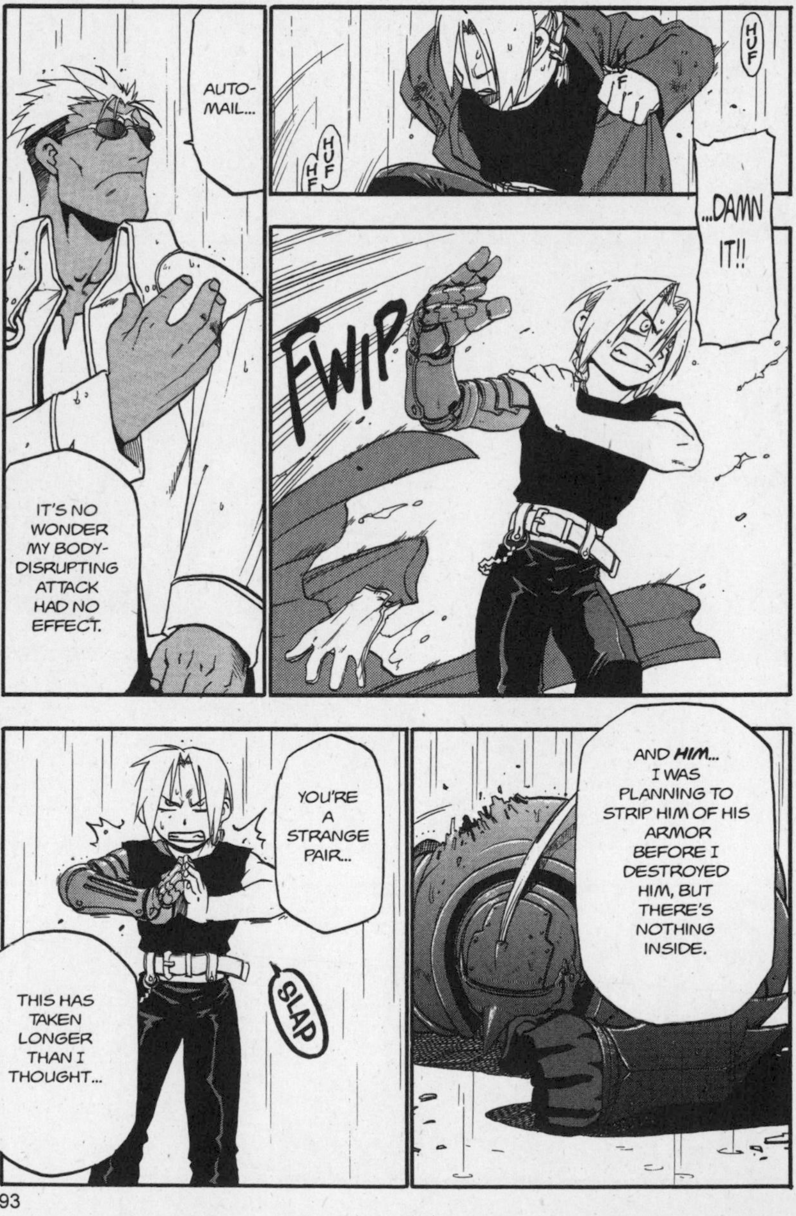
HUF F
HUF HUF
...DAMN IT!!
FWIP
AUTO-MAIL...
IT'S NO WONDER MY BODY-DISRUPTING ATTACK HAD NO EFFECT.
AND HIM... I WAS PLANNING TO STRIP HIM OF HIS ARMOR BEFORE I DESTROYED HIM, BUT THERE'S NOTHING INSIDE.
YOU'RE A STRANGE PAIR...
SLAP
THIS HAS TAKEN LONGER THAN I THOUGHT...

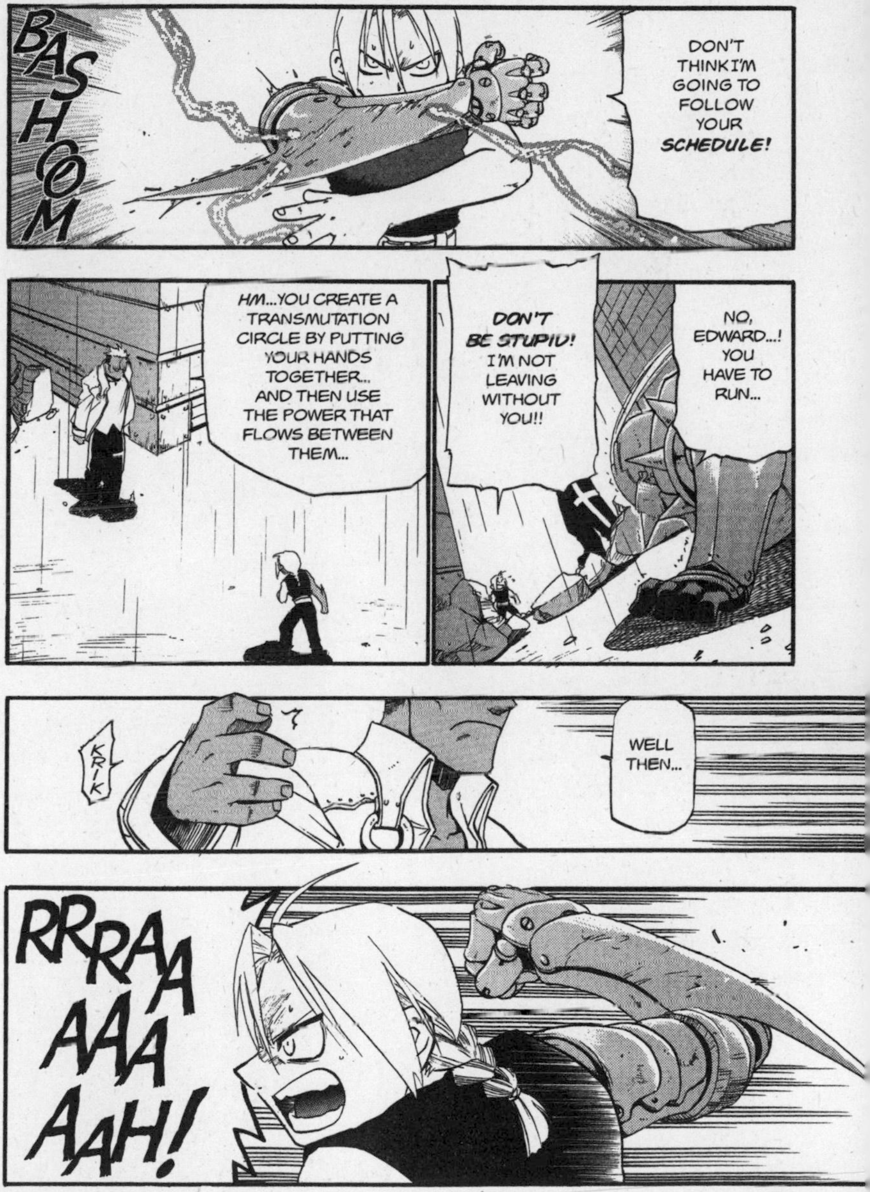
DON'T THINK I'M GOING TO FOLLOW YOUR SCHEDULE!
BASHOOM
NO, EDWARD...! YOU HAVE TO RUN...
DON'T BE STUPID! I'M NOT LEAVING WITHOUT YOU!!
HM...YOU CREATE A TRANSMUTATION CIRCLE BY PUTTING YOUR HANDS TOGETHER... AND THEN USE THE POWER THAT FLOWS BETWEEN THEM...
WELL THEN...
KRIK
RRRAAAAAAAH!

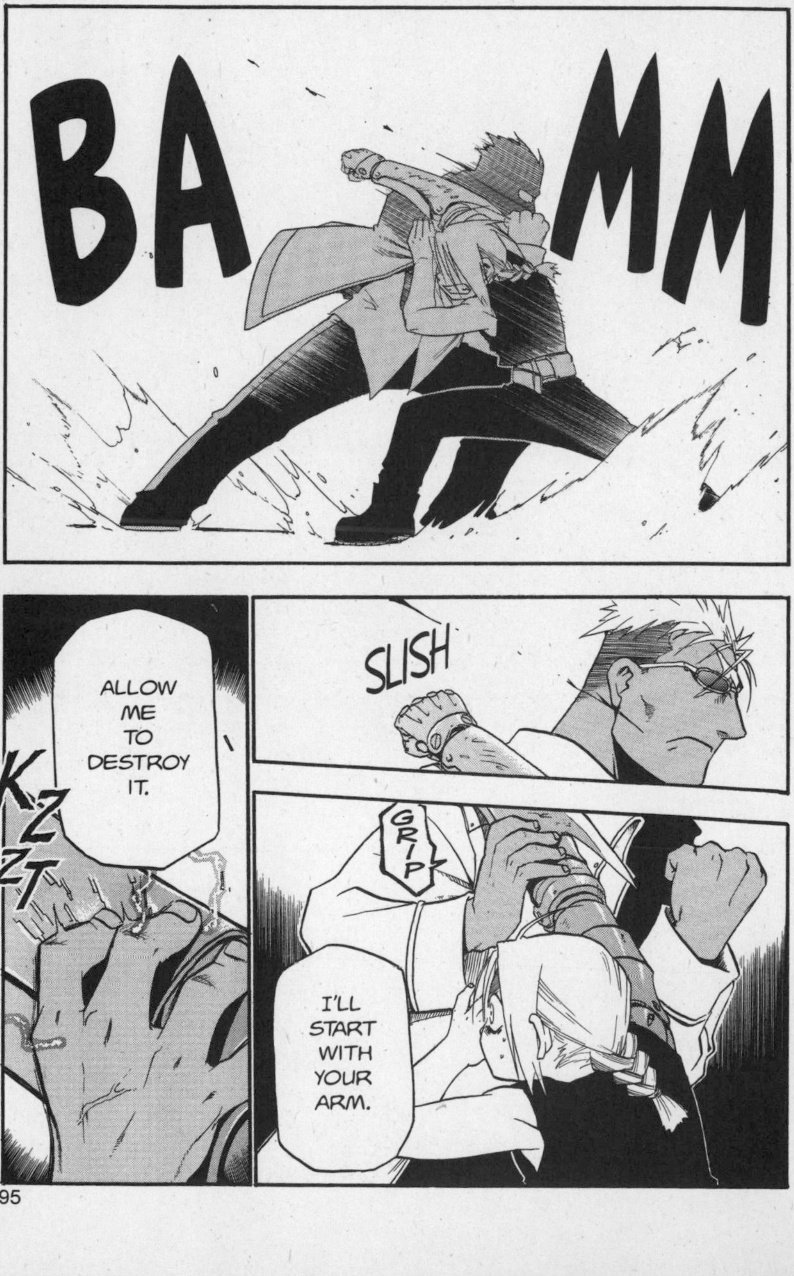
BAMM
SLISH
GRIP
I'LL START WITH YOUR ARM.
ALLOW ME TO DESTROY IT.
KZZT

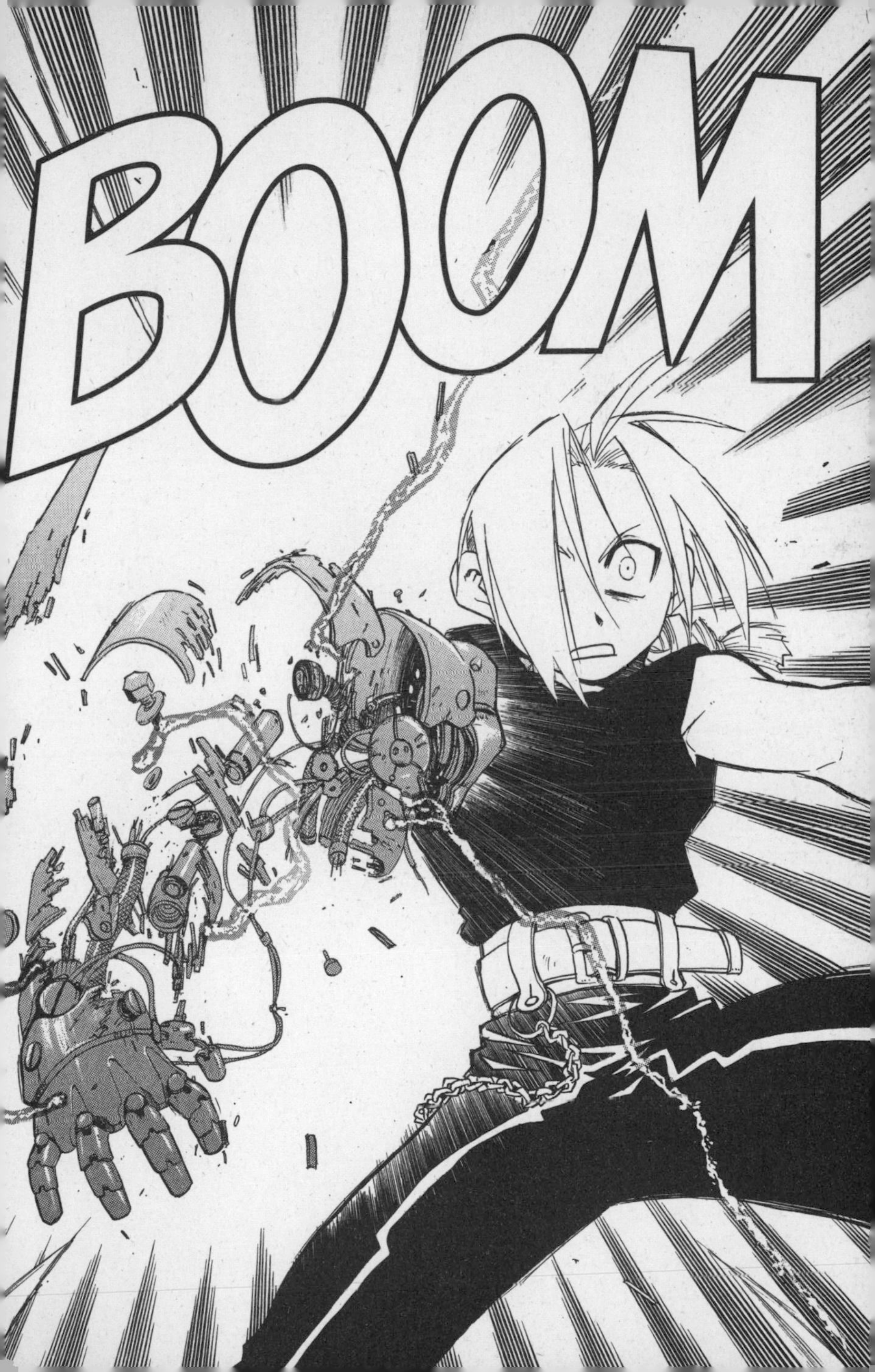
BOOM

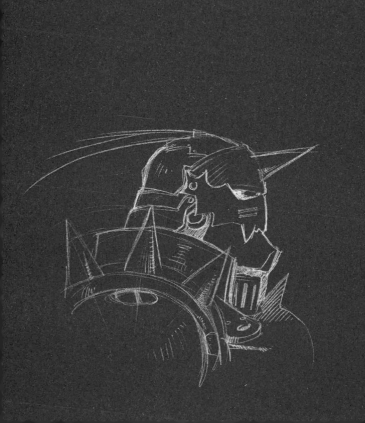

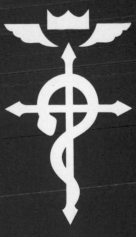

FULLMETAL
ALCHEMIST

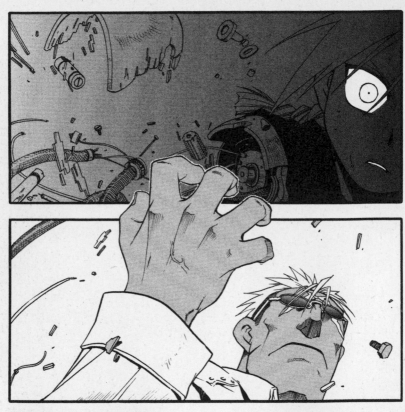

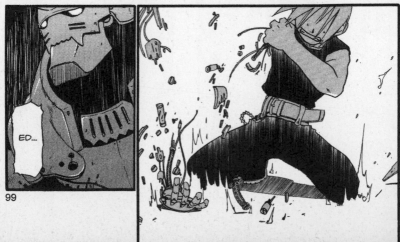

ED...

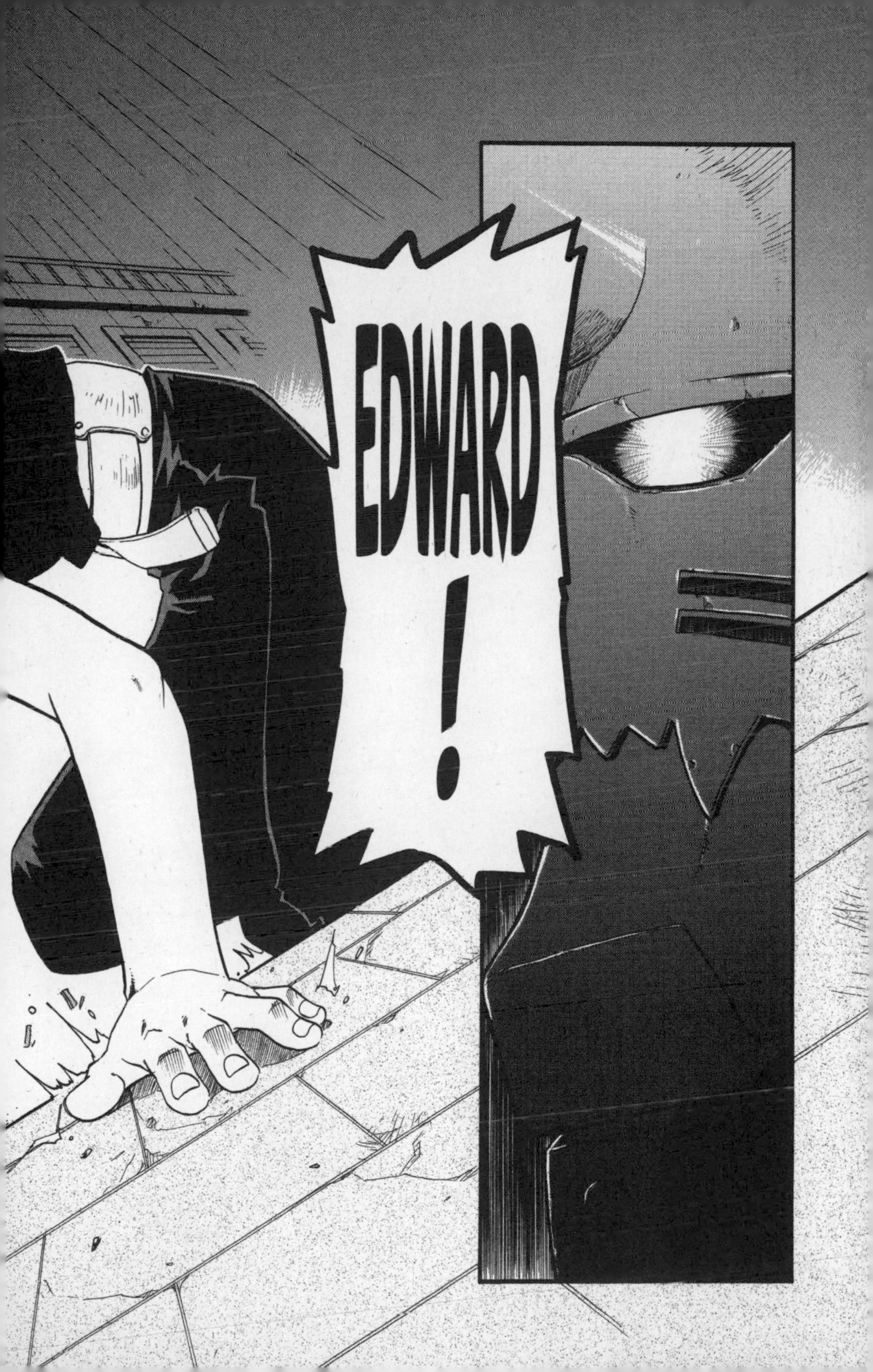
EDWARD!

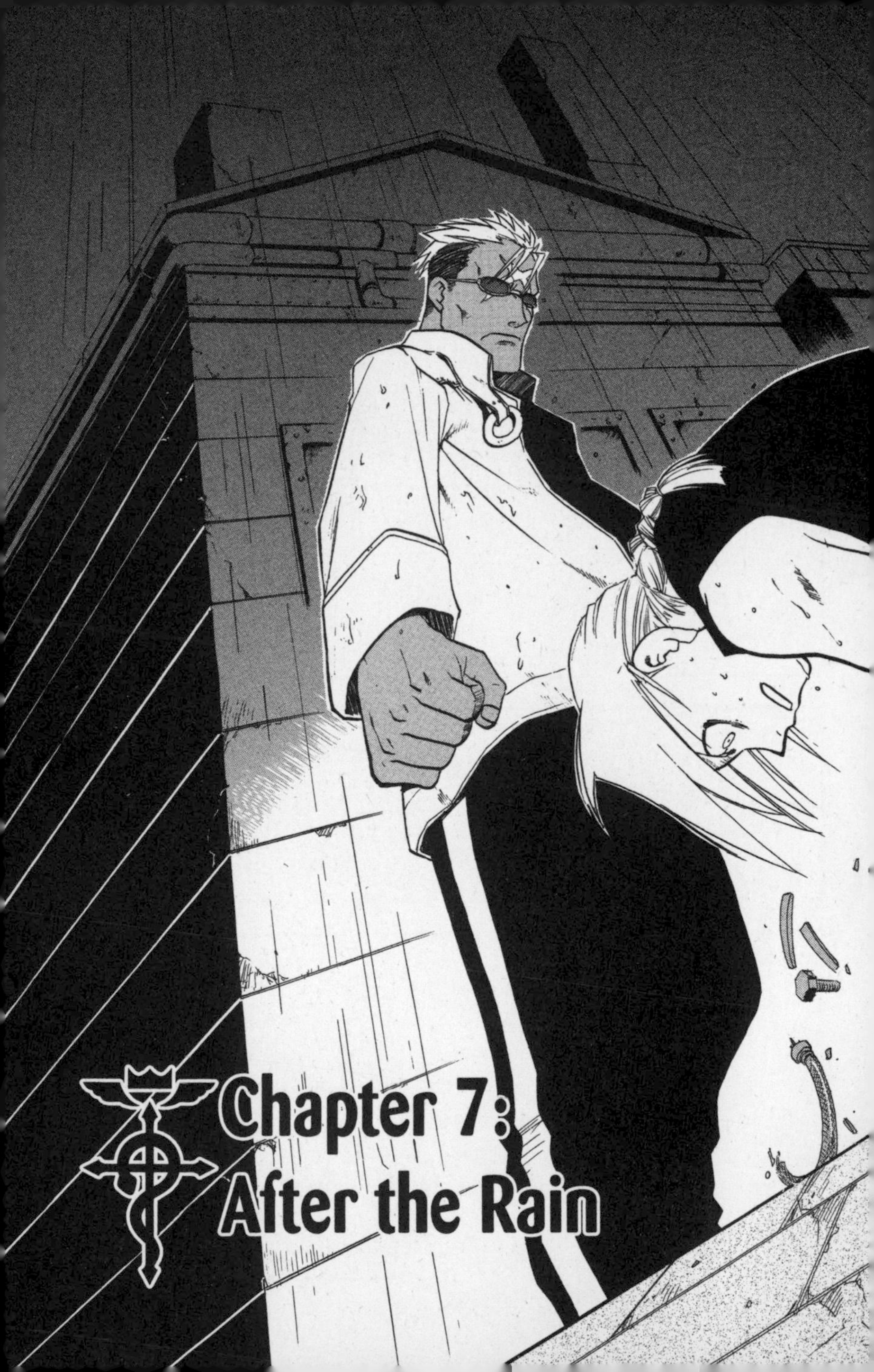
Chapter 7:
After the Rain

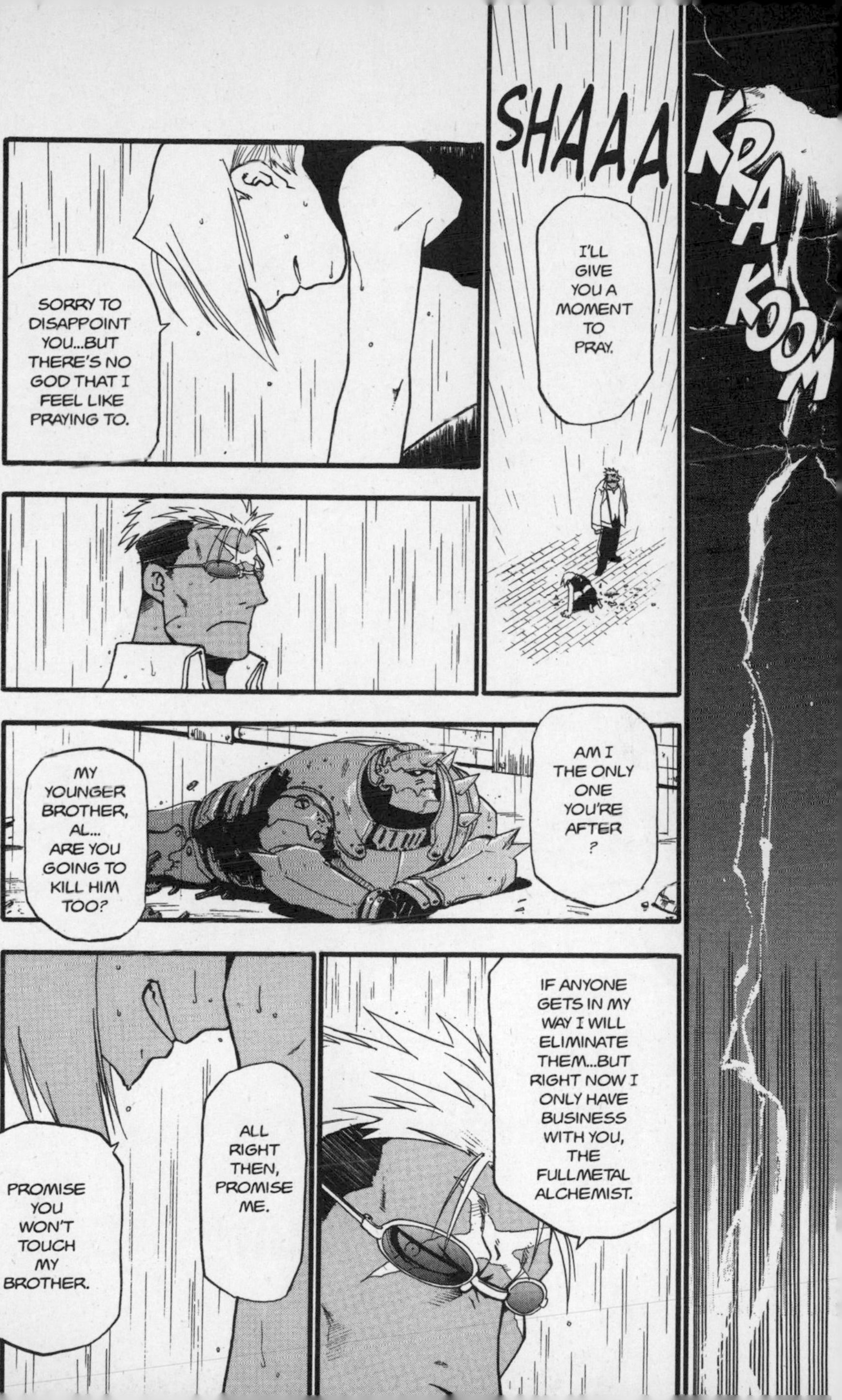
KRAKOOM
SHAAA
I'LL GIVE YOU A MOMENT TO PRAY.
SORRY TO DISAPPOINT YOU...BUT THERE'S NO GOD THAT I FEEL LIKE PRAYING TO.
AM I THE ONLY ONE YOU'RE AFTER?
MY YOUNGER BROTHER, AL... ARE YOU GOING TO KILL HIM TOO?
IF ANYONE GETS IN MY WAY I WILL ELIMINATE THEM...BUT RIGHT NOW I ONLY HAVE BUSINESS WITH YOU, THE FULLMETAL ALCHEMIST.
ALL RIGHT THEN, PROMISE ME.
PROMISE YOU WON'T TOUCH MY BROTHER.

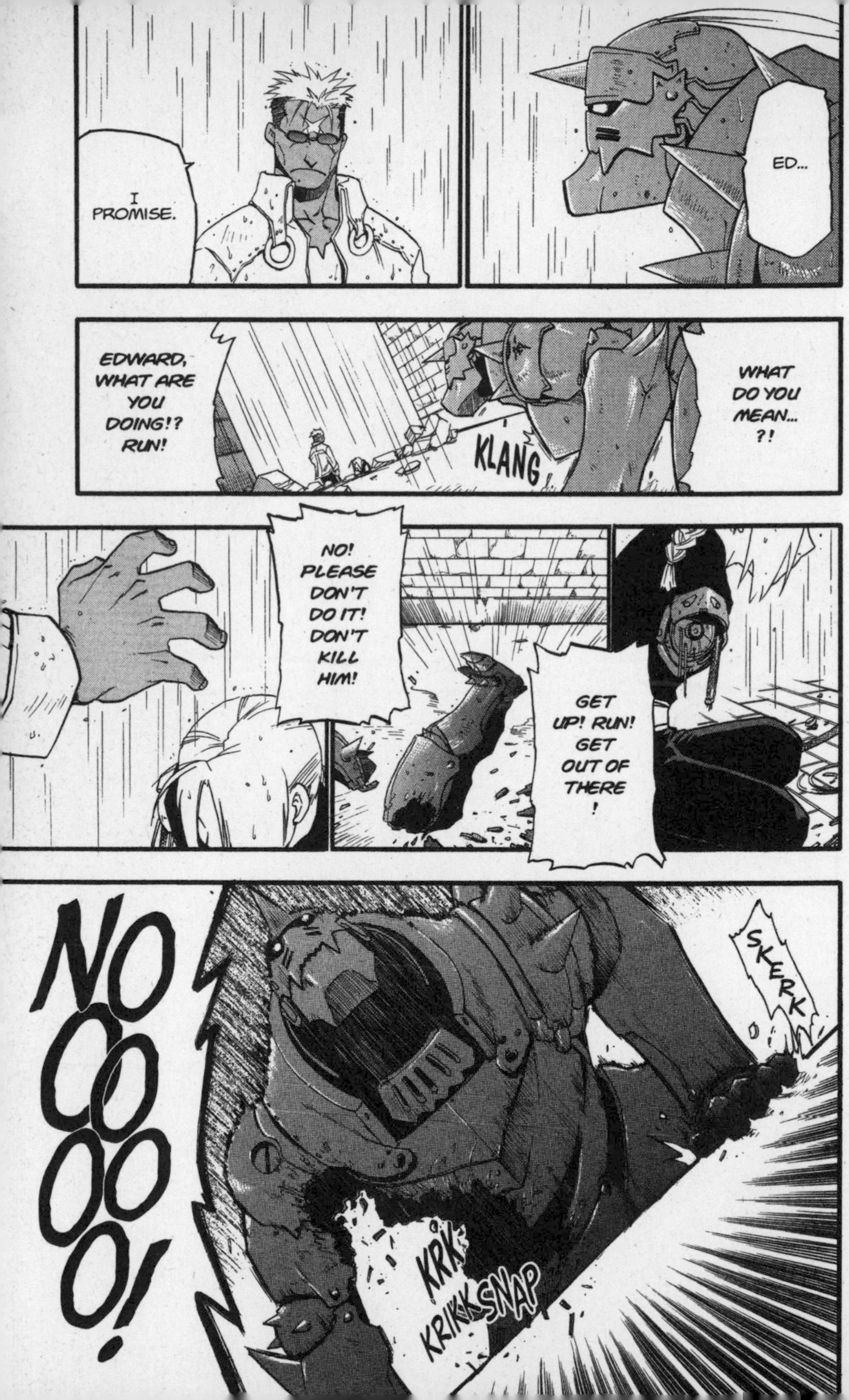
ED...
I PROMISE.
WHAT DO YOU MEAN...?!
EDWARD, WHAT ARE YOU DOING!? RUN!
KLANG
GET UP! RUN! GET OUT OF THERE!
NO! PLEASE DON'T DO IT! DON'T KILL HIM!
SKERK
KRK KRIKK SNAP
NOOOOOO!

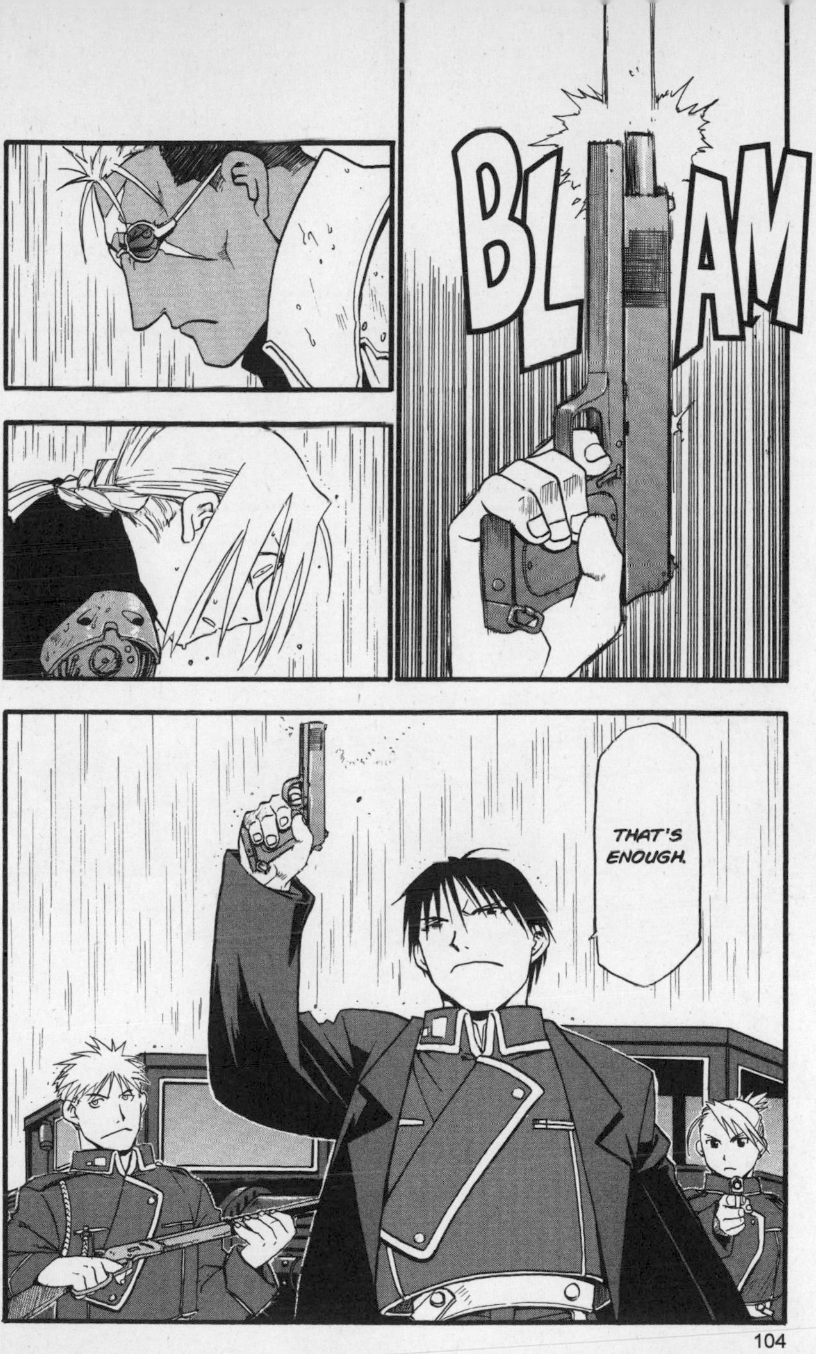
BLAM
THAT'S ENOUGH.

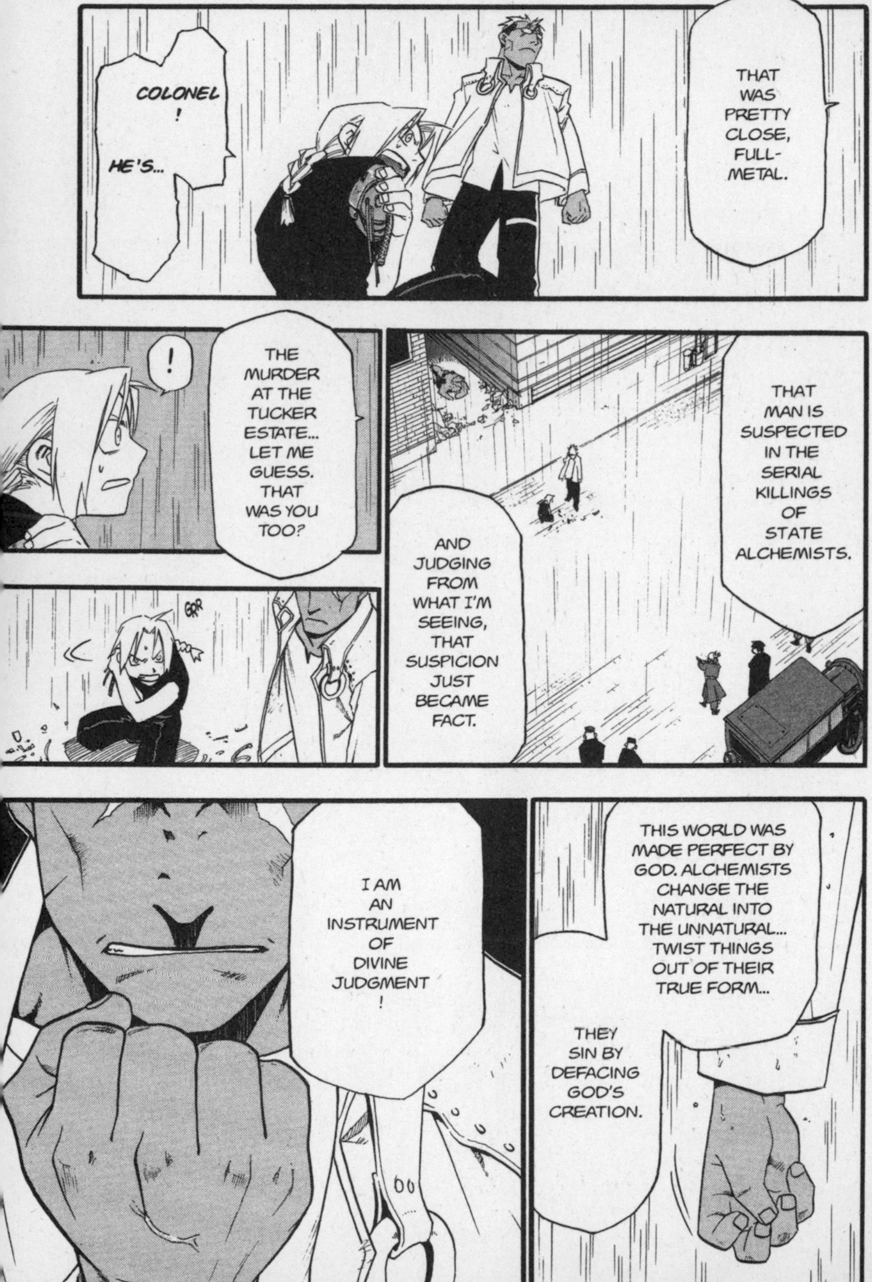
THAT WAS PRETTY CLOSE, FULL-METAL.
COLONEL! HE'S...
THAT MAN IS SUSPECTED IN THE SERIAL KILLINGS OF STATE ALCHEMISTS.
AND JUDGING FROM WHAT I'M SEEING, THAT SUSPICION JUST BECAME FACT.
!
THE MURDER AT THE TUCKER ESTATE... LET ME GUESS. THAT WAS YOU TOO?
GRR
THIS WORLD WAS MADE PERFECT BY GOD. ALCHEMISTS CHANGE THE NATURAL INTO THE UNNATURAL... TWIST THINGS OUT OF THEIR TRUE FORM...
THEY SIN BY DEFACING GOD'S CREATION.
I AM AN INSTRUMENT OF DIVINE JUDGMENT!

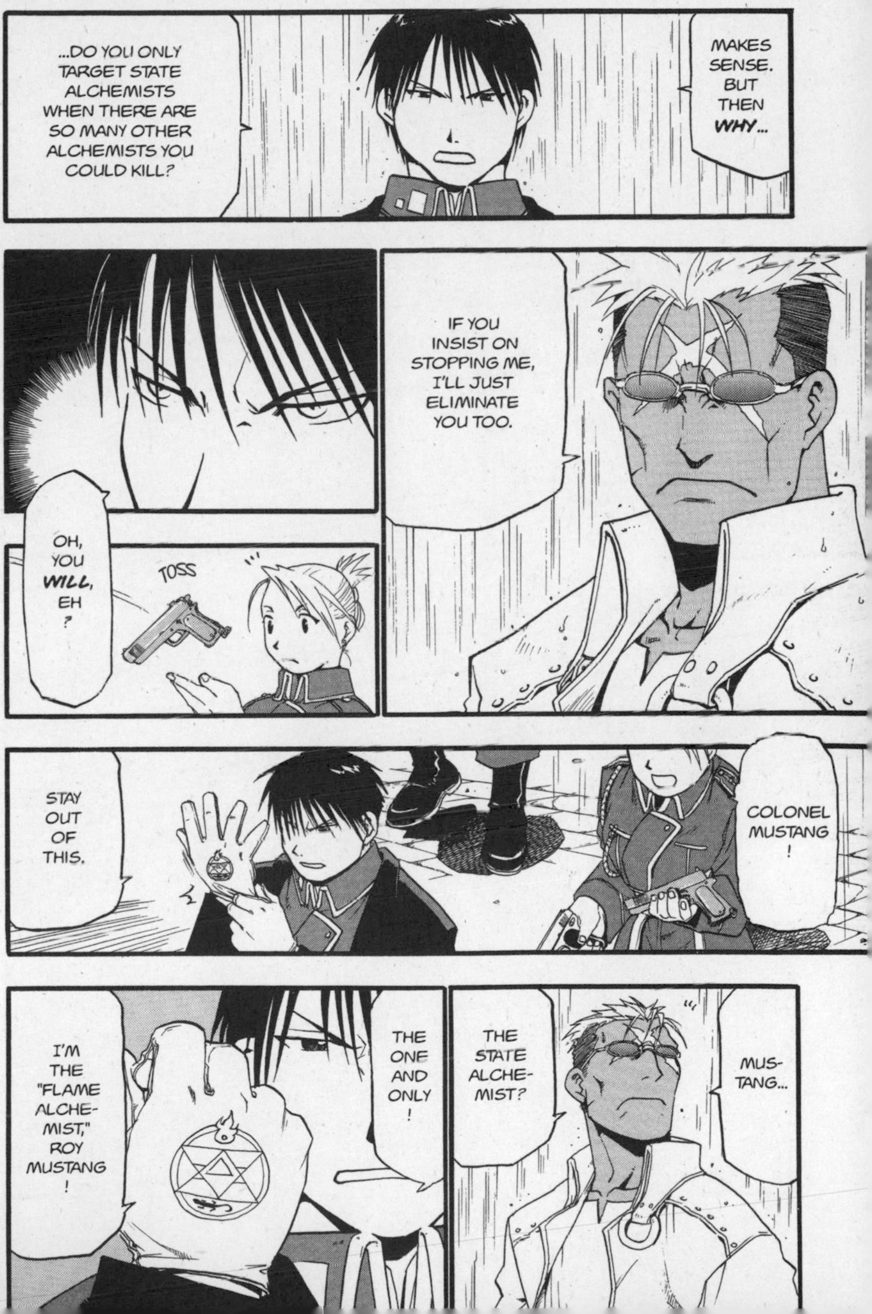
MAKES SENSE. BUT THEN WHY...
...DO YOU ONLY TARGET STATE ALCHEMISTS WHEN THERE ARE SO MANY OTHER ALCHEMISTS YOU COULD KILL?
IF YOU INSIST ON STOPPING ME, I'LL JUST ELIMINATE YOU TOO.
OH, YOU WILL, EH?
TOSS
COLONEL MUSTANG!
STAY OUT OF THIS.
MUSTANG...
THE STATE ALCHEMIST?
THE ONE AND ONLY!
I'M THE "FLAME ALCHEMIST," ROY MUSTANG!

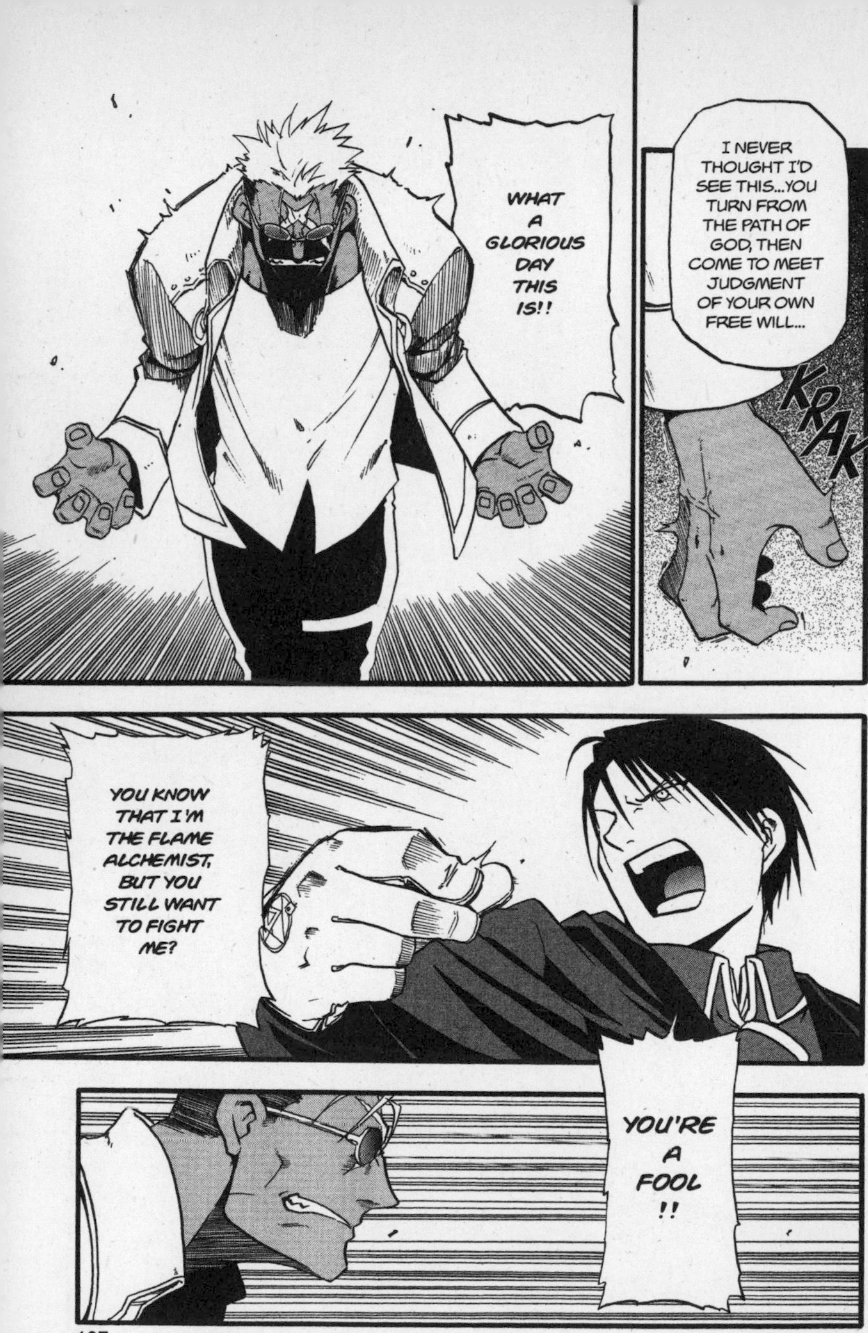
I NEVER THOUGHT I'D SEE THIS...YOU TURN FROM THE PATH OF GOD, THEN COME TO MEET JUDGMENT OF YOUR OWN FREE WILL...
KRAK
WHAT A GLORIOUS DAY THIS IS!!
YOU KNOW THAT I'M THE FLAME ALCHEMIST, BUT YOU STILL WANT TO FIGHT ME?
YOU'RE A FOOL !!

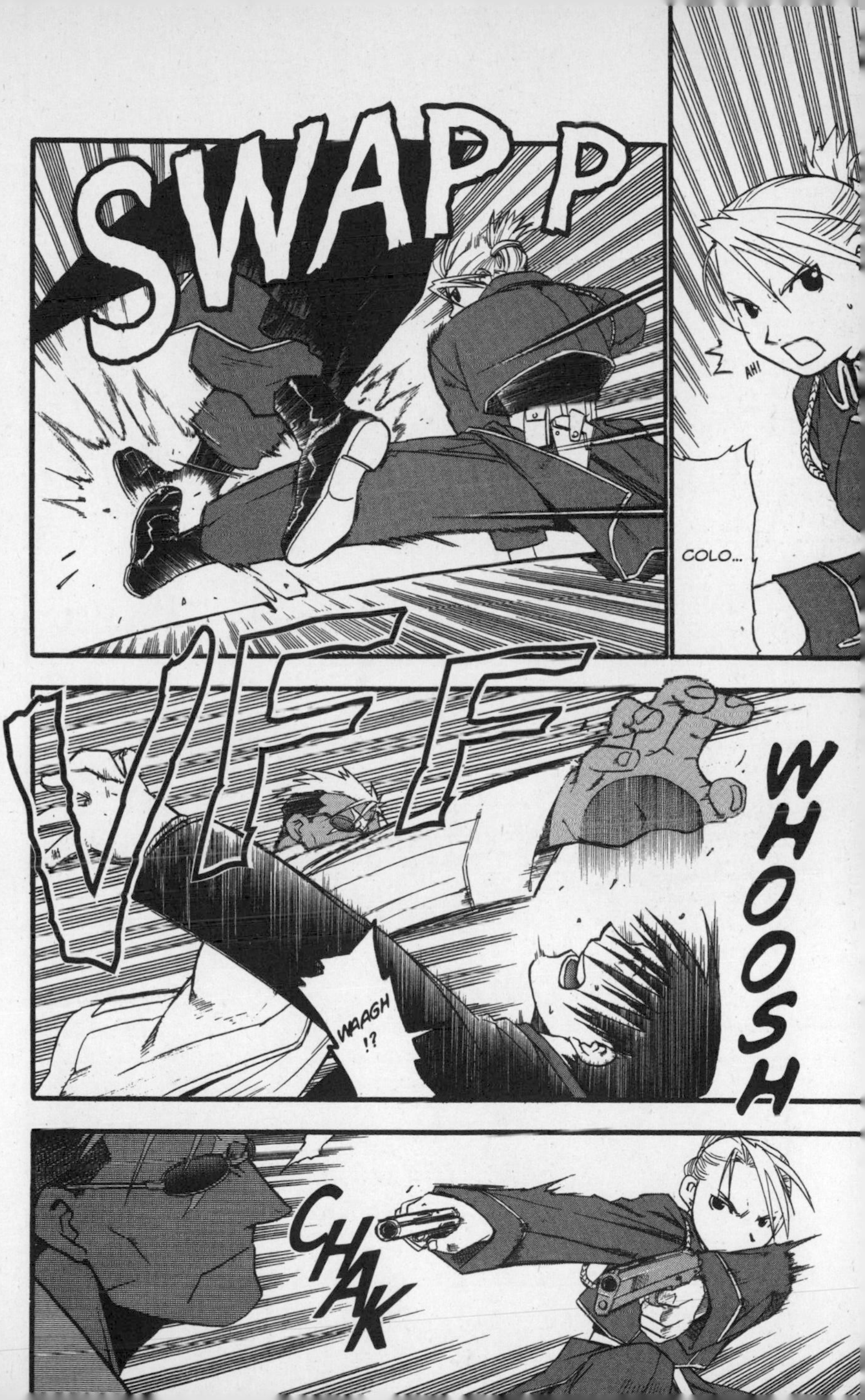
AH!
COLO...
SWAPP
WHOOSH
VIFF
WAAGH !?
CHAK

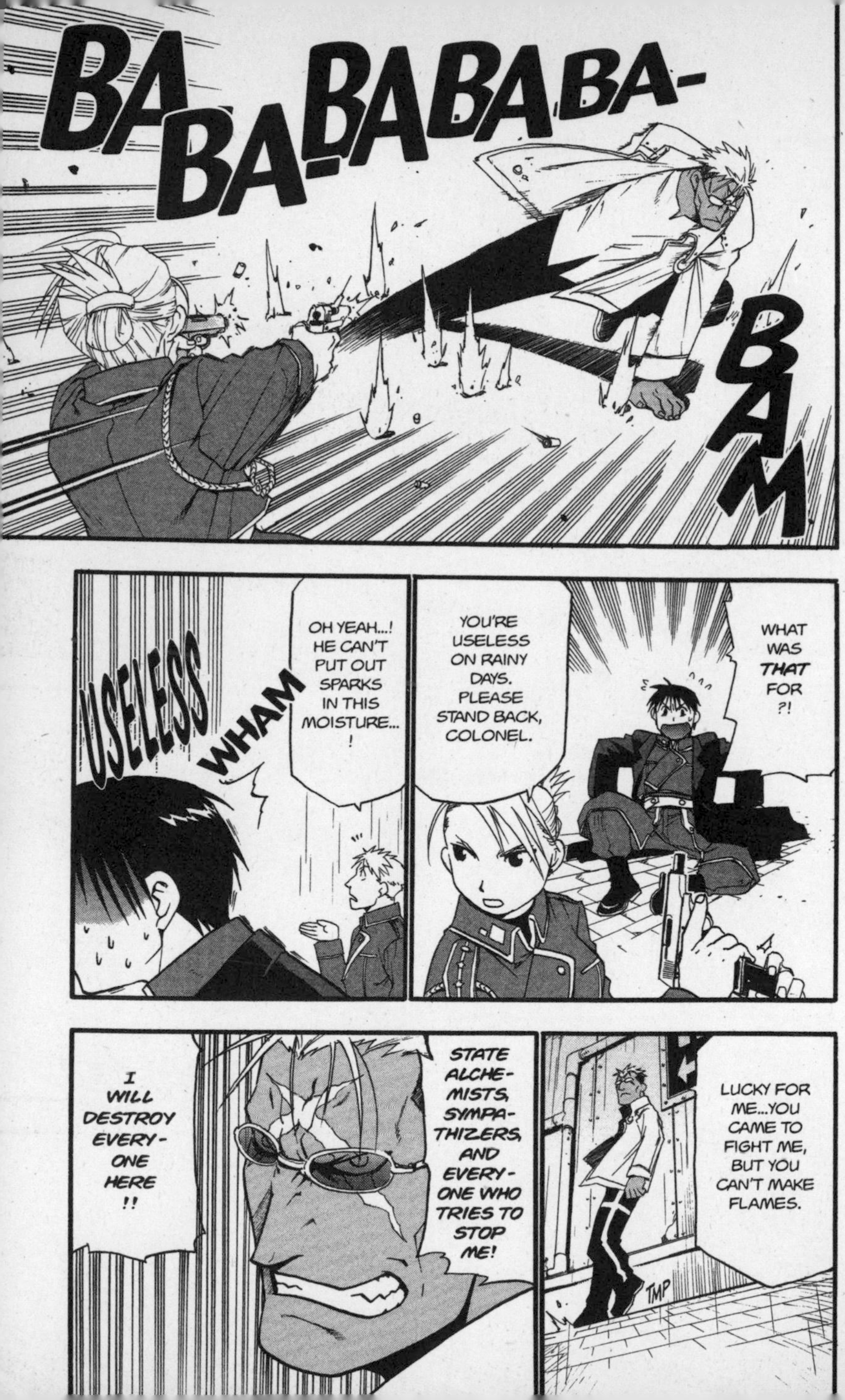
BA-BA-BA-BA-BA-BA-
BLAM
WHAT WAS THAT FOR?!
YOU'RE USELESS ON RAINY DAYS. PLEASE STAND BACK, COLONEL.
OH YEAH...! HE CAN'T PUT OUT SPARKS IN THIS MOISTURE...!
WHAM
USELESS
LUCKY FOR ME...YOU CAME TO FIGHT ME, BUT YOU CAN'T MAKE FLAMES.
TMP
STATE ALCHEMISTS, SYMPATHIZERS, AND EVERYONE WHO TRIES TO STOP ME!
I WILL DESTROY EVERYONE HERE!!

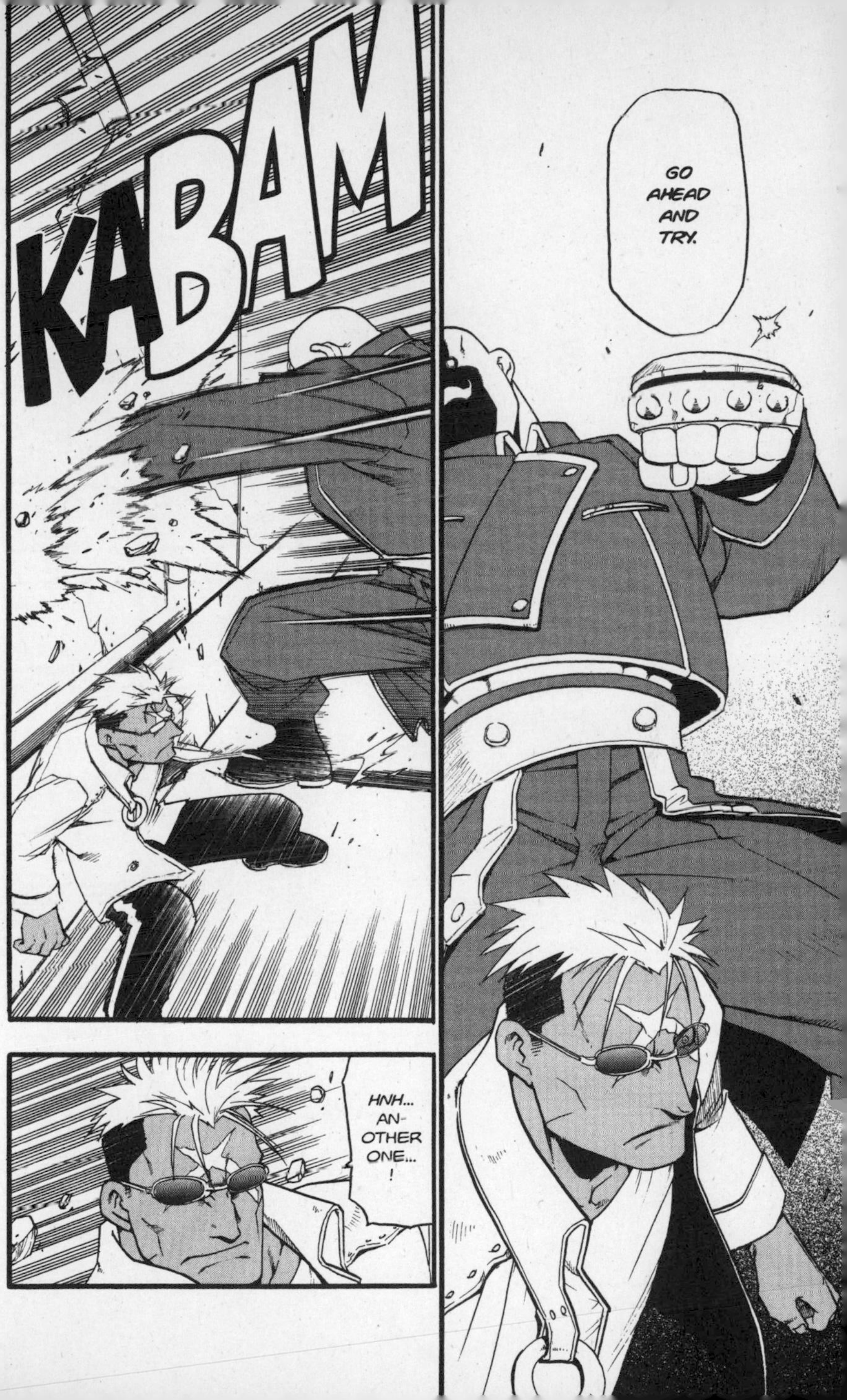
GO AHEAD AND TRY.
KABAM
HNH... AN-OTHER ONE...!

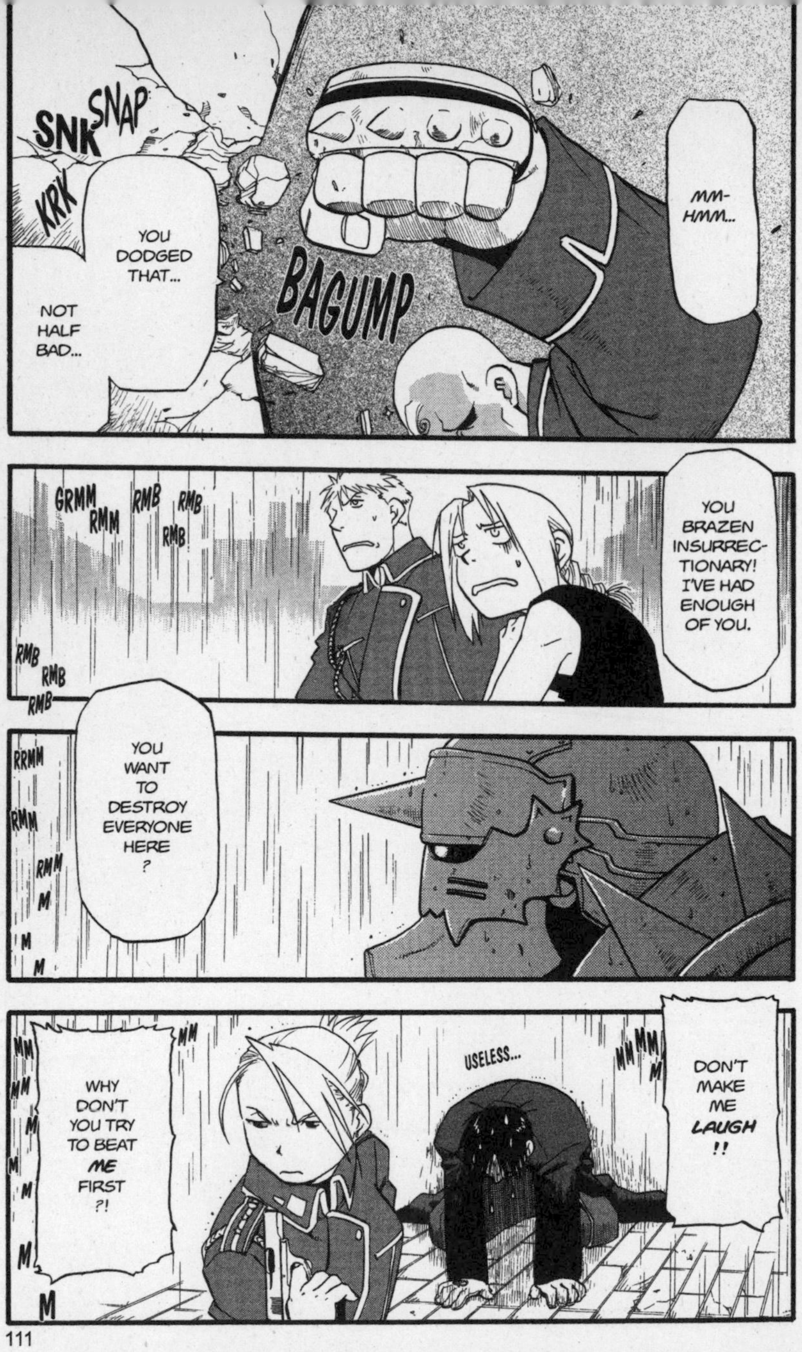
MM-HMM...
BAGUMP
SNAP
SNK
KRK
YOU DODGED THAT...
NOT HALF BAD...
YOU BRAZEN INSURRECTIONARY! I'VE HAD ENOUGH OF YOU.
RMB RMB
RMB
RMM
GRMM
RMB RMB RMB
YOU WANT TO DESTROY EVERYONE HERE?
RRMM RMM RMMMMM
DON'T MAKE ME LAUGH!!
MMMMM
USELESS...
MM
WHY DON'T YOU TRY TO BEAT ME FIRST?!
MMMMMMMMM

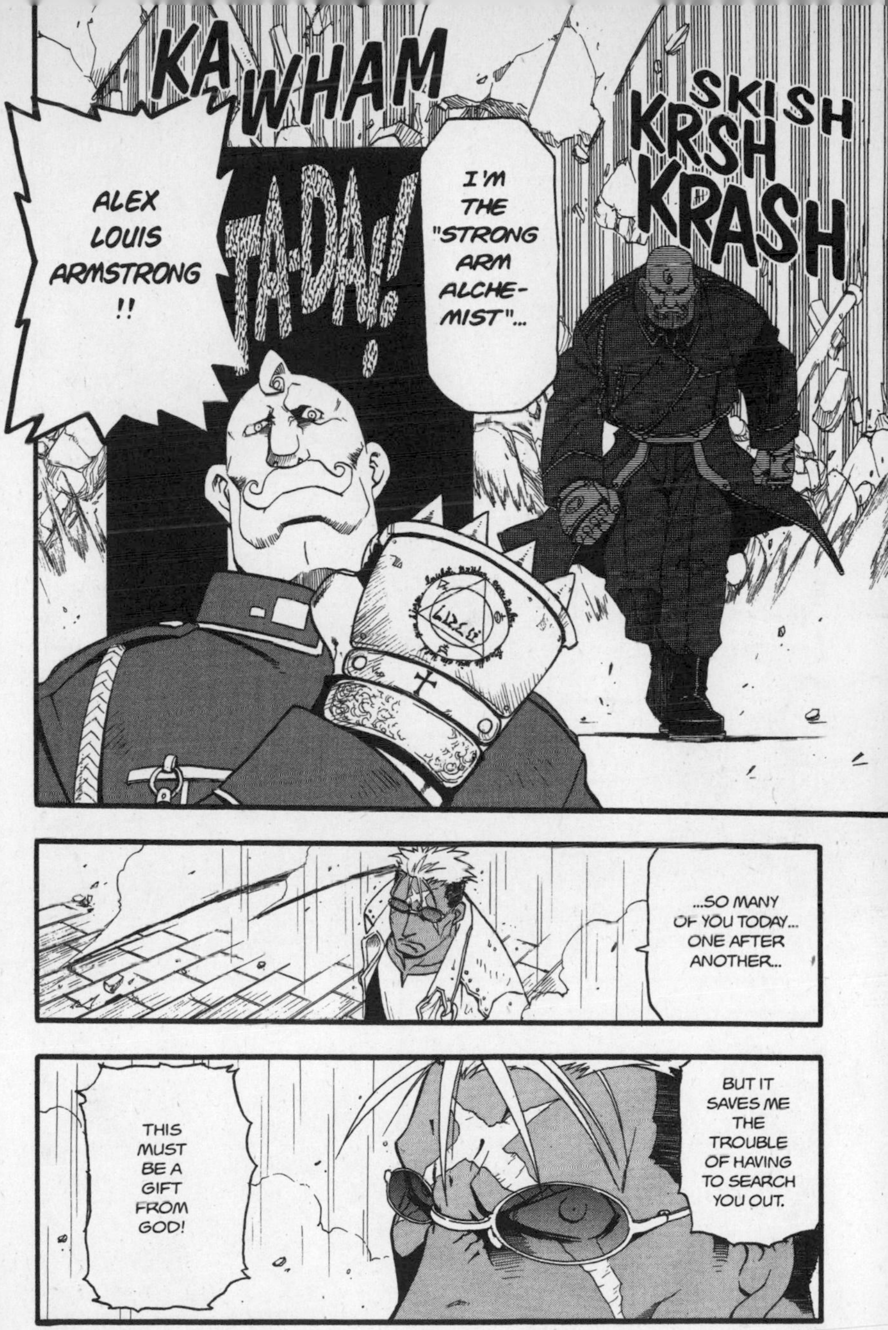
SKISH KRSH KRASH
KA WHAM
I'M THE "STRONG ARM ALCHE- MIST"...
TA-DA!
ALEX LOUIS ARMSTRONG !!
...SO MANY OF YOU TODAY... ONE AFTER ANOTHER...
BUT IT SAVES ME THE TROUBLE OF HAVING TO SEARCH YOU OUT.
THIS MUST BE A GIFT FROM GOD!

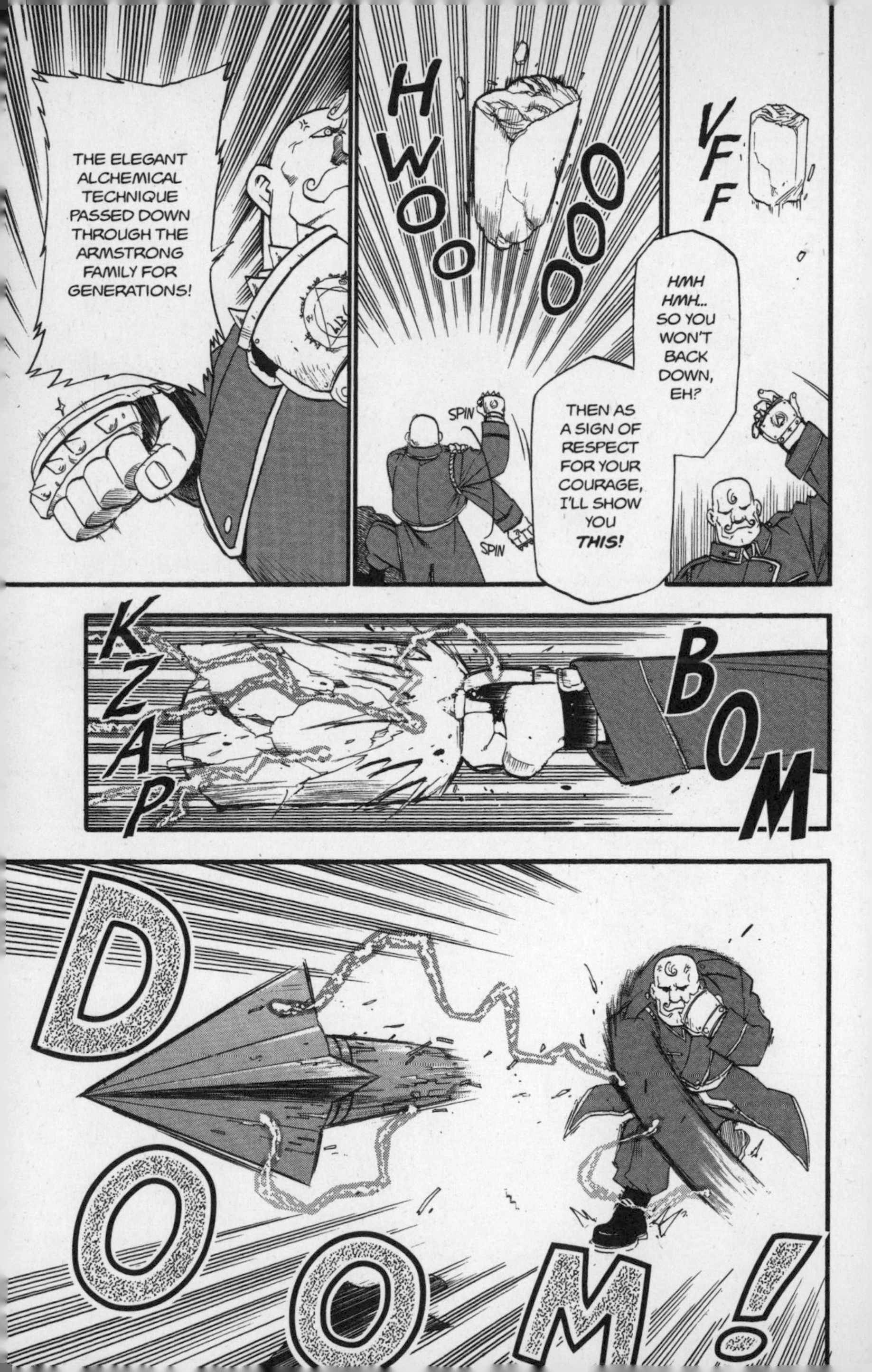
VFF
HMH HMH... SO YOU WON'T BACK DOWN, EH?
THEN AS A SIGN OF RESPECT FOR YOUR COURAGE, I'LL SHOW YOU *THIS!*
HWOOOOOO
SPIN
SPIN
THE ELEGANT ALCHEMICAL TECHNIQUE PASSED DOWN THROUGH THE ARMSTRONG FAMILY FOR GENERATIONS!
BOM
KZAP
DOOM!

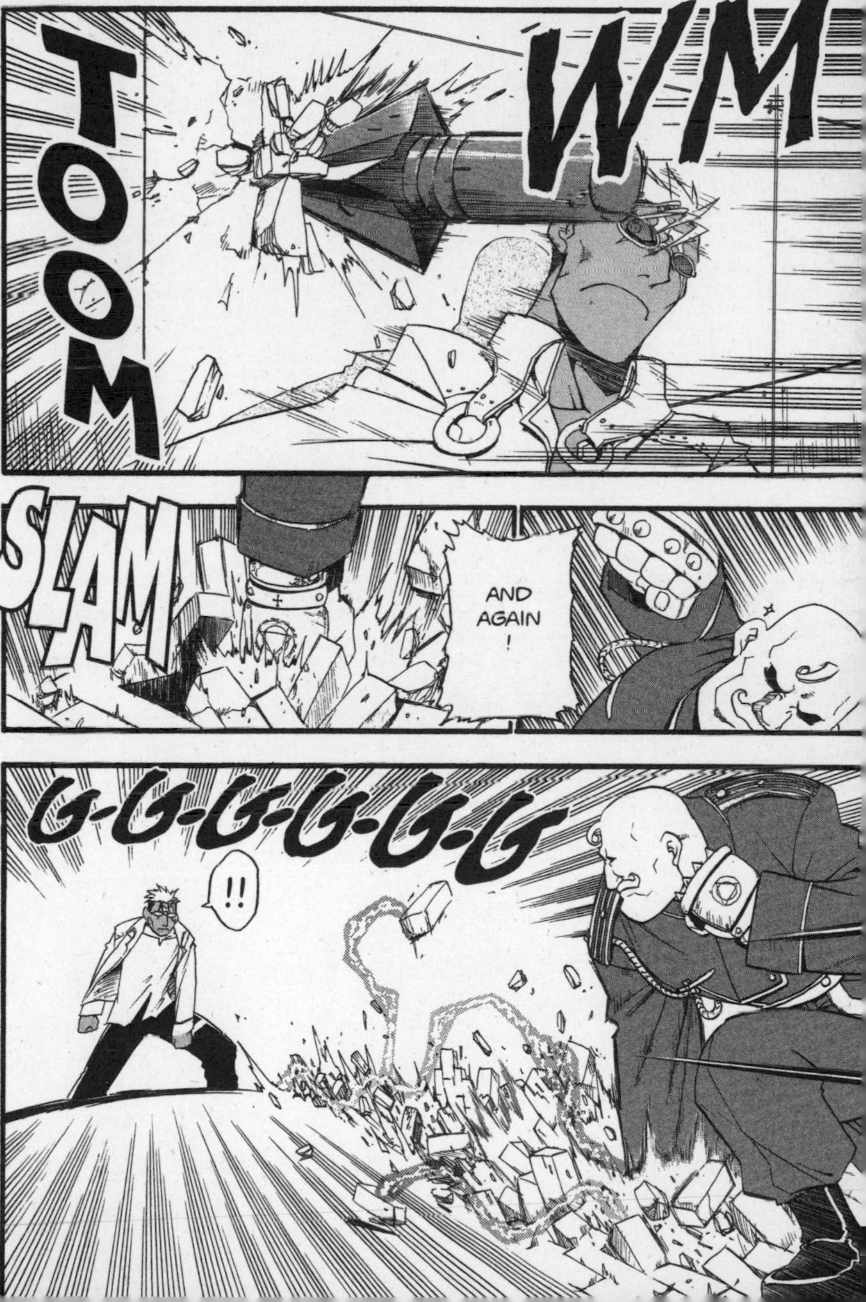
WM
TOOOM
AND AGAIN !
SLAM
G-G-G-G-G-G
!!

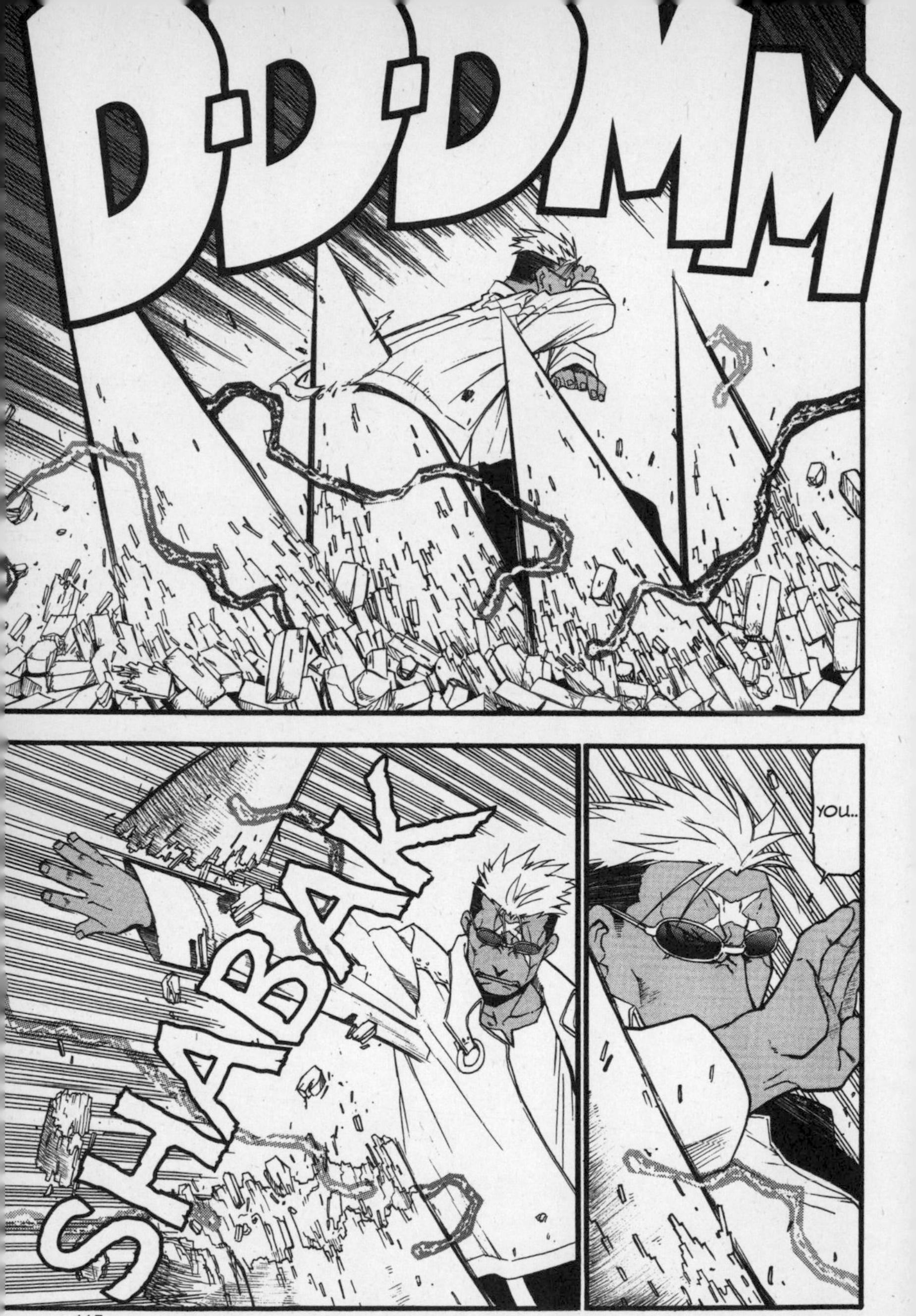
D-D-DMM
YOU...
SHABAK

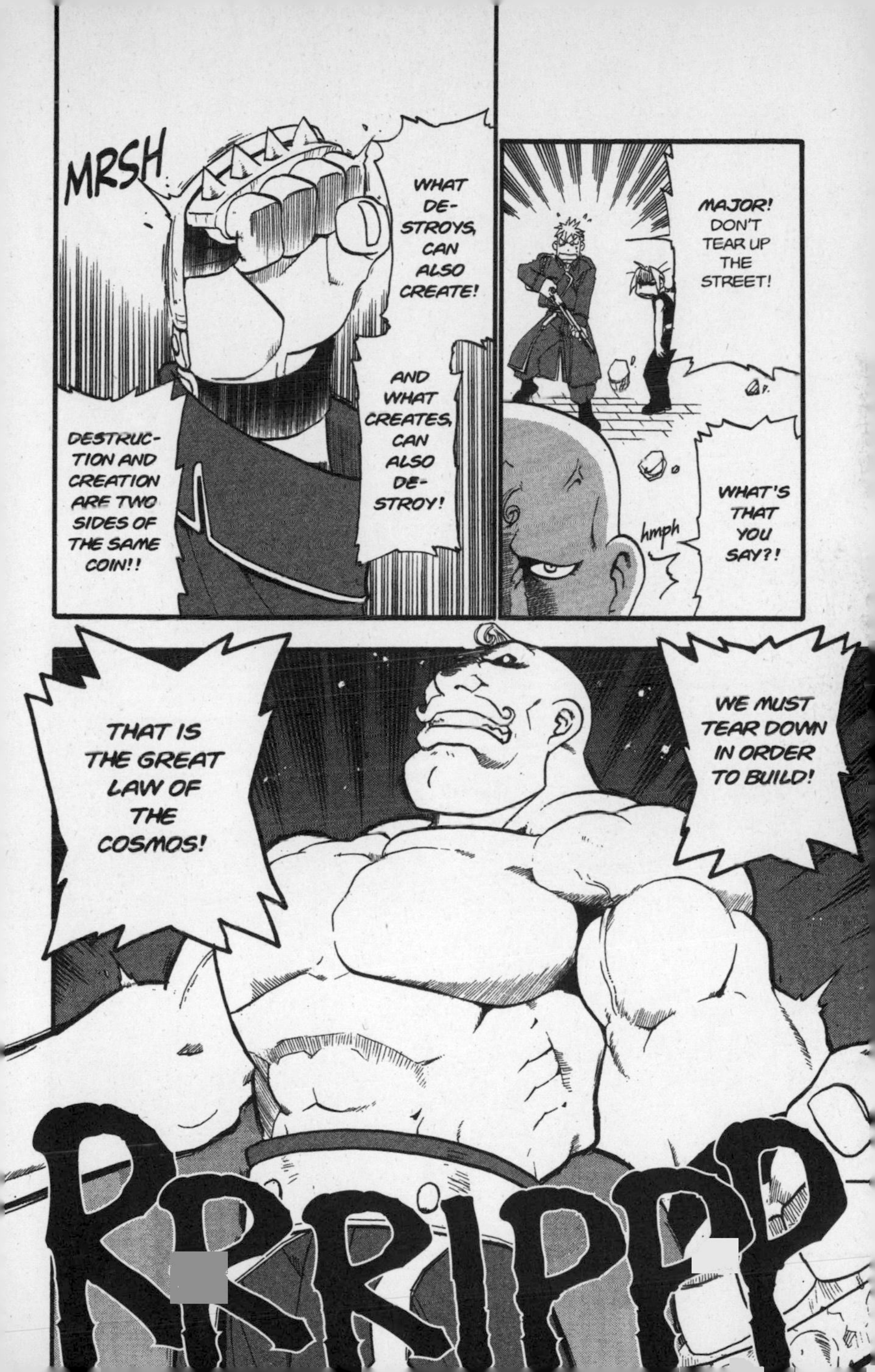

MAJOR! DON'T TEAR UP THE STREET!
hmph
WHAT'S THAT YOU SAY?!
WHAT DE-STROYS, CAN ALSO CREATE!
AND WHAT CREATES, CAN ALSO DE-STROY!
MRSH
DESTRUC-TION AND CREATION ARE TWO SIDES OF THE SAME COIN!!
WE MUST TEAR DOWN IN ORDER TO BUILD!
THAT IS THE GREAT LAW OF THE COSMOS!
RRRIPPP

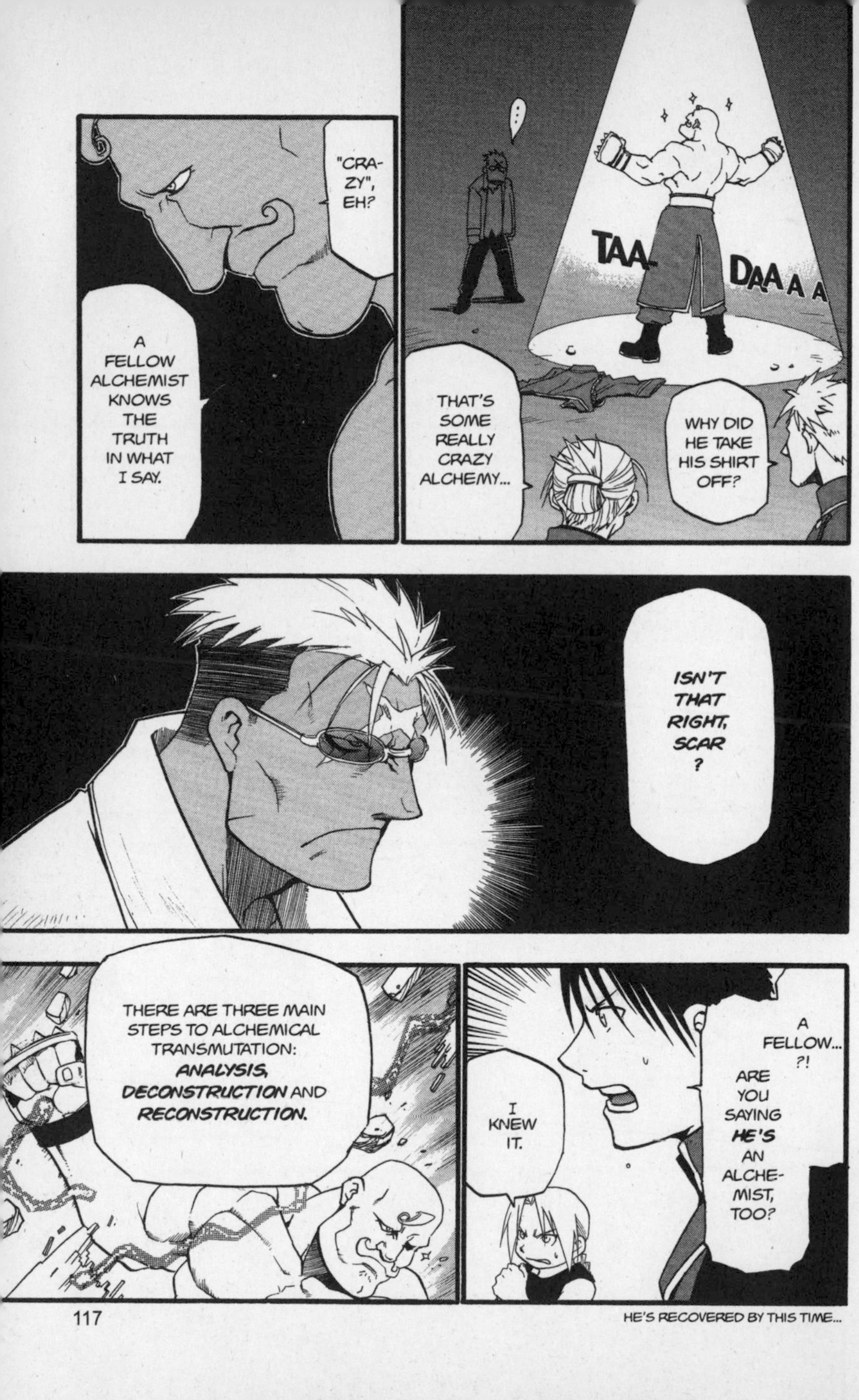

TAA DAAAA
WHY DID HE TAKE HIS SHIRT OFF?
THAT'S SOME REALLY CRAZY ALCHEMY...
"CRAZY", EH?
A FELLOW ALCHEMIST KNOWS THE TRUTH IN WHAT I SAY.
ISN'T THAT RIGHT, SCAR?
A FELLOW...?!
ARE YOU SAYING HE'S AN ALCHEMIST, TOO?
I KNEW IT.
THERE ARE THREE MAIN STEPS TO ALCHEMICAL TRANSMUTATION: ANALYSIS, DECONSTRUCTION AND RECONSTRUCTION.

HE'S RECOVERED BY THIS TIME...

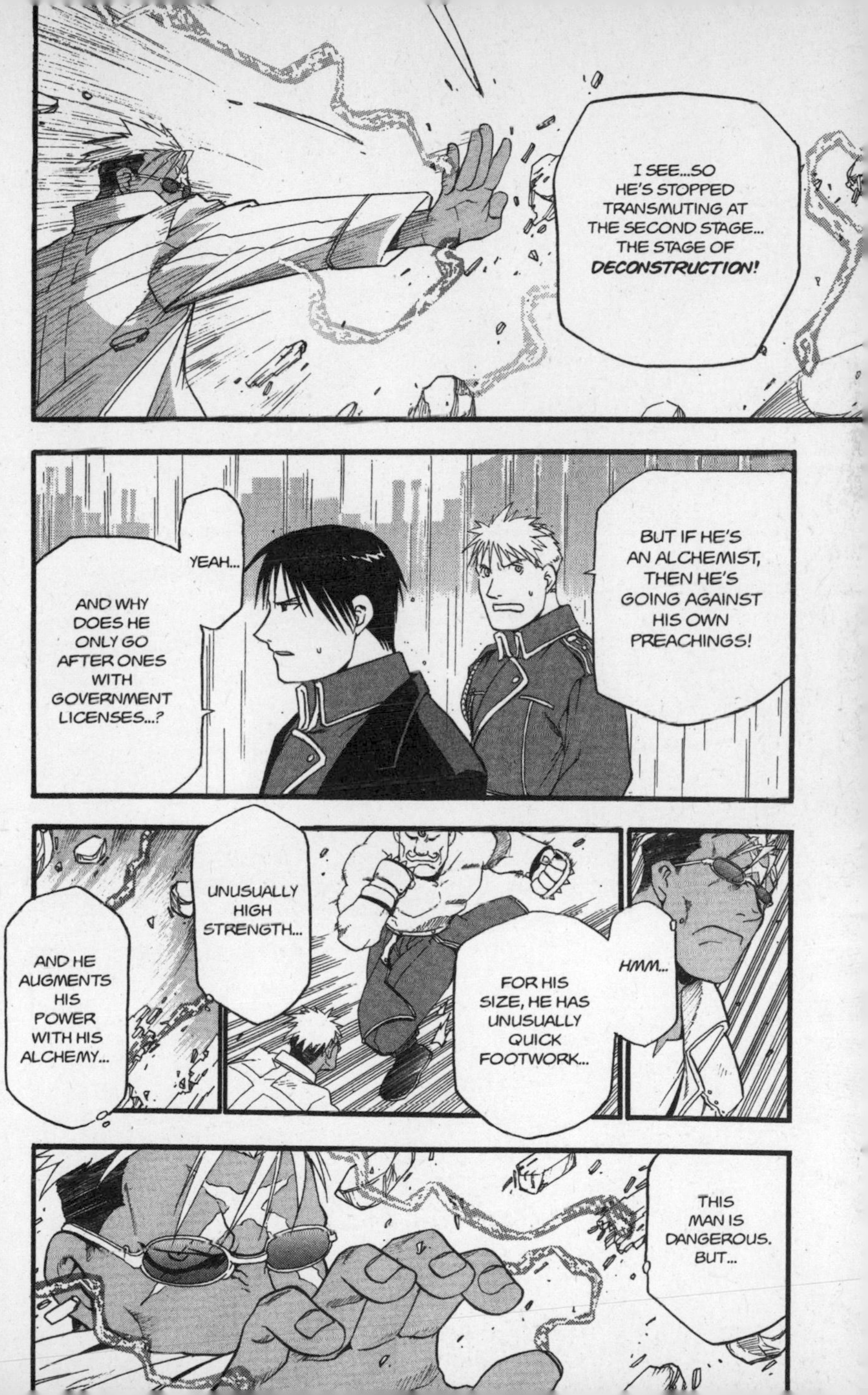
I SEE...SO HE'S STOPPED TRANSMUTING AT THE SECOND STAGE... THE STAGE OF **DECONSTRUCTION!**
BUT IF HE'S AN ALCHEMIST, THEN HE'S GOING AGAINST HIS OWN PREACHINGS!
YEAH...
AND WHY DOES HE ONLY GO AFTER ONES WITH GOVERNMENT LICENSES...?
HMM...
FOR HIS SIZE, HE HAS UNUSUALLY QUICK FOOTWORK...
UNUSUALLY HIGH STRENGTH...
AND HE AUGMENTS HIS POWER WITH HIS ALCHEMY...
THIS MAN IS DANGEROUS. BUT...

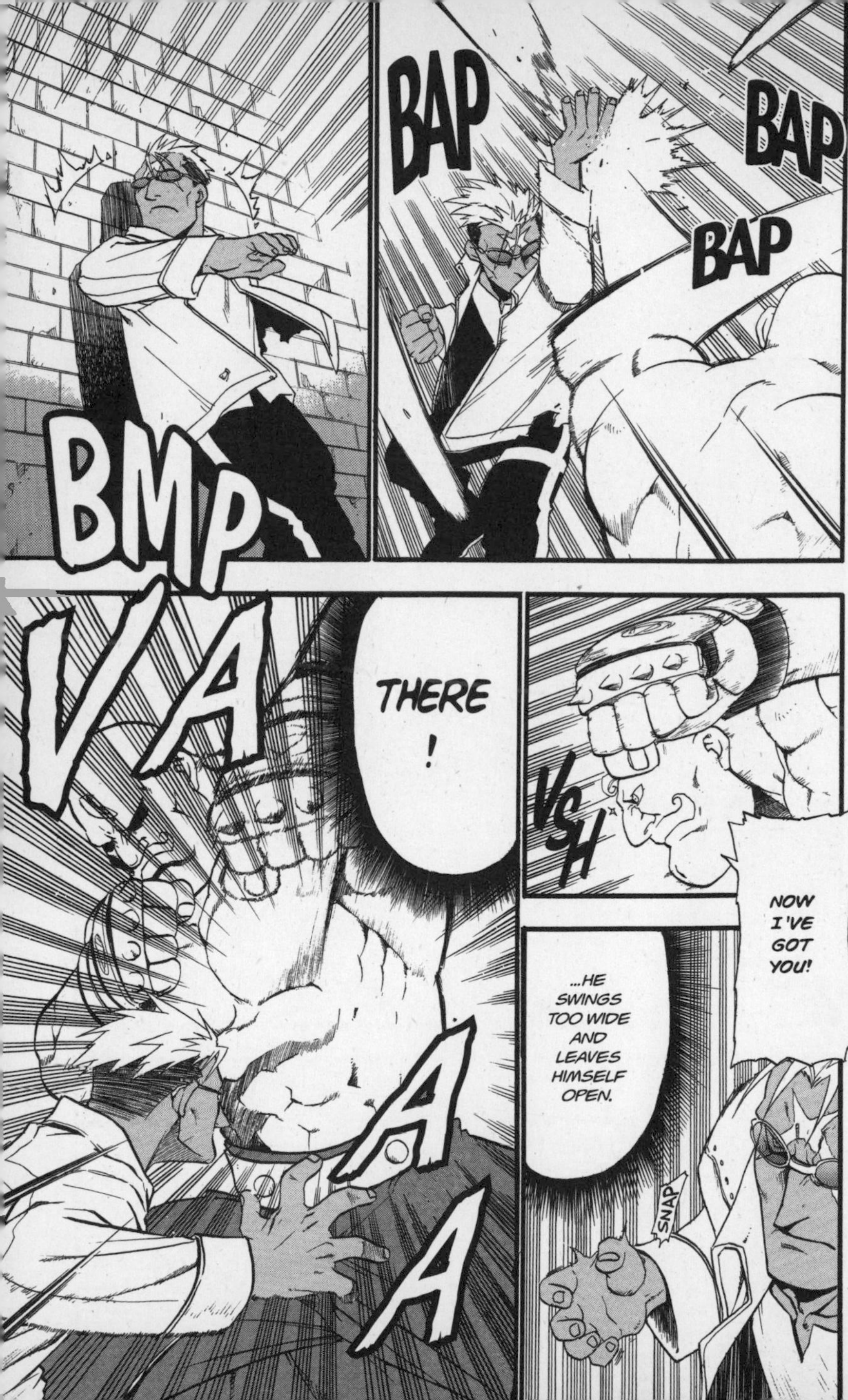
BAP
BAP
BAP
BMP
VSH
NOW I'VE GOT YOU!
...HE SWINGS TOO WIDE AND LEAVES HIMSELF OPEN.
SNAP
VA
THERE!
AA

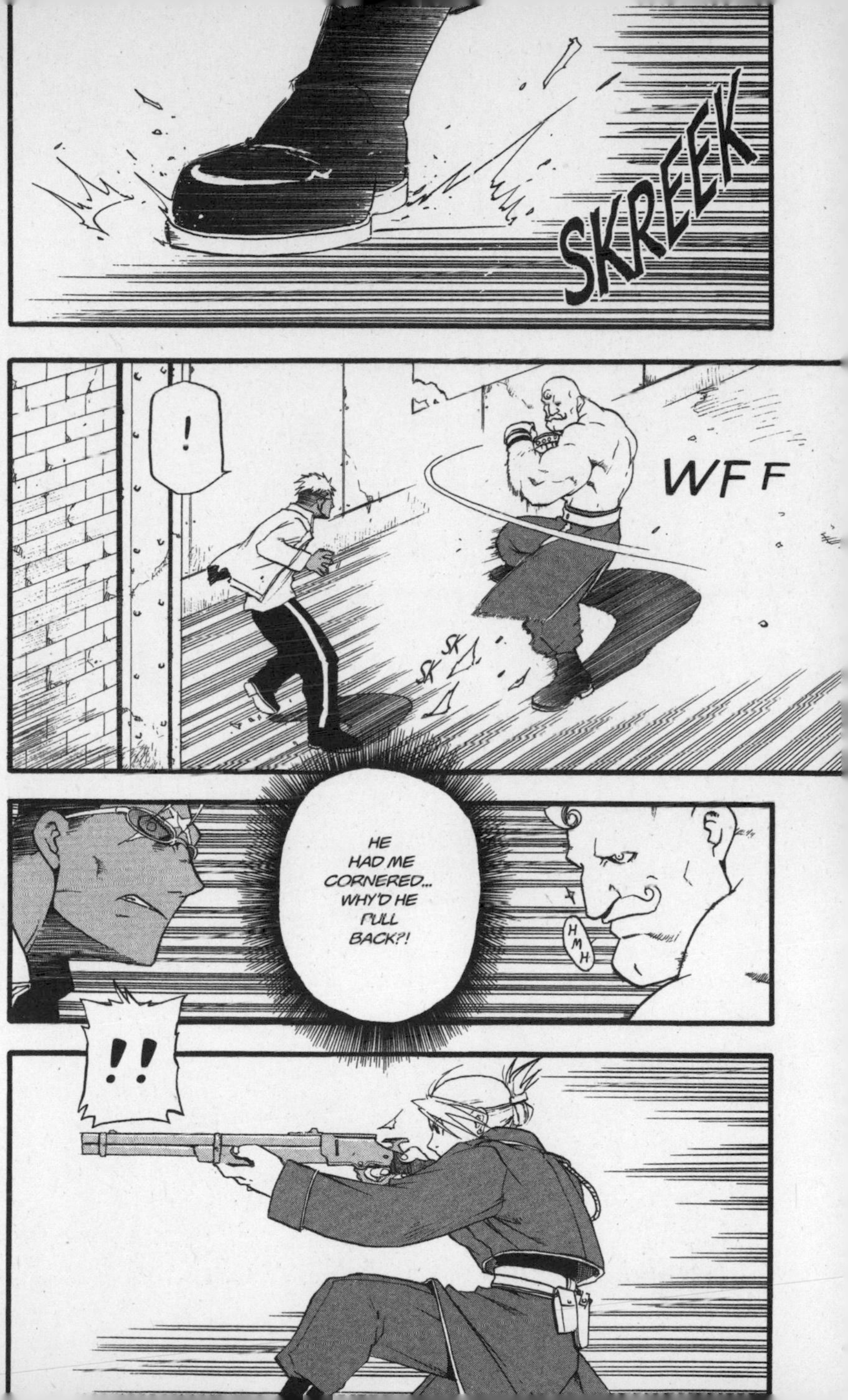
SKREEK
WFF
SK SK
!
HMH
HE HAD ME CORNERED... WHY'D HE PULL BACK?!
!!

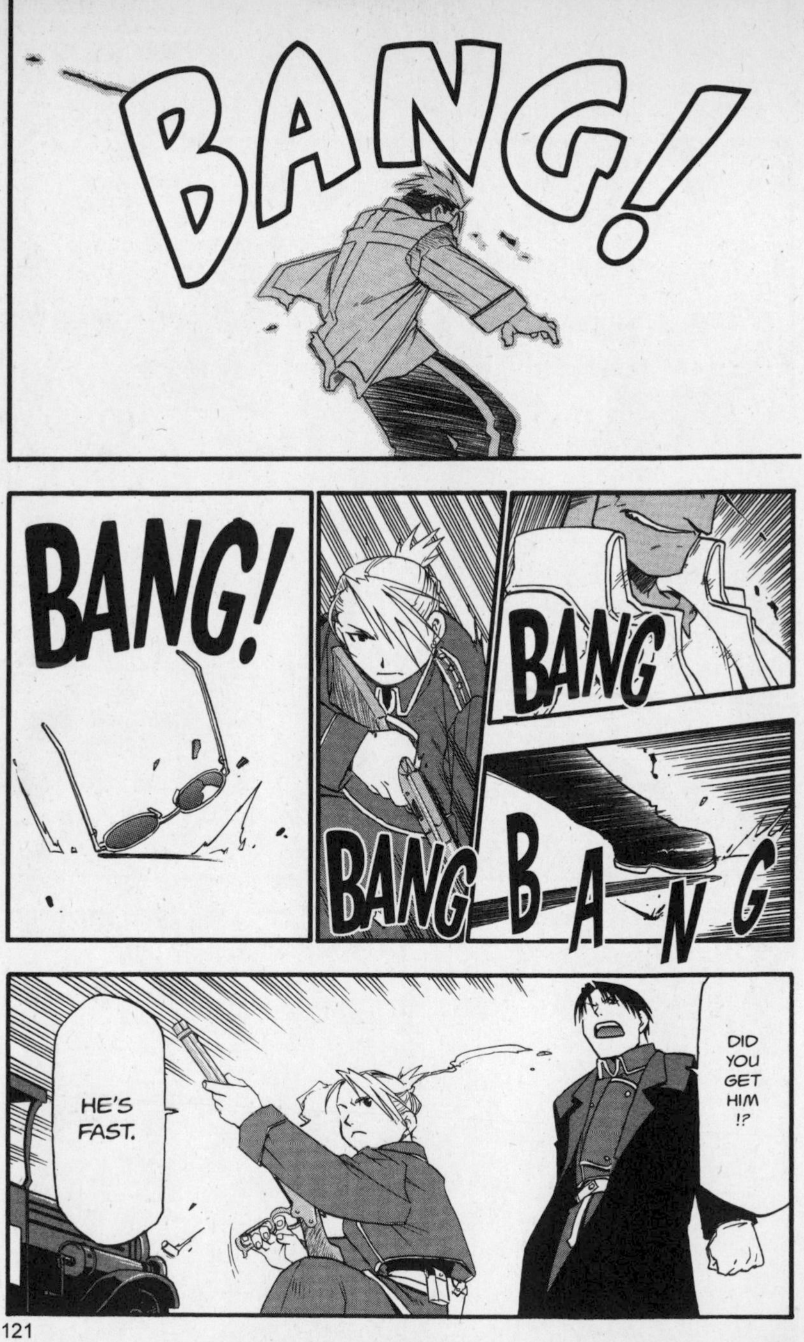
BANG!
BANG
BANG
BANG
BANG!
DID YOU GET HIM !?
HE'S FAST.

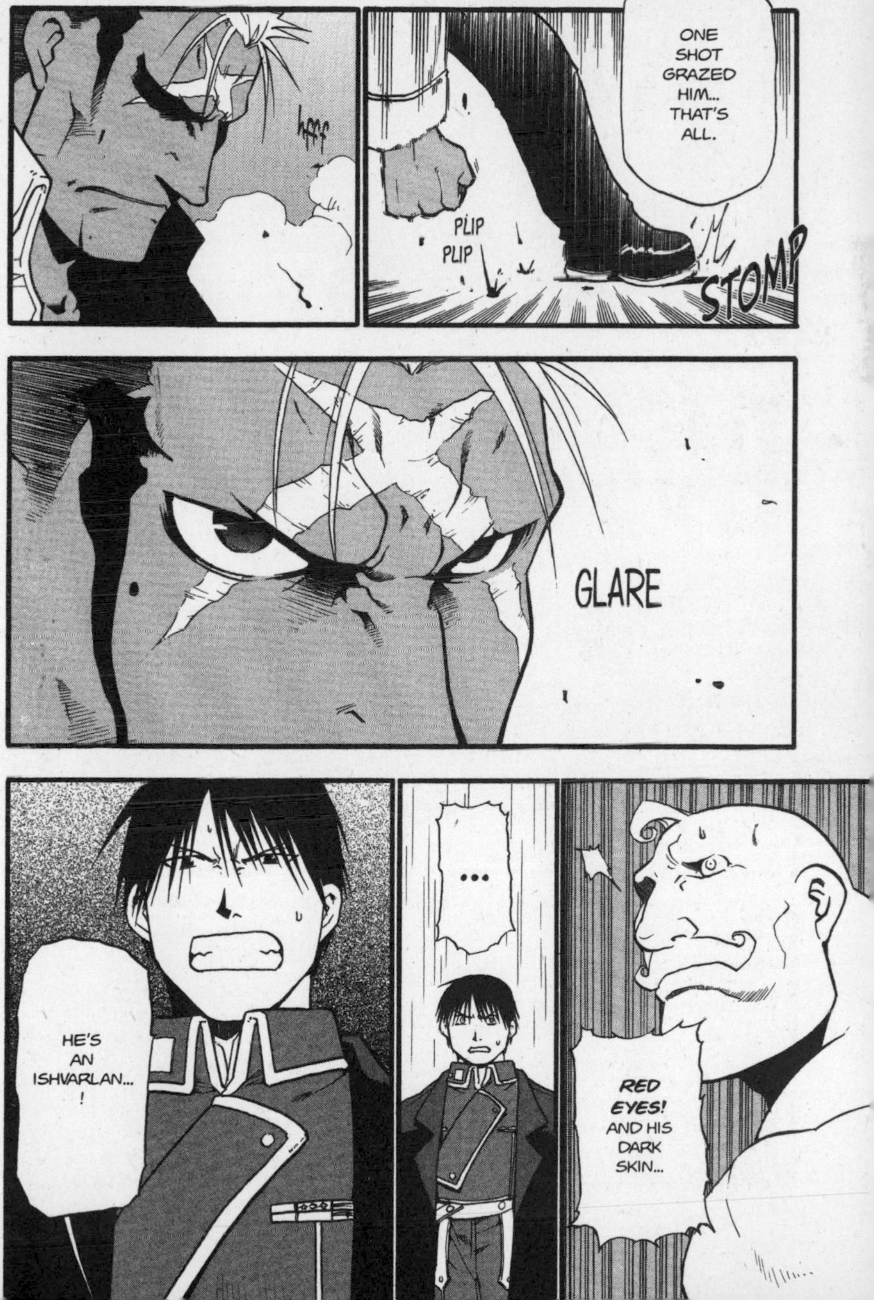
ONE SHOT GRAZED HIM... THAT'S ALL.
PLIP PLIP
STOMP
hff
GLARE
RED EYES! AND HIS DARK SKIN...
...
HE'S AN ISHVARLAN... !

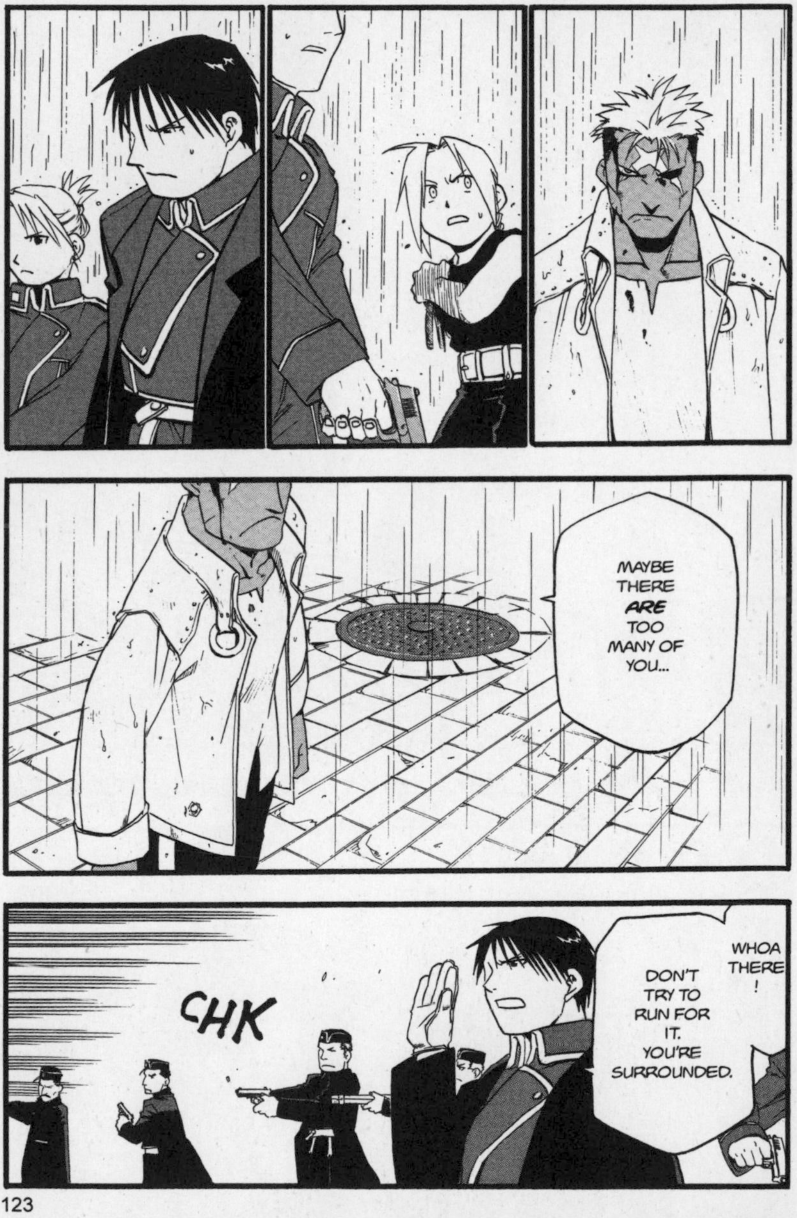
MAYBE THERE ***ARE*** TOO MANY OF YOU...
WHOA THERE!
DON'T TRY TO RUN FOR IT. YOU'RE SURROUNDED.
CHK

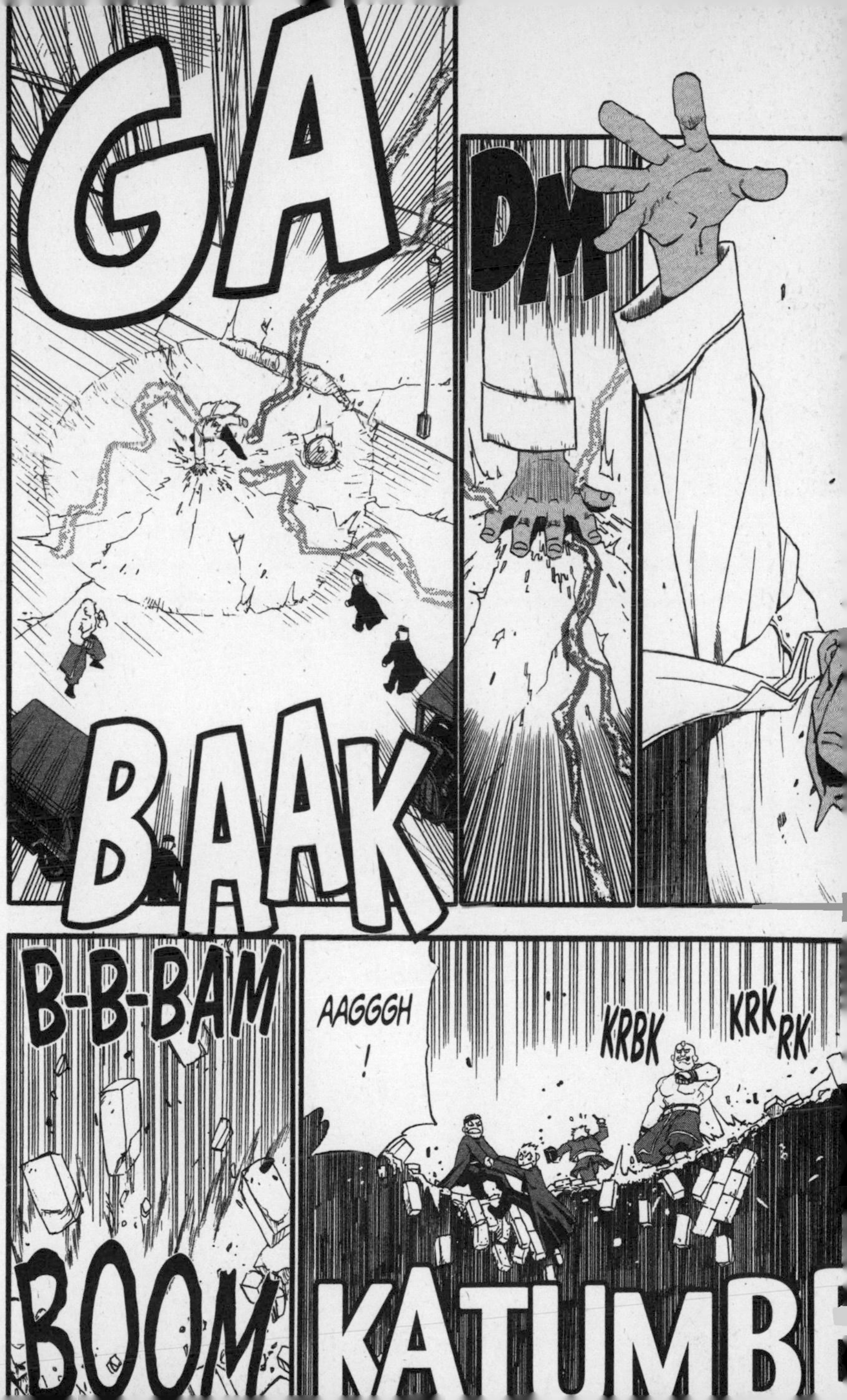
DM
GA
BAAK
KRK RK
KRBK
AAGGGH !
KATUMBE
B-B-BAM
BOOM

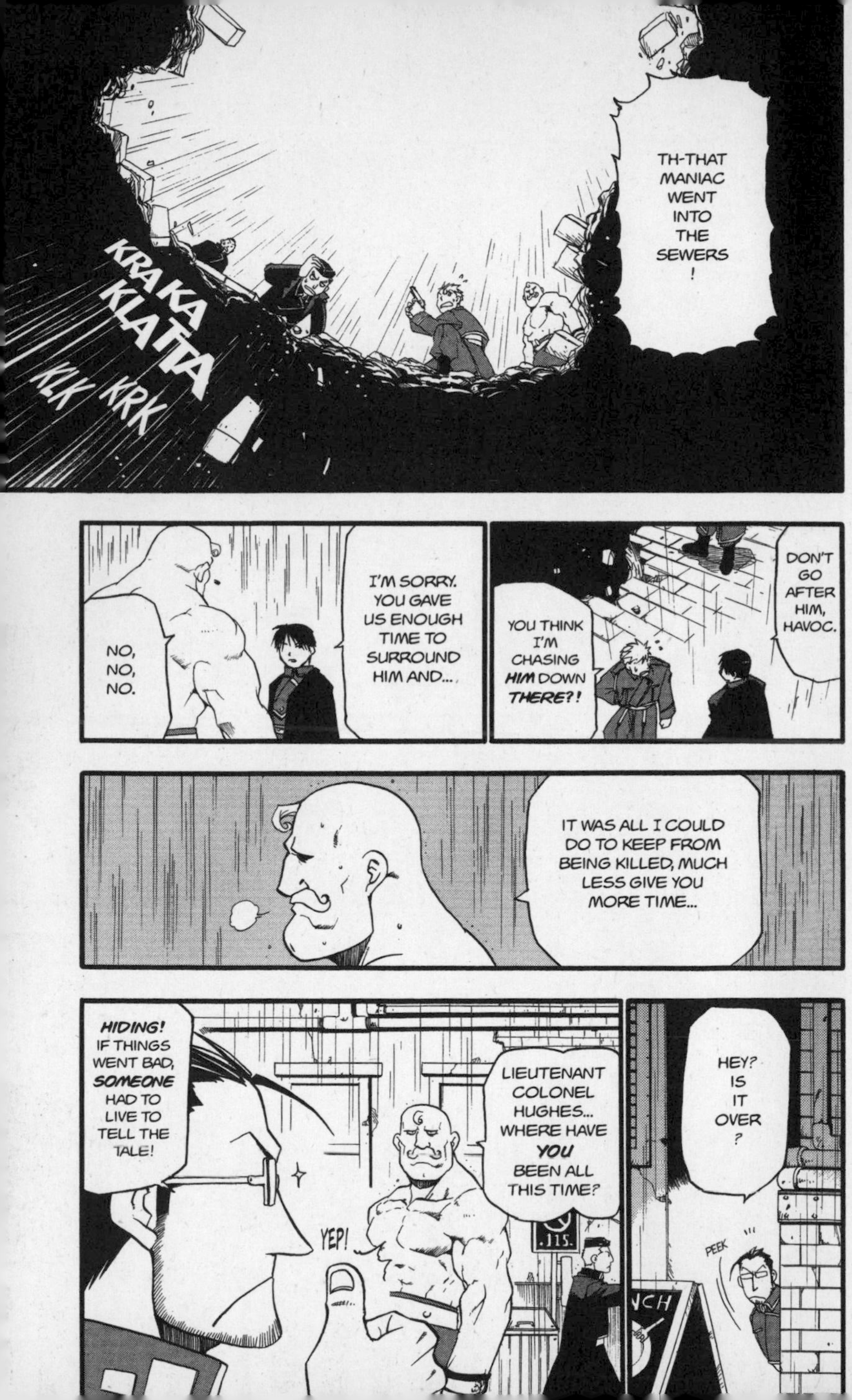
TH-THAT MANIAC WENT INTO THE SEWERS!
KRA KA KLATTA
KLK KRK
DON'T GO AFTER HIM, HAVOC.
YOU THINK I'M CHASING HIM DOWN THERE?!
I'M SORRY. YOU GAVE US ENOUGH TIME TO SURROUND HIM AND...
NO, NO, NO.
IT WAS ALL I COULD DO TO KEEP FROM BEING KILLED, MUCH LESS GIVE YOU MORE TIME...
HEY? IS IT OVER?
PEEK
LIEUTENANT COLONEL HUGHES... WHERE HAVE YOU BEEN ALL THIS TIME?
.115.
HIDING! IF THINGS WENT BAD, SOMEONE HAD TO LIVE TO TELL THE TALE!
YEP!

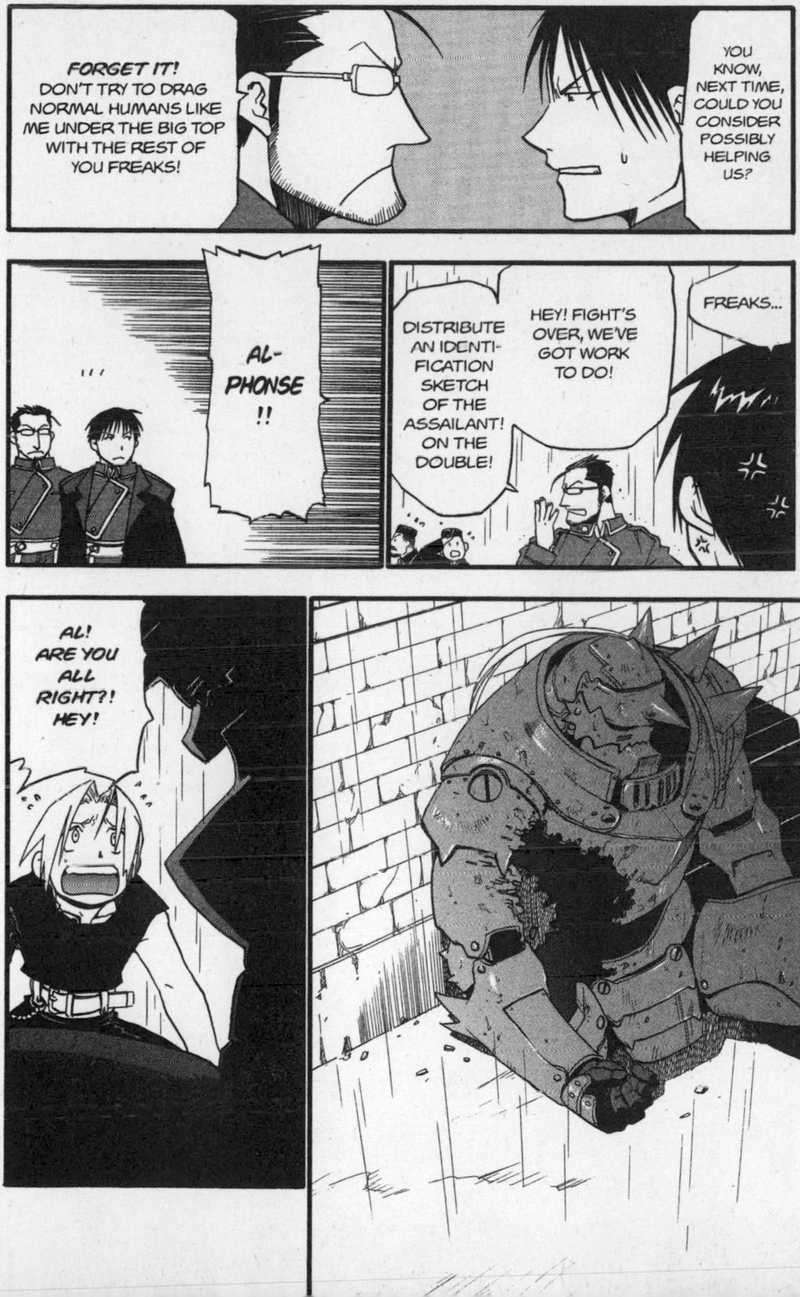
YOU KNOW, NEXT TIME, COULD YOU CONSIDER POSSIBLY HELPING US?
FORGET IT! DON'T TRY TO DRAG NORMAL HUMANS LIKE ME UNDER THE BIG TOP WITH THE REST OF YOU FREAKS!
FREAKS...
HEY! FIGHT'S OVER, WE'VE GOT WORK TO DO!
DISTRIBUTE AN IDENTIFICATION SKETCH OF THE ASSAILANT! ON THE DOUBLE!
AL-PHONSE !!
AL! ARE YOU ALL RIGHT?! HEY!

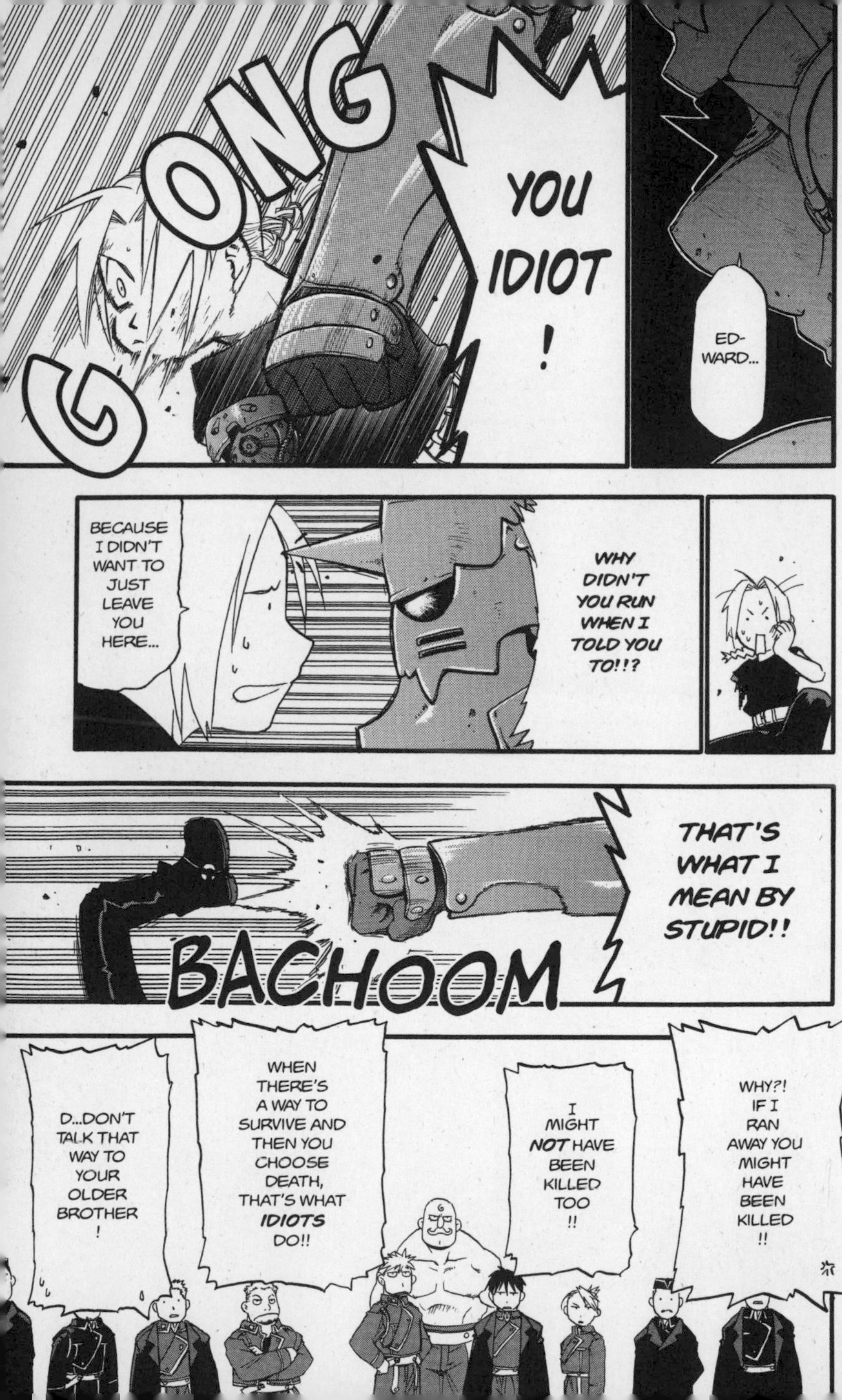
ED-WARD...
YOU IDIOT !
GONG
WHY DIDN'T YOU RUN WHEN I TOLD YOU TO!!?
BECAUSE I DIDN'T WANT TO JUST LEAVE YOU HERE...
THAT'S WHAT I MEAN BY STUPID!!
BACHOOM
WHY?! IF I RAN AWAY YOU MIGHT HAVE BEEN KILLED !!
I MIGHT NOT HAVE BEEN KILLED TOO !!
WHEN THERE'S A WAY TO SURVIVE AND THEN YOU CHOOSE DEATH, THAT'S WHAT IDIOTS DO!!
D...DON'T TALK THAT WAY TO YOUR OLDER BROTHER !

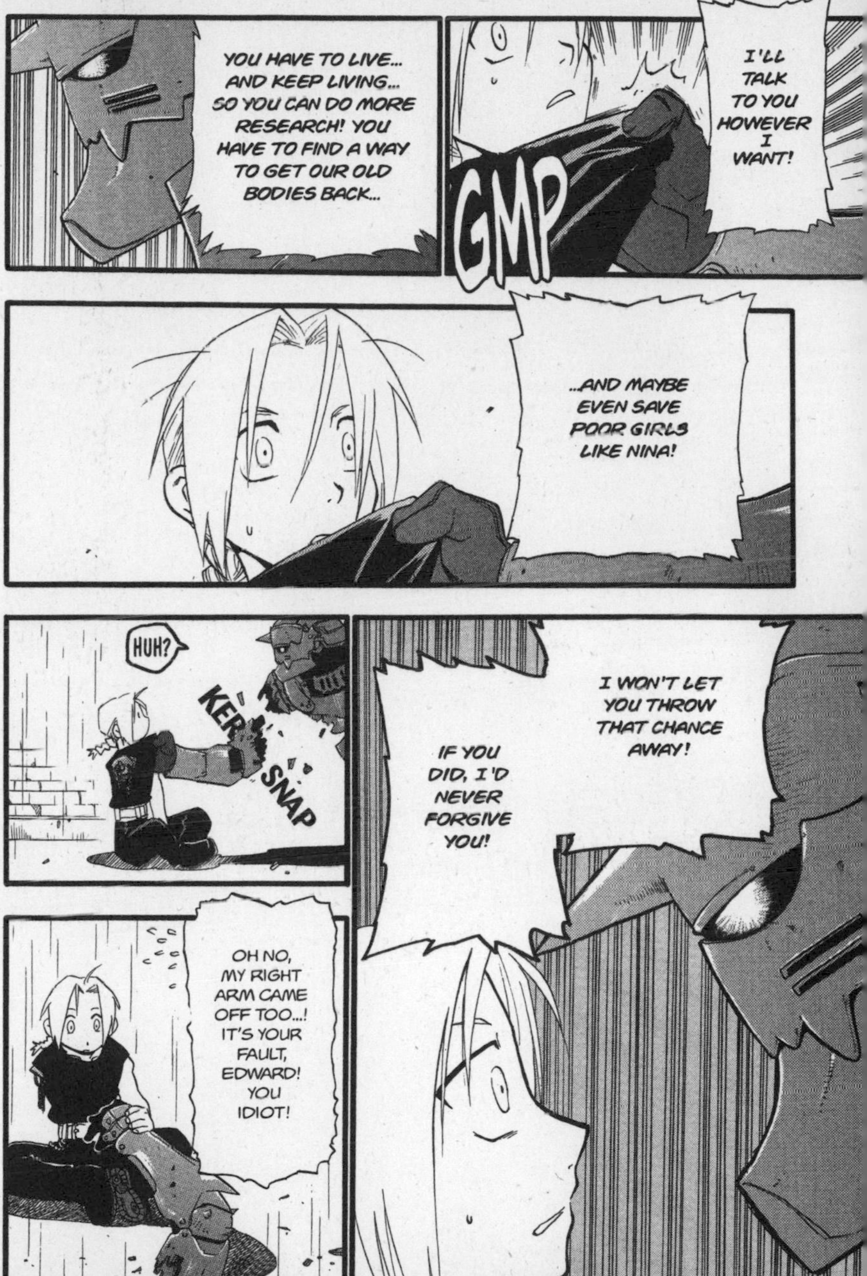
I'LL TALK TO YOU HOWEVER I WANT!
GMP
YOU HAVE TO LIVE... AND KEEP LIVING... SO YOU CAN DO MORE RESEARCH! YOU HAVE TO FIND A WAY TO GET OUR OLD BODIES BACK...
...AND MAYBE EVEN SAVE POOR GIRLS LIKE NINA!
I WON'T LET YOU THROW THAT CHANCE AWAY!
IF YOU DID, I'D NEVER FORGIVE YOU!
HUH?
KER
SNAP
OH NO, MY RIGHT ARM CAME OFF TOO...! IT'S YOUR FAULT, EDWARD! YOU IDIOT!

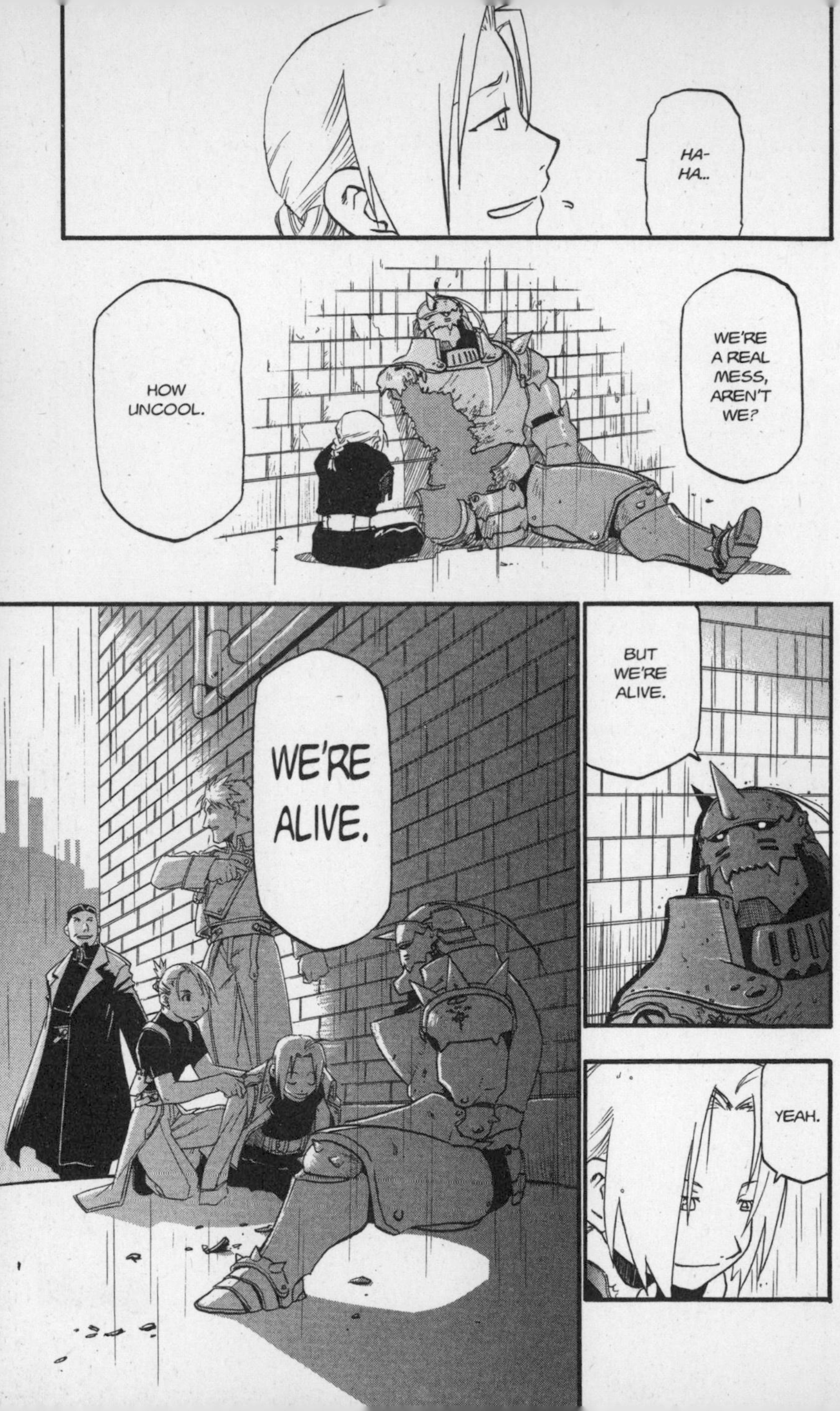
HA-HA...
WE'RE A REAL MESS, AREN'T WE?
HOW UNCOOL.
BUT WE'RE ALIVE.
YEAH.
WE'RE ALIVE.

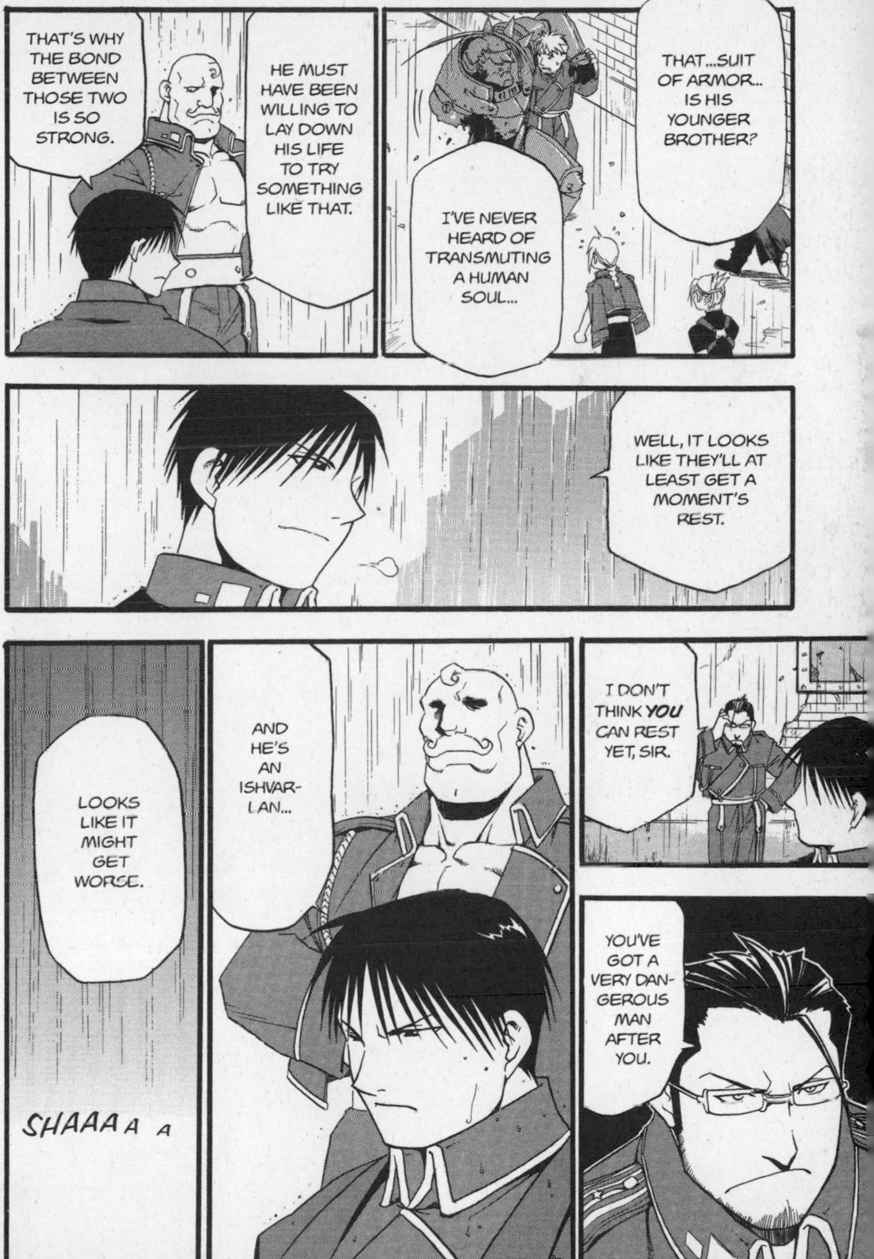
THAT...SUIT OF ARMOR... IS HIS YOUNGER BROTHER?
I'VE NEVER HEARD OF TRANSMUTING A HUMAN SOUL...
HE MUST HAVE BEEN WILLING TO LAY DOWN HIS LIFE TO TRY SOMETHING LIKE THAT.
THAT'S WHY THE BOND BETWEEN THOSE TWO IS SO STRONG.
WELL, IT LOOKS LIKE THEY'LL AT LEAST GET A MOMENT'S REST.
I DON'T THINK *YOU* CAN REST YET, SIR.
YOU'VE GOT A VERY DAN-GEROUS MAN AFTER YOU.
AND HE'S AN ISHVAR-LAN...
LOOKS LIKE IT MIGHT GET WORSE.
SHAAA A A

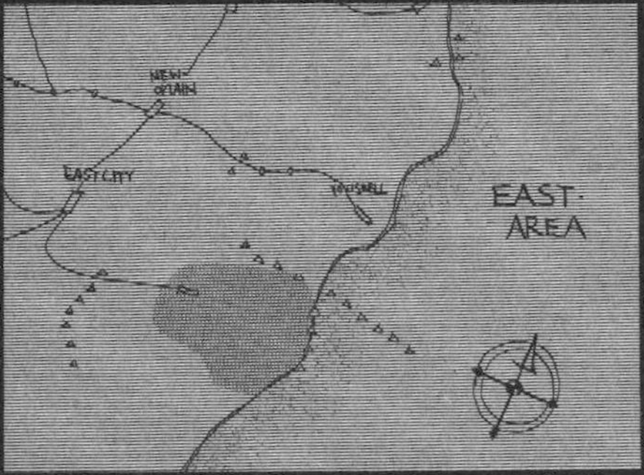
EAST CITY
EAST AREA

THE
ISHVARLANS
ARE A PEOPLE
FROM THE
EAST, WHO
BELIEVE IN
ONE GOD,
ISHVARA.

DUE TO RELIGIOUS
DIFFERENCES,
THEY'D ALWAYS
BEEN IN CONFLICT
WITH THE CENTRAL
GOVERNMENT...

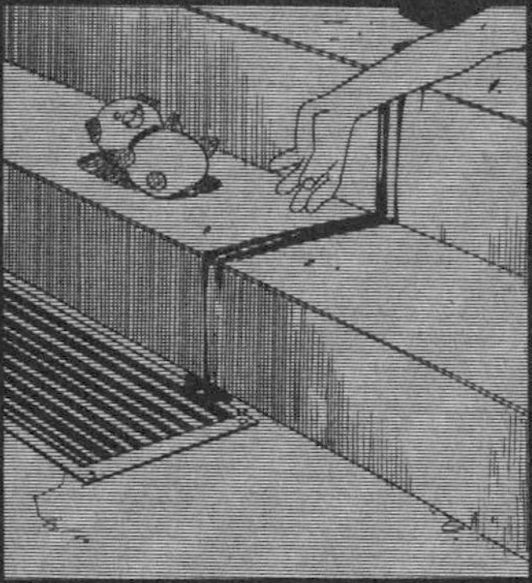

BUT THIRTEEN
YEARS AGO, WHEN
AN ARMY OFFICER
ACCIDENTALLY
SHOT AN ISHVARLAN
CHILD, THE INCIDENT
EXPLODED INTO
CIVIL WAR.

RIOT LED TO RIOT, AND SOON
THE FIRES OF CIVIL WAR SPREAD
THROUGHOUT THE ENTIRE EAST AREA.
AFTER SEVEN FRUSTRATING YEARS,
THE MILITARY COMMANDERS TOOK
A NEW TACTIC...

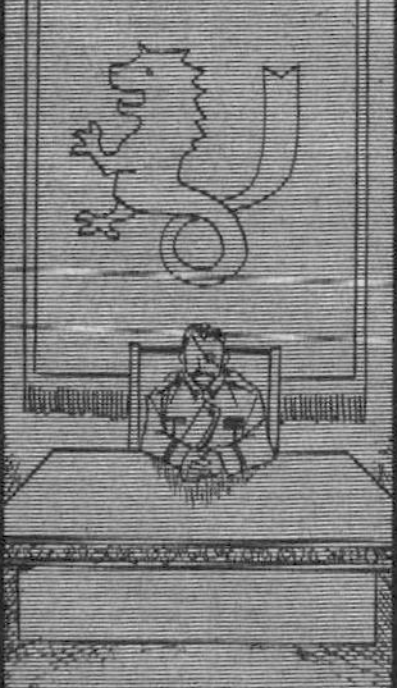

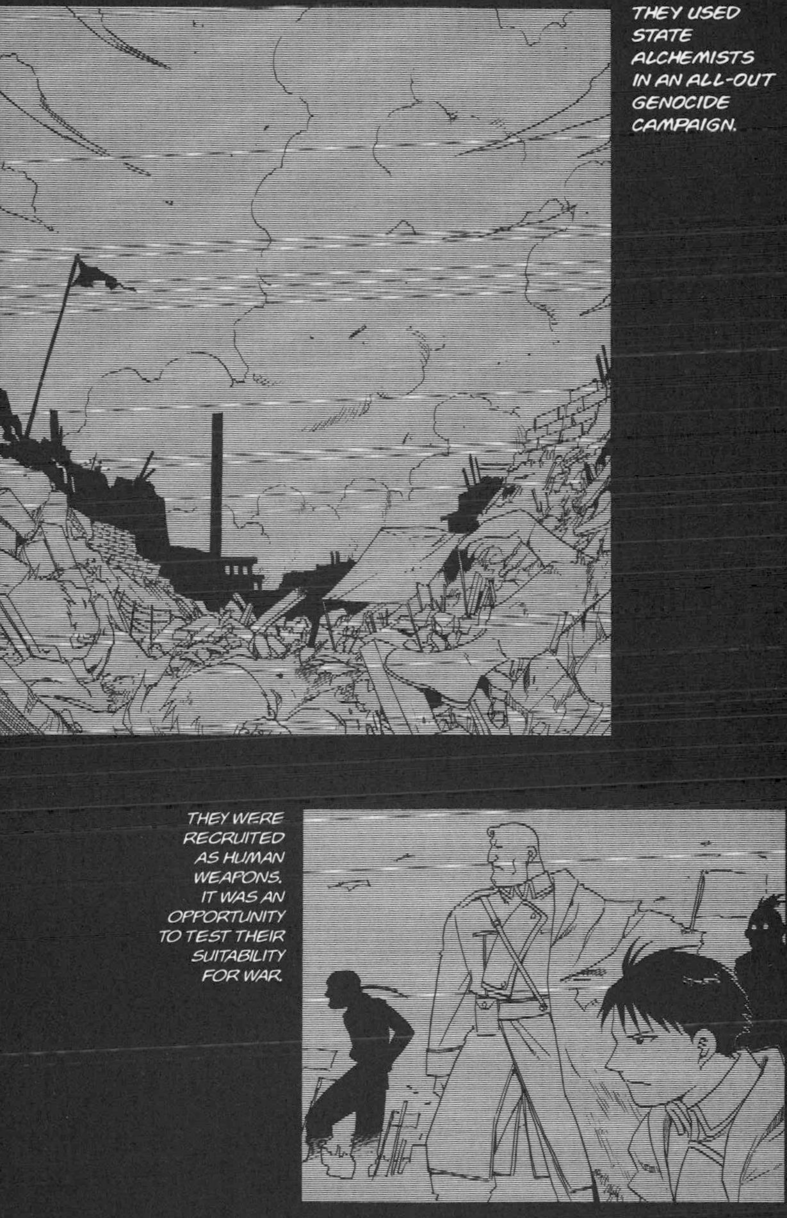
THEY USED STATE ALCHEMISTS IN AN ALL-OUT GENOCIDE CAMPAIGN.
THEY WERE RECRUITED AS HUMAN WEAPONS. IT WAS AN OPPORTUNITY TO TEST THEIR SUITABILITY FOR WAR.

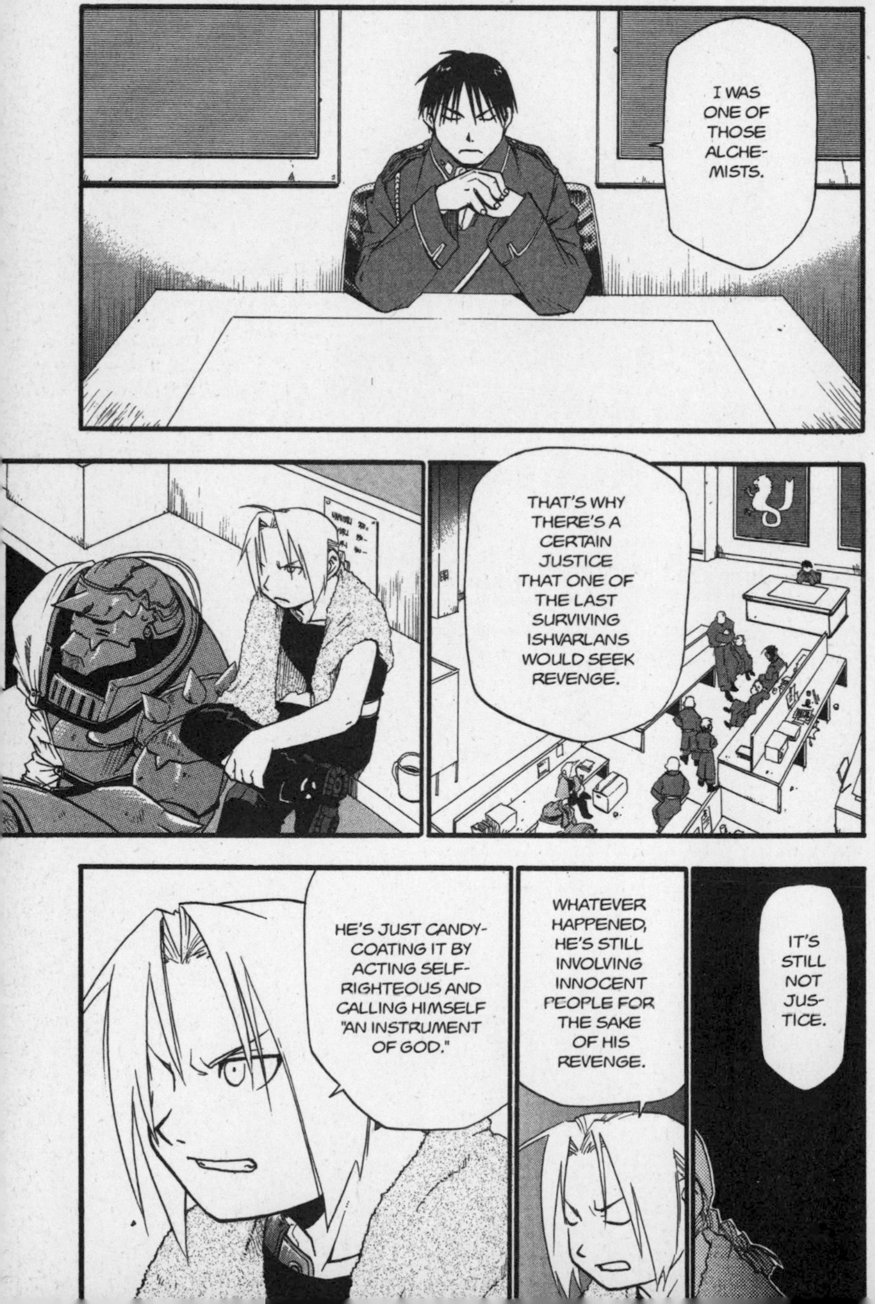
I WAS ONE OF THOSE ALCHE-MISTS.
THAT'S WHY THERE'S A CERTAIN JUSTICE THAT ONE OF THE LAST SURVIVING ISHVARLANS WOULD SEEK REVENGE.
IT'S STILL NOT JUS-TICE.
WHATEVER HAPPENED, HE'S STILL INVOLVING INNOCENT PEOPLE FOR THE SAKE OF HIS REVENGE.
HE'S JUST CANDY-COATING IT BY ACTING SELF-RIGHTEOUS AND CALLING HIMSELF "AN INSTRUMENT OF GOD."

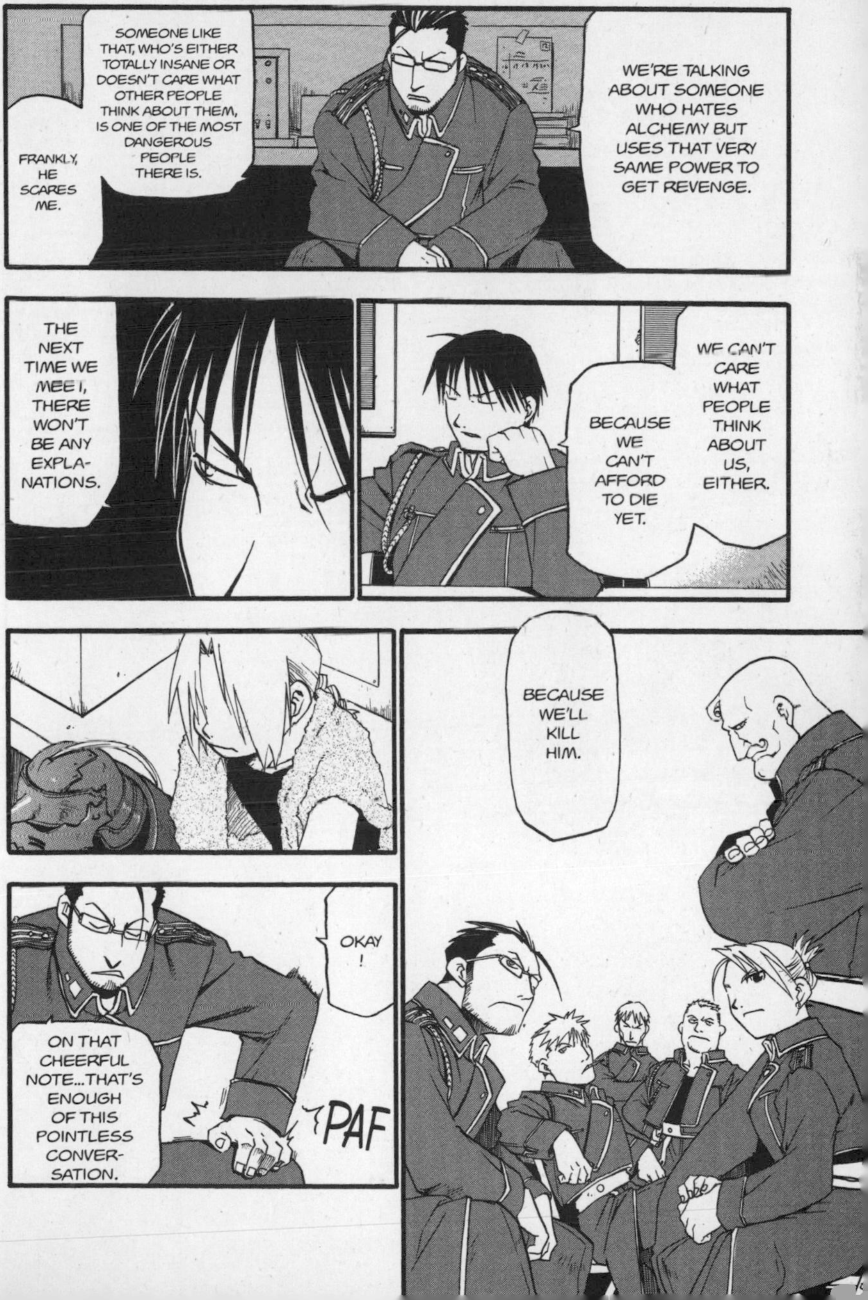
WE'RE TALKING ABOUT SOMEONE WHO HATES ALCHEMY BUT USES THAT VERY SAME POWER TO GET REVENGE.
SOMEONE LIKE THAT, WHO'S EITHER TOTALLY INSANE OR DOESN'T CARE WHAT OTHER PEOPLE THINK ABOUT THEM, IS ONE OF THE MOST DANGEROUS PEOPLE THERE IS.
FRANKLY, HE SCARES ME.
WE CAN'T CARE WHAT PEOPLE THINK ABOUT US, EITHER.
BECAUSE WE CAN'T AFFORD TO DIE YET.
THE NEXT TIME WE MEET, THERE WON'T BE ANY EXPLANATIONS.
BECAUSE WE'LL KILL HIM.
OKAY!
ON THAT CHEERFUL NOTE...THAT'S ENOUGH OF THIS POINTLESS CONVERSATION.
PAF

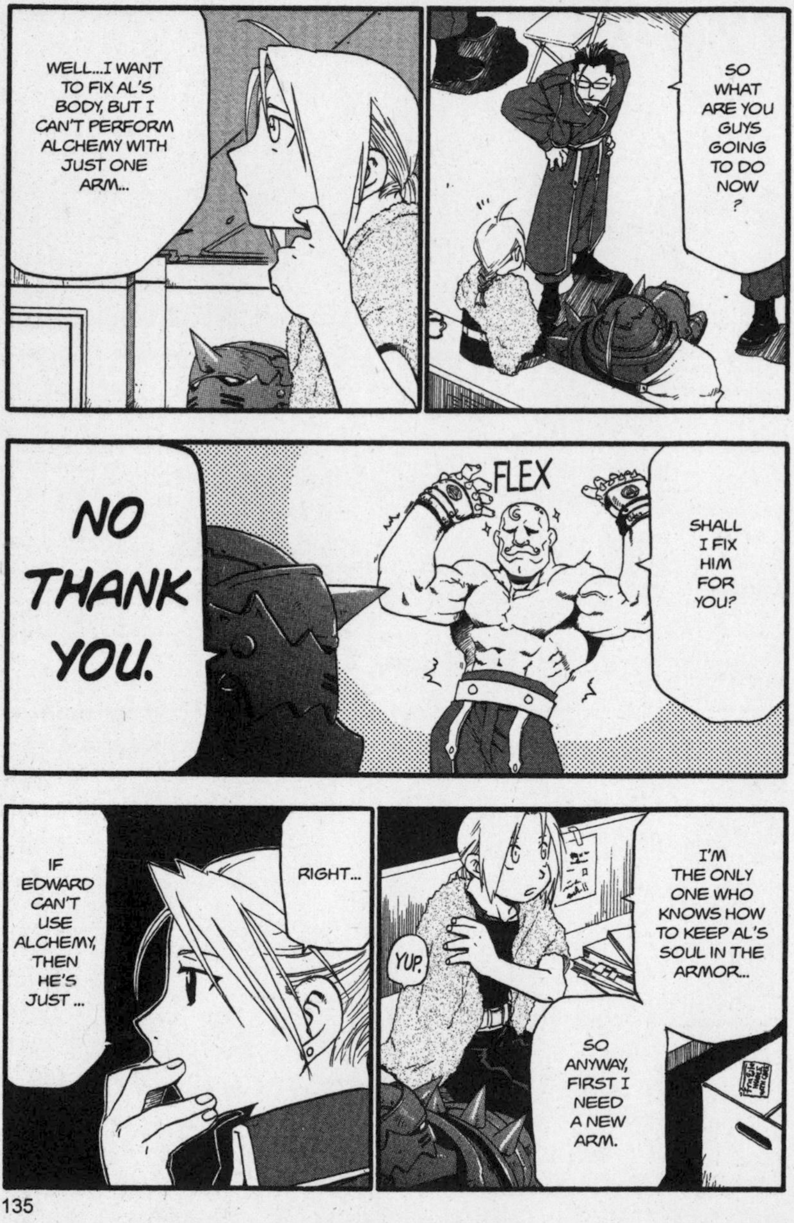
SO WHAT ARE YOU GUYS GOING TO DO NOW?
WELL...I WANT TO FIX AL'S BODY, BUT I CAN'T PERFORM ALCHEMY WITH JUST ONE ARM...
FLEX
SHALL I FIX HIM FOR YOU?
NO THANK YOU.
I'M THE ONLY ONE WHO KNOWS HOW TO KEEP AL'S SOUL IN THE ARMOR...
YUP.
SO ANYWAY, FIRST I NEED A NEW ARM.
RIGHT...
IF EDWARD CAN'T USE ALCHEMY, THEN HE'S JUST ...

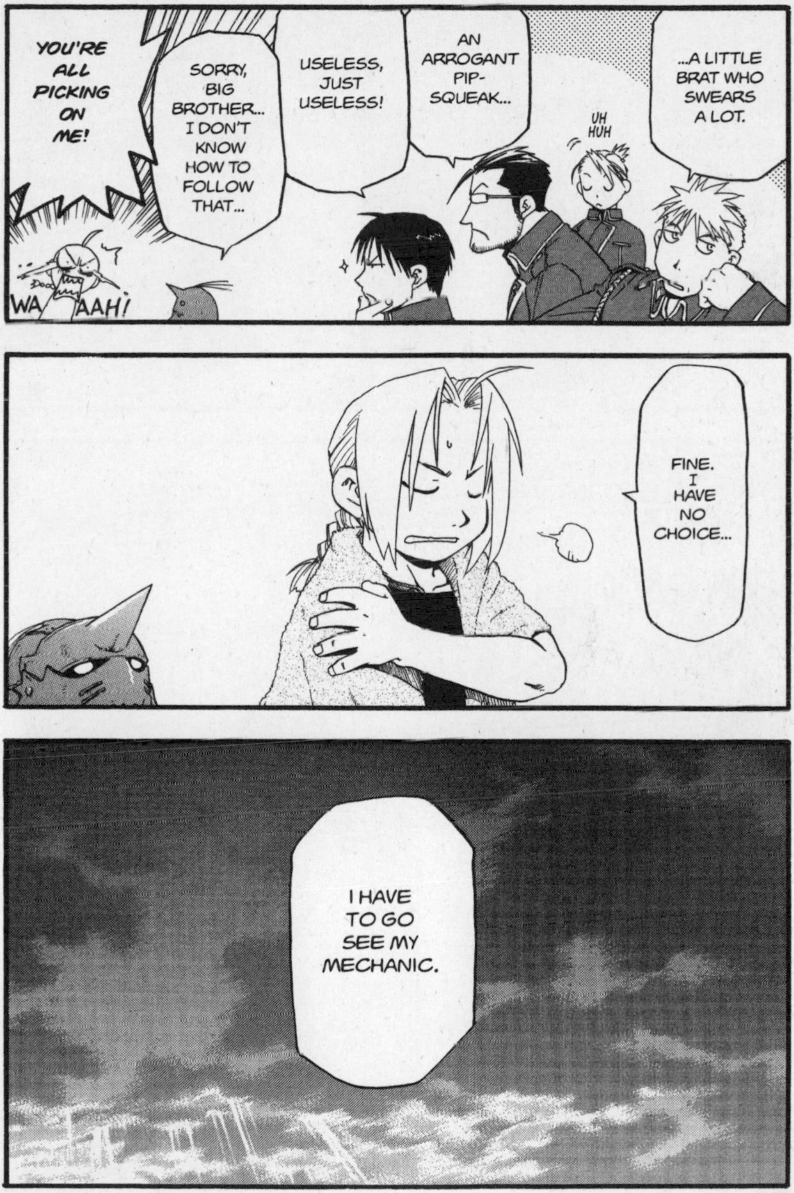
...A LITTLE BRAT WHO SWEARS A LOT.
UH HUH
AN ARROGANT PIP-SQUEAK...
USELESS, JUST USELESS!
SORRY, BIG BROTHER... I DON'T KNOW HOW TO FOLLOW THAT...
YOU'RE ALL PICKING ON ME!
WA AAH!
FINE. I HAVE NO CHOICE...
I HAVE TO GO SEE MY MECHANIC.

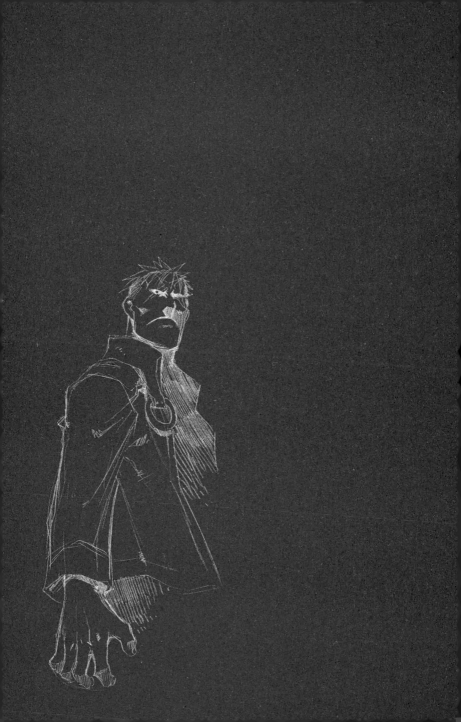

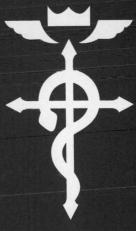

FULLMETAL
ALCHEMIST

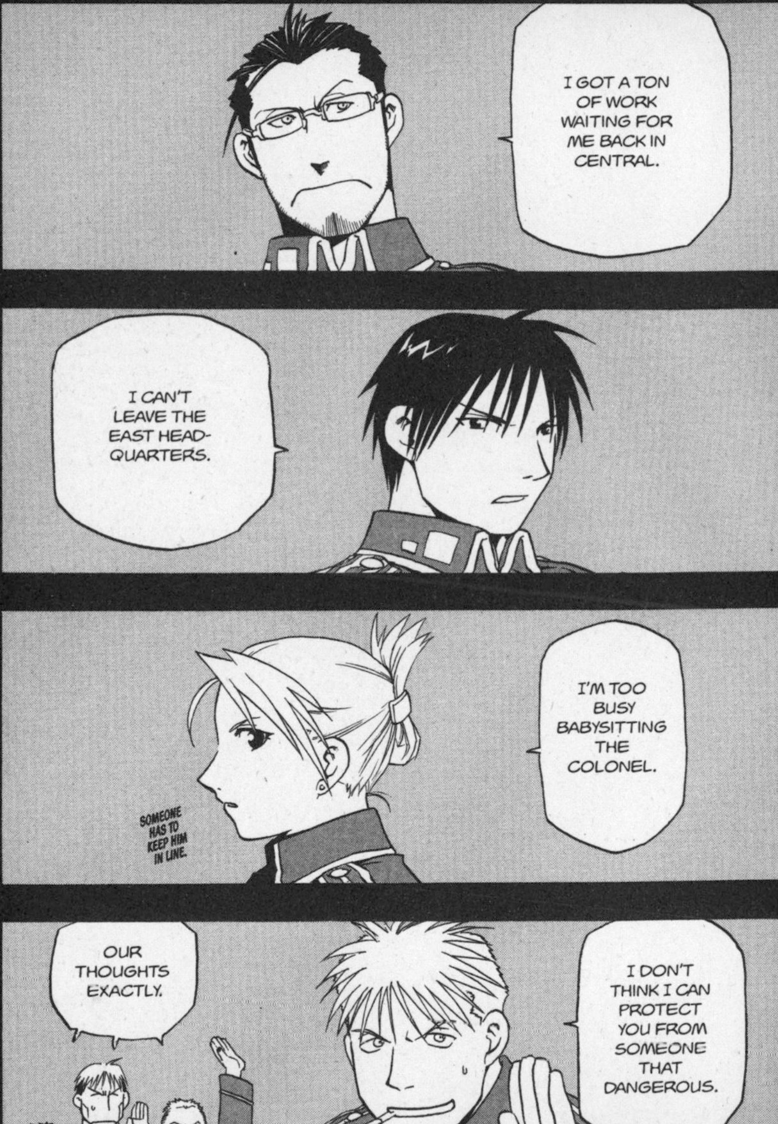
I GOT A TON OF WORK WAITING FOR ME BACK IN CENTRAL.
I CAN'T LEAVE THE EAST HEAD-QUARTERS.
I'M TOO BUSY BABYSITTING THE COLONEL.
SOMEONE HAS TO KEEP HIM IN LINE.
I DON'T THINK I CAN PROTECT YOU FROM SOMEONE THAT DANGEROUS.
OUR THOUGHTS EXACTLY.

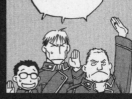

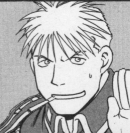

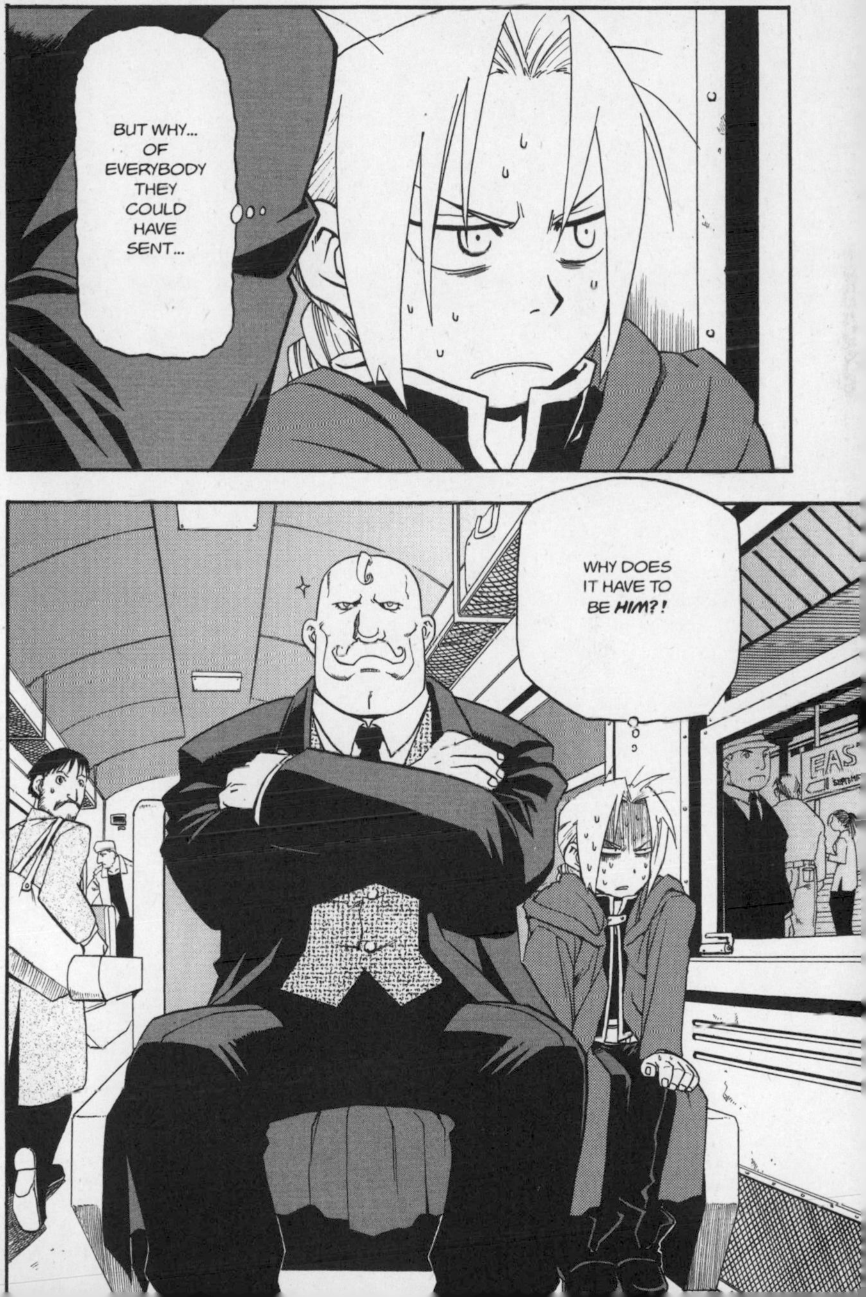
BUT WHY... OF EVERYBODY THEY COULD HAVE SENT...
WHY DOES IT HAVE TO BE *HIM?!*

Chapter 8: The Road of Hope

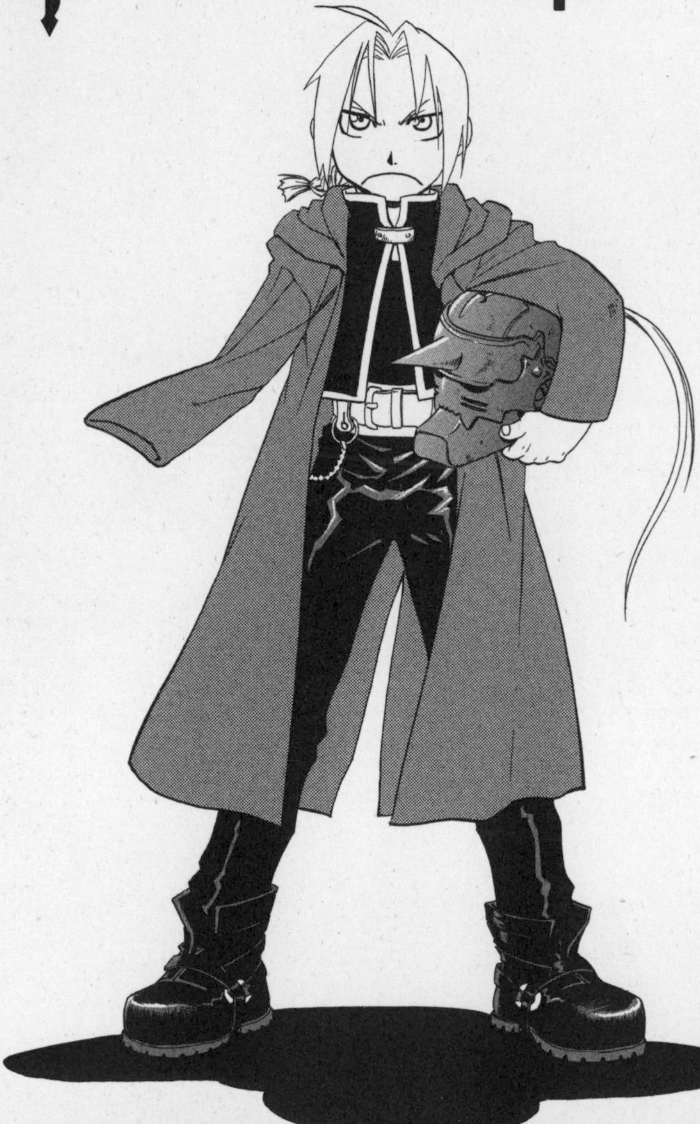

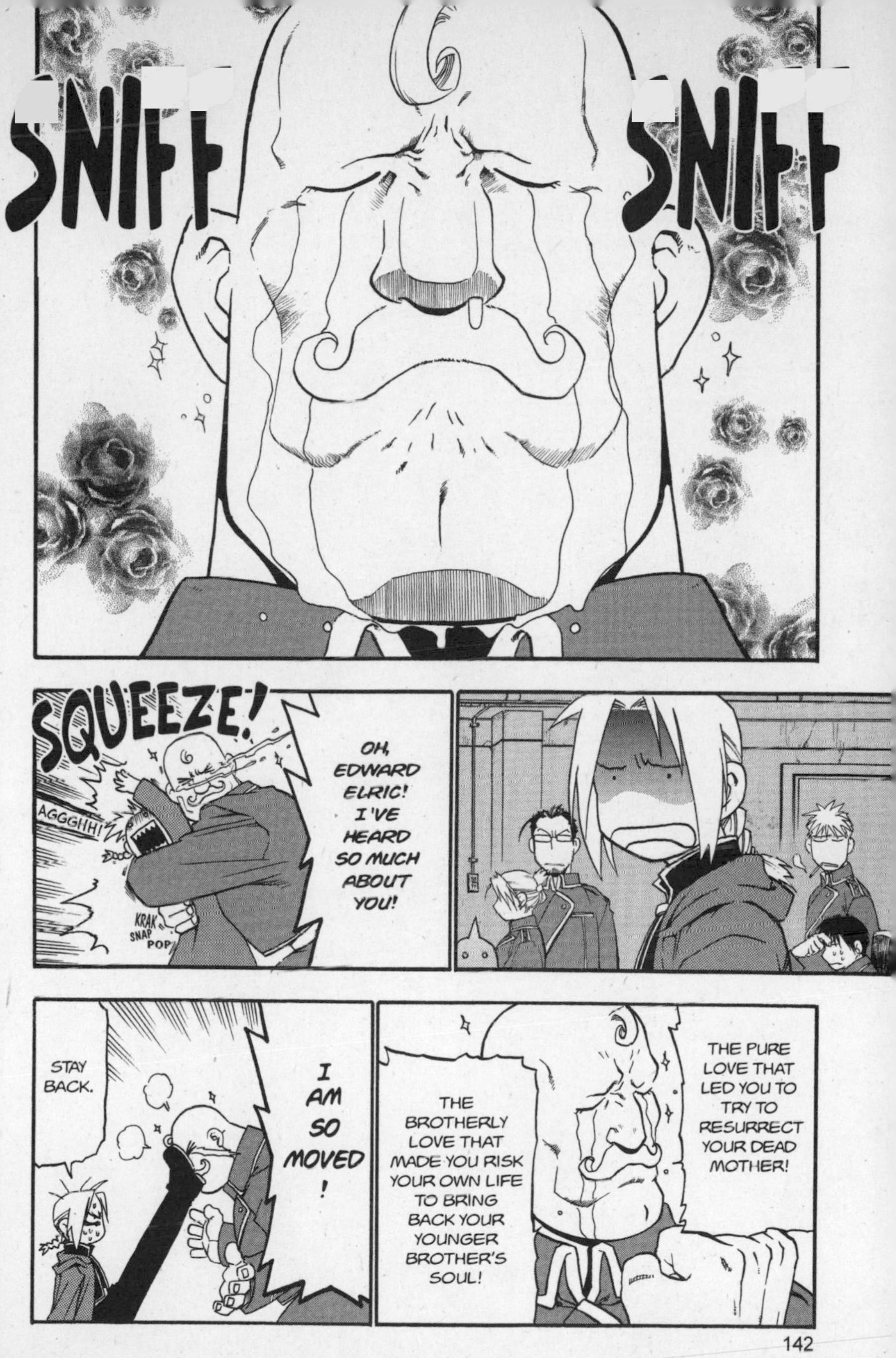
SNIFF
SNIFF
SQUEEZE!
OH, EDWARD ELRIC! I'VE HEARD SO MUCH ABOUT YOU!
AGGGHH!
KRAK SNAP POP
THE PURE LOVE THAT LED YOU TO TRY TO RESURRECT YOUR DEAD MOTHER!
THE BROTHERLY LOVE THAT MADE YOU RISK YOUR OWN LIFE TO BRING BACK YOUR YOUNGER BROTHER'S SOUL!
I AM SO MOVED!
STAY BACK.

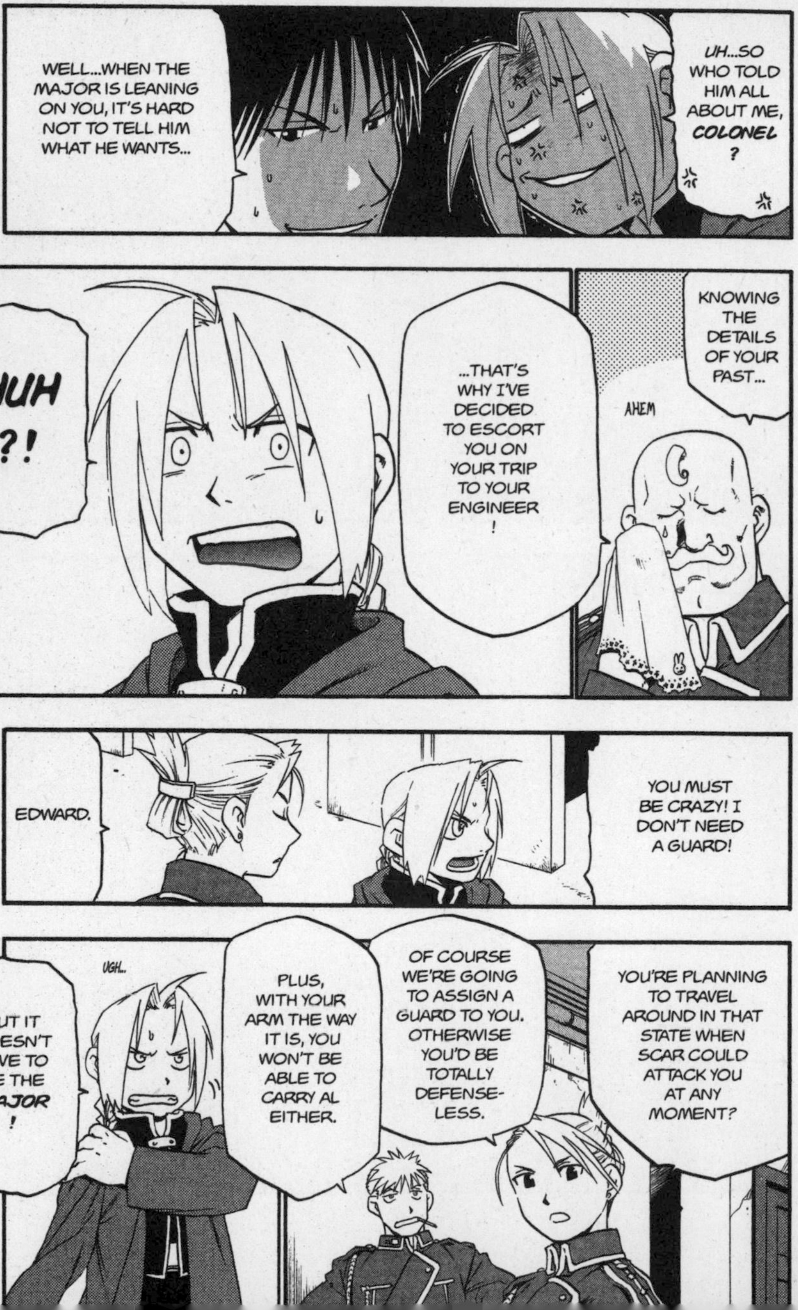
UH...SO WHO TOLD HIM ALL ABOUT ME, COLONEL?
WELL...WHEN THE MAJOR IS LEANING ON YOU, IT'S HARD NOT TO TELL HIM WHAT HE WANTS...
KNOWING THE DETAILS OF YOUR PAST...
AHEM
...THAT'S WHY I'VE DECIDED TO ESCORT YOU ON YOUR TRIP TO YOUR ENGINEER!
HUH?!
YOU MUST BE CRAZY! I DON'T NEED A GUARD!
EDWARD.
YOU'RE PLANNING TO TRAVEL AROUND IN THAT STATE WHEN SCAR COULD ATTACK YOU AT ANY MOMENT?
OF COURSE WE'RE GOING TO ASSIGN A GUARD TO YOU. OTHERWISE YOU'D BE TOTALLY DEFENSE-LESS.
PLUS, WITH YOUR ARM THE WAY IT IS, YOU WON'T BE ABLE TO CARRY AL EITHER.
UGH...
BUT IT DOESN'T HAVE TO BE THE MAJOR!

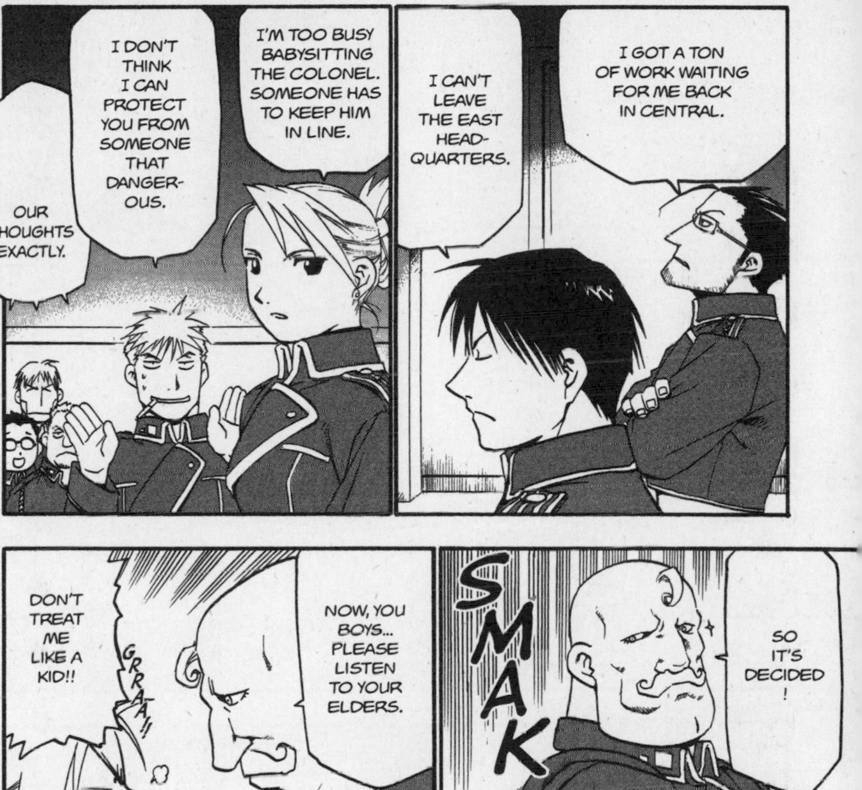
I GOT A TON OF WORK WAITING FOR ME BACK IN CENTRAL.
I CAN'T LEAVE THE EAST HEAD-QUARTERS.
I'M TOO BUSY BABYSITTING THE COLONEL. SOMEONE HAS TO KEEP HIM IN LINE.
I DON'T THINK I CAN PROTECT YOU FROM SOMEONE THAT DANGER-OUS.
OUR THOUGHTS EXACTLY.
SO IT'S DECIDED!
SMAK
NOTHING'S "DECIDED"!
NOW, YOU BOYS... PLEASE LISTEN TO YOUR ELDERS.
GRRAAA!!
DON'T TREAT ME LIKE A KID!!
WHY YOU...
HEY AL! ARE YOU GONNA TAKE THAT?!

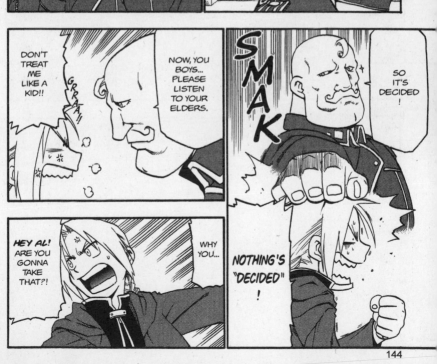

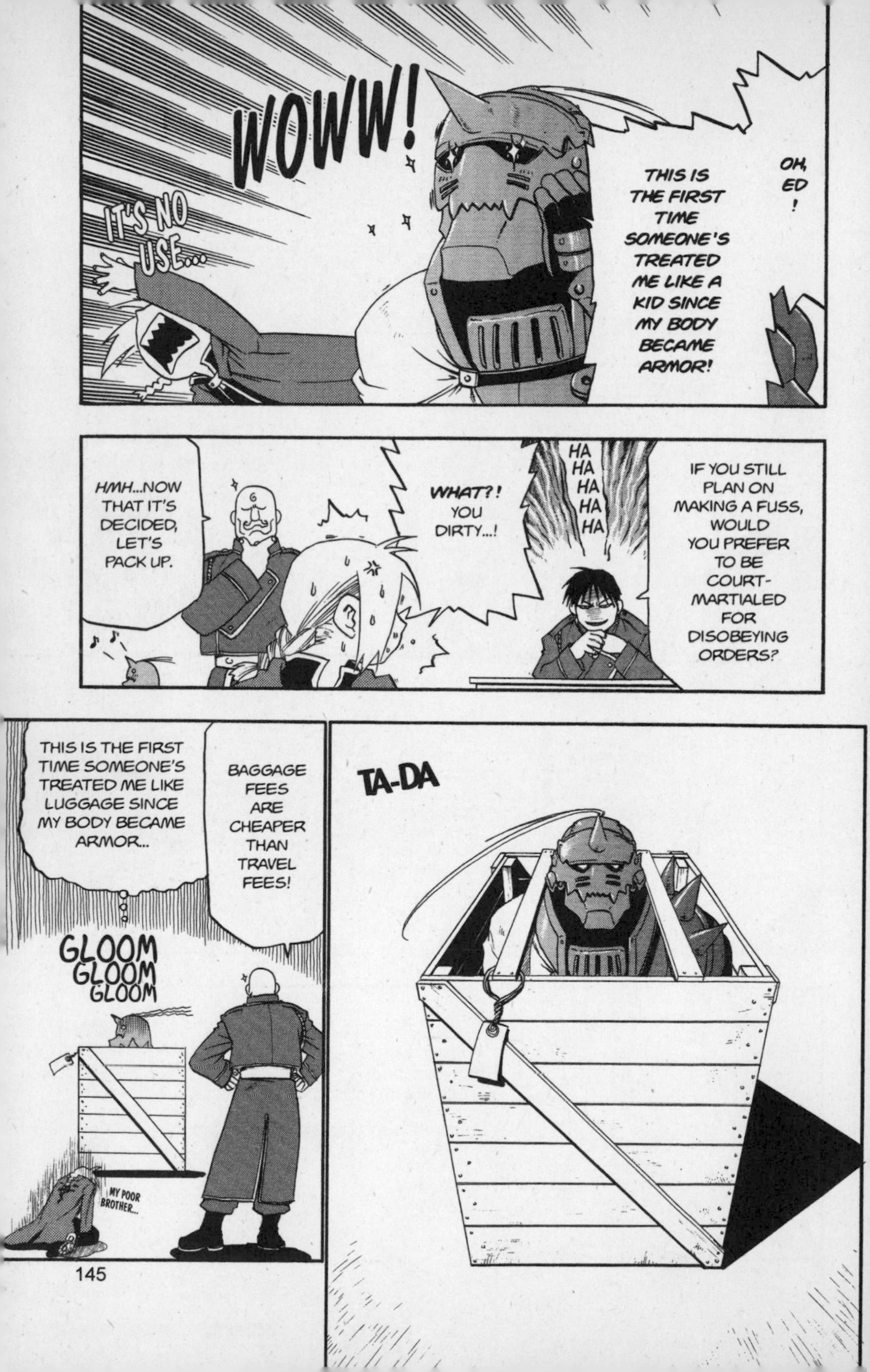
OH, ED!
THIS IS THE FIRST TIME SOMEONE'S TREATED ME LIKE A KID SINCE MY BODY BECAME ARMOR!
WOWW!
IT'S NO USE...
IF YOU STILL PLAN ON MAKING A FUSS, WOULD YOU PREFER TO BE COURT-MARTIALED FOR DISOBEYING ORDERS?
HA HA HA HA HA
WHAT?! YOU DIRTY...!
HMH...NOW THAT IT'S DECIDED, LET'S PACK UP.
TA-DA
BAGGAGE FEES ARE CHEAPER THAN TRAVEL FEES!
THIS IS THE FIRST TIME SOMEONE'S TREATED ME LIKE LUGGAGE SINCE MY BODY BECAME ARMOR...
GLOOM GLOOM GLOOM
MY POOR BROTHER...

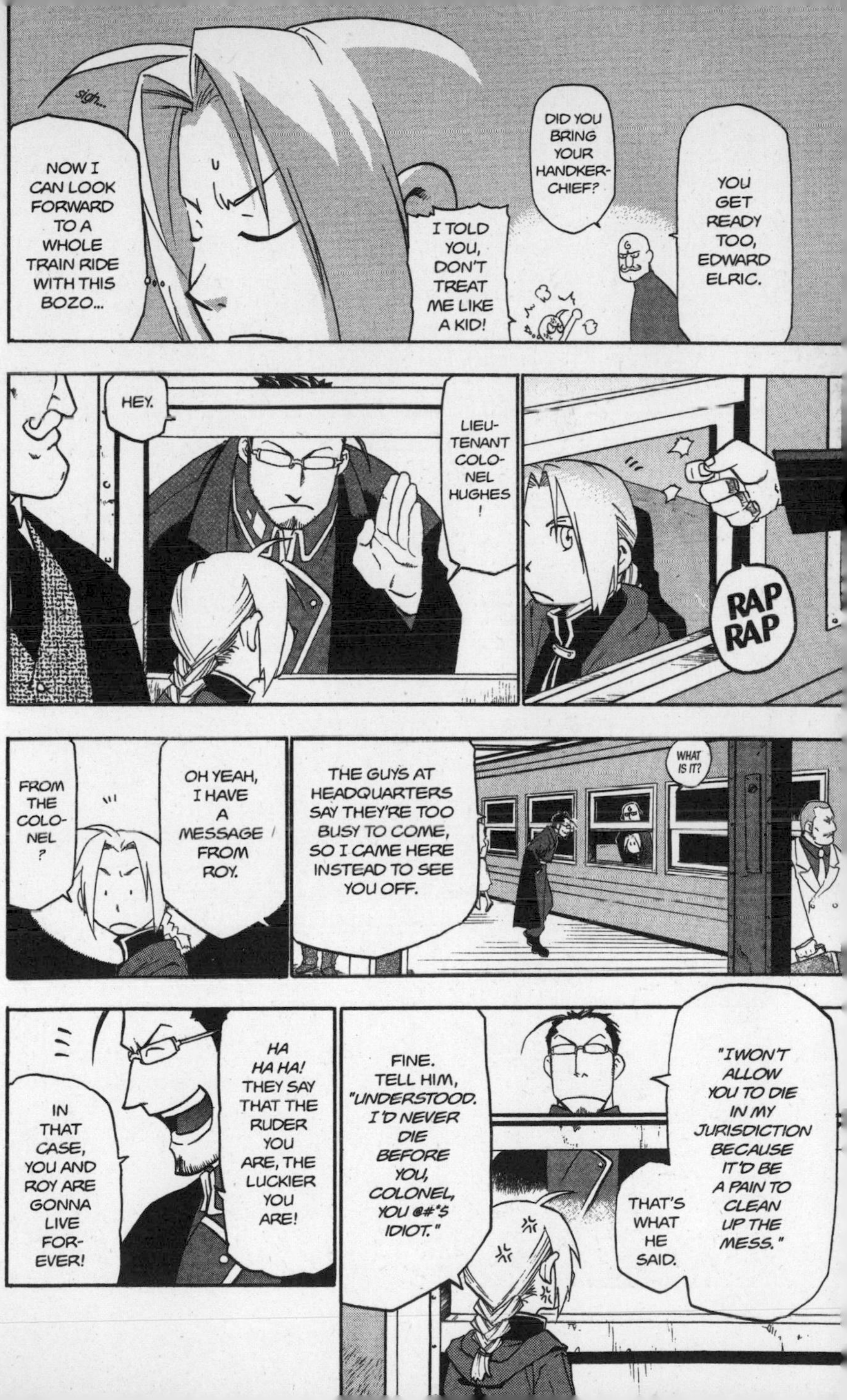
YOU GET READY TOO, EDWARD ELRIC.
DID YOU BRING YOUR HANDKERCHIEF?
I TOLD YOU, DON'T TREAT ME LIKE A KID!
sigh...
NOW I CAN LOOK FORWARD TO A WHOLE TRAIN RIDE WITH THIS BOZO...
RAP RAP
LIEUTENANT COLONEL HUGHES!
HEY.
WHAT IS IT?
THE GUYS AT HEADQUARTERS SAY THEY'RE TOO BUSY TO COME, SO I CAME HERE INSTEAD TO SEE YOU OFF.
OH YEAH, I HAVE A MESSAGE FROM ROY.
FROM THE COLONEL?
"I WON'T ALLOW YOU TO DIE IN MY JURISDICTION BECAUSE IT'D BE A PAIN TO CLEAN UP THE MESS."
THAT'S WHAT HE SAID.
FINE. TELL HIM, "UNDERSTOOD. I'D NEVER DIE BEFORE YOU, COLONEL, YOU @#*S IDIOT."
HA HA HA! THEY SAY THAT THE RUDER YOU ARE, THE LUCKIER YOU ARE!
IN THAT CASE, YOU AND ROY ARE GONNA LIVE FOREVER!

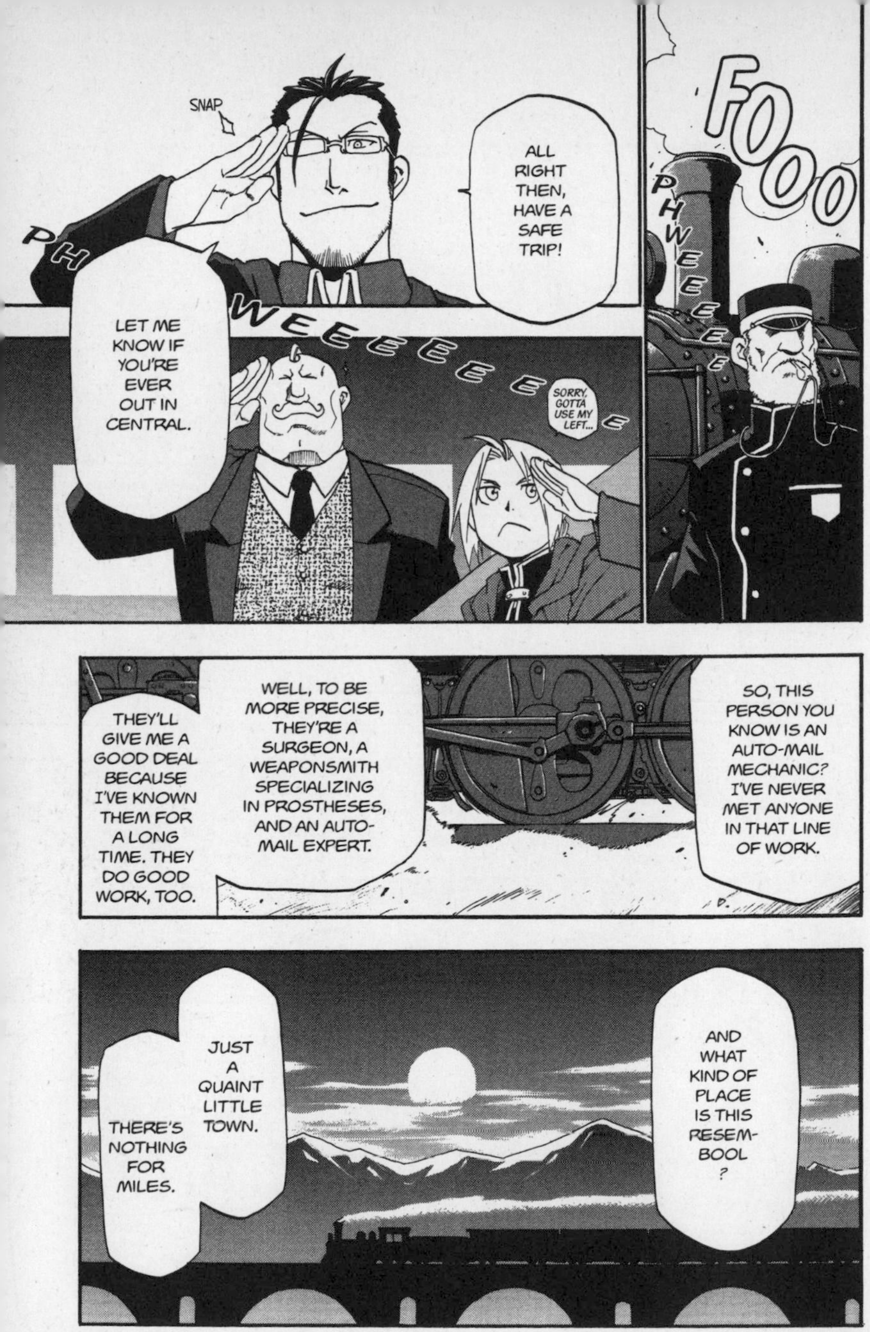
FOOO
PHWEEEEE
ALL RIGHT THEN, HAVE A SAFE TRIP!
SNAP
PHWEEEEEEEEEE
LET ME KNOW IF YOU'RE EVER OUT IN CENTRAL.
SORRY, GOTTA USE MY LEFT...
SO, THIS PERSON YOU KNOW IS AN AUTO-MAIL MECHANIC? I'VE NEVER MET ANYONE IN THAT LINE OF WORK.
WELL, TO BE MORE PRECISE, THEY'RE A SURGEON, A WEAPONSMITH SPECIALIZING IN PROSTHESES, AND AN AUTO-MAIL EXPERT.
THEY'LL GIVE ME A GOOD DEAL BECAUSE I'VE KNOWN THEM FOR A LONG TIME. THEY DO GOOD WORK, TOO.
AND WHAT KIND OF PLACE IS THIS RESEMBOOL?
JUST A QUAINT LITTLE TOWN.
THERE'S NOTHING FOR MILES.

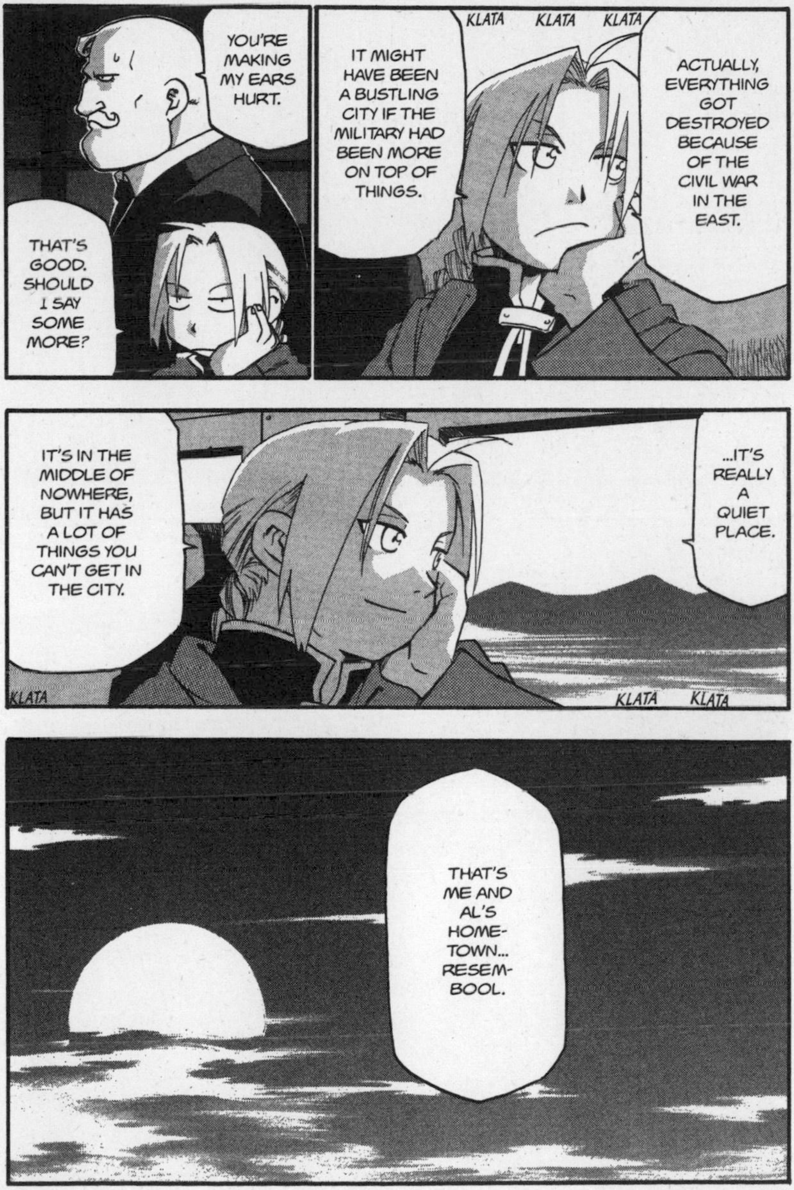
KLATA KLATA KLATA
ACTUALLY, EVERYTHING GOT DESTROYED BECAUSE OF THE CIVIL WAR IN THE EAST.
IT MIGHT HAVE BEEN A BUSTLING CITY IF THE MILITARY HAD BEEN MORE ON TOP OF THINGS.
YOU'RE MAKING MY EARS HURT.
THAT'S GOOD. SHOULD I SAY SOME MORE?
...IT'S REALLY A QUIET PLACE.
IT'S IN THE MIDDLE OF NOWHERE, BUT IT HAS A LOT OF THINGS YOU CAN'T GET IN THE CITY.
KLATA KLATA
KLATA
THAT'S ME AND AL'S HOME-TOWN... RESEM-BOOL.

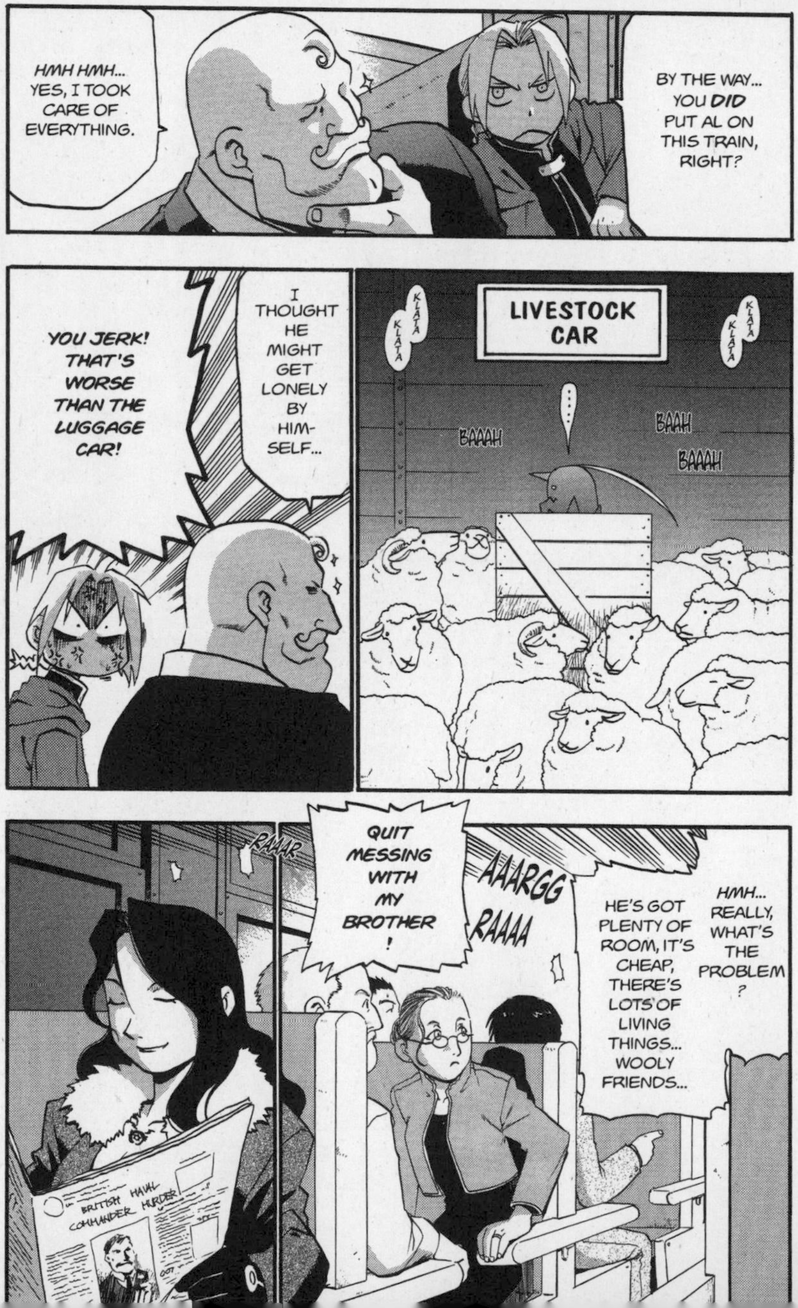
BY THE WAY... YOU **DID** PUT AL ON THIS TRAIN, RIGHT?
HMH HMH... YES, I TOOK CARE OF EVERYTHING.
KLATA KLATA
LIVESTOCK CAR
KLATA KLATA
BAAH
BAAAH
BAAAH
...
I THOUGHT HE MIGHT GET LONELY BY HIMSELF...
YOU JERK! THAT'S WORSE THAN THE LUGGAGE CAR!
HMH... REALLY, WHAT'S THE PROBLEM?
HE'S GOT PLENTY OF ROOM, IT'S CHEAP, THERE'S LOTS OF LIVING THINGS... WOOLY FRIENDS...
AAARGG
RAAAA
QUIT MESSING WITH MY BROTHER!
RAAAR
BRITISH HAVAL
COMMANDER MURDER

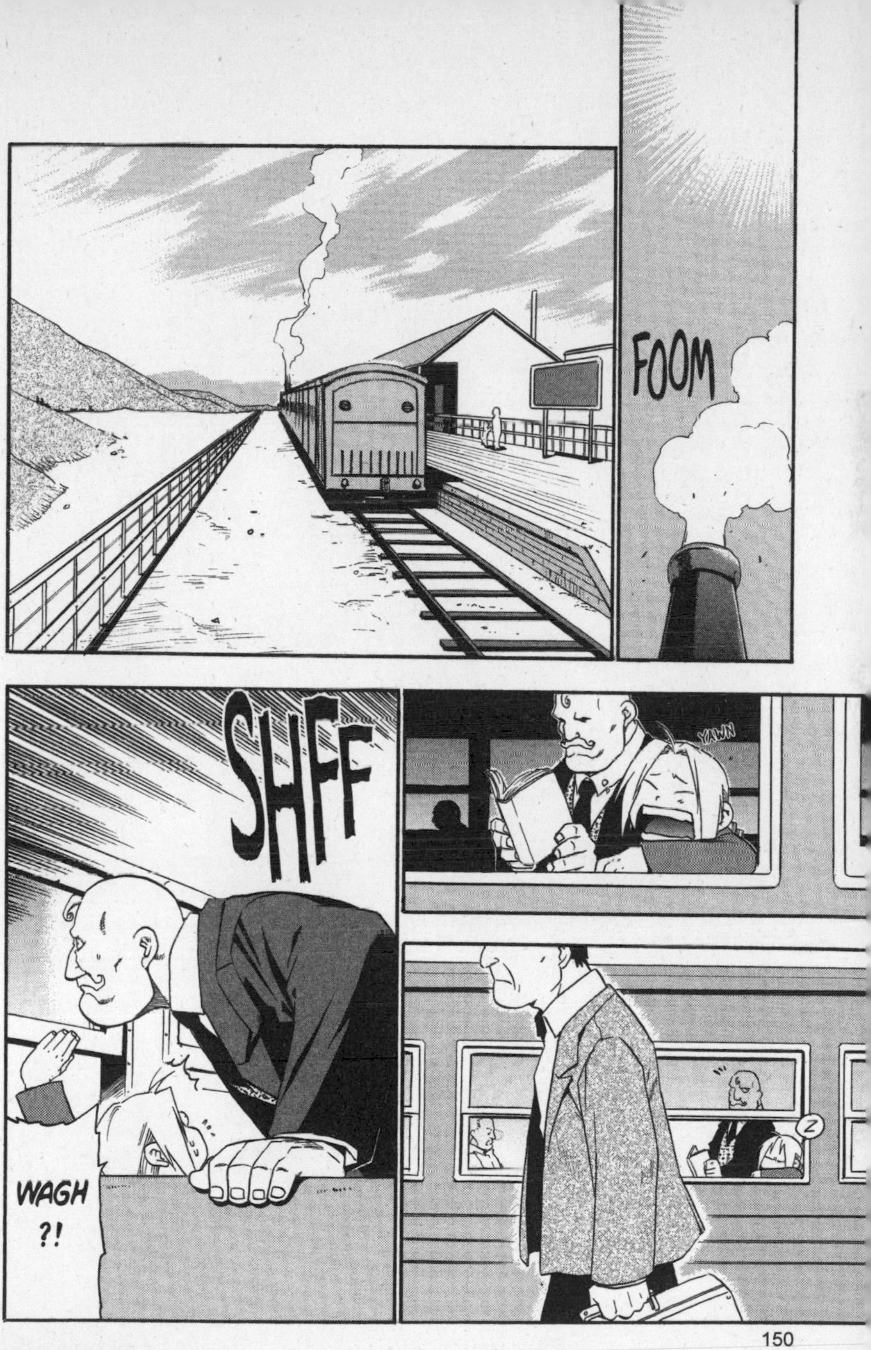
FOOM
YAWN
Z
SHFF
WAGH ?!

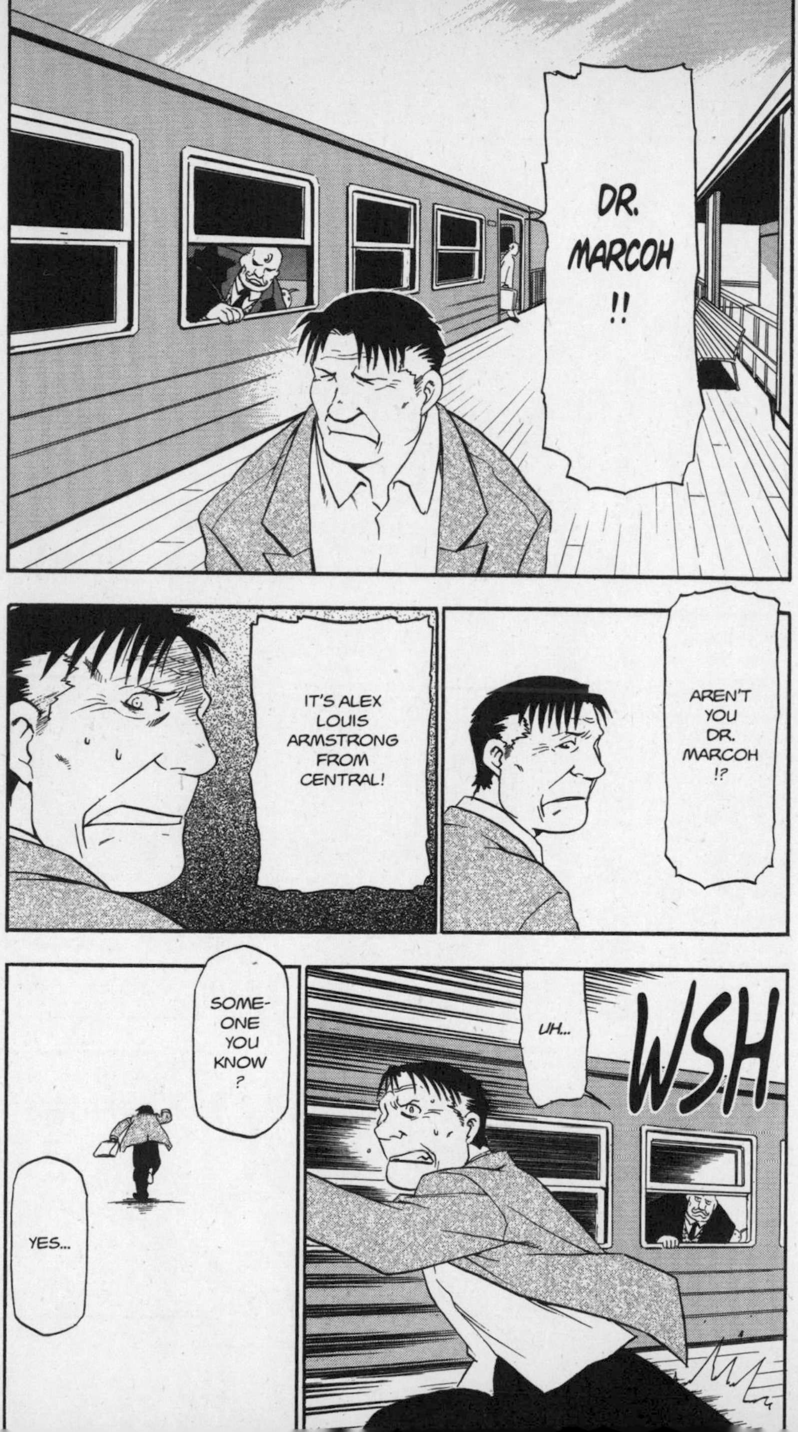
DR. MARCOH !!
AREN'T YOU DR. MARCOH !?
IT'S ALEX LOUIS ARMSTRONG FROM CENTRAL!
UH...
WSH
SOME-ONE YOU KNOW ?
YES...

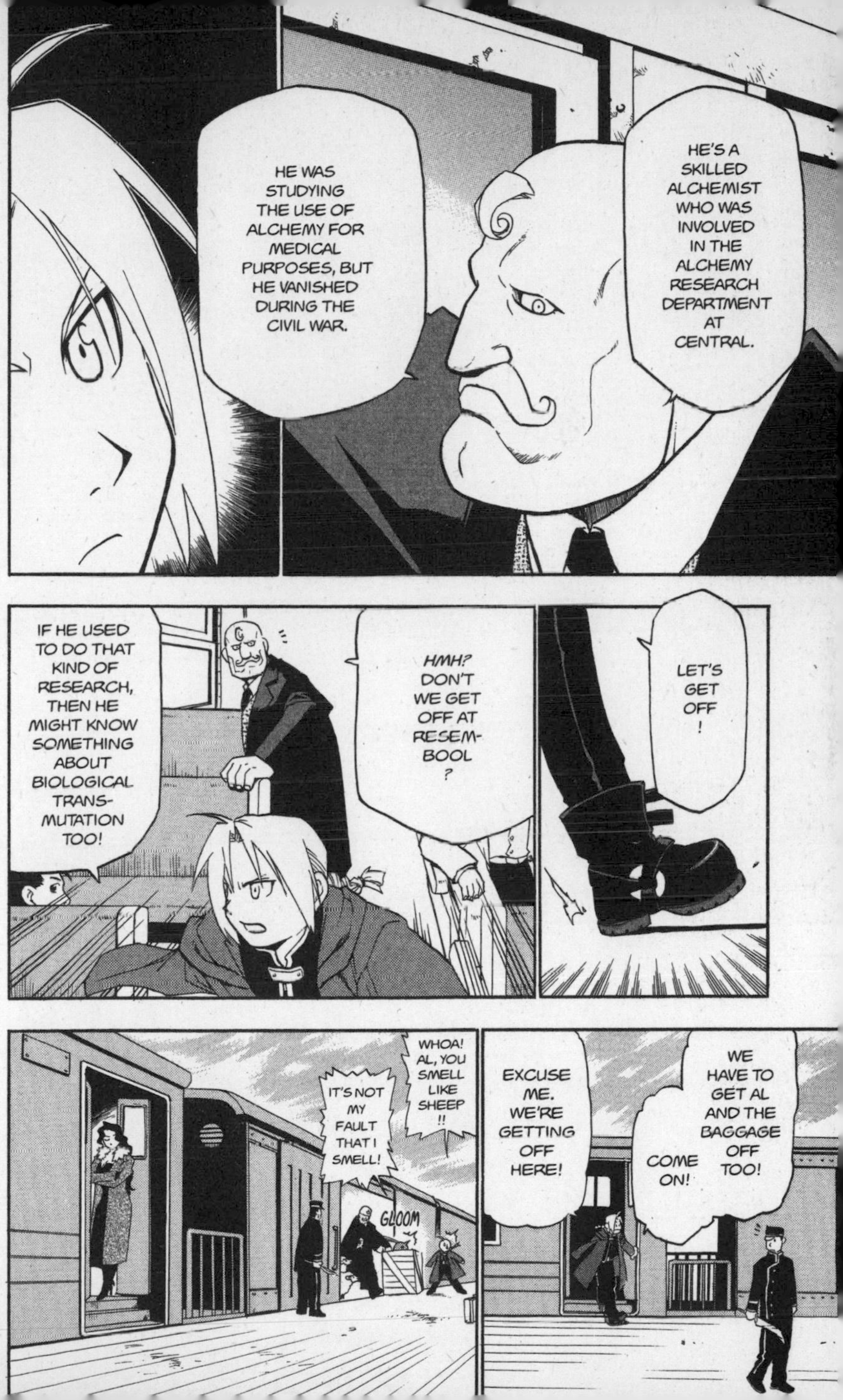
HE'S A SKILLED ALCHEMIST WHO WAS INVOLVED IN THE ALCHEMY RESEARCH DEPARTMENT AT CENTRAL.
HE WAS STUDYING THE USE OF ALCHEMY FOR MEDICAL PURPOSES, BUT HE VANISHED DURING THE CIVIL WAR.
LET'S GET OFF!
HMH? DON'T WE GET OFF AT RESEMBOOL?
IF HE USED TO DO THAT KIND OF RESEARCH, THEN HE MIGHT KNOW SOMETHING ABOUT BIOLOGICAL TRANSMUTATION TOO!
WE HAVE TO GET AL AND THE BAGGAGE OFF TOO!
COME ON!
EXCUSE ME. WE'RE GETTING OFF HERE!
WHOA! AL, YOU SMELL LIKE SHEEP!!
IT'S NOT MY FAULT THAT I SMELL!
GLOOM

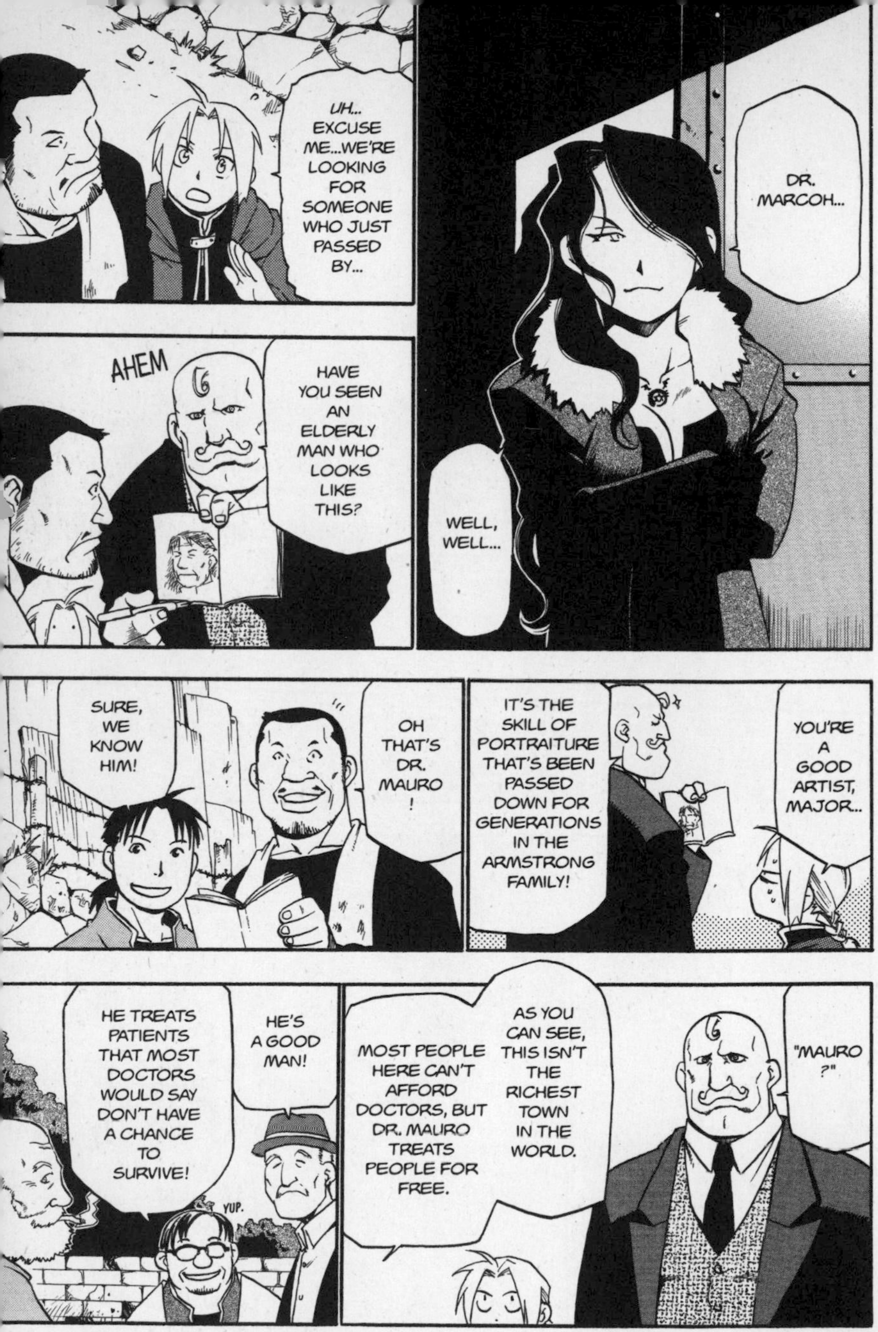
DR. MARCOH...
WELL, WELL...
UH... EXCUSE ME...WE'RE LOOKING FOR SOMEONE WHO JUST PASSED BY...
AHEM
HAVE YOU SEEN AN ELDERLY MAN WHO LOOKS LIKE THIS?
YOU'RE A GOOD ARTIST, MAJOR...
IT'S THE SKILL OF PORTRAITURE THAT'S BEEN PASSED DOWN FOR GENERATIONS IN THE ARMSTRONG FAMILY!
OH THAT'S DR. MAURO!
SURE, WE KNOW HIM!
"MAURO?"
AS YOU CAN SEE, THIS ISN'T THE RICHEST TOWN IN THE WORLD.
MOST PEOPLE HERE CAN'T AFFORD DOCTORS, BUT DR. MAURO TREATS PEOPLE FOR FREE.
HE'S A GOOD MAN!
HE TREATS PATIENTS THAT MOST DOCTORS WOULD SAY DON'T HAVE A CHANCE TO SURVIVE!
YUP.

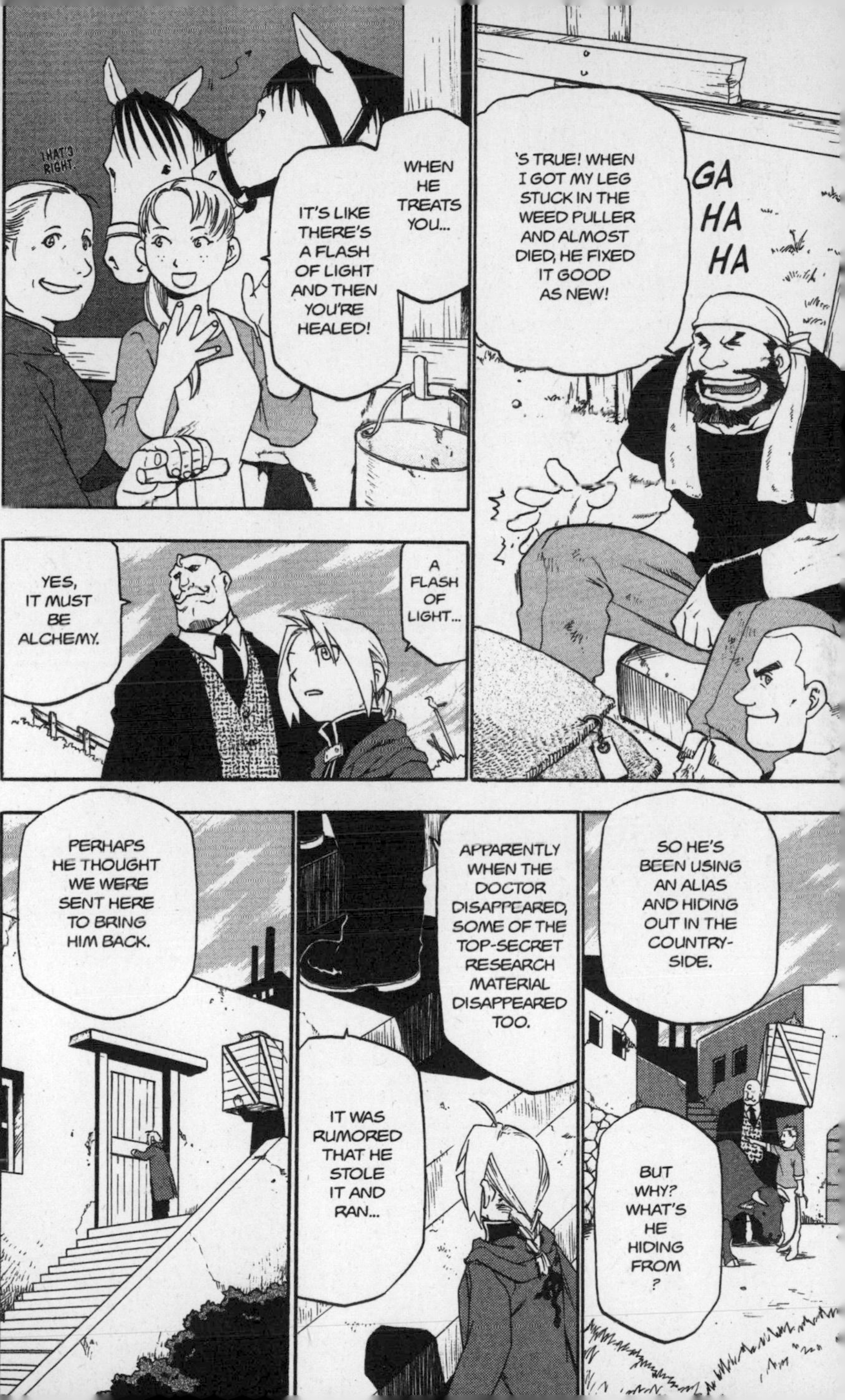
'S TRUE! WHEN I GOT MY LEG STUCK IN THE WEED PULLER AND ALMOST DIED, HE FIXED IT GOOD AS NEW!
GA HA HA
WHEN HE TREATS YOU...
IT'S LIKE THERE'S A FLASH OF LIGHT AND THEN YOU'RE HEALED!
THAT'S RIGHT.
A FLASH OF LIGHT...
YES, IT MUST BE ALCHEMY.
SO HE'S BEEN USING AN ALIAS AND HIDING OUT IN THE COUNTRY-SIDE.
BUT WHY? WHAT'S HE HIDING FROM?
APPARENTLY WHEN THE DOCTOR DISAPPEARED, SOME OF THE TOP-SECRET RESEARCH MATERIAL DISAPPEARED TOO.
IT WAS RUMORED THAT HE STOLE IT AND RAN...
PERHAPS HE THOUGHT WE WERE SENT HERE TO BRING HIM BACK.

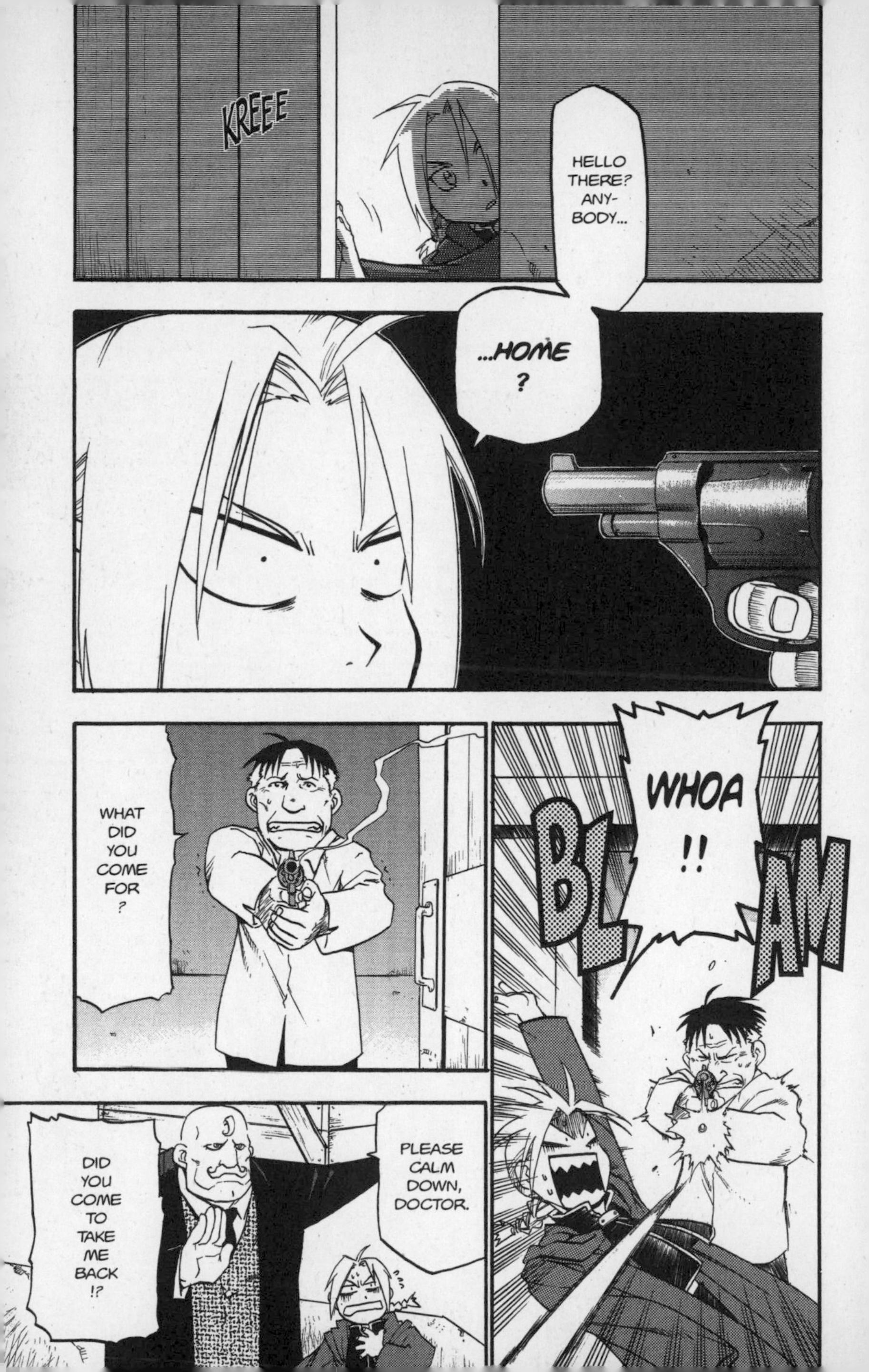

KREEE
HELLO THERE? ANY-BODY...
...HOME ?
WHOA !!
BLAM
WHAT DID YOU COME FOR ?
PLEASE CALM DOWN, DOCTOR.
DID YOU COME TO TAKE ME BACK !?

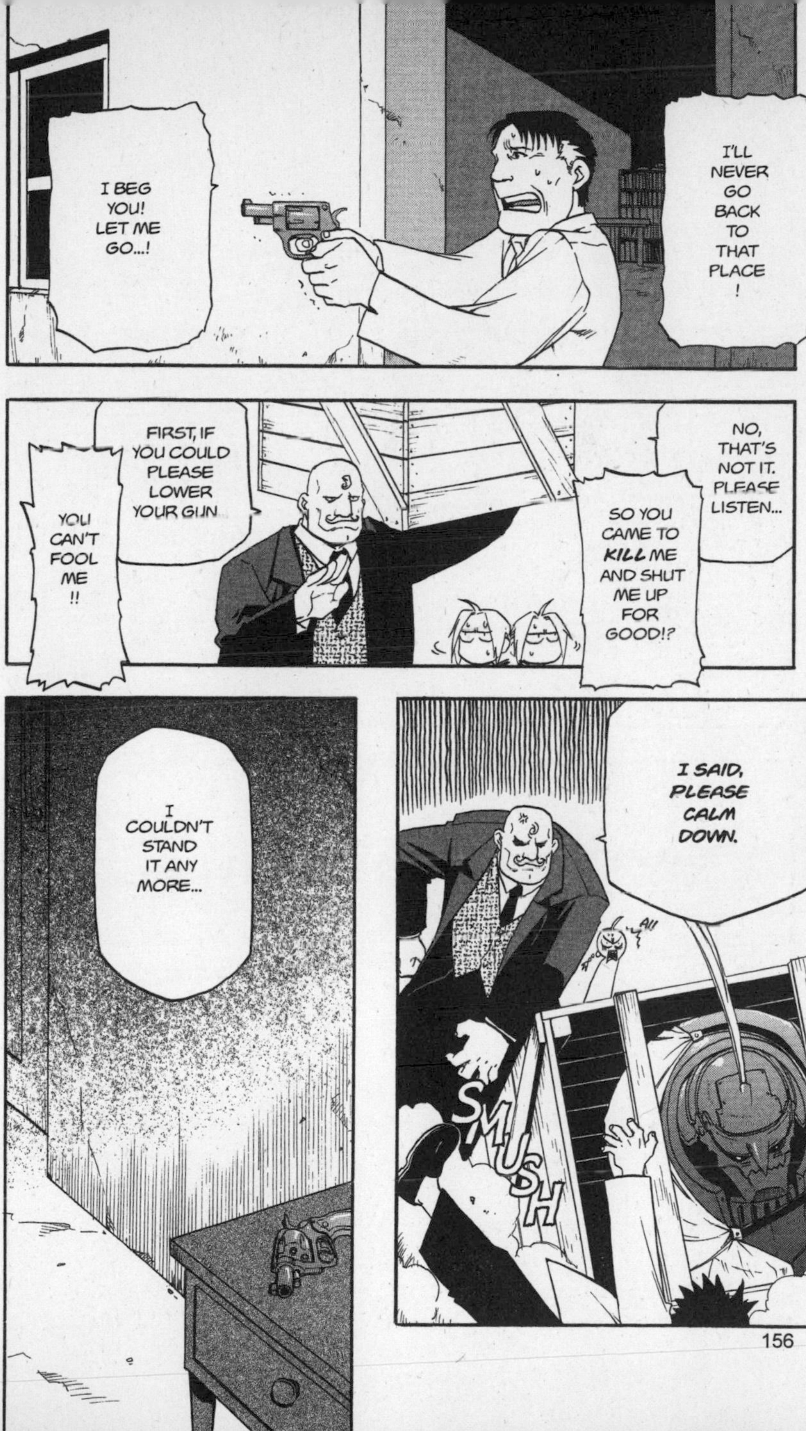
I'LL NEVER GO BACK TO THAT PLACE!
I BEG YOU! LET ME GO...!
NO, THAT'S NOT IT. PLEASE LISTEN...
SO YOU CAME TO KILL ME AND SHUT ME UP FOR GOOD!?
FIRST, IF YOU COULD PLEASE LOWER YOUR GUN
YOU CAN'T FOOL ME!!
I SAID, PLEASE CALM DOWN.
SMUSH
I COULDN'T STAND IT ANY MORE...

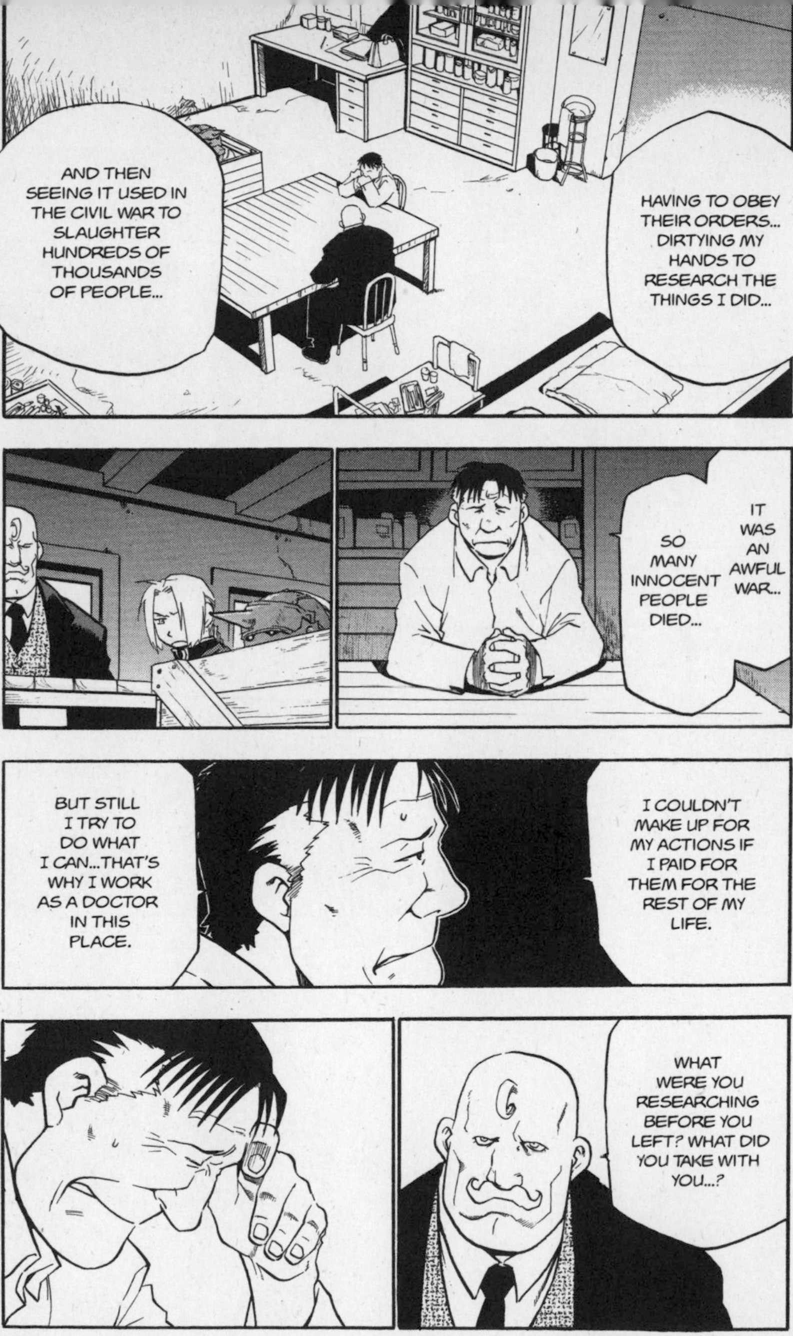
HAVING TO OBEY THEIR ORDERS... DIRTYING MY HANDS TO RESEARCH THE THINGS I DID...
AND THEN SEEING IT USED IN THE CIVIL WAR TO SLAUGHTER HUNDREDS OF THOUSANDS OF PEOPLE...
IT WAS AN AWFUL WAR...
SO MANY INNOCENT PEOPLE DIED...
I COULDN'T MAKE UP FOR MY ACTIONS IF I PAID FOR THEM FOR THE REST OF MY LIFE.
BUT STILL I TRY TO DO WHAT I CAN...THAT'S WHY I WORK AS A DOCTOR IN THIS PLACE.
WHAT WERE YOU RESEARCHING BEFORE YOU LEFT? WHAT DID YOU TAKE WITH YOU...?

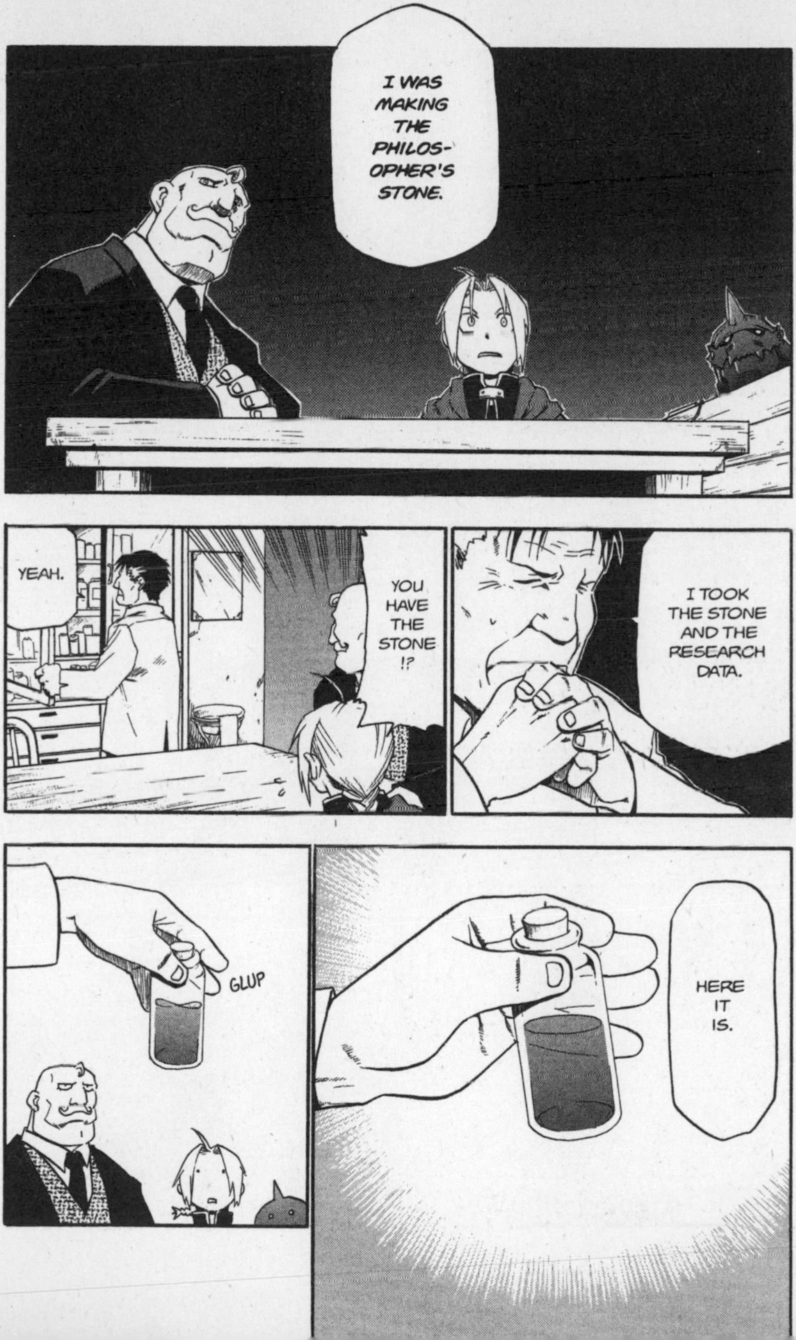
I WAS MAKING THE PHILOS-OPHER'S STONE.
I TOOK THE STONE AND THE RESEARCH DATA.
YOU HAVE THE STONE !?
YEAH.
HERE IT IS.
GLUP

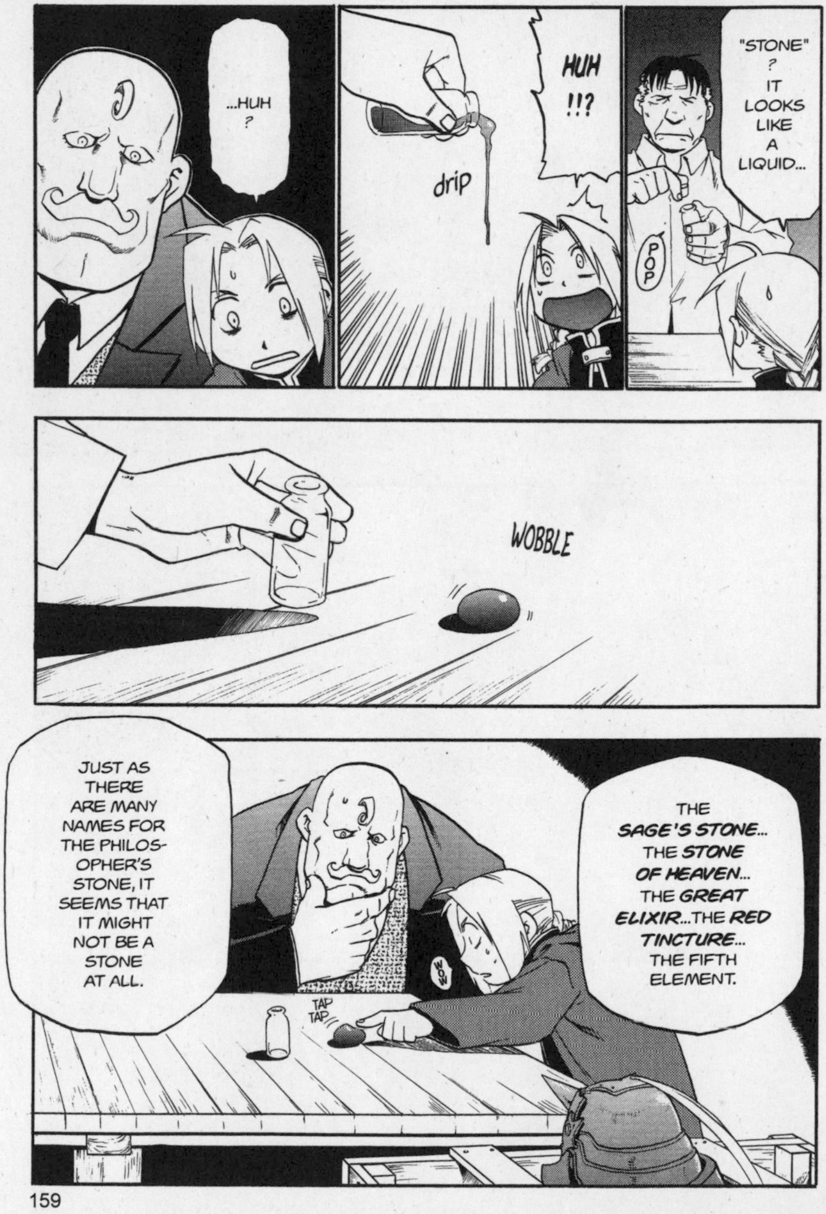

"STONE"? IT LOOKS LIKE A LIQUID...
POP
HUH!!?
drip
...HUH?
WOBBLE
THE *SAGE'S STONE*... THE *STONE OF HEAVEN*... THE *GREAT ELIXIR*...THE *RED TINCTURE*... THE FIFTH ELEMENT.
JUST AS THERE ARE MANY NAMES FOR THE PHILOSOPHER'S STONE, IT SEEMS THAT IT MIGHT NOT BE A STONE AT ALL.
WOW
TAP TAP

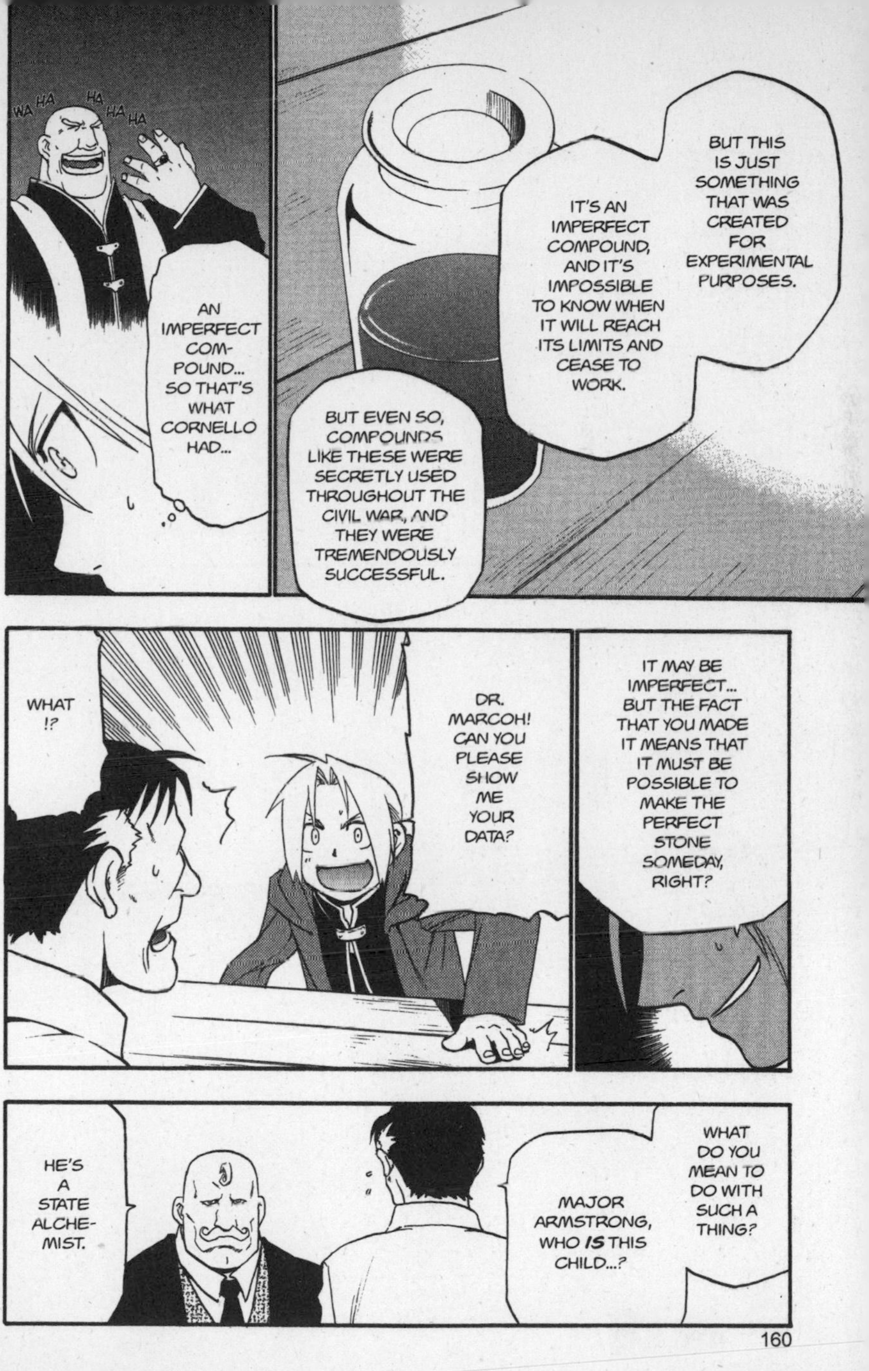
BUT THIS IS JUST SOMETHING THAT WAS CREATED FOR EXPERIMENTAL PURPOSES.
IT'S AN IMPERFECT COMPOUND, AND IT'S IMPOSSIBLE TO KNOW WHEN IT WILL REACH ITS LIMITS AND CEASE TO WORK.
BUT EVEN SO, COMPOUNDS LIKE THESE WERE SECRETLY USED THROUGHOUT THE CIVIL WAR, AND THEY WERE TREMENDOUSLY SUCCESSFUL.
WA HA HA HA HA
AN IMPERFECT COMPOUND... SO THAT'S WHAT CORNELLO HAD...
IT MAY BE IMPERFECT... BUT THE FACT THAT YOU MADE IT MEANS THAT IT MUST BE POSSIBLE TO MAKE THE PERFECT STONE SOMEDAY, RIGHT?
DR. MARCOH! CAN YOU PLEASE SHOW ME YOUR DATA?
WHAT!?
WHAT DO YOU MEAN TO DO WITH SUCH A THING?
MAJOR ARMSTRONG, WHO *IS* THIS CHILD...?
HE'S A STATE ALCHEMIST.

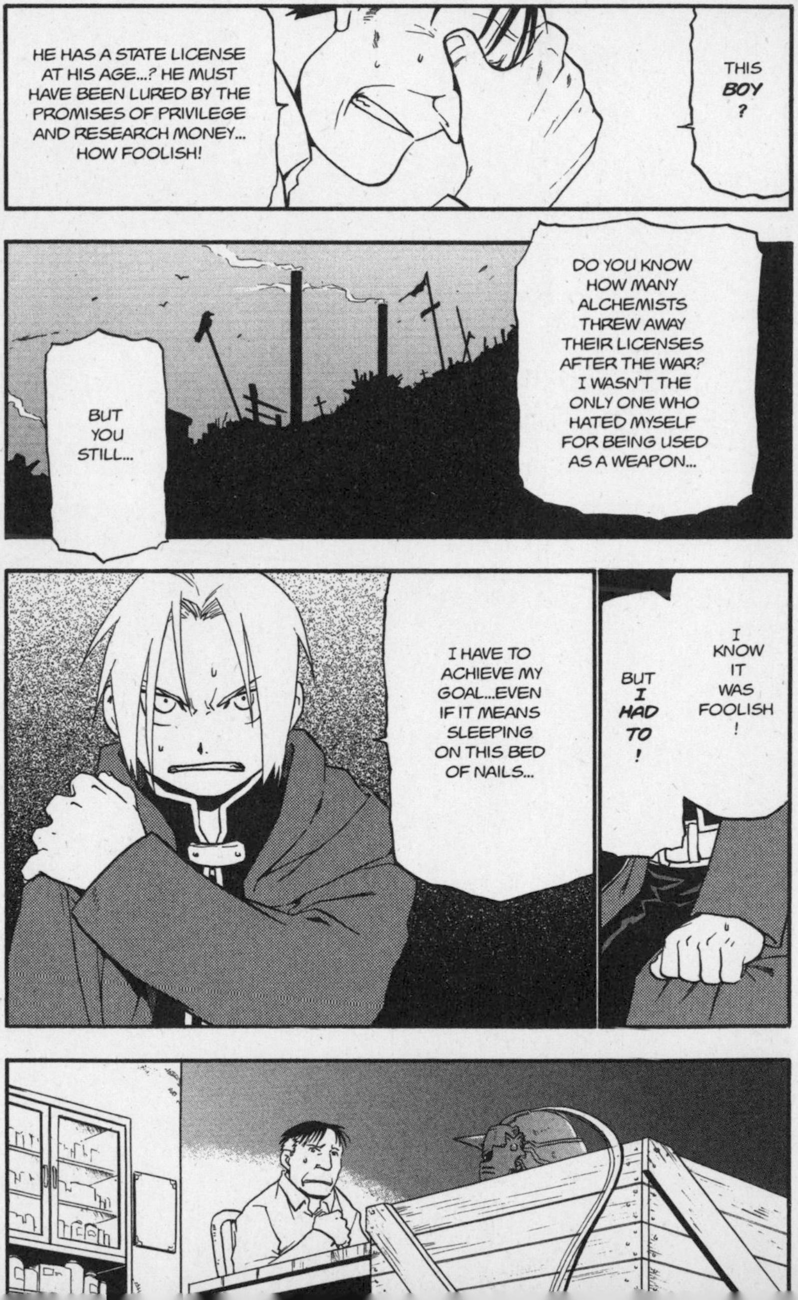
THIS BOY?
HE HAS A STATE LICENSE AT HIS AGE...? HE MUST HAVE BEEN LURED BY THE PROMISES OF PRIVILEGE AND RESEARCH MONEY... HOW FOOLISH!
DO YOU KNOW HOW MANY ALCHEMISTS THREW AWAY THEIR LICENSES AFTER THE WAR? I WASN'T THE ONLY ONE WHO HATED MYSELF FOR BEING USED AS A WEAPON...
BUT YOU STILL...
I KNOW IT WAS FOOLISH!
BUT I HAD TO!
I HAVE TO ACHIEVE MY GOAL...EVEN IF IT MEANS SLEEPING ON THIS BED OF NAILS...

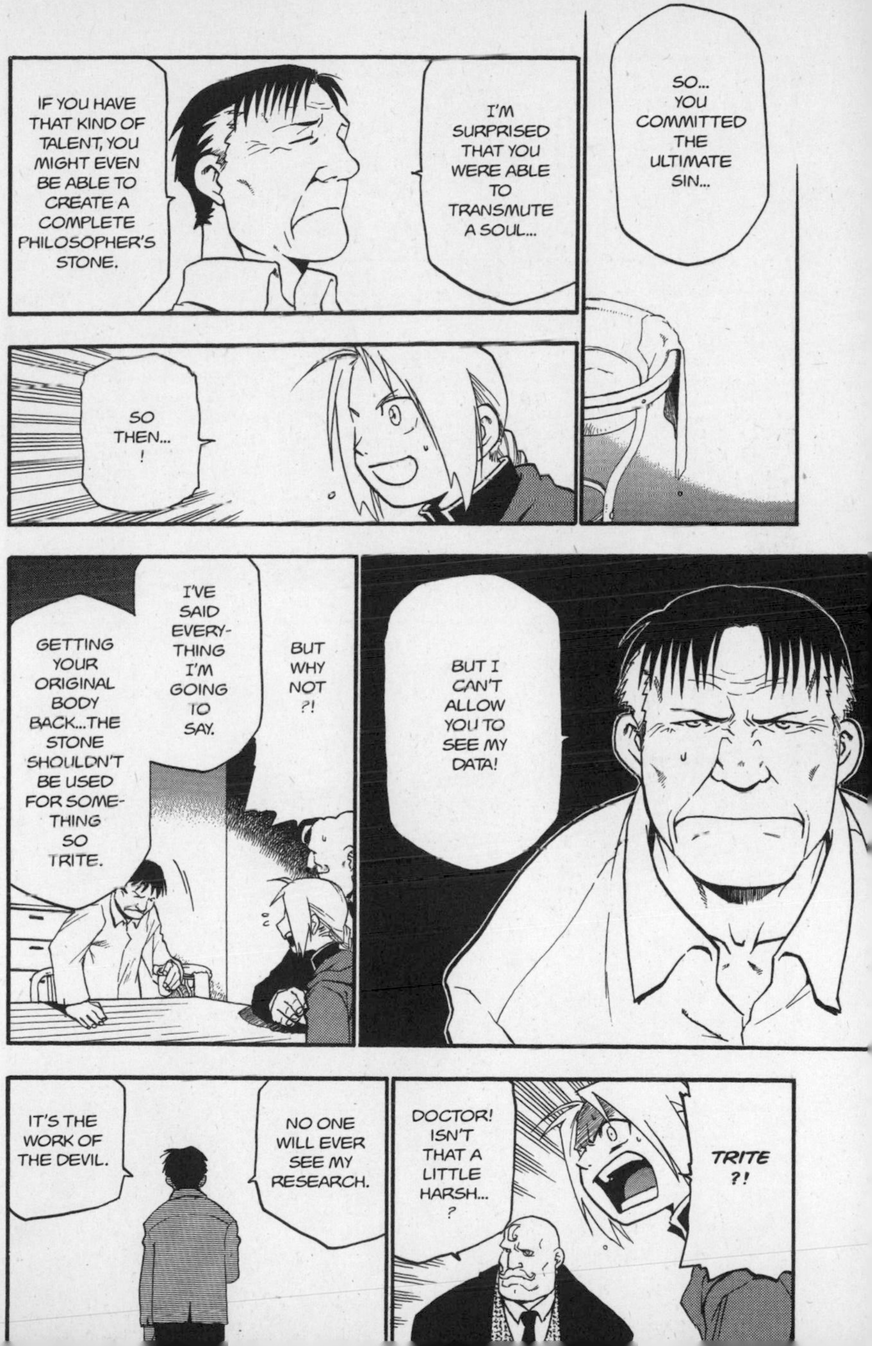
SO... YOU COMMITTED THE ULTIMATE SIN...
I'M SURPRISED THAT YOU WERE ABLE TO TRANSMUTE A SOUL...
IF YOU HAVE THAT KIND OF TALENT, YOU MIGHT EVEN BE ABLE TO CREATE A COMPLETE PHILOSOPHER'S STONE.
SO THEN...!
BUT I CAN'T ALLOW YOU TO SEE MY DATA!
BUT WHY NOT?!
I'VE SAID EVERYTHING I'M GOING TO SAY.
GETTING YOUR ORIGINAL BODY BACK...THE STONE SHOULDN'T BE USED FOR SOMETHING SO TRITE.
TRITE?!
DOCTOR! ISN'T THAT A LITTLE HARSH...?
NO ONE WILL EVER SEE MY RESEARCH.
IT'S THE WORK OF THE DEVIL.

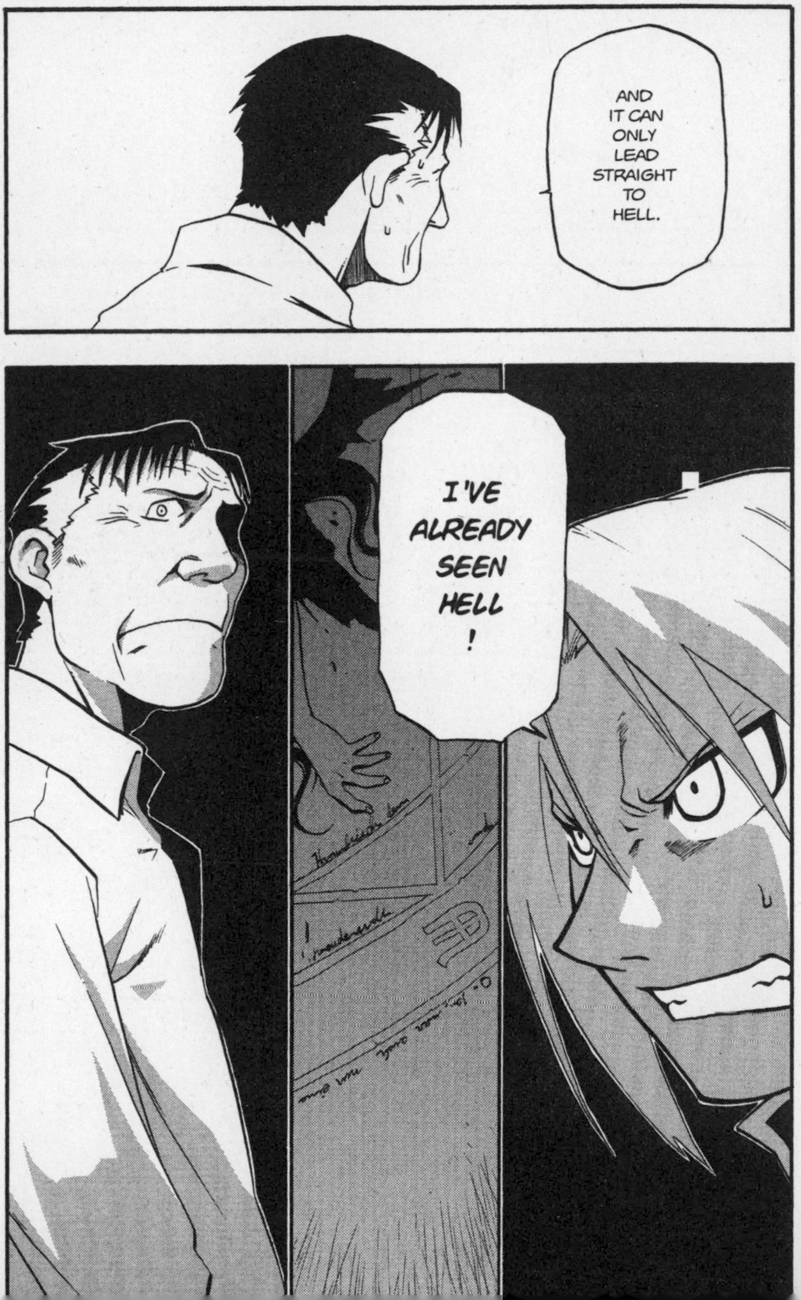
AND IT CAN ONLY LEAD STRAIGHT TO HELL.
I'VE ALREADY SEEN HELL!

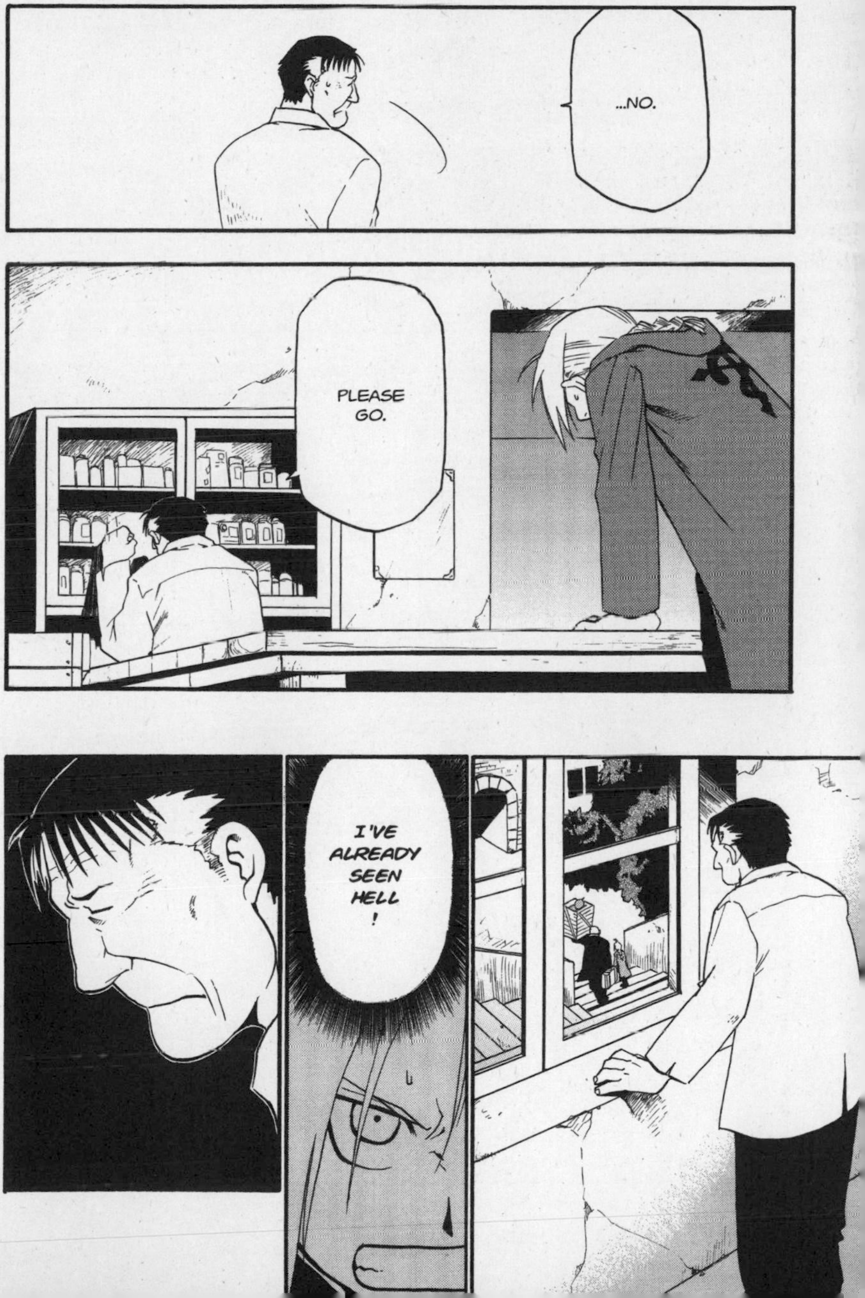
...NO.
PLEASE GO.
I'VE ALREADY SEEN HELL!

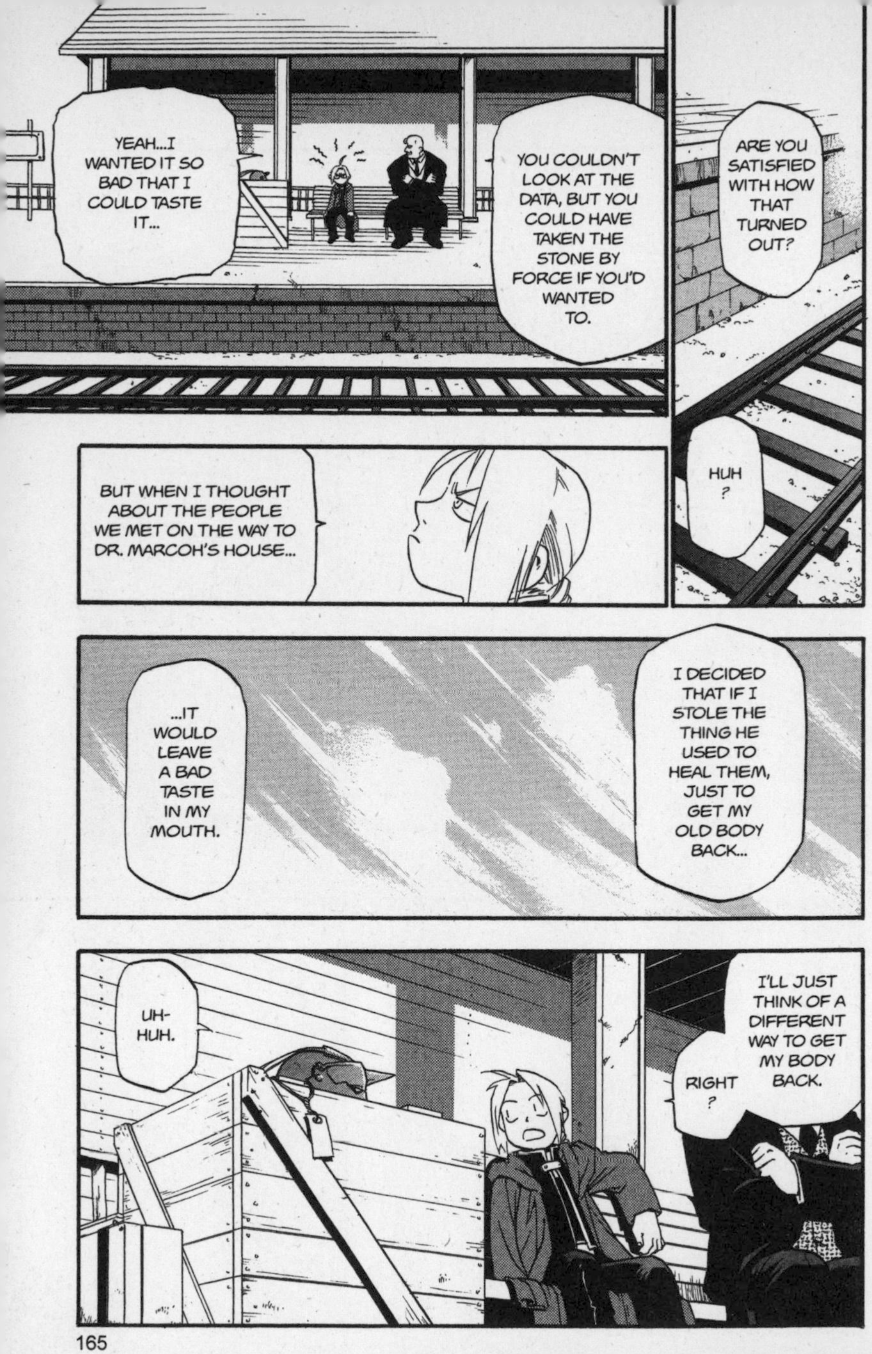
ARE YOU SATISFIED WITH HOW THAT TURNED OUT?
HUH?
YOU COULDN'T LOOK AT THE DATA, BUT YOU COULD HAVE TAKEN THE STONE BY FORCE IF YOU'D WANTED TO.
YEAH...I WANTED IT SO BAD THAT I COULD TASTE IT...
BUT WHEN I THOUGHT ABOUT THE PEOPLE WE MET ON THE WAY TO DR. MARCOH'S HOUSE...
I DECIDED THAT IF I STOLE THE THING HE USED TO HEAL THEM, JUST TO GET MY OLD BODY BACK...
...IT WOULD LEAVE A BAD TASTE IN MY MOUTH.
I'LL JUST THINK OF A DIFFERENT WAY TO GET MY BODY BACK.
RIGHT?
UH-HUH.

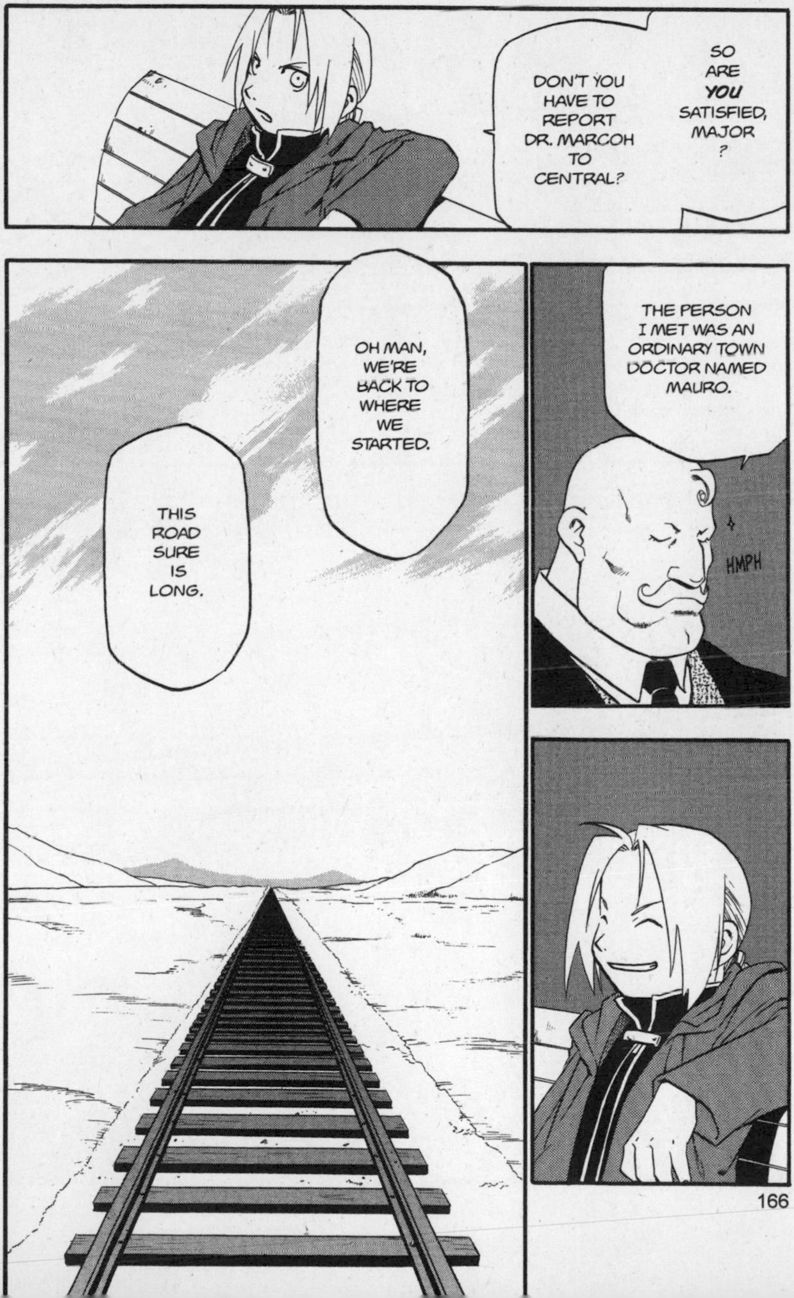
SO ARE ***YOU*** SATISFIED, MAJOR?
DON'T YOU HAVE TO REPORT DR. MARCOH TO CENTRAL?
THE PERSON I MET WAS AN ORDINARY TOWN DOCTOR NAMED MAURO.
HMPH
OH MAN, WE'RE BACK TO WHERE WE STARTED.
THIS ROAD SURE IS LONG.

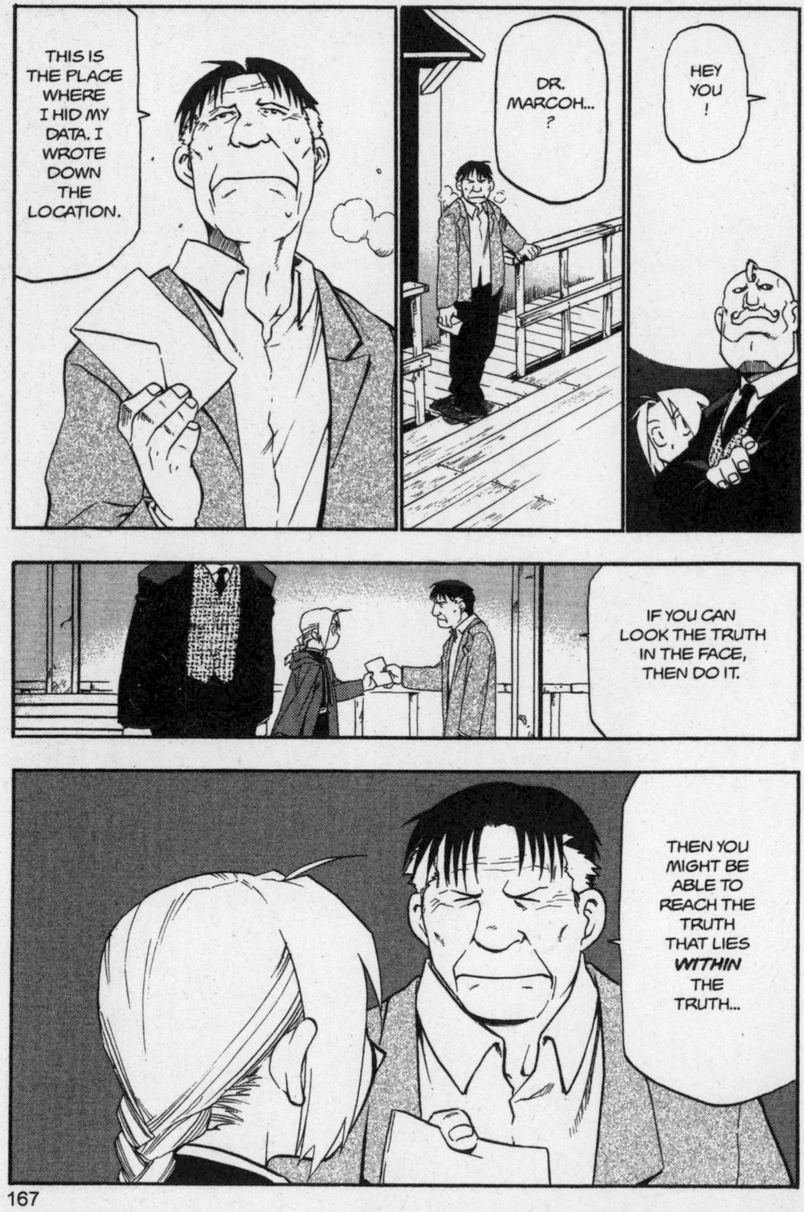
HEY YOU !
DR. MARCOH... ?
THIS IS THE PLACE WHERE I HID MY DATA. I WROTE DOWN THE LOCATION.
IF YOU CAN LOOK THE TRUTH IN THE FACE, THEN DO IT.
THEN YOU MIGHT BE ABLE TO REACH THE TRUTH THAT LIES ***WITHIN*** THE TRUTH...

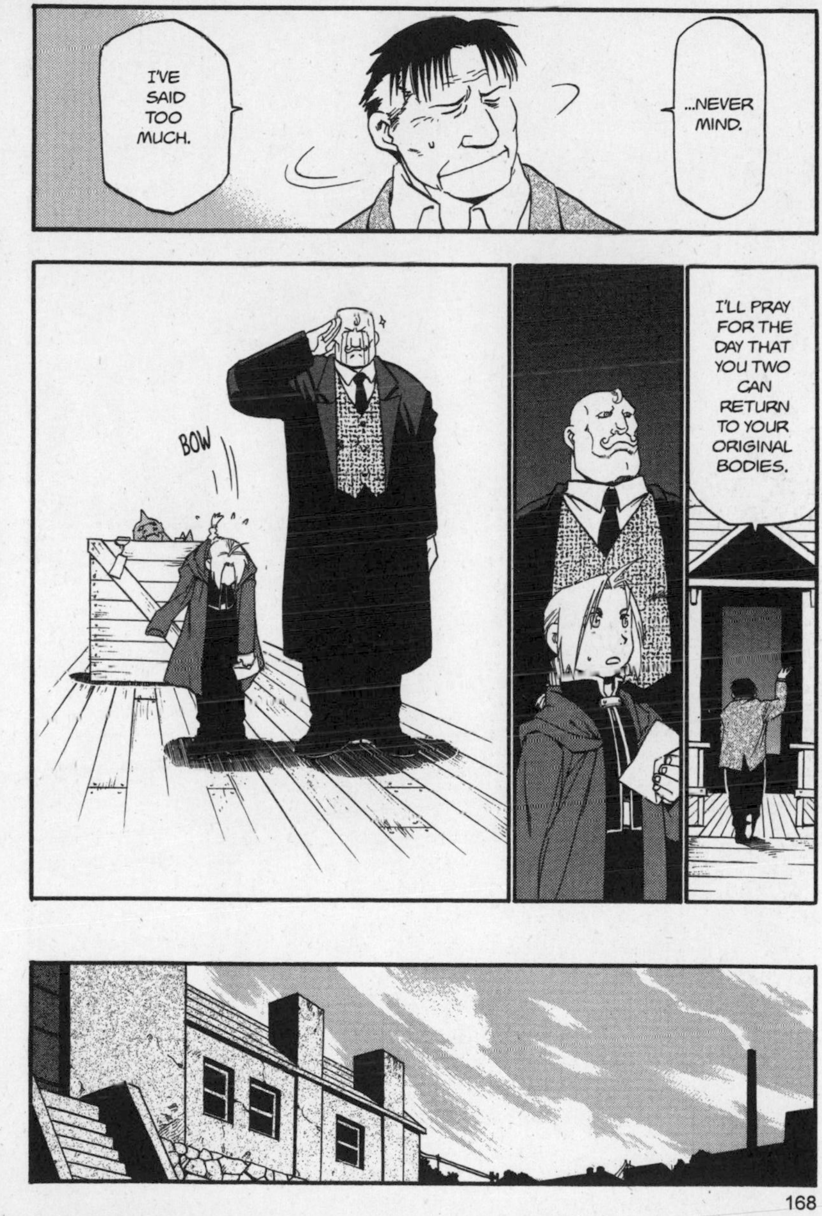
...NEVER MIND.
I'VE SAID TOO MUCH.
I'LL PRAY FOR THE DAY THAT YOU TWO CAN RETURN TO YOUR ORIGINAL BODIES.
BOW

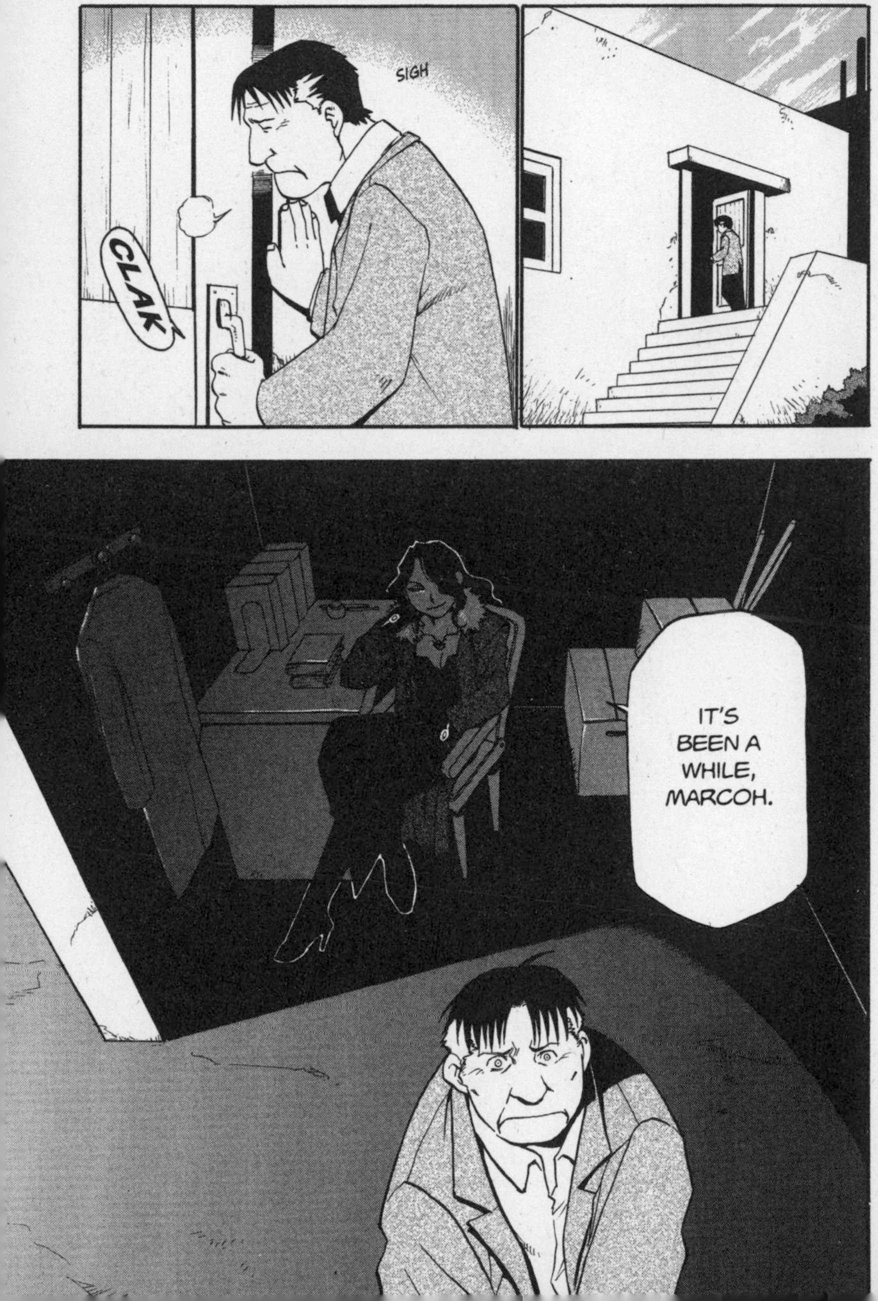
SIGH
CLAK
IT'S BEEN A WHILE, MARCOH.

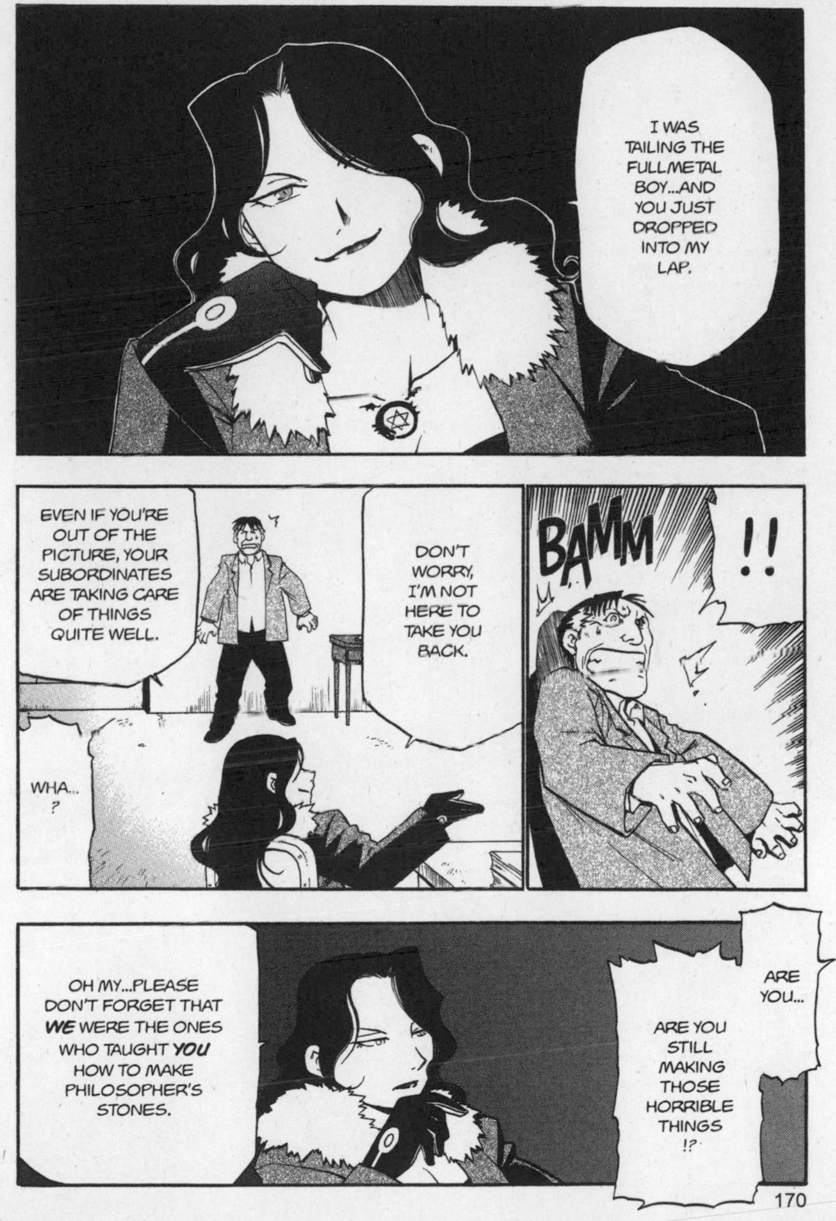
I WAS TAILING THE FULLMETAL BOY...AND YOU JUST DROPPED INTO MY LAP.
BAMM
!!
DON'T WORRY, I'M NOT HERE TO TAKE YOU BACK.
EVEN IF YOU'RE OUT OF THE PICTURE, YOUR SUBORDINATES ARE TAKING CARE OF THINGS QUITE WELL.
WHA... ?
ARE YOU...
ARE YOU STILL MAKING THOSE HORRIBLE THINGS !?
OH MY...PLEASE DON'T FORGET THAT *WE* WERE THE ONES WHO TAUGHT *YOU* HOW TO MAKE PHILOSOPHER'S STONES.

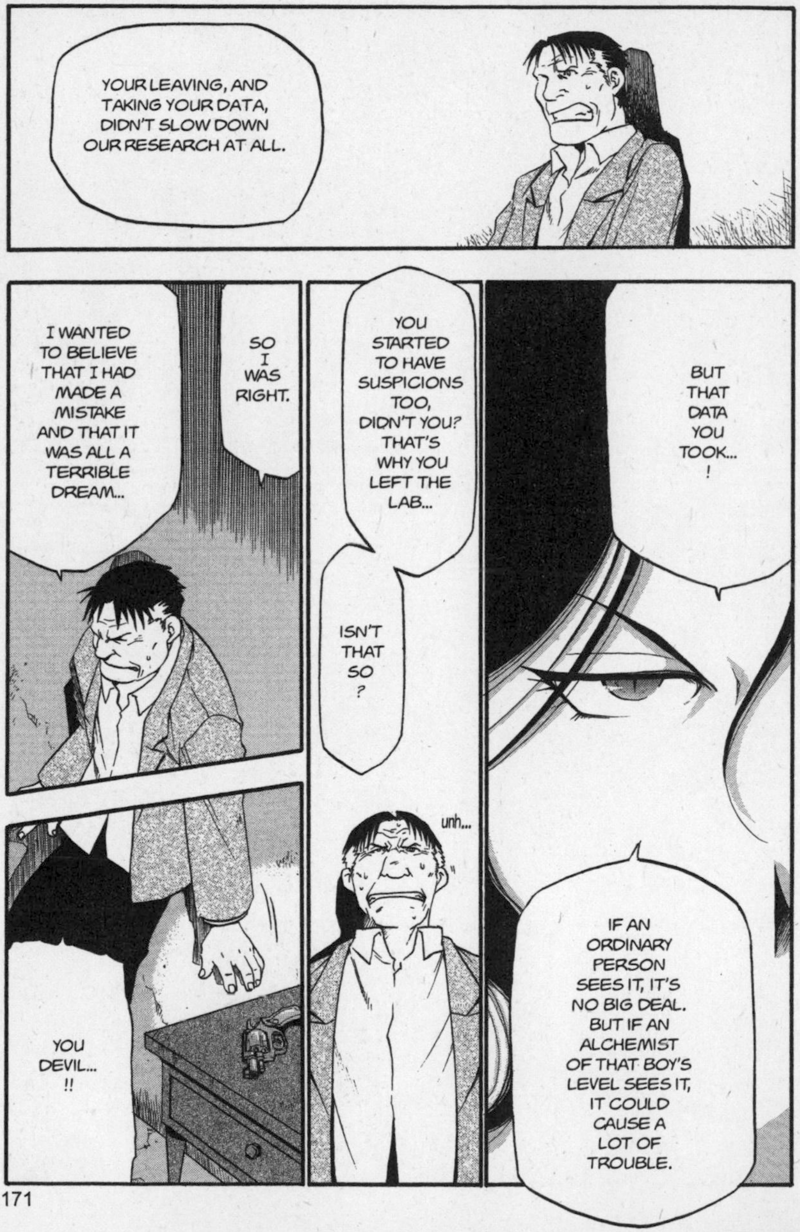
YOUR LEAVING, AND TAKING YOUR DATA, DIDN'T SLOW DOWN OUR RESEARCH AT ALL.
BUT THAT DATA YOU TOOK...!
IF AN ORDINARY PERSON SEES IT, IT'S NO BIG DEAL. BUT IF AN ALCHEMIST OF THAT BOY'S LEVEL SEES IT, IT COULD CAUSE A LOT OF TROUBLE.
YOU STARTED TO HAVE SUSPICIONS TOO, DIDN'T YOU? THAT'S WHY YOU LEFT THE LAB...
ISN'T THAT SO?
unh...
SO I WAS RIGHT.
I WANTED TO BELIEVE THAT I HAD MADE A MISTAKE AND THAT IT WAS ALL A TERRIBLE DREAM...
YOU DEVIL... !!

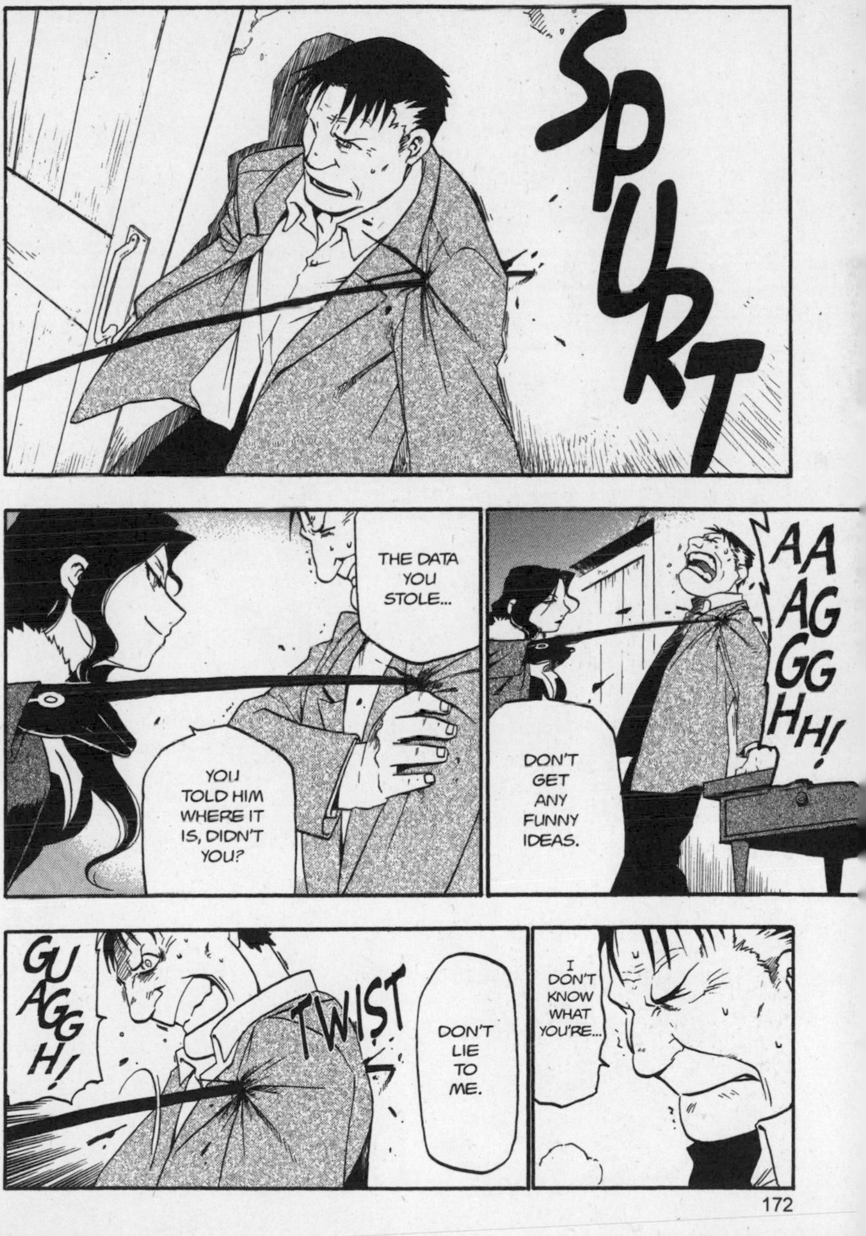
SPURT
AAAGGHH!
DON'T GET ANY FUNNY IDEAS.
THE DATA YOU STOLE...
YOU TOLD HIM WHERE IT IS, DIDN'T YOU?
I DON'T KNOW WHAT YOU'RE...
DON'T LIE TO ME.
TWIST
GUAGGH!

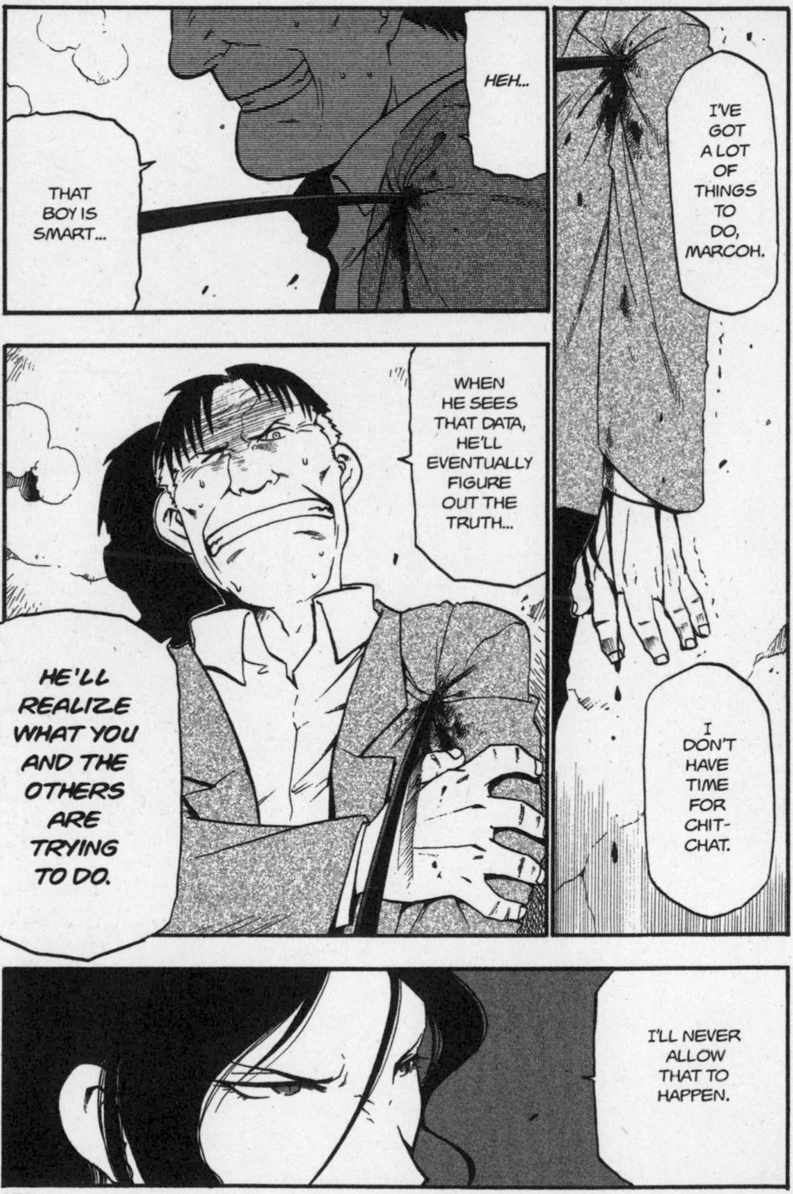
I'VE GOT A LOT OF THINGS TO DO, MARCOH.
I DON'T HAVE TIME FOR CHIT-CHAT.
HEH...
THAT BOY IS SMART...
WHEN HE SEES THAT DATA, HE'LL EVENTUALLY FIGURE OUT THE TRUTH...
HE'LL REALIZE WHAT YOU AND THE OTHERS ARE TRYING TO DO.
I'LL NEVER ALLOW THAT TO HAPPEN.

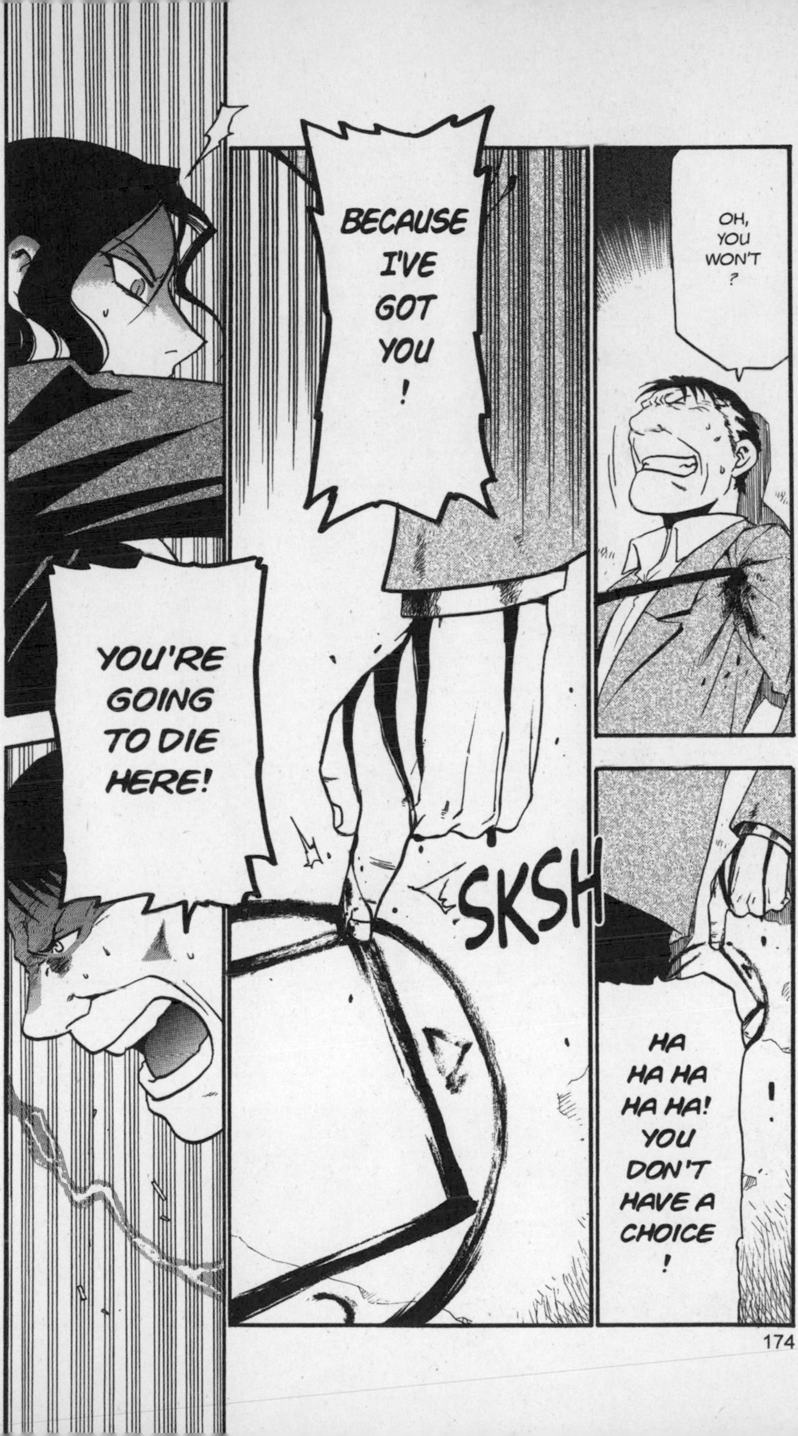
OH, YOU WON'T?
HA HA HA HA HA! YOU DON'T HAVE A CHOICE!
BECAUSE I'VE GOT YOU!
SKSH
YOU'RE GOING TO DIE HERE!

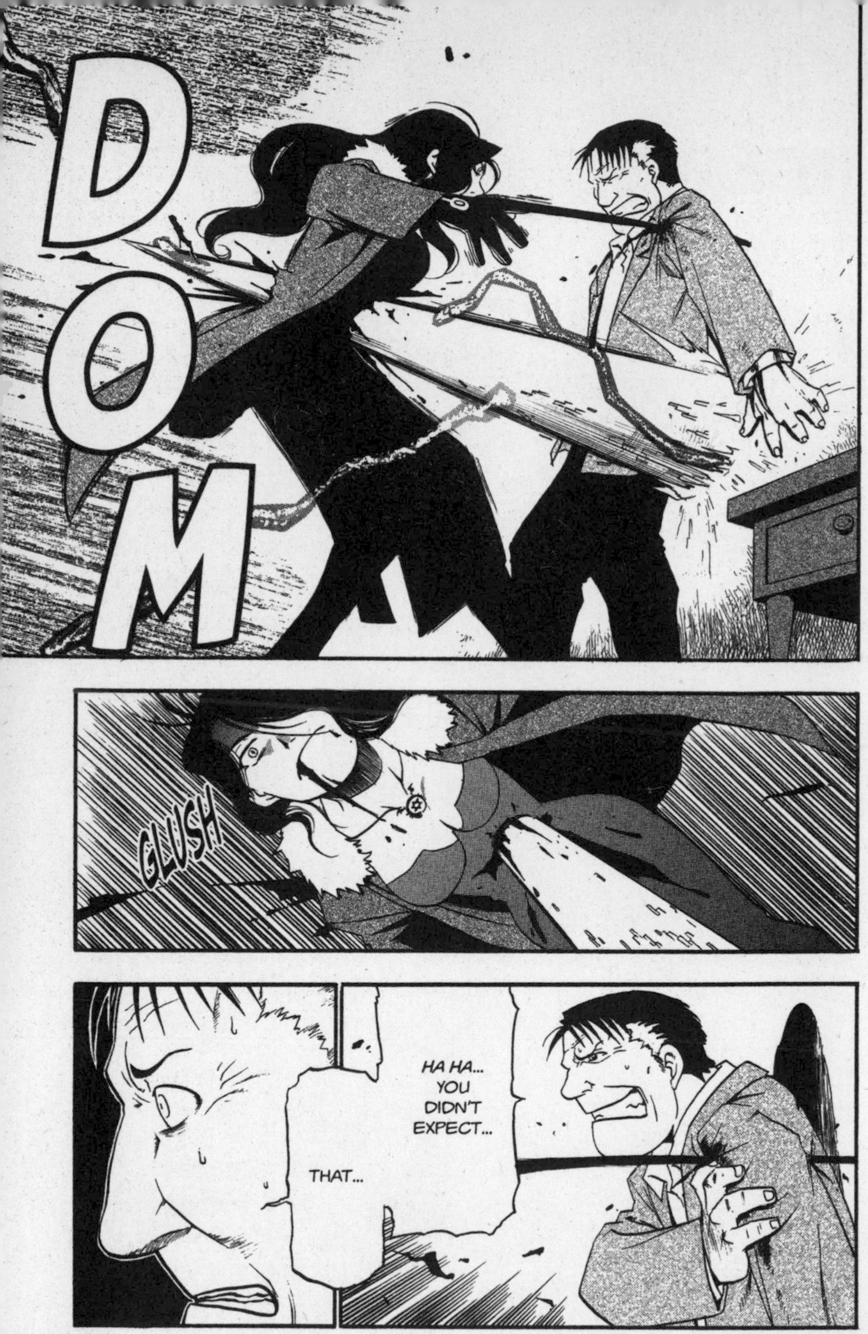
DOM
GLUSH
HA HA... YOU DIDN'T EXPECT...
THAT...

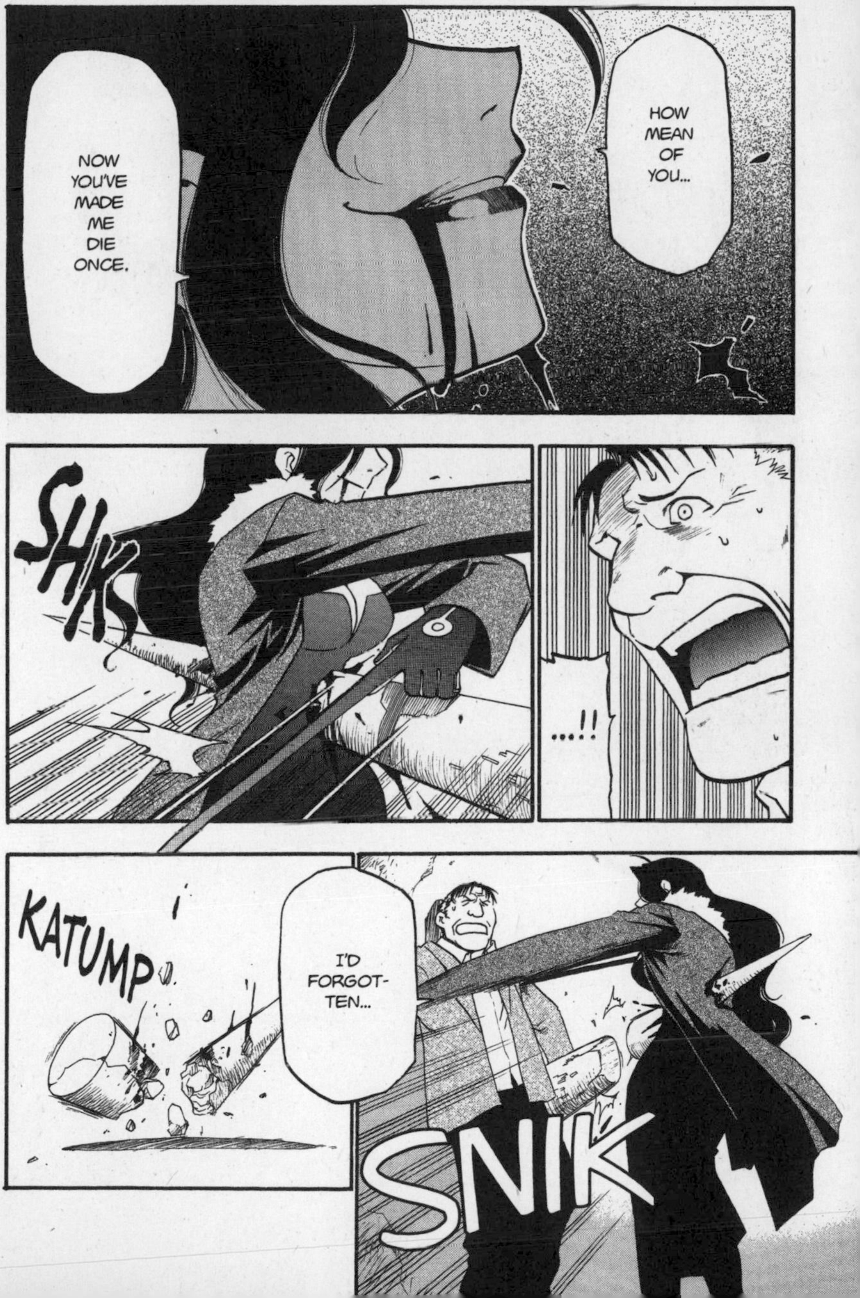
HOW MEAN OF YOU...
NOW YOU'VE MADE ME DIE ONCE.
...!!
SHK
I'D FORGOT-TEN...
SNIK
KATUMP

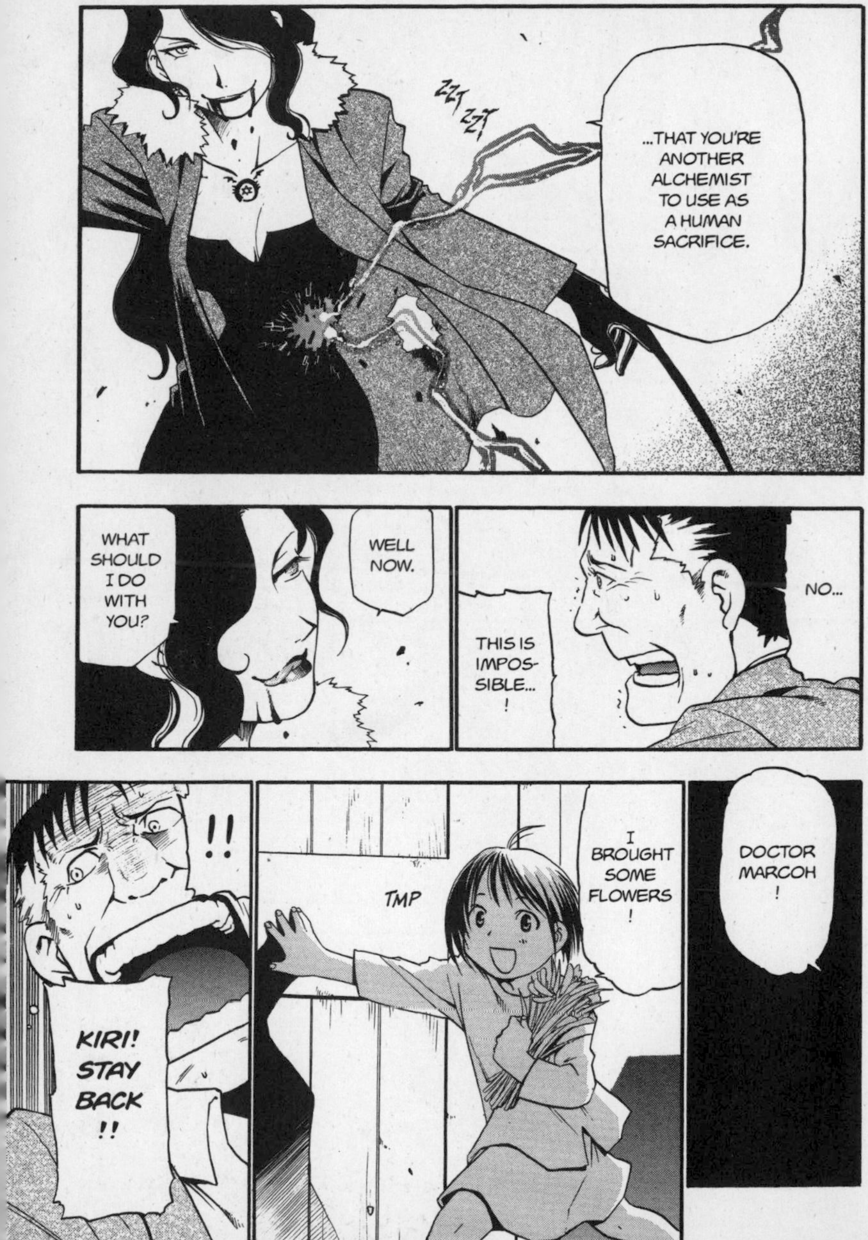
ZZT ZZT
...THAT YOU'RE ANOTHER ALCHEMIST TO USE AS A HUMAN SACRIFICE.
NO...
THIS IS IMPOSSIBLE...!
WELL NOW.
WHAT SHOULD I DO WITH YOU?
DOCTOR MARCOH!
I BROUGHT SOME FLOWERS!
TMP
!!
KIRI! STAY BACK!!

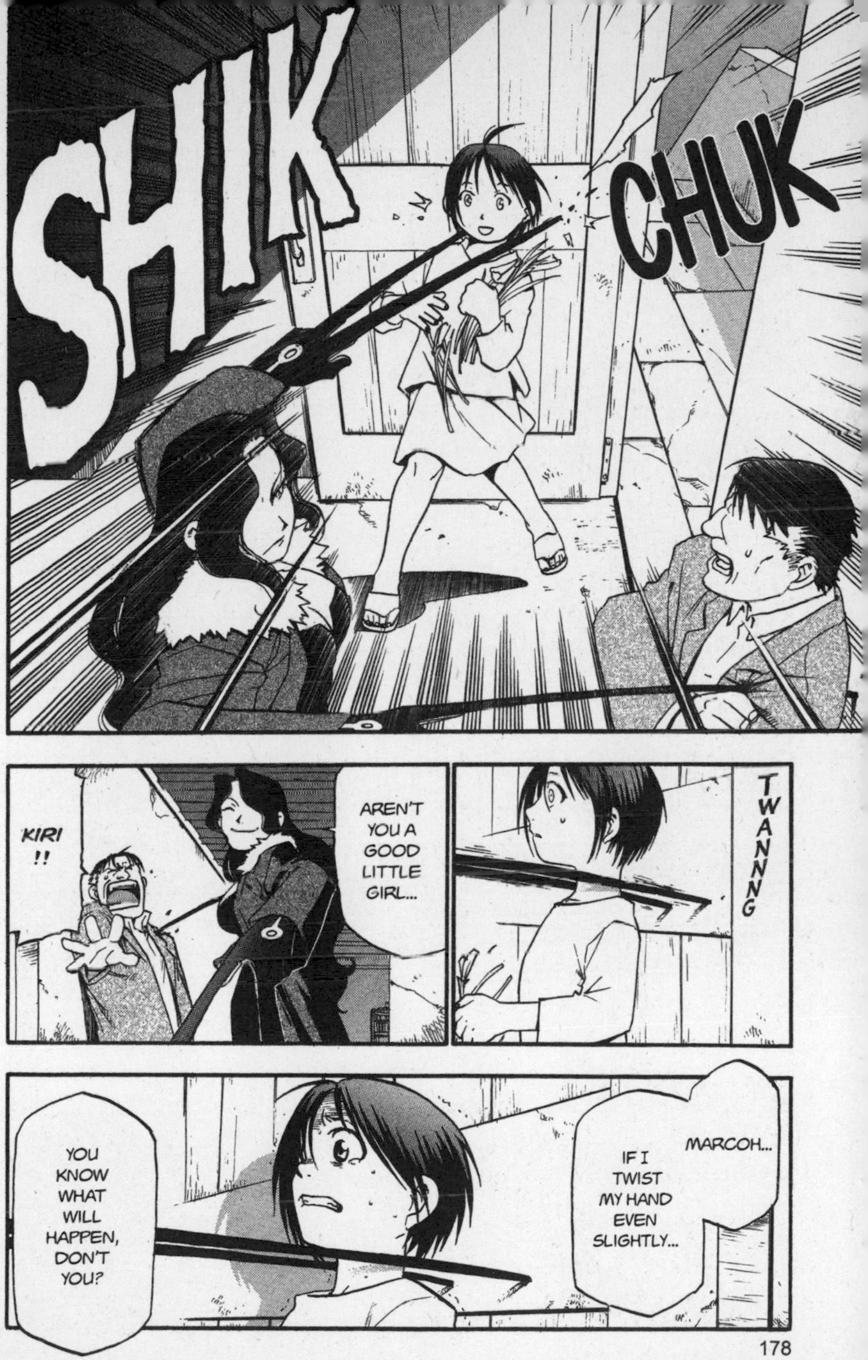
CHUK
SHIK
TWANNNG
AREN'T YOU A GOOD LITTLE GIRL...
KIRI !!
MARCOH...
IF I TWIST MY HAND EVEN SLIGHTLY...
YOU KNOW WHAT WILL HAPPEN, DON'T YOU?

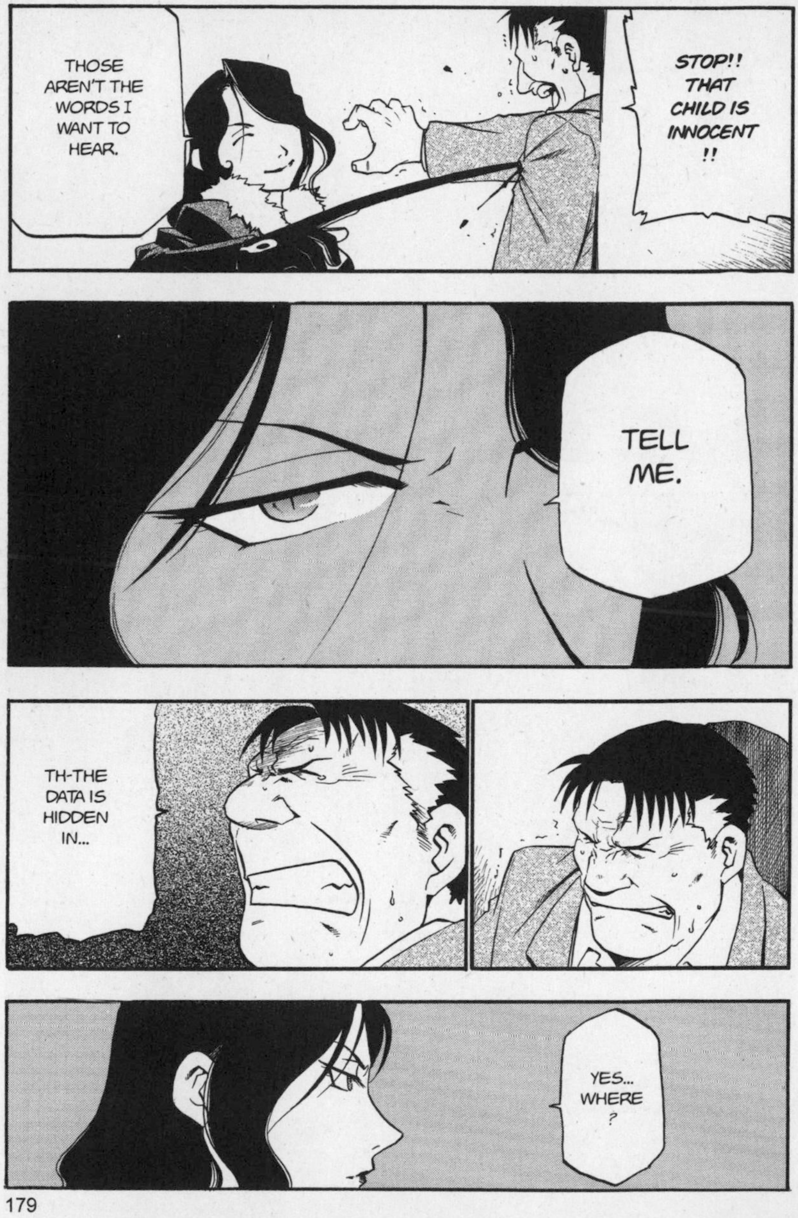
STOP!! THAT CHILD IS INNOCENT!!
THOSE AREN'T THE WORDS I WANT TO HEAR.
TELL ME.
TH-THE DATA IS HIDDEN IN...
YES... WHERE?

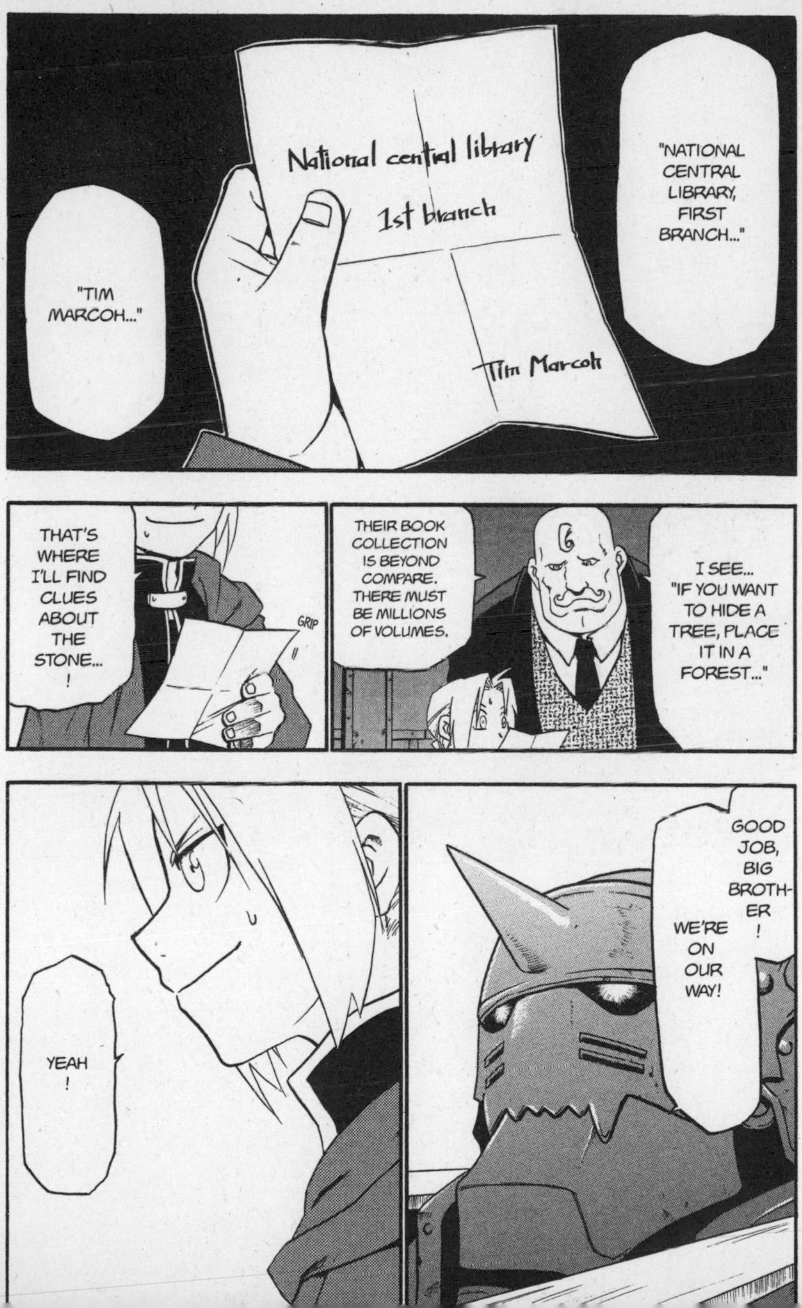
National central library
1st branch
Tim Marcoh
"NATIONAL CENTRAL LIBRARY, FIRST BRANCH..."
"TIM MARCOH..."
I SEE... "IF YOU WANT TO HIDE A TREE, PLACE IT IN A FOREST..."
THEIR BOOK COLLECTION IS BEYOND COMPARE. THERE MUST BE MILLIONS OF VOLUMES.
GRIP
THAT'S WHERE I'LL FIND CLUES ABOUT THE STONE...
!
GOOD JOB, BIG BROTHER!
WE'RE ON OUR WAY!
YEAH!

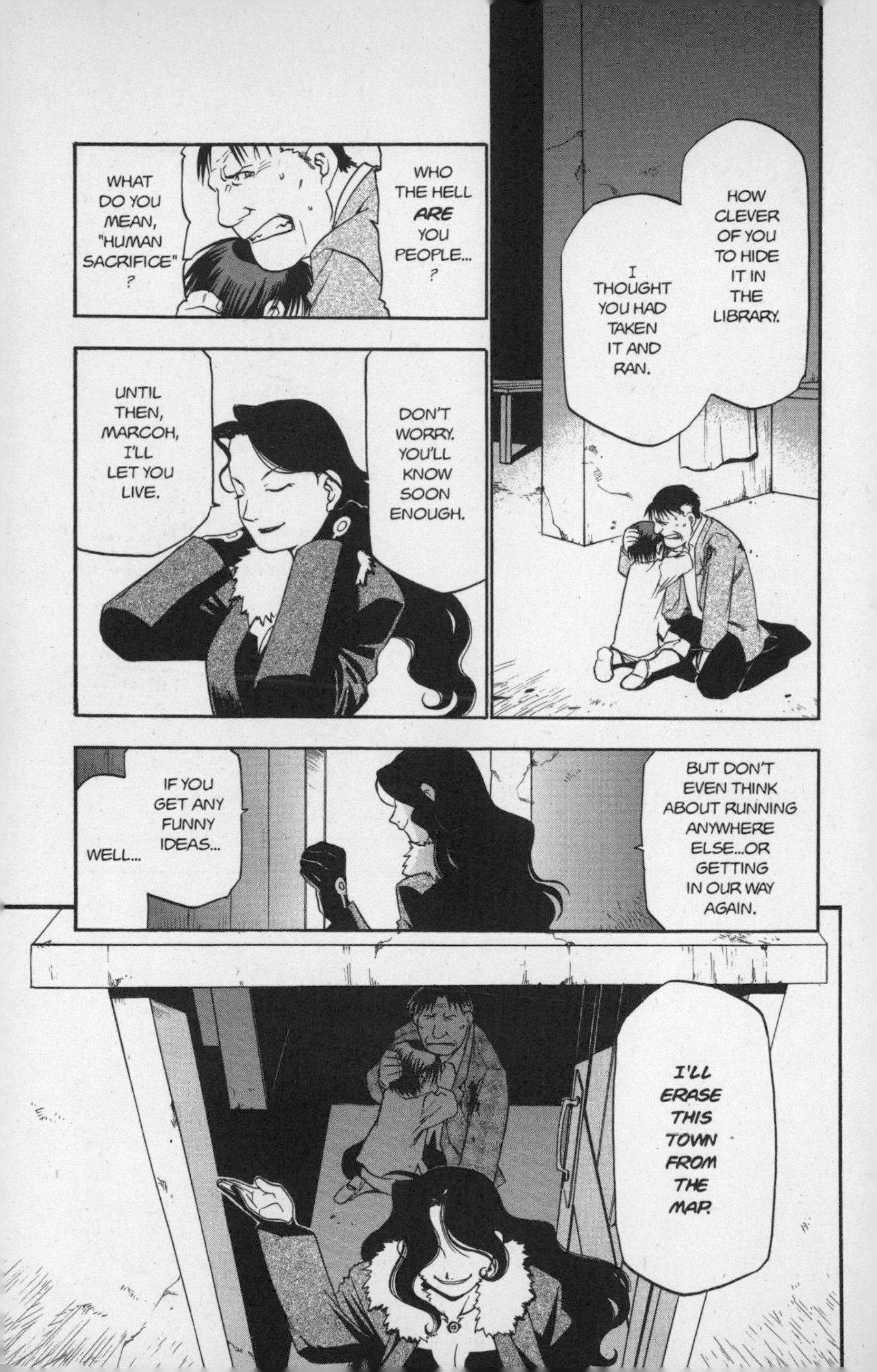
HOW CLEVER OF YOU TO HIDE IT IN THE LIBRARY.
I THOUGHT YOU HAD TAKEN IT AND RAN.
WHO THE HELL *ARE* YOU PEOPLE...?
WHAT DO YOU MEAN, "HUMAN SACRIFICE"?
DON'T WORRY. YOU'LL KNOW SOON ENOUGH.
UNTIL THEN, MARCOH, I'LL LET YOU LIVE.
BUT DON'T EVEN THINK ABOUT RUNNING ANYWHERE ELSE...OR GETTING IN OUR WAY AGAIN.
IF YOU GET ANY FUNNY IDEAS...
WELL...
I'LL ERASE THIS TOWN FROM THE MAP.

THIS MANGA WAS ORIGINALLY PRINTED IN MONTHLY **SHONEN GANGAN**, DECEMBER 2001 THROUGH MARCH 2002.

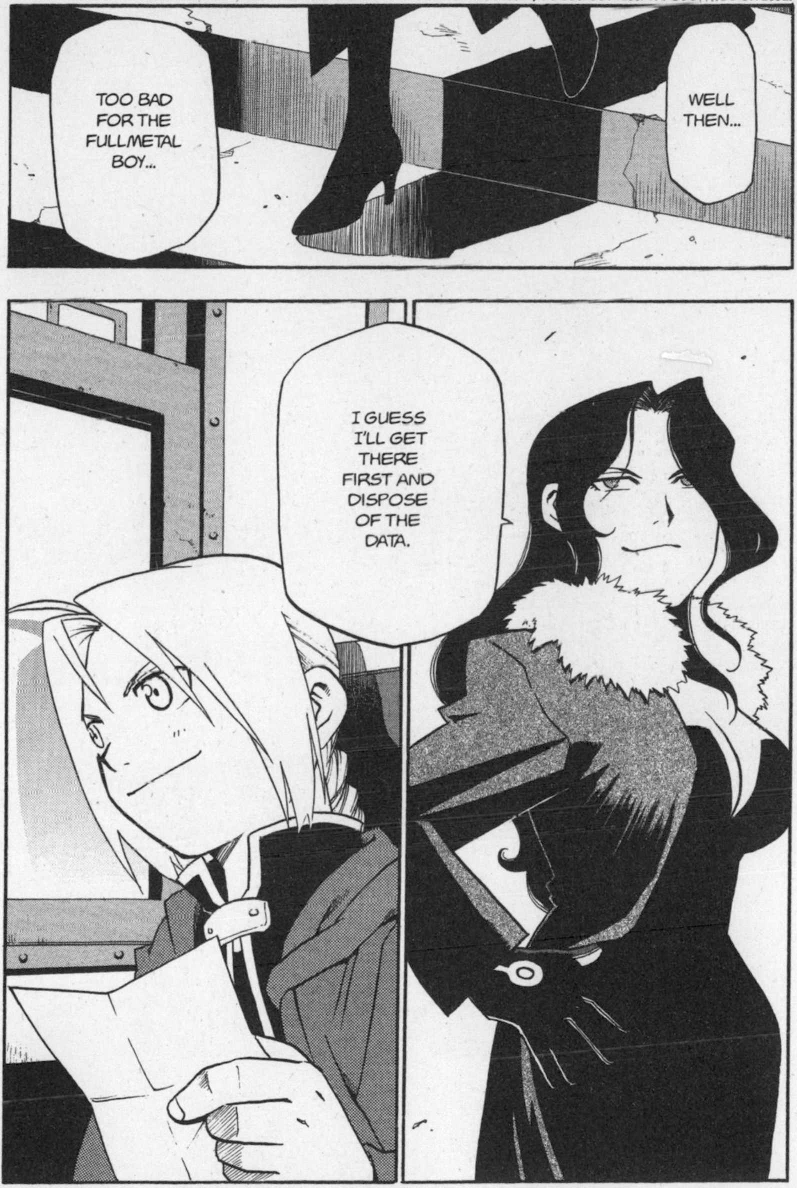
WELL THEN...
TOO BAD FOR THE FULLMETAL BOY...
I GUESS I'LL GET THERE FIRST AND DISPOSE OF THE DATA.

TO BE CONTINUED IN **FULLMETAL ALCHEMIST** VOL. 3...

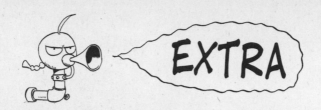

EXTRA

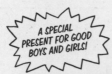

A SPECIAL PRESENT FOR GOOD BOYS AND GIRLS!

MAJOR ARMSTRONG
LUCKY CHARM

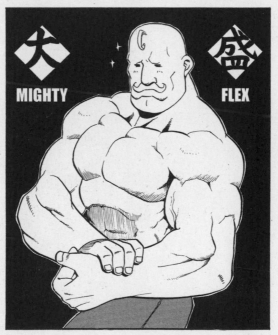

✳ Please be extra careful when using it.

POPULARITY EMPIRE

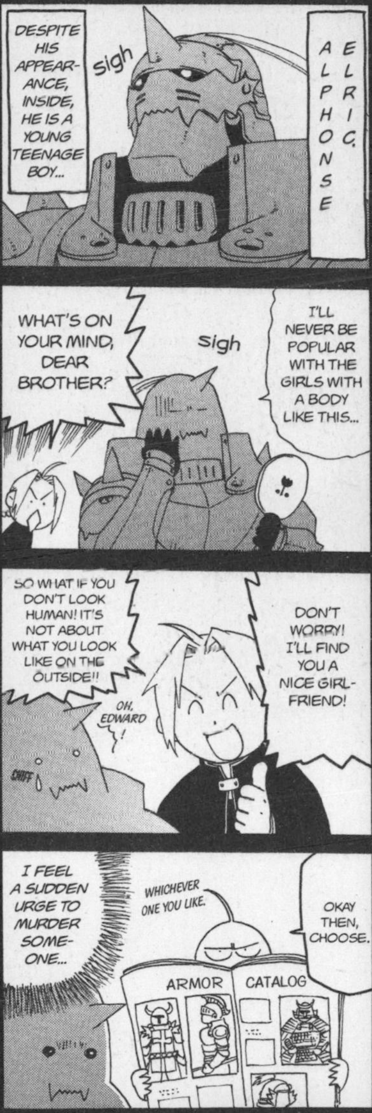
ALPHONSE ELRIC.
sigh
DESPITE HIS APPEARANCE, INSIDE, HE IS A YOUNG TEENAGE BOY...
I'LL NEVER BE POPULAR WITH THE GIRLS WITH A BODY LIKE THIS...
sigh
WHAT'S ON YOUR MIND, DEAR BROTHER?
DON'T WORRY! I'LL FIND YOU A NICE GIRL-FRIEND!
SO WHAT IF YOU DON'T LOOK HUMAN! IT'S NOT ABOUT WHAT YOU LOOK LIKE ON THE OUTSIDE!!
OH, EDWARD!
OKAY THEN, CHOOSE.
WHICHEVER ONE YOU LIKE.
ARMOR CATALOG
I FEEL A SUDDEN URGE TO MURDER SOME-ONE...

FIRST, DO SOMETHING ABOUT THE LOINCLOTH

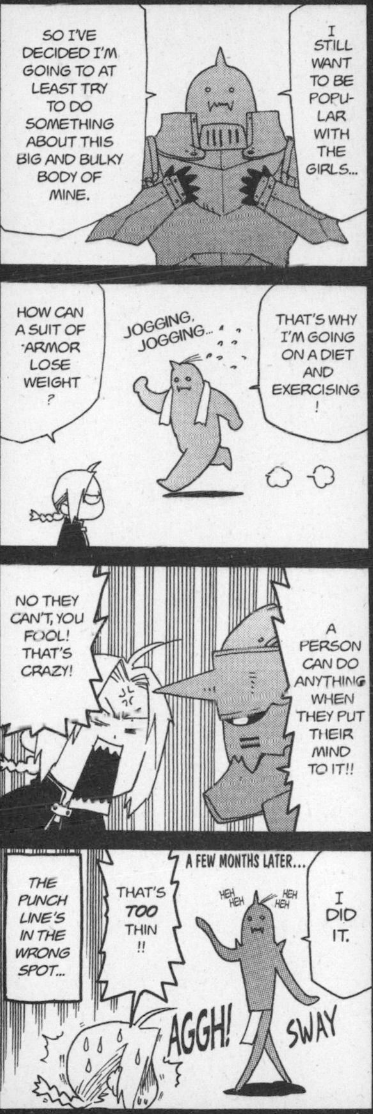
I STILL WANT TO BE POPU-LAR WITH THE GIRLS...
SO I'VE DECIDED I'M GOING TO AT LEAST TRY TO DO SOMETHING ABOUT THIS BIG AND BULKY BODY OF MINE.
THAT'S WHY I'M GOING ON A DIET AND EXERCISING!
JOGGING, JOGGING...
HOW CAN A SUIT OF ARMOR LOSE WEIGHT?
A PERSON CAN DO ANYTHING WHEN THEY PUT THEIR MIND TO IT!!
NO THEY CAN'T, YOU FOOL! THAT'S CRAZY!
A FEW MONTHS LATER...
I DID IT.
HEH HEH HEH HEH
SWAY
AGGH!
THAT'S TOO THIN!!
THE PUNCH LINE'S IN THE WRONG SPOT...

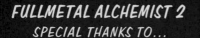

THE PITIFUL TRUTH

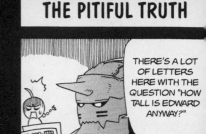

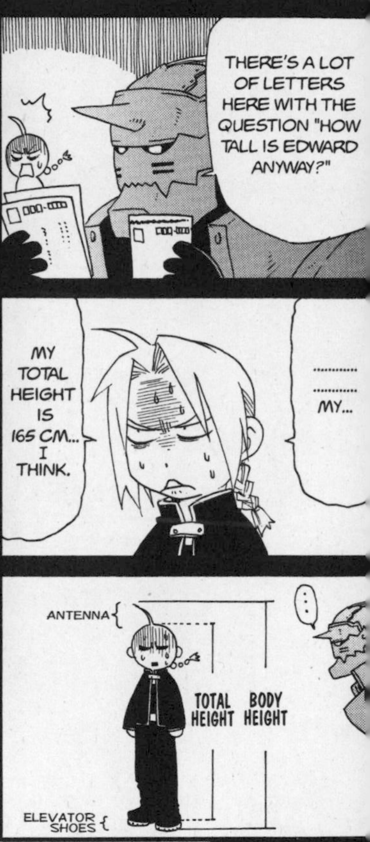
THERE'S A LOT OF LETTERS HERE WITH THE QUESTION "HOW TALL IS EDWARD ANYWAY?"
....
....
MY...
MY TOTAL HEIGHT IS 165 CM... I THINK.
...
ANTENNA
TOTAL HEIGHT
BODY HEIGHT
ELEVATOR SHOES
THE MEASURE'S ALL SET TO GO...
NOOO! LET ME GOOOOOOO!
PLUNK
DRAG DRAG

FULLMETAL ALCHEMIST 2
SPECIAL THANKS TO...

KEISUI TAKAEDA-SAN

SANKICHI HINODEYA-CHAN

JUN MORIYASU-SAN

YUICHI SHIMOMURA-SHI
(MANAGER)

AND YOU!!

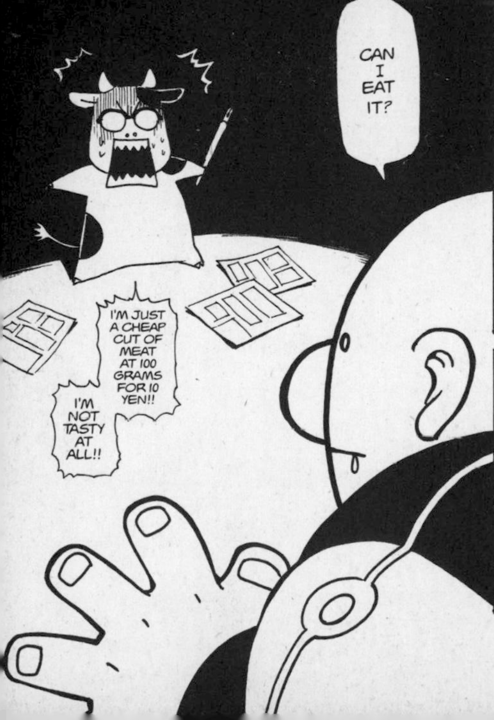
CAN I EAT IT?
I'M JUST A CHEAP CUT OF MEAT AT 100 GRAMS FOR 10 YEN!!
I'M NOT TASTY AT ALL!!

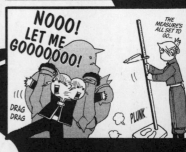

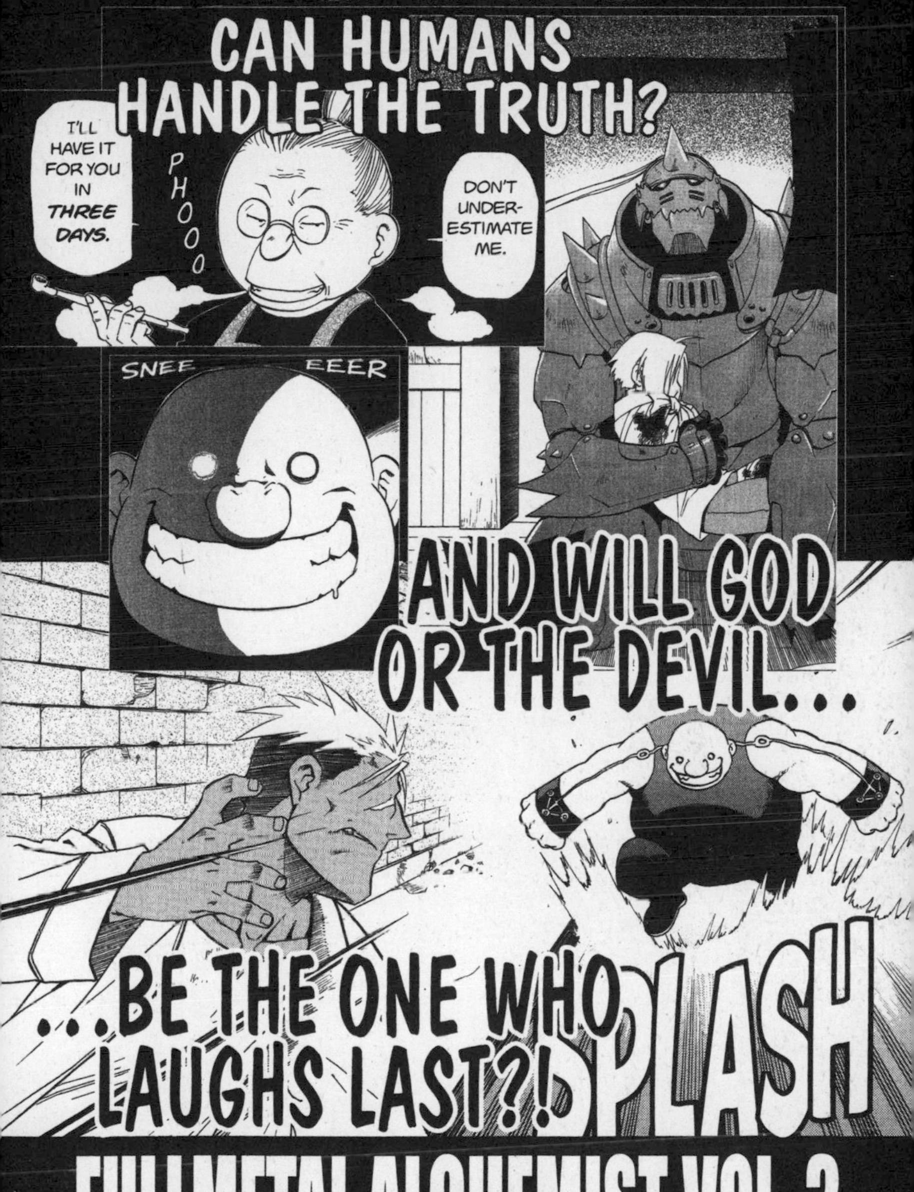
CAN HUMANS HANDLE THE TRUTH?
DON'T UNDER-ESTIMATE ME.
PHOOOO
I'LL HAVE IT FOR YOU IN THREE DAYS.
SNEEEEER
AND WILL GOD OR THE DEVIL...
...BE THE ONE WHO LAUGHS LAST?!
SPLASH

FULLMETAL ALCHEMIST VOL. 3
COMING IN SEPTEMBER 2005!

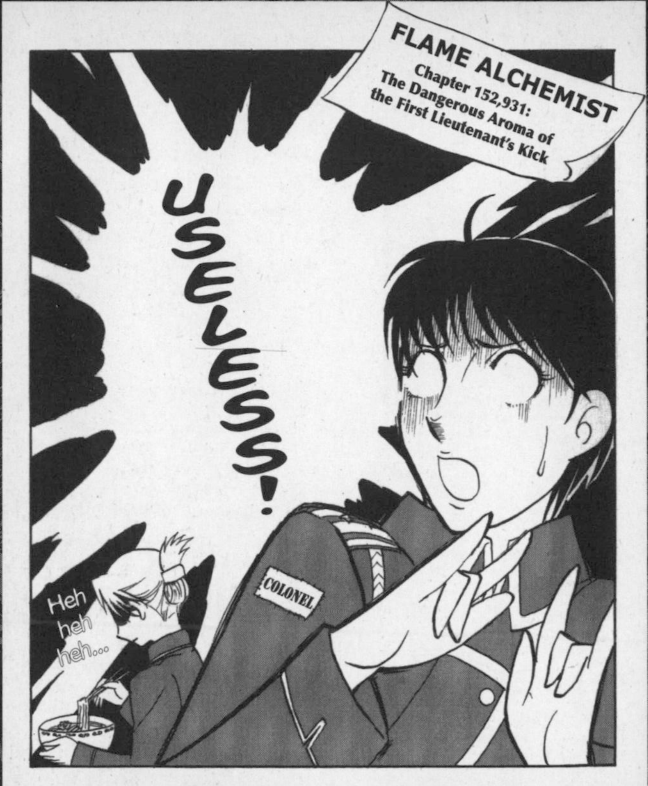
FLAME ALCHEMIST
Chapter 152,931:
The Dangerous Aroma of the First Lieutenant's Kick
USELESS!
COLONEL
Heh heh heh...

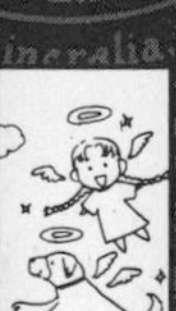
Aaggh
HELL

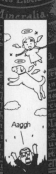

In Memoriam

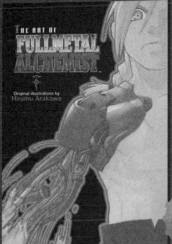
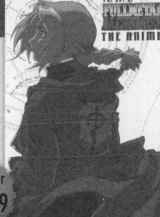

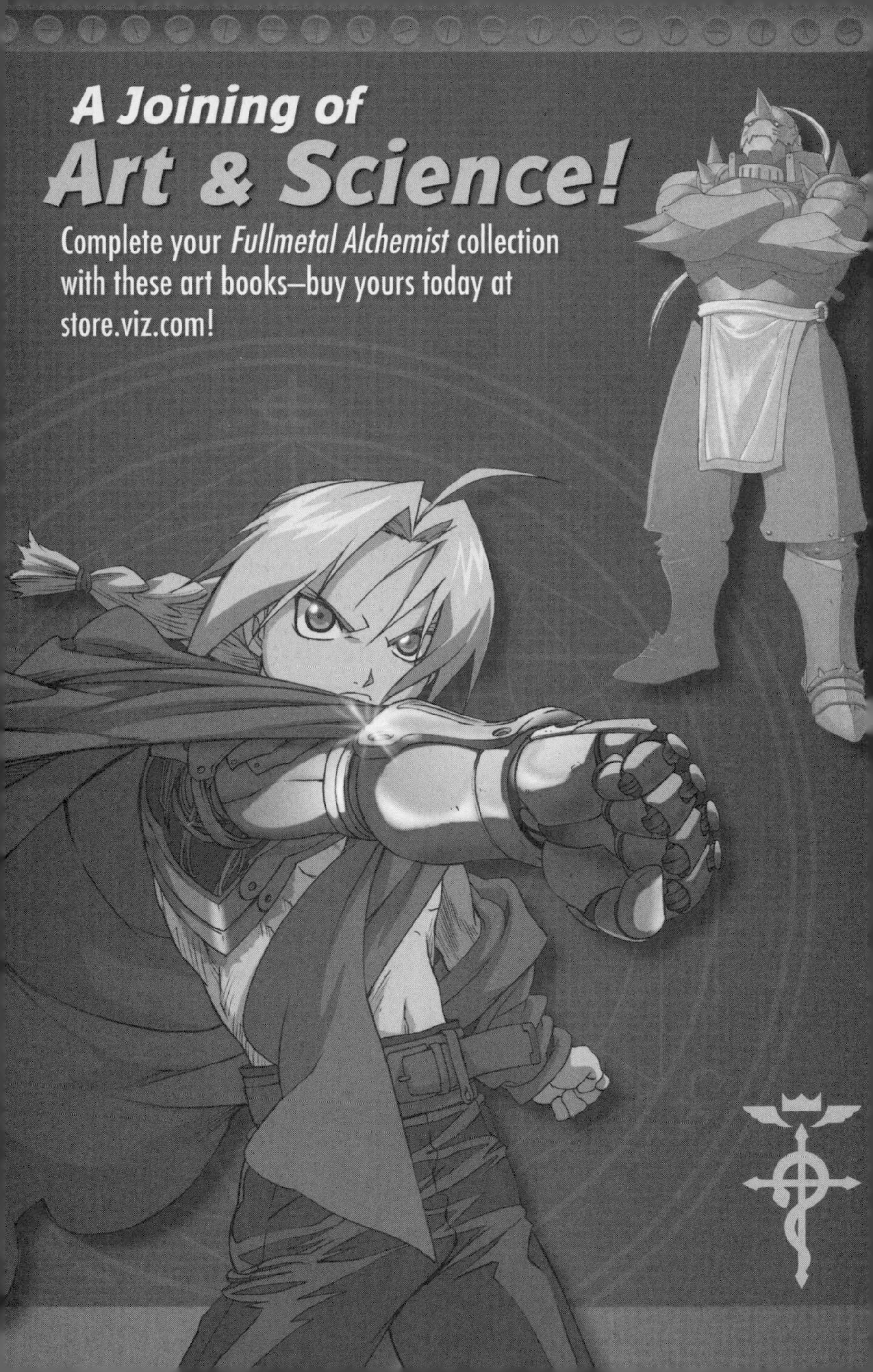
A Joining of
Art & Science!
Complete your *Fullmetal Alchemist* collection with these art books—buy yours today at store.viz.com!

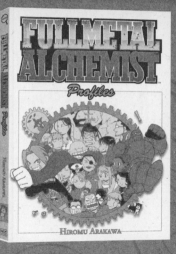
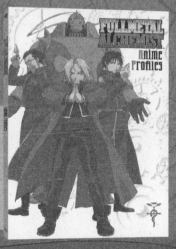
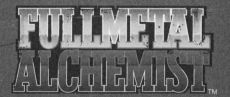

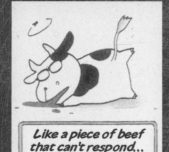

Like a piece of beef
that can't respond...

It's been a few years since I left home, saying, "I won't come back here until I can make a living drawing manga." I got my wish but now I'm so busy that I don't have time to go home. I feel happy and sad at the same time.

—Hiromu Arakawa, 2002

D0311059

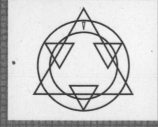

Born in Hokkaido (northern Japan), Hiromu Arakawa first attracted national attention in 1999 with her award-winning manga **Stray Dog**. Her series **Fullmetal Alchemist** debuted in 2001 in Square Enix's monthly manga anthology **Shonen Gangan**.